Lecture Notes in Computer Science 12442

More information about this series at http://www.springer.com/series/7407

Galina Jirásková · Giovanni Pighizzini (Eds.)

Descriptional Complexity of Formal Systems

22nd International Conference, DCFS 2020
Vienna, Austria, August 24–26, 2020
Proceedings

Springer

Editors
Galina Jirásková
Slovak Academy of Sciences
Košice, Slovakia

Giovanni Pighizzini iD
University of Milan
Milan, Italy

ISSN 0302-9743 ISSN 1611-3349 (electronic)
Lecture Notes in Computer Science
ISBN 978-3-030-62535-1 ISBN 978-3-030-62536-8 (eBook)
https://doi.org/10.1007/978-3-030-62536-8

LNCS Sublibrary: SL1 – Theoretical Computer Science and General Issues

This Springer imprint is published by the registered company Springer Nature Switzerland AG
The registered company address is: Gewerbestrasse 11, 6330 Cham, Switzerland

Preface

The 22nd International Conference on Descriptional Complexity of Formal Systems (DCFS 2020) was expected to be organized by Rudolf Freund at the TU Wien as part of the Summer of Formal Languages 2020 in Wien, Austria, and by the International Federation for Information Processing (IFIP) Working Group 1.02 "Descriptional Complexity." Unfortunately, due to development of the crisis caused by COVID-19, the conference had to be canceled. However, in order to allow researchers in the area of descriptional complexity to still present their recent results in some form, the DCFS Steering Committee decided to prepare this volume, collecting papers that have been selected by a committee after a standard review process.

Descriptional complexity is a field in computer science that deals with the size of all kinds of objects that occur in computational models, such as Turing machines, finite automata, grammars, splicing systems, and others. The topics of DCFS conferences are related to all aspects of descriptional complexity and include, but are not limited to:

- Automata, grammars, languages, and other formal systems; various modes of operations and complexity measures.
- Succinctness of description of objects, state-explosion-like phenomena.
- Circuit complexity of Boolean functions and related measures.
- Size complexity of formal systems.
- Structural complexity of formal systems.
- Trade-offs between computational models and mode of operation.
- Applications of formal systems – for instance in software and hardware testing, in dialogue systems, in systems modeling, or in modeling natural languages – and their complexity constraints.
- Cooperating formal systems.
- Size or structural complexity of formal systems for modeling natural languages.
- Complexity aspects related to the combinatorics of words.
- Descriptional complexity in resource-bounded or structure-bounded environments.
- Structural complexity as related to descriptional complexity.
- Frontiers between decidability and undecidability.
- Universality and reversibility.
- Nature-motivated (bio-inspired) architectures and unconventional models of computing.
- Blum static (Kolmogorov/Chaitin) complexity, algorithmic information.

DCFS became an IFIP working conference in 2016, continuing the former Workshop on Descriptional Complexity of Formal Systems, which was a merger in 2002 of two other workshops: Formal Descriptions and Software Reliability (FDSR) and Descriptional Complexity of Automata, Grammars and Related Structures (DCAGRS). DCAGRS was previously held in Magdeburg, Germany (1999), London, UK (2000), and Vienna, Austria (2001). FDSR was previously held in Paderborn, Germany (1998),

Boca Raton, USA (1999), and San Jose, USA (2000). Since 2002, DCFS has been successively held in London, Ontario, Canada (2002), Budapest, Hungary (2003), London, Ontario, Canada (2004), Como, Italy (2005), Las Cruces, New Mexico, USA (2006), Nový Smokovec, High Tatras, Slovakia (2007), Charlottetown, Prince Edward Island, Canada (2008), Magdeburg, Germany (2009), Saskatoon, Canada (2010), Gießen, Germany (2011), Braga, Portugal (2012), London, Ontario, Canada (2013), Turku, Finland (2014), Waterloo, Ontario, Canada (2015), Bucharest, Romania (2016), Milano, Italy (2017), Halifax, Nova Scotia, Canada (2018), and Košice, Slovakia (2019).

This volume contains 19 contributed papers, selected by the Selection Committee out of a total of 31 submissions, by a total of 54 authors from 17 countries (61.3% acceptance rate). The selection was done on the basis of three reviews per submission, with the exception of a few papers for which we received only two reviews. The selection process was carried out by taking into account originality, quality, significance, pertinence with DCFS topics, and presentation. We thank all authors who submitted their works for consideration in this volume. We wish to thank all Selection Committee members and external reviewers for their competent and timely handling of the submissions. The scientific level of the volume is guaranteed by their hard work.

During the selection process, we used the EasyChair conference management system, which provided excellent support. We wish to thank the editorial team at Springer, for the efficient production of this volume.

Unfortunately, the conference could not take place this year. Anyway, we hope that this volume will be of inspiration for new research and cooperations. We really hope to restart our series of conferences very soon, hopefully in 2021, when DCFS is planned to take place in Seoul, South Korea.

October 2020   Galina Jirásková
                                                                                 Giovanni Pighizzini

Organization

Steering Committee

Cezar Câmpeanu	University of Prince Edward Island, Canada
Erzsébet Csuhaj-Varjú	Eötvös Loránd University, Hungary
Stavros Konstantinidis	Saint Mary's University, Canada
Martin Kutrib (Chair)	Justus Liebig University, Germany
Giovanni Pighizzini	University of Milan, Italy
Rogério Reis	University of Porto, Portugal

Selection Committee

Cezar Cámpeanu	University of Prince Edward Island, Canada
Pawel Gawrychowski	University of Wrocław, Poland
Dora Giammarresi	University of Rome Tor Vergata, Italy
Galina Jirásková (Co-chair)	Slovak Academy of Sciences, Slovakia
Martin Kutrib	Justus Liebig University, Germany
Florin Manea	University of Göttingen, Germany
František Mráz	Charles University, Czech Republic
Dana Pardubská	Comenius University, Slovakia
Andrei Păun	University of Bucharest, Romania
Giovanni Pighizzini (Co-chair)	University of Milan, Italy
Rogério Reis	University of Porto, Portugal
Michel Rigo	University of Liège, Belgium
Marinella Sciortino	University of Palermo, Italy
Shinnosuke Seki	The University of Electro-Communications, Japan
Klaus Sutner	Carnegie Mellon University, USA
Bianca Truthe	Justus Liebig University, Germany
György Vaszil	University of Debrecen, Hungary

Additional Reviewers

Broda, Sabine
Catalano, Costanza
Charlier, Émilie
Cisternino, Célia
Day, Joel
Fleischmann, Pamela
Giannakis, Konstantinos
Holzer, Markus

Jajcayova, Tatiana
Janczewski, Wojciech
Kapoutsis, Christos
Kari, Jarkko
Kostolányi, Peter
Lejeune, Marie
Leroy, Julien
Loff, Bruno

Machiavelo, António
Madonia, Maria
Malcher, Andreas
Marsault, Victor
Massuir, Adeline
Mercaş, Robert
Mereghetti, Carlo
Mitrana, Victor
Monmege, Benjamin
Moreira, Nelma
Peltomäki, Jarkko

Pokorski, Karol
Prigioniero, Luca
Průša, Daniel
Rampersad, Narad
Salomaa, Kai
Schmid, Markus L.
Selmi, Carla
Volkov, Mikhail
Yakaryılmaz, Abuzer
Yamakami, Tomoyuki

Contents

Mutually Accepting Capacitated Automata

Ravid Alon[(✉)] and Orna Kupferman

The Hebrew University, Jerusalem, Israel
{ravid.alon,orna}@cs.huji.ac.il

Abstract. We study *capacitated automata* (CAs) [10], where transitions correspond to resources and have capacities, bounding the number of times they may be traversed. We follow the *utilization semantics* of CAs and view them as recognizers of *multi-languages* – sets of multisets of words, where a multiset S of words is in the multi-language of a CA A if all the words in S can be mutually accepted by A: the multiset of runs on all the words in S together respects the bounds induced by the capacities. Thus, capacitated automata model possible utilizations of systems with bounded resources. We study the basic properties of CAs: their expressive power in the nondeterministic and deterministic models, closure under classical operations, and the complexity of basic decision problems.

1 Introduction

Finite state automata are used in the modelling and design of finite-state systems and their behaviors, with applications in engineering, databases, linguistics, biology, and many more. The traditional definition of an automaton does not refer to its transitions as consumable resources. Indeed, a run of an automaton is a sequence of successive transitions, and there is no bound whatsoever on the number of times that a transition may be traversed. In some settings, the use of a transition may correspond to the use of some resource. For example, it may be associated with the usage of some energy-consuming machine, application of some material, or consumption of bandwidth.

In [6], the authors introduced *Parikh automata*, which do impose restrictions related to consumption. Essentially, a Parikh automaton is a pair $\langle A, C \rangle$, where A is a nondeterministic finite automaton (NFA) over alphabet Σ, and $C \subseteq \mathbb{N}^\Sigma$ is a set of "allowed occurrences". A word w is accepted by $\langle A, C \rangle$ if A accepts w and the Parikh's commutative image of w, which maps each letter in Σ to its number of occurrences in w, is in C. Thus, the semantics views occurrences of letters as consumable resources. Several variants of Parikh automata have seen studied. In particular, [3] studied *constrained automata*, a variant that counts traversals of transitions and requires the vector of counters to belong to C, now a semi-linear set of allowed vectors. Additional models include *multiple counters automata* [4], where transitions can be taken only if guards referring to traversals so far

G. Jiráskóvá and G. Pighizzini (Eds.): DCFS 2020, LNCS 12442, pp. 1–12, 2020.
https://doi.org/10.1007/978-3-030-62536-8_1

are satisfied, and *queue-content decision diagrams*, which are used to represent queue content of FIFO-channel systems [1, 2].

In [10], the authors introduced *capacitated automata* (CAs).[1] In this model, transitions correspond to resources and may have bounded capacities. Formally, each transition is associated with a (possibly infinite) integral bound on the number of times it may be traversed. A word w is accepted by a CA A if A has an accepting run on w; one that reaches an accepting state and respects the bounds on the transitions. The study of CAs considers two possible semantics to them. The first, which is more related to the models described above, views CAs as recognizers of formal languages (see also [9]). The second, referred to in [10] as the *utilization semantics*, is related to traditional resource-allocation theory, and views CAs as labeled flow networks.

Our work here focuses on the second view. In order to understand and motivate it, let us consider a simple example. Consider the CA A appearing in Fig. 1. In the first semantics, we view A as a recognizer of a language of words. Then, for example, the word ab is accepted by A, as the run q_0, q_0, q_2 on it "consumes" the selfloop in q_0 and the transition from q_0 to q_2. Likewise, the word ac is accepted by A, by its run q_0, q_1, q_3, and so does the word aac, by the run q_0, q_0, q_1, q_3. On the other hand, the word aab is not accepted by A, as an accepting run on it has to traverse the selfloop in q_0 twice, yet the capacity of this selfloop in only 1.

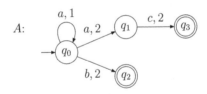

Fig. 1. A CA that mutually accepts $\{b, b, ac, ac\}$, $\{ab, b, ac, ac\}$, $\{b, b, aac, ac\}$, and their sub-multisets.

We now proceed to the utilization semantics. Recall that both ab and ac are accepted by A. In fact, since the transitions consumed by both runs together respect the capacity bounds, the A *mutually accepts* the multiset $\{ab, ac\}$. We use the term *multiset*, namely a set with possible re-occurrences of elements, as words may be accepted by A several times, and we care about the number of times that each word is accepted. For example, since the capacity of the transitions $\langle q_0, a, q_1 \rangle$ and $\langle q_1, c, q_2 \rangle$ is 2, then A mutually accepts also the multiset $\{ac, ac\}$, in which the word ac appears twice. On the other hand, A cannot mutually accept $\{ab, aac\}$, as the accepting runs on both words traverse the selfloop q_0, whose capacity is 1.

As the example above demonstrates, the utilization semantics enables reasoning about the utilization of systems with consumable resources. Its applications

---

[1] Not to be confused with *finite capacity automata* [12], which model the control of an automated manufacturing system, and are more related to Petri nets.

depend on the setting modeled by the CA. If, for example, the CA models a communication network, with transitions corresponding to channels and capacities corresponding to bounds on the number of times a channel may be used, then the CA accepts multisets of communication routes that can be transmitted simultanously in the network. Likewise, if the CA models a production system, then it accepts multisets of chains of services that can be processed mutually in the system.

The study of the utilization semantics in [10] focuses on the *maximal utilization* problem for CA: Given a CA A, return a multiset S of words, such that A mutually accepts all the words in S, and $|S|$ is maximal. The max-utilization problem can be viewed as a generalization of the max-flow problem in networks [5]. In the max-flow problem, the network is utilized by units of flow, each routed from the source to the target. The CA model enables a rich description of the feasible routes. The labels along a path correspond to a sequence of applications of resources. In particular, paths from an initial state to a final state correspond to feasible such sequences, and the goal is to mutually process as many of them as possible. It is shown in [10] that the problem can be solved in polynomial time, yet if we restrict the set of possible routes by a regular language, it becomes APX-complete, thus hard to approximate in polynomial time.

Here, we study theoretical properties of CAs as recognizers of *multi-languages*. A multi-language over an alphabet Σ is a set of multisets of words in Σ^*. The multi-language recognized by a CA A is the set $\mathcal{M}(A)$ of multisets S such that A mutually accepts S. For example the CA A from Fig. 1 has in $\mathcal{M}(A)$ the multisets $\{b, b, ac, ac\}$, $\{ab, b, ac, ac\}$, and $\{b, b, aac, ac\}$, as well as all multisets contained in one of them.

We say that a multi-language $\mathcal{M}$ is *regular* if there is a CA A such that $\mathcal{M}(A) = \mathcal{M}$. We first study the expressive power of CAs, show that not all *finite* multi-languages are regular, and that nondeterministic CAs are strictly more expressive than deterministic ones (DCAs, for short). For example, there is no DCA that recognizes the multi-language of the CA from Fig. 1. We then study closure properties for CAs. In addition to the usual union and intersection operators, we consider *pairwise* union and intersection, where the operations are applied to the multisets in the multi-language. We study closure in both the nondeterministic and deterministic setting. We show that while regular multi-languages are closed under pairwise union, they are not closed under the other operators. Moreover, the deterministic fragment is not closed even under pairwise union.

Finally, we study the basic *decision problems* for CAs. We start with the membership problem, of deciding whether a given multiset is in the multi-language of a given CA. In practice, this problem is relevant for checking, for example, whether a certain list of tasks can be accomplished by a manufacturing system with bounded resources. We show that when the input is given explicitly (that is, the multiset is given by a list of its elements, and the capacities in the CA are given in unary), the problem can be solved in linear time for DCAs and is NP-complete for CAs. We continue with the containment problem, namely deciding, given CAs A and B, whether $\mathcal{M}(A) \subseteq \mathcal{M}(B)$. In practice, this problem is relevant for checking, for example, whether every multisets of routes that can be transmitted simultanously in a communication network A can also be transmitted in B. We show that the problem is EXPSPACE-complete in the general setting, going down to co-NP-complete when B is deterministic. The upper bounds in these latter results are the most technically challenging results in the paper, as they involve a careful analysis of the length of words in accepted and rejected multisets in CAs with transitions with infinite capacities.

Due to the lack of space, some proofs are omitted and can be found in the full version, at the authors' URLs.

2   Preliminaries

A *capacitated automaton* (CA, for short) [10] is a tuple $A = \langle \Sigma, Q, Q_0, \Delta, F, c \rangle$, where Σ is a finite alphabet, Q is a finite set of states, $Q_0 \subseteq Q$ is a set of initial states, $\Delta \subseteq Q \times \Sigma \times Q$ is a transition relation, $F \subseteq Q$ is a set of final states, and $c : \Delta \to \mathbb{N} \cup \{\infty\}$ is a capacity function on transitions. If $|Q_0| = 1$, and for all $q \in Q$ and $\sigma \in \Sigma$, there is at most one $q' \in Q$ such that $\langle q, \sigma, q' \rangle \in \Delta$, then we say that A is a deterministic CA (DCA, for short).

A *multiset* is a generalization of a set in which each element may appear more than once. The number of repetitions of an element is called its *multiplicity*. A multiset over a set X of elements can be represented by a list (with repetitions) of its elements or by a function $S : X \to \mathbb{N} \cup \{\infty\}$, where $S(x)$ is the multiplicity of the element $x \in X$. We focus here on multisets of words over some finite alphabet Σ, and use CAs to define and recognize such multisets. Essentially, a CA A recognizes a multiset S of words if A can accept all the words in S simultaneously without exceeding the allowed capacities. Formally, we have the following.

Let $S = \{w_1, \ldots, w_n\}$ be a (possibly infinite) multiset of finite words, with $w_i = \sigma_1^i \cdots \sigma_{k_i}^i$. An *operation* of a CA A on S is a multiset of runs $O = \{r_1, \ldots, r_n\}$, such that the following hold.

1. The operation consists of legal runs: For all $1 \le i \le n$, we have that $r_i = q_0^i, \ldots, q_{k_i}^i$ is a run of A on w_i: it starts in an initial state, thus $q_0^i \in Q_0$, and it obeys the transition function, thus for all $0 \le j \le k_i - 1$, we have that $\langle q_j^i, \sigma_{j+1}^i, q_{j+1}^i \rangle \in \Delta$.
2. The operation respects the capacities: For each run r_i, let $t_i : \Delta \to \mathbb{N}$ map each transition $e \in \Delta$ to the number of times it is traversed in r_i, thus $t_i(e) = |\{j : e = \langle q_j^i, \sigma_{j+1}^i, q_{j+1}^i \rangle\}|$. Then, the number of times each transition is traversed in all the runs in O is bounded by its capacity. Formally, for all $e \in \Delta$, it holds that $\sum_{i=1}^n t_i(e) \le c(e)$.

We say that the operation O is *accepting* if the final states of all its runs are accepting, thus, $q_{k_i}^i \in F$, for all $1 \le i \le n$. When this happens, we say that A *mutually accepts* S with the operation O.

Note that if A is nondeterministic, it may have several operations on S. In contrast, a DCA has a single operation on each multiset. We say that A *mutually accepts* the multiset S if there exists an operation O such that A mutually accepts S with O.

A *multi-language* over an alphabet Σ is a set of multisets of words from Σ^*. The multi-language recognized by a CA A is the set $\mathcal{M}(A) = \{S : A$ mutually accepts $S\}$ of all multisets of words in Σ^* that can be mutually accepted by A.

Example 1. Consider the DCA A described in Fig. 2.

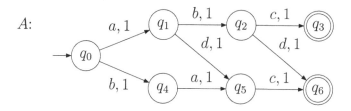

Fig. 2. A DCA A with $\mathcal{M}(A) = \{\{abc, bac\}, \{abd, bac\}, \{abc\}, \{abd\}, \{adc\}, \{bac\}, \emptyset\}$.

Consider the runs $r_0 = q_0, q_4, q_5, q_6$ and $r_1 = q_0, q_1, q_2, q_3$ of A on the words bac and abc, respectively. Both runs respect the capacity function and end in an accepting state. Since the runs are disjoint, the multiset of runs $\{r_0, r_1\}$ is a legal operation, it accepts the multiset $\{abc, bac\}$, and so $\{abc, bac\} \in \mathcal{M}(A)$

Consider now the run $r_2 = q_0, q_1, q_5, q_6$ of A on adc. It respects the capacity function and ends in an accepting state, and so $\{adc\} \in \mathcal{M}(A)$. The run r_2 shares the transition $e = \langle q_5, c, q_6 \rangle$ with r_0. This transition has capacity 1. Thus, the multiset $\{r_0, r_2\}$ does not respect the capacity function and is not a legal operation, and so $\{bac, adc\} \notin \mathcal{M}(A)$.

Using similar considerations, it is easy to see that $\mathcal{M}(A) = \{\{abc, bac\}, \{abd, bac\}, \{abc\}, \{abd\}, \{adc\}, \{bac\}, \emptyset\}$.   □

3   Expressive Power

A multi-language $\mathcal{M}$ is *regular* if there is a CA that recognizes $\mathcal{M}$. We denote by MREG the classes of regular multi-languages. In this section we study the expressive power of CAs. We show that not all finite multi-languages are regular, that nondeterministic CAs are strictly more expressive than deterministic one, and that the picture of closure properties in MREG is involved.

We first need some definitions and observations. Given two multisets S_1 and S_2 over a set X of elements, we say that S_1 is a *submultiset* of S_2, denoted by $S_1 \subseteq S_2$, if every element in X appears in S_1 (weakly) fewer times than in S_2. That is, for every element $x \in X$, it holds that $S_1(x) \leq S_2(x)$. Since a submultiset of an accepting operation is an accepting operation, we have the following (see full proof in the full version).

Theorem 1. *Regular multi-languages are closed downwards: Consider a regular multi-language $\mathcal{M}$ and a multiset $S \in \mathcal{M}$. For all $S' \subseteq S$, it holds that $S' \in \mathcal{M}$.*

Given a CA A, we say that a multiset S *saturates* A if S is mutually accepted by A and it is maximal with respect to containment in $\mathcal{M}(A)$. That is, $S \in \mathcal{M}(A)$, and for every $S' \in \mathcal{M}(A)$, it holds that $S \not\subseteq S'$. Theorem 1 implies that regular multi-languages are characterized uniquely by maximal multisets, which are the saturating multisets of the CA. Accordingly, we define the *saturating language* of a CA A, denoted $\mathcal{SM}(A)$, as the set of all saturating multisets of the CA.

Given a set $\mathcal{M}$ of multisets, we denote by $sub(\mathcal{M})$ the set of all submultisets of the multisets in $\mathcal{M}$. Formally, $sub(\mathcal{M}) = \{S' : \text{there exists } S \in \mathcal{M} \text{ such that } S' \subseteq S\}$. Note that for every CA A, we have that $\mathcal{M}(A) = sub(\mathcal{SM}(A))$.

Example 2. Recall the CA A appearing in Fig. 2. It is easy to see that $\mathcal{SM}(A) = \{\{abc, bac\}, \{abd, bac\}, \{adc\}\}$. □

3.1 Regularity

Given a CA A, the *language* of A, denoted $L(A)$, is the set of all words that can be accepted by A while respecting the capacity function. It is easy to see that for every word $w \in \Sigma^*$, we have that $w \in L(A)$ iff $\{w\} \in \mathcal{M}(A)$. By the closure property we study in Sect. 3.3, this implies that for every finite multiset S of words, there is a CA A with $\mathcal{M}(A) = sub(\{S\})$. Essentially, the proof is similar to the proof showing that all finite languages are regular: a nondeterministic automaton for a finite language $L \subseteq \Sigma^*$ may consist of $|L|$ components, each for a word in L. Likewise, a CA for $sub(\{S\})$ may consist of $|S|$ components, each for a word in S. On the other hand, as we show below, there are finite multi-languages that are not regular.

Theorem 2. *Not all finite multi-languages are regular.*

Proof: Consider the finite multi-language $sub(\{\{ab, ac\}, \{ad\}\}) = \{\{ab, ac\}, \{ad\}, \{ab\}, \{ac\}, \emptyset\}$. In the full version, we prove that it is not regular. Essentially, this follows from the fact that every CA that has both an accepting operation on $\{ab, ac\}$ and an accepting operation on $\{ad\}$, should also have an accepting operation on $\{ab, ad\}$ or $\{ac, ad\}$. Yet, these multisets are not in $sub(\{\{ab, ac\}, \{ad\}\})$. □

3.2 Determinism

A *deterministic regular multi-language* is a multi-language that can be recognized by a DCA. We denote by DMREG the class of deterministic regular multi-languages.

Theorem 3. *CAs are strictly more expressive than DCAs.*

Proof: Clearly, every DCA is a CA. In order to prove strictness, consider the multi-language $sub(\{\{a, ab\}\})$. As we show in the full version, a CA for $sub(\{\{a, ab\}\})$ can nondeterministically chooses between reading a and ab, and so $sub(\{\{a, ab\}\}) \in$ MREG. On the other hand, $sub(\{\{a, ab\}\}) \notin$ DMREG. Intuitively, a DCA that mutually accepts $sub(\{\{a, ab\}\})$ should be able to traverse a twice, and should reach an accepting state while reading a. Yet, $sub(\{\{a, ab\}\})$ contains only one occurrence of a.   □

Essentially, the reason no DCA can recognize $sub(\{\{a, ab\}\})$ is that the DCA should traverse twice a prefix of two different words, yet may accept only one occurrence of this prefix. Trying to generalize this to a characterization of languages in MREG $\setminus$ DMREG, we say that a multi-language $\mathcal{M}$ is *prefix-replaceable* if whenever a word and its prefix are in a multiset in $\mathcal{M}$, then the multiset obtained by replacing the word by the prefix is also in $\mathcal{M}$. Formally, for every multiset of words $S \in \mathcal{M}$ and every word $w \in S$ that is a prefix of another word $w \cdot x \in S$, with $x \neq \epsilon$, it holds that $(S \setminus \{w \cdot x\}) \cup \{w\} \in \mathcal{M}$.

For example, the multi-language $sub(\{\{a, ab\}\})$ is not prefix-replaceable. Indeed, for $S = \{a, ab\}$, the word a is a prefix of the word ab, it is in S, and yet $(S \setminus \{ab\}) \cup \{a\} = \{a, a\}$ is not in $sub(\{\{a, ab\}\})$.

In the full version, we prove that prefix-replacability is a necessary yet insufficient condition for membership in DMREG. Another attempt to characterize DMREG, in particular for solving the problem of deciding whether a given CA has an equivalent DCA, considers *powerset-typeness*. Researchers have studied typeness for automata in various setting [7,8]. In particular, a class γ of automata is powerset type if whenever a nondeterministic automaton A in the class γ has an equivalent deterministic automaton, then an equivalent deterministic automaton can be defined on top of the subset construction of A. It is well known, for example, that finite automata are powerset type. So are nondeterministic weak automata on infinite words [8]. On the other hand, Büchi automata are not powerset type [11].

Theorem 4. *CAs are not powerset type.*

Proof: Consider the CA A described in Fig. 3. It is easy to see that $\mathcal{M}(A) \in$ DMREG. Indeed, the DCA D recognizes $\mathcal{M}(A)$. On the other hand, applying the subset construction on A results on the the structure A', and there is no way to define initial and final states and capacities on top of it and obtain a DCA for $\mathcal{M}(A)$.   □

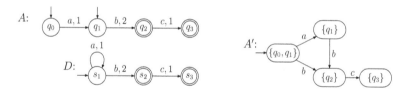

Fig. 3. The CA A has an equivalent DCA D, yet no equivalent DCA can be defined on top of its subset construction A'.

3.3 Closure Properties

In this section we study closure properties for MREG and DMREG. Since all regular multi-languages are closed downwards, complementation is not interesting in the context of MREG. On the other hand, in addition to the usual union and intersection operators, we consider *pairwise* union and intersection, to be defined below.

Consider a set X of elements. The union of multisets over X is naturally defined by summing the repetitions of each element. That is, for two multistes S_1 and S_2, we define their union $S_1 \cup S_2$ such that for every element $x \in X$, we have that $(S_1 \cup S_2)(x) = S_1(x) + S_2(x)$. Then, the intersection of multisets is defined by taking the minimal number of repetitions of each element. That is, for two multistes S_1 and S_2, we define their intersection $S_1 \cap S_2$ such that for every element $x \in X$, we have that $(S_1 \cap S_2)(x) = \min\{S_1(x), S_2(x)\}$.

We continue to the pairwise operators, where we apply union and intersection between the multisets in the two sets of multisets. Formally, for two multi-languages $\mathcal{M}_1$ and $\mathcal{M}_2$, we define their pairwise union by $\mathcal{M}_1 \uplus \mathcal{M}_2 = \{S_1 \cup S_2 : S_1 \in \mathcal{M}_1 \text{ and } S_2 \in \mathcal{M}_2\}$, and their pairwise intersection by $\mathcal{M}_1 \pitchfork \mathcal{M}_2 = \{S_1 \cap S_2 : S_1 \in \mathcal{M}_1 \text{ and } S_2 \in \mathcal{M}_2\}$.

Example 3. Let $\mathcal{M}_1 = \{\{a\}, \{ab, ac\}\}$ and $\mathcal{M}_2 = \{\{ac\}, \{a, ab, ac\}$. Then,

- $\mathcal{M}_1 \cup \mathcal{M}_2 = \{\{a\}, \{ab, ac\}, \{ac\}, \{a, ab, ac\}\}$.
- $\mathcal{M}_1 \cap \mathcal{M}_2 = \emptyset$.
- $\mathcal{M}_1 \uplus \mathcal{M}_2 = \{\{a, ac\}, \{a, a, ab, ac\}, \{ab, ac, ac\}, \{ab, ac, a, ab, ac\}\}$.
- $\mathcal{M}_1 \pitchfork \mathcal{M}_2 = \{\emptyset, \{a\}, \{ac\}, \{ab, ac\}\}$.

When we focus on regular multi-languages, it is useful to observe that for all multisets $\mathcal{M}_1$ and $\mathcal{M}_2$, it follows directly from the definition that $sub(\mathcal{M}_1) \cup sub(\mathcal{M}_2) = sub(\mathcal{M}_1 \cup \mathcal{M}_2)$ and $sub(\mathcal{M}_1) \uplus sub(\mathcal{M}_2) = sub(S_1 \cup S_2)_{S_1 \in \mathcal{M}_1, S_2 \in \mathcal{M}_2}$. In addition, we have the following.

Lemma 1. *If $\mathcal{M}_1$ and $\mathcal{M}_2$ are closed downwards, then $\mathcal{M}_1 \pitchfork \mathcal{M}_2 = \mathcal{M}_1 \cap \mathcal{M}_2$.*

Proof: First, by definition, $\mathcal{M}_1 \cap \mathcal{M}_2 \subseteq \mathcal{M}_1 \pitchfork \mathcal{M}_2$ regardless of $\mathcal{M}_1$ and $\mathcal{M}_2$ being closed downwards. We prove that $\mathcal{M}_1 \pitchfork \mathcal{M}_2 \subseteq \mathcal{M}_1 \cap \mathcal{M}_2$. Consider a multiset $S = S_1 \cap S_2$ for $S_1 \in \mathcal{M}_1$ and $S_2 \in \mathcal{M}_2$. Clearly, $S_1 \cap S_2 \subseteq S_1$. Therefore, as $\mathcal{M}_1$ is closed downwards, we have that $S_1 \cap S_2 \in \mathcal{M}_1$. Similarly, $S_1 \cap S_2 \in \mathcal{M}_2$, and so $S_1 \cap S_2 \in \mathcal{M}_1 \cap \mathcal{M}_2$, and we are done.

As MREG and DMREG are closed downwards, Lemma 1 implies that in the context of MREG and DMREG, pairwise intersection coincides with intersection. For union, this is not true.

We can now state our results about closure properties. See full proofs in the full version.

Theorem 5. – DMREG *and* MREG *are not closed under union.*
- MREG *is closed under pairwise union.*
- DMREG *is not closed under pairwise union.*
- DMREG *and* MREG *are not closed under intersection.*

4   Decision Problems

In this section we study the following decision problems for CAs in the utilization semantics:

1. Membership: given a CA A and a finite multiset S, decide whether $S \in \mathcal{M}(A)$.
2. Containment: given two CAs A and B, decide whether $\mathcal{M}(A) \subseteq \mathcal{M}(B)$.

Remark 1. A classical decision problem for automata is *nonemptiness*, namely deciding whether their language is not empty. In the setting of CA, we need to decide, given a CA A, whether $\mathcal{M}(A) \neq \emptyset$. Since all regular multi-languages are nonempty, as they contain $\emptyset$, this question is not of much interest. Alternatively, one may ask, in the nonemptiness problem for CA, whether $\mathcal{M}(A) \neq \{\emptyset\}$. It is easy to see that the latter holds iff the language of A is not empty, which is NLOGSPACE-complete [10].   □

Studying the complexities of decision problems on CAs, it is important to specify how the input to the problems is given. For a multiset S of words, we define the *length* of S, denoted $\|S\|$, as the sum of lengths of words in S. We also refer to the *size* of S, denoted $|S|$, which is the number of words in S. Alternative definitions represent a multiset by a list of its words along with their multiplicity, in unary or binary. Note that in either case, the "list with multiplicity" representation is more succinct than our "list with repetition" representation. For a CA $A = \langle \Sigma, Q, Q_0, \Delta, F, c \rangle$, we define the size of A by $\sum_{e \in \Delta} c'(e)$, where $c'(e)$ is $c(e) + 1$ if $c(e) \neq \infty$, and is 1 if $c(e) = \infty$. Note that our definition corresponds to a representation of A with capacities given in unary.

For traditional automata, the membership problem is to decide, given a word w and an NFA or DFA A, whether $w \in L(A)$. In both cases, the problem can be solved in linear time and is NLOGSPACE-complete. For the traditional semantics of CAs, namely when we care about $L(A)$, the membership problem can be solved in linear time for DCAs and is NP-complete for CAs [10]. For the containment problem, the complexity depends on whether the containing automaton is deterministic. For a CA A, the complexity of deciding whether $L(A) \subseteq L(B)$ is co-NP-complete for a DCA B and is EXPSPACE-complete for a CA B [9].

We now study the complexity of the problems for CAs in the utilization semantics. We start with membership.

Theorem 6. *The membership problem in the utilization semantics can be solved in linear time for DCAs and is NP-complete for CAs.*

Proof: Given a DCA A and a finite multiset S, we trace the single run of A on each word in S and maintain for each transition a counter of the number of times it is traversed. Clearly, $S \in \mathcal{M}(A)$ iff all runs end in an accepting state, and the counters are bounded by the corresponding capacities.

For a CA A and a finite multiset S, a witness to the membership of S in $\mathcal{M}(A)$ is an operation that accepts S. The length of the operation agrees with that of S, and as in the case of DCAs, it can be checked in linear time.

For the lower bound, recall that given a CA A and a word w, we have that $w \in L(A)$ iff $\{w\} \in \mathcal{M}(A)$. Thus, the lower bound follows from the NP-hardness of the membership problem in the traditional semantics for CAs [10]. $\square$

We continue to the containment problem. Recall that $\mathcal{M}(A)$ and $\mathcal{M}(B)$ may be infinite and may contain infinite multisets, which makes the setting challenging. Indeed, if all capacities are finite, then all multisets accepted by a CA A are of length linear in A. As we now show, we are able to bound the length of a multiset in $\mathcal{M}(A) \setminus \mathcal{M}(B)$ even when both may contain transitions with an infinite capacity. Intuitively, long words must traverse cycles all whose transitions have infinite capacity, and can be shortened.

Lemma 2. *Consider CAs A and B. If $\mathcal{M}(A) \not\subseteq \mathcal{M}(B)$, then there is a finite multiset in $\mathcal{M}(A) \setminus \mathcal{M}(B)$ whose size is linear in the size of B and whose length is polynomial in A and doubly exponential in B in the general case, and polynomial in both A and B when B is a DCA.*

Proof: Let $A = \langle \Sigma, Q, Q_0, \Delta, F, c \rangle$ and $B = \langle \Sigma, Q', Q_0', \Delta', F', c' \rangle$. As $\mathcal{M}(A) \not\subseteq \mathcal{M}(B)$, there is a multiset $S \in \mathcal{M}(A) \setminus \mathcal{M}(B)$. Since $\mathcal{M}(B)$ is closed downwards and $\emptyset \in \mathcal{M}(B)$, there is a submultiset $S' \subseteq S$ such that $S' \notin \mathcal{M}(B)$ and for every $S'' \subset S'$, it holds that $S'' \in \mathcal{M}(B)$. That is, S' is a minimal submultiset of S that is not in $\mathcal{M}(B)$. Note that since $S' \subseteq S$ and $S \in \mathcal{M}(A)$, we have that $S' \in \mathcal{M}(A)$. Hence, $S' \in \mathcal{M}(A) \setminus \mathcal{M}(B)$.

We claim that S' is of a finite size, linear in B. Since S' is a minimal submultiset of S that is not in $\mathcal{M}(B)$, it does not contain words that can be accepted via a run that only uses transitions with infinite capacities. To see this, assume by way of contradiction that S' contains a word w that is read in B along a path π from Q_0' to F' all whose transitions have capacity ∞. By the minimality of S', we have that $S' \setminus \{w\} \in \mathcal{M}(B)$. But then, by adding to the operation that mutually accepts $S' \setminus \{w\}$ an accepting run on w along the path π, we obtain an operation that respects the capacities and mutually accepts S', contradicting the fact that $S' \notin \mathcal{M}(B)$. Now, consider a word $w \in S'$ and consider the operation O of B that mutually accepts $S' \setminus \{w\}$. Since S' does not contain words that can be accepted via a run that only uses transitions with infinite capacities, we know that every run in O consumes at least 1 from the capacity of some transition. Hence, $|S' \setminus \{w\}| = |S'| - 1 \leq |B|$, and we are done.

We continue to the length argument and show that we can replace every word in S' by a word whose length is polynomial in A and doubly exponential in B in the general case, and is polynomial in both A and B when B is a DCA, while maintaining that $S' \in \mathcal{M}(A) \setminus \mathcal{M}(B)$. Recall that $S' = \{w_1, \ldots, w_n\}$. For $i = 1, 2, \ldots, n$, we proceed iteratively and replace w_i by w_i', defined so that $S'' = S' \cup \{w_i'\} \setminus \{w_i\}$ still satisfies $S'' \in \mathcal{M}(A) \setminus \mathcal{M}(B)$. Also, if S'' is no longer minimal, we take a minimal submultiset of S'', namely one for which $S'' \setminus \{w\} \in \mathcal{M}(B)$ for all $w \in S''$. Once this is done, we update S' to S'', and continue to the next word in S'.

It is left to point to w_i'. First, if w_i is of the required length, then $w_i' = w_i$. Otherwise, as detailed in the full version, we distinguish between the case B is nondeterministic and the case it is deterministic. In the first, we obtain w_i' from w_i by removing subwords that traverse cycles in the product $A \times B'$, where B' is a DFA with $L(B') = L(B)$. In the second, reasoning about the product $A \times B$ is not sufficient, yet we can reason about the product of the CAs obtained from A and B by reducing the capacities of transitions consumed by w_i. In both cases, the bound on the size of the product gives the desire bound on w_i'.   □

Lemma 3. *The containment problem for CAs in the utilization semantics is at least as hard as the containment problem for CAs in the traditional semantics.*

Proof: We describe a logspace reduction from the containment problem in the traditional semantics to the containment problem in the utilization semantics. Consider a CA $A = \langle \Sigma, Q, Q_0, \Delta, F, c \rangle$, and let \$ be a letter not in Σ. We define the \$\$-*padding* of A as the CA $A' = \langle \Sigma \cup \{\$\}, Q \cup \{q_0, q_1\}, \{q_0\}, \Delta', F, c' \rangle$, where Δ' and c' are defined as follows.

- The transition relation Δ' is obtained from Δ by adding one \$-transition from q_0 to q_1 and $|Q_0|$ \$-transitions from q_1 to all initial states in A. That is, $\Delta' = \Delta \cup \{\langle q_0, \$, q_1 \rangle\} \cup \{\langle q_1, \$, q' \rangle : q' \in Q_0\}$.
- The capacity of all new transitions is 1, and the capacity of the transitions in Δ stays as in A. That is, $c' : \Delta' \to \mathbb{N} \cup \{\infty\}$ is such that $c'(e) = c(e)$ if $e \in \Delta$, and $c'(e) = 1$ otherwise.

Note that the construction preserves determinism: the CA A' has a single initial state and there is nondeterminism in the transitions from q_1 only when $|Q_0| > 1$.

Now, given CAs A and B – an input to the containment problem in the traditional semantics, our reduction returns their \$\$-paddings CAs A' and B'. Clearly, the reduction can be done in logspace. We prove that the reduction is correct, thus $L(A) \subseteq L(B)$ iff $\mathcal{M}(A') \subseteq \mathcal{M}(B')$.

First note that $L(A') = \$\$ \cdot L(A)$. Indeed, every run of A' is of the form q_0, q_1, r, for a run r of A, and the first two transitions in it can only be traversed while reading \$\$. Similarly, $L(B') = \$\$ \cdot L(B)$, and thus we get that $L(A) \subseteq L(B)$ iff $L(A') \subseteq L(B')$.

Now, since the only transition from the initial state has capacity 1, all multisets in A' contain at most one word. Since, in addition, we know that for every $w \in (\Sigma \cup \{\$\})^*$, we have that $w \in L(A')$ iff $\{w\} \in \mathcal{M}(A')$, it follows that $\mathcal{M}(A') = \{\emptyset\} \cup \{\{w\} : w \in L(A')\}$. Likewise, $\mathcal{M}(B') = \{\emptyset\} \cup \{\{w\} : w \in L(B')\}$. Accordingly, $\mathcal{M}(A') \subseteq \mathcal{M}(B')$ iff $L(A') \subseteq L(B')$ iff $L(A) \subseteq L(B)$, and we are done.   □

Theorem 7. *The containment problem $\mathcal{M}(A) \subseteq \mathcal{M}(B)$ is EXPSPACE-complete for a CA or a DCA A and a CA B, and is co-NP-complete for a CA or a DCA A and a DCA B.*

Proof: As detailed in the full version, the upper bounds follow from Lemma 2 and we can check that a guessed finite multiset S is indeed in $\mathcal{M}(A) \setminus \mathcal{M}(B)$ in the desired complexity. The lower bounds follow from the known lower bounds in the traditional semantics, namely EXPSPEC-hard for a CA B and co-NP-hard for a DCA B, and Lemma 3.   □

References

1. Boigelot, B., Godefroid, P.: Symbolic verification of communication protocols with infinite state spaces using QDDs. In: Alur, R., Henzinger, T.A. (eds.) CAV 1996. LNCS, vol. 1102, pp. 1–12. Springer, Heidelberg (1996). https://doi.org/10.1007/3-540-61474-5_53

2. Bouajjani, A., Habermehl, P., Vojnar, T.: Verification of parametric concurrent systems with prioritised FIFO resource management. Formal Methods Syst. Des. **32**(2), 129–172 (2008)

3. Cadilhac, M., Finkel, A., McKenzie, P.: On the expressiveness of Parikh automata and related models. In: 3rd Workshop on Non-Classical Models for Automata and Applications - NCMA, pp. 103–119 (2011)

4. Comon, H., Jurski, Y.: Multiple counters automata, safety analysis and presburger arithmetic. In: Hu, A.J., Vardi, M.Y. (eds.) CAV 1998. LNCS, vol. 1427, pp. 268–279. Springer, Heidelberg (1998). https://doi.org/10.1007/BFb0028751

5. Ford, L., Fulkerson, D.: Flows in Networks. Princeton University Press, Princeton (1962)

6. Klaedtke, F., Rueß, H.: Monadic second-order logics with cardinalities. In: Baeten, J.C.M., Lenstra, J.K., Parrow, J., Woeginger, G.J. (eds.) ICALP 2003. LNCS, vol. 2719, pp. 681–696. Springer, Heidelberg (2003). https://doi.org/10.1007/3-540-45061-0_54

7. Krishnan, S., Puri, A., Brayton, R.: Deterministic ω-automata vis-a-vis deterministic Büchi automata. In: Algorithms and Computations. Lecture Notes in Computer Science, vol. 834, pp. 378–386. Springer (1994)

8. Kupferman, O., Morgenstern, G., Murano, A.: Typeness for ω-regular automata. Int. J. Found. Comput. Sci. **17**(4), 869–884 (2006)

9. Kupferman, O., Sheinvald, S.: Capacitated automata and systems. Inf. Comput. **961**, 269 (2019)

10. Kupferman, O., Tamir, T.: Properties and utilization of capacitated automata. In: Proceedings 34th Conference on Foundations of Software Technology and Theoretical Computer Science. LIPIcs, vol. 29, pp. 33–44. Schloss Dagstuhl - Leibniz-Zentrum fuer Informatik, Germany (2014)

11. Löding, C.: Optimal bounds for the transformation of ω-automata. In: Proceedings 19th Conference on Foundations of Software Technology and Theoretical Computer Science. Lecture Notes in Computer Science, vol. 1738, pp. 97–109 (1999)

12. Qiu, R., Joshi, S.: Deterministic finite capacity automata: a solution to reduce the complexity of modeling and control of automated manufacturing systems. In: Proceedings Symposium on Computer-Aided Control System Design, pp. 218–223 (1996)

Bad Pictures: Some Structural Properties Related to Overlaps

Marcella Anselmo[1], Dora Giammarresi[2(✉)], Maria Madonia[3], and Carla Selmi[4]

[1] Dipartimento di Informatica, Università di Salerno, Via Giovanni Paolo II, 132, 84084 Fisciano, SA, Italy
manselmo@unisa.it

[2] Dipartimento di Matematica, Università Roma "Tor Vergata", via della Ricerca Scientifica, 00133 Roma, Italy
giammarr@mat.uniroma2.it

[3] Dipartimento di Matematica e Informatica,, Università di Catania, Viale Andrea Doria 6/a, 95125 Catania, Italy
madonia@dmi.unict.it

[4] LITIS, Université de Rouen Normandie, Saint Etienne du Rouvray, 76830 Rouen, France
carla.selmi@univ-rouen.fr

Abstract. Given two pictures p and f, p is f-free if f is not a subpicture of p. A binary picture f is *good* if for any pair of f-free pictures p and q there exists a bit-to-bit transformation from p to q such that any picture in the intermediate steps is f-free. Such transformation is called *f-free transformation*. A binary picture is *bad* if it is not good. These notions generalize to pictures the corresponding ones for strings. We study some properties of bad binary pictures in terms of overlaps and give some examples. Furthermore, we discuss the properties of an *index* of a bad picture f, that is a minimal picture size (h, k) for which two pictures of such size do not admit a f-free transformation.

Keywords: Bad pictures · Overlap · Index

1 Introduction

In combinatorics of strings the leading actors are all particular strings that generate interesting and useful patterns. Most of the pecularities of such strings are based on specific attributes regarding their factors (substrings) or, more specifically, their prefixes and suffixes. Important properties can be found also studying strings with overlap (also called *bifix* or *border*); they are often crucial to prove

Partially supported by INdAM-GNCS Projects 2019–2020, FARB Project ORSA190149 of University of Salerno and CREAMS Project of University of Catania. The second author acknowledges the MIUR Excellence Department Project awarded to the Department of Mathematics, University of Rome Tor Vergata, CUP E83C18000100006.

G. Jirásková and G. Pighizzini (Eds.): DCFS 2020, LNCS 12442, pp. 13–25, 2020.
https://doi.org/10.1007/978-3-030-62536-8_2

important structural properties as well as to design algorithms for coding or pattern matching. Recall that, given a string s, an *overlap* of s is a substring x that is both prefix and suffix of s.

An interesting notion is the one of *good* strings as defined for example in [7]; they are special binary strings that never appear as factors in some string transformations. More precisely, let $\Sigma = \{0, 1\}$ and let f be a string over Σ. A string w is said f-*free* if it does not contain f as factor. Given two f-free strings u and v of the same length d, an f-*free transformation* from u to v is a succession of f-free strings $x_1, x_2, \ldots, x_n$, $n \geq 1$ such that $x_1 = u$, $x_n = v$ and x_i differs from x_{i+1} only in one position (i.e. the Hamming distance between x_i and x_{i+1} is 1). A string f is called d-*good* if for any pair of f-free words of length d there exists an f-free transformation between them. A string is *good* if it s d-good for any d while a string is *bad* if it is not good. The *index* of a word f is the smallest integer d for which f is not d-good. Bounding the index of a word is useful to test whether a given word is good or bad. In [7–11] the structure of bad words is characterized and related to particular properties on overlaps.

Good strings are also called *isometric* because they are related to isometric subgraphs of the n-cube Q_n, that is the graph whose vertices consist of the (binary) words of length n, two vertices being adjacent when the corresponding words differ in exactly one symbol. Then an f-free transformation of a string corresponds to a path in this graph through vertices corresponding to strings that do not contain f. Moreover if f is good, then the subgraph $Q_n(f)$ of all vertices corresponding to f-free strings is isometric to Q_n. Such $Q_n(f)$ graphs are also called generalized Fibonacci cubes. Other applications of good strings are in the problem of pattern matching with errors and also in the context of studies of strings avoiding special factors.

In this paper, we deal with combinatorics of two-dimensional strings called *pictures*. A *picture* is a rectangular array of symbols taken from a finite alphabet Σ. The size of a picture is a pair (m, n) corresponding to the number of rows and columns. The set of all pictures over Σ is usually denoted by Σ^{**}; a two-dimensional language is thus a subset of Σ^{**}. Extending results from the formal (string) languages theory to two dimensions is often a challenging task. The two-dimensional structure in fact imposes some intrinsic difficulties even when trying to generalize the basic concepts. Nevertheless during the last fifty years, and still intensively nowadays, several results from string language theory were extended to pictures.

For what concerns combinatorics on pictures, the notions of factor, prefix ad suffix can be transposed from strings either in a "light" or in a general version. Given a picture p of size (m, n) we could consider only portions (sub-pictures) of p of size either (h, n) of (m, k) with $h < m$ and $k < n$. This corresponds to the particular cases of subpictures/ prefixes /suffixes that are a block of rows or columns, resp., of the picture p. This version is certainly more consistent with the case of strings. More generally, by exploiting the two-dimensional structure, we can use sub-pictures of any size (h, k). Then, for example, a prefix of a picture can be *any* top-left portion of p. However, in this case if one deletes a prefix from a picture, the remaining part is not a picture anymore (while, with the light definition, deleting any sub-pictures leaves rectangular pictures). Adopting this general definition of sub-picture leads to more interesting results but also to much involved proof techniques.

The notion of overlap extends very naturally from strings to pictures since it is not related to any scanning direction. Informally we can say that a picture p has an *overlap* if a copy p' of p can be put on p by placing a corner of p' somewhere on a position of p in a way that the superposed positions match. The overlap of p will be the sub-picture corresponding to the portion where p and p' match. Because of the two dimensions there are several possibilities to specialize this notion. The simplest one is when the matching is checked only by sliding the two picture copies with a horizontal or a vertical move; in this case we allow only overlap with the same number of columns or rows of the picture p itself. Notice that this case corresponds to the light version of definition for prefixes and suffixes. In some sense, pictures can be handled as they were thick strings on the alphabet either of the columns or of the rows. More general overlaps can be obtained by putting the top-left corner of p inside the copy p' (called tl-overlap) or by taking the bottom-left corner (called bl-overlap); and these corresponds to two different situations. Definition and properties of picture overlaps were recently studied in [1–5].

We extend the mentioned notion of good string to pictures. The basic definition can be given naturally by generalizing the corresponding ones for strings. The alphabet will be always the binary alphabet $\Sigma = \{0,1\}$. Let f be a picture of size (m,n) and p a picture of bigger size (h,k) (i.e. $h \geq m$ and $k \geq n$), we say that p is *f-free* if p does not contain f as sub-picture. Given two f-free pictures p and q of the same size, we say that there is an f-free transformation from p to q if p can be transformed into q by switching one by one all the bits on which p differs from q and all of the new pictures obtained in this process are f-free. Then a picture f is *(h,k)-good* if for any pair of f-free pictures p and q of size (h,k), there exists a f-free transformation from p to q. A picture is *good* if it is (h,k)-good for any positive pair (h,k). Finally, a picture is *bad* if it is not good.

We study some structural properties of bad pictures. We demonstrate that the property of being a bad picture is related to the fact of having some kind of error overlaps i.e. overlaps where some positions do not match. The most difficult part of the proof is to show that if a picture has a 2-error overlap then it is bad. For that all possible overlap cases are carefully analyzed. The last part of the paper considers the problem of finding a minimal (h,k) for which a bad picture f of given size (m,n) is not (h,k)-good. Such pair is called *index* of the picture f. This study can have applications in the context of two-dimensional pattern matching with errors. Some examples of good and bad pictures are also given.

2 Preliminaries

In this section, we first report some definitions and results on good and bad strings. Then, we collect all the notions for the two-dimensional setting (i.e.

pictures) needed for the main results. Throughout the paper, Σ denotes the binary alphabet $\{0, 1\}$.

2.1   Basic Notions and Results on Strings

A string s is a sequence of zero or more symbols from the alphabet Σ. The number n of symbols that compose s is referred to as the length (or the size) of s while the positions of such symbols are numbered from 1 to n. We also write $s = s_1 s_2 \ldots s_n$ with $s_i \in \Sigma$. A string w is a substring of s if $s = uwv$ for some $u, v \in \Sigma^*$.

Moreover, we say that w of length h occurs at position j of s if and only if $w = s_j \ldots s_{j+h-1}$. A string u is a *prefix* of s if u is a substring that occurs in s at position 1; a string v of length $h \leq n$ is a *suffix* of s if it is a substrings that occurs in s at position $n - h + 1$. A string x that is both prefix and suffix of s is called an *overlap* (also *border* or *bifix*) of s. Note that the empty string and s itself are *trivial* overlaps of s. Note that the name "overlap" comes from the fact that we can put a copy s' of s on s itself in a way that the corresponding positions match. A string s has an r-error overlap, $0 \leq r < n$, if there exist a prefix x and a suffix y of s that differ in exactly r positions (i.e., the Hamming distance between x and y is equal to r).

In [7], it is considered the interesting notion of *good* strings; they are special binary strings that never appear as factors in some string transformations. More precisely, let $\Sigma = \{0, 1\}$ and let f be a string over Σ. A string s is said f-*free* if it does not contain f as factor.

Given two f-free strings, u and v of the same length d, we can transform u in v by switching one-by-one all the bits in which they differ. This results in a sequence of strings $x_1, x_2, \ldots, x_n$ such that $x_1 = u$, $x_n = v$ and x_i differs from x_{i+1} only in one position. If each string x_i is f-free, we call it an f-*free transformation* from u to v. The length n of the succession is exactly the Hamming distance between u and v.

A string f is called d-*good* if for any pair of f-free words of length d there exists an f-free transformation between them. A string is *good* if it is d-good for any d. A string is *bad* if it is not good. The structure of bad words is characterized in [7–11]. In particular we mention the following results.

Proposition 1. *A string f is bad if and only if f has a 2-error overlap.*

The *index* of a bad word f, usually denoted by $B(f)$, is defined as the smallest integer d for which f is not d-good. If f is good then its index is ∞. Bounding the index of a word, as in the following proposition, is useful to test whether a given word is good or bad. In [11] it is proved the following result.

Proposition 2. *Let $f \in \Sigma^n$ be a bad string. Then $n + 1 \leq B(f) \leq 2n - 1$.*

2.2   Basic Notions on Pictures

We recall some definitions about pictures (see [6]). A *picture* over a finite alphabet Σ is a two-dimensional rectangular array of elements of Σ. Given a picture p with m rows and n columns, the *size* of p is the pair $size(p) = (m, n)$. The pictures of size $(m, 0)$ or $(0, n)$ for all $m, n \geq 0$, called *empty* pictures, will be never considered in this paper. The set of all pictures over Σ of fixed size (m, n) is denoted by $\Sigma^{m,n}$, while the set of all pictures over Σ is denoted by Σ^{**}.

Let p be a picture of size (m, n). The set of coordinates $dom(p) = \{1, 2, \ldots, m\} \times \{1, 2, \ldots, n\}$ is referred to as the *domain* of a picture p. We let $p(i, j)$ denote the symbol in p at coordinates (i, j). We assume the top-left corner of the picture to be at position $(1, 1)$. Moreover, to easily detect border positions of pictures, we use initials of words "top", "bottom", "left" and "right": then, for example, the *tl-corner* of p refers to position $(1, 1)$ while the *br-corner* refers to position (m, n).

A *sub-domain* of $dom(p)$ is a set d of the form $\{i, i + 1, \ldots, i'\} \times \{j, j + 1, \ldots, j'\}$, where $1 \leq i \leq i' \leq m$, $1 \leq j \leq j' \leq n$, also specified by the pair $[(i, j), (i', j')]$. The portion of p corresponding to positions in subdomain $[(i, j), (i', j')]$ is denoted by $p[(i, j), (i', j')]$. Then a non-empty picture x is *sub-picture of p* if $x = p[(i, j), (i', j')]$, for some $1 \leq i \leq i' \leq m$, $1 \leq j \leq j' \leq n$; if it is so, we say that x *occurs* at position (i, j) (its tl-corner).

Given two pictures, p and q, of size (m, n) and (m', n'), respectively, they can be concatenated both horizontally by juxtaposing the last column of p with the first column of q or vertically by juxtaposing the last row of p with the first row of q. These operations are called the *column concatenation* of p and q $(p \oplus q)$ and the *row concatenation* of p and q $(p \ominus q)$ are partial operations, defined only if $m = m'$ and if $n = n'$, respectively.

$$p \oplus q = \boxed{\begin{array}{c|c} p & q \end{array}} \qquad\qquad p \ominus q = \boxed{\begin{array}{c} p \\ \hline q \end{array}}$$

Note that any string $s = y_1 y_2 \cdots y_n$ can be identified either with a single-row or with a single-column picture, i.e. a picture of size $(1, n)$ or $(n, 1)$.

We now consider the notion of overlap as generalization from strings to pictures (see for example [4]). Informally, as for strings, we say that a picture p has an overlap if we can put a copy p' somewhere over p in a way that the corresponding positions match. This implies p has an overlap if and only if we can find the same rectangular portion at two opposite corners. Note that there are two different kinds of overlaps depending on the pair of opposite corners that hold the overlap. We state the following definition.

Definition 3. *Given pictures $p \in \Sigma^{m,n}$ and $x \in \Sigma^{m',n'}$, with $1 \leq m' \leq m$ and $1 \leq n' \leq n$, the picture x is a tl-overlap of p, if x is a sub-picture of p occurring at position $(1, 1)$ and at position $(m - m' + 1, n - n' + 1)$; picture x is a bl-overlap of p, if x is a sub-picture of p occurring at position $(m - m' + 1, 1)$ and at position $(1, n - n' + 1)$. Moreover x is an overlap of p if it is either a tl- or a bl-overlap.*

As special cases, p is a *trivial overlap* of itself, and x is a *proper overlap* of p if it is not trivial. Other particular cases are when the overlap x has the same number of rows or columns of p: these particular cases are referred to as *horizontal* or *vertical overlaps*, respectively and correspond to the horizontal or vertical slide movement to put a copy of p into p. A *diagonal overlap* is an overlap neither horizontal nor vertical.

Note that a tl-overlap x of a picture p of size (m, n) can be univocally detected either by giving the position where its tl-corner occurs in p or by giving its size. The analogous holds for the bl-overlap. Examples of pictures together with their overlaps are given below; p has a tl-overlap, q and r have a bl-overlap while s has a vertical overlap.

$$
p = \begin{array}{|cc c|c cc|}
\hline
0 & 1 & 0 & 0 & 0 & 0 \\
1 & 1 & 0 & 1 & 1 & 1 \\
\hline
0 & 0 & 1 & 1 & 1 & 0 \\
0 & 1 & 1 & 0 & 1 & 0 \\
1 & 1 & 1 & 1 & 1 & 0 \\
\hline
\end{array}
\qquad
q = \begin{array}{|c cc|c c|}
\hline
1 & 0 & 0 & 1 & 0 \\
1 & 1 & 0 & 1 & 1 \\
1 & 1 & 1 & 0 & 0 \\
\hline
1 & 0 & 1 & 1 & 0 \\
1 & 1 & 1 & 1 & 0 \\
0 & 0 & 0 & 1 & 0 \\
\hline
\end{array}
\qquad
r = \begin{array}{ccc}
0 & 0 & 1 \\
0 & 1 & 1 \\
1 & 1 & 1 \\
\end{array}
\qquad
s = \begin{array}{|cccc|}
\hline
0 & 1 & 0 & 0 \\
1 & 1 & 1 & 1 \\
0 & 0 & 1 & 1 \\
0 & 1 & 0 & 0 \\
1 & 1 & 1 & 1 \\
\hline
\end{array}
$$

For the sequel, given two pictures p and q of the same size, we will be interested in the number of positions in which they differ. By borrowing the terminology from string theory, we will refer to this number as the Hamming distance between p and q and denote it by $dist_\mathcal{H}(p, q)$.

3   Good and Bad Pictures

We introduce the notions of good and bad pictures and prove some properties of bad pictures based on overlaps with errors. The definitions and the results extend to two dimensions the corresponding theory for strings given in [8].

Definition 4. *Let p and f be two pictures on Σ. The picture p is* f-free *if p does not contain f as sub-picture.*

We now consider two f-free pictures p and q of the same size (h, k). Let d be the number of positions in which they differ, i.e. $d = dist_\mathcal{H}(p, q)$. We can "transform" p into q by switching one-by-one the symbols in these positions in exactly d steps and denote by p_i the picture obtained after i changes. If all such p_i are f-free, this sequence of pictures p_i, with $p_0 = p$ and $p_d = q$, is called an *f-free transformation* from p to q. More formally, we give the following definition.

Definition 5. *Let f be a picture over Σ and let $p, q \in \Sigma^{h,k}$ be two f-free pictures. A f-free tranformation from p to q, which we denote $p \rightsquigarrow q$, is a sequence of pictures $p_0 = p, p_1, \ldots, p_d = q$ such that:*

1. *$p_i \in \Sigma^{h,k}$ $0 \le i \le h$,*
2. *$dist_\mathcal{H}(p_i, p_{i+1}) = 1$, for all $0 \le i \le d - 1$,*
3. *$d = dist_\mathcal{H}(p, q)$,*
4. *p_i is f-free, for all $0 \le i \le d$.*

Definition 6. *A picture $f \in \Sigma^{**}$ is (h,k)-good if, for all pairs of f-free pictures $p, q \in \Sigma^{h,k}$, there exists a f-free transformation from p to q. A picture f on Σ is* good *if f is (h, k)-good, for all $h, k \geq 1$.*

Definition 7. *A picture $f \in \Sigma^{**}$ is (h,k)-bad if there exist f-free pictures $p, q \in \Sigma^{h,k}$ for which no f-free transformation from p to q exists. A picture $f \in \Sigma^{**}$ is* bad *if it is not good i.e. if f is (h, k)-bad, for some $h, k \geq 1$.*

Let us now introduce the notion of overlap with errors that will be used to prove properties of binary bad pictures. A picture p has an *r-error tl-overlap* if p has a tl-overlap in the sense of Definition 3 where the two subpictures in the corners match everywhere except in exactly r positions. Similarly, p has an *r-error bl-overlap* if p has a bl-overlap where exactly r points do not match. A picture p has an *r-error overlap* if p has an r-error tl-overlap or an r-error bl-overlap. Note that, trivially, a 0-error overlap is an overlap.

We now show that the notion of 2-error overlap is related to the property of being bad. For lack of space we do not give all the details of the proof.

Proposition 8. *Let f be a picture on $\Sigma^{m,n}$. If f has a 2-error overlap then f is bad.*

Proof. Let $f \in \Sigma^{m,n}$ be a picture with a 2-error tl-overlap. The proof goes similarly if f has a 2-error bl-overlap. Suppose that the size of the 2-error tl-overlap is (k, l), for some $1 \leq k \leq m$ and $1 \leq l \leq n$, and denote $r = m - k$ and $s = n - l$. Hence, the subpicture $ov \in \Sigma^{k,l}$ of f occurring at position $(1, 1)$ and the subpicture $ov' \in \Sigma^{k,l}$ of f occurring at position $(r + 1, s + 1)$ coincide in all positions except for two, say (i_1, j_1) and (i_2, j_2). Let $f(i_1, j_1) = ov(i_1, j_1) = x$ and $f(i_2, j_2) = ov(i_2, j_2) = y$, for some $x, y \in \Sigma$. Then, $f(r + i_1, s + j_1) = ov'(i_1, j_1) = \overline{x}$ and $f(r + i_2, s + j_2) = ov'(i_2, j_2) = \overline{y}$.

The proof is split in three parts, following that the 2-error overlap is a diagonal, a horizontal, or a vertical 2-error overlap.

First, consider the case that the 2-error overlap of size (k, l) is a diagonal one. Just to fix ideas, suppose that $i_1 \leq i_2$ and $j_1 \leq j_2$, $(i_1, j_1) \neq (i_2, j_2)$ The other cases can be handled in a similar way. We are going to construct two f-free pictures for which there does not exist a f-free transformation, thus showing that f is bad.

Let $f(1, n) = c$ and $f(m, 1) = e$, for some $c, e \in \Sigma$. Consider the picture α, of size $(m + r, n + s)$, constructed as follows. Imagine to take two copies of f and let the tl-corner of a copy of f coincide with position $(r + 1, s + 1)$ of the other one. In this way, picture ov is superposed to picture ov'. Thus, the symbols in all positions match, except for the symbols in two positions that we set as follows: $\alpha(r + i_1, s + j_1) = \overline{x}$, and $\alpha(r + i_2, s + j_2) = y$. The remaining positions in the domain $d_{tr} = [(1, n + 1), (r, n + s)]$ are filled with $\overline{c}$, while the positions in the domain $d_{bl} = [(m + 1, 1), (m + r, s)]$ are filled with $\overline{e}$. The construction of α is depicted in the following figure.

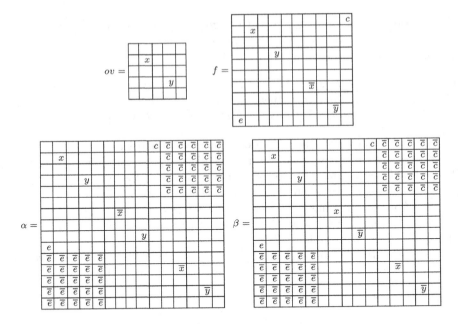

We show that α is f-free. In fact, f cannot occur in α with its tl-corner at position $(1,1)$, since $\alpha(r + i_2, s + j_2) = y$ while $f(r + i_2, s + j_2) = \overline{y}$. Picture f cannot occur even with its br-corner at position $(m + r, n + s)$, since $\alpha(r + i_1, s + j_1) = \overline{x}$ while $f(i_1, j_1) = x$. Finally, f cannot occur elsewhere, because either the tr-corner of this occurrence of f would fall in d_{tr}, or the bl-corner of this occurrence of f would fall in d_{bl}, or both. In any case this would cause a mismatch.

Let β the picture of size $(m + r, n + s)$ that differs from α only in positions $(r+i_1, s+j_1)$ and $(r+i_2, s+j_2)$. Actually, $\beta(r+i_1, s+j_1) = x$ and $\beta(r+i_2, s+j_2) = \overline{y}$, as shown in the previous figure.

Using similar arguments as for α, we can prove that β is f-free. Note that the pictures α and β differ only in positions $(r + i_1, s + j_1)$ and $(r + i_2, s + j_2)$, and that each time one of these positions is switched, an occurrence of f appears. Hence, there is no f-free transformation from α to β. This concludes the proof in the case of a diagonal 2-error overlap in f.

The remaining two cases when the 2-error overlap in f is an horizontal one and a vertical one, respectively, are very technical; they are not given for lack of space. □

Following the construction of the pictures α, β in the previous theorem, we can say something more about the size of these pictures.

Remark 9. If $f \in \Sigma^{m,n}$ has a 2-error overlap then f is (s,t)-bad, with $s \leq 2m-1$ and $t \leq 2n - 1$ and $(s,t) \neq (2m - 1, 2n - 1)$. Let ov be such 2-error overlap. Following the construction in the proof of Proposition 8, there exists a pair of f-free pictures in $\Sigma^{s,t}$, (either α and β) such that no f-free transformation from one picture to the other one exists. Note that, if ov is a horizontal (vertical, resp.) 2-error overlap, then $s = m$ and $t \leq 2n - 1$ ($s \leq 2m - 1$ and $t = n$, resp.). If instead $ov \in \Sigma^{\overline{h},\overline{k}}$ is a diagonal 2-error overlap, then $s = 2m - \overline{h}$ and $t = 2n - \overline{k}$. Moreover, since ov is a 2-error overlap, we have $area(p) \geq 2$ (i.e. it cannot be $\overline{h} = 1$ and $\overline{k} = 1$) and, therefore, we cannot have $s = 2m - 1$ and $t = 2n - 1$.

Remark 10. The previous proposition suggests a method to construct a family of bad pictures. Let p be a picture on a binary alphabet. We choose two positions in p, switch the symbols in these two positions, and denote by p' the picture obtained from p in this way. Any picture f having p and p' as tl- and br-corners, respectively, has 2-error overlap and then it is a bad picture applying Proposition 8.

Unfortunately the vice versa of Proposition 8 is not true and then the presence of a 2-error overlap does not characterize bad pictures as it holds for strings. Here is a counterexample.

Example 11. The binary picture $f = \begin{array}{|c|c|c|} \hline 1 & 0 & 1 \\ \hline 0 & 1 & 0 \\ \hline \end{array}$ has not a 2-error ovelap but it is a bad picture. In fact, the following pictures p and q are f-free and any transformation from p to q is not f-free.

$$p = \begin{array}{|c|c|c|c|c|c|c|} \hline 1 & 1 & 1 & 0 & 1 & 1 & 1 \\ \hline 1 & 0 & 1 & 1 & \mathbf{0} & \mathbf{0} & 1 \\ \hline 0 & 1 & 1 & 0 & \mathbf{0} & 1 & 0 \\ \hline 1 & 1 & 0 & 1 & 0 & 1 & 0 \\ \hline \end{array} \qquad q = \begin{array}{|c|c|c|c|c|c|c|} \hline 1 & 1 & 1 & 0 & 1 & 1 & 1 \\ \hline 1 & 0 & 0 & 1 & \mathbf{1} & \mathbf{0} & 1 \\ \hline 0 & 1 & 0 & 0 & \mathbf{1} & 1 & 0 \\ \hline 1 & 1 & 0 & 1 & 0 & 1 & 0 \\ \hline \end{array}$$

The bits in which p and q differ are written in bold. Switching each of the bold written bit of p, an occurence of f is generated. So the transformation from p to q is not f-free.

Very interestlingly, we can prove a weak version of the vice versa of Proposition 8. In fact we demostrate that if a picture is bad then either it has a 2-error overlap or it has both a 1-error tl-overlap and a 1-error bl-overlap (somehow again 2 errors in total). We prove first the following lemma.

Lemma 12. *Let $f \in \Sigma^{m,n}$ be a bad picture and let $p, q \in \Sigma^{s,t}$ be two f-free pictures of minimal Hamming distance among the pictures of that size with no f-free transformation. Let V be the set of all positions in which p differs from q. It holds the following.*

1. *The distance $dist_{\mathcal{H}}(p, q) = d \geq 2$,*
2. *Switching any symbol in p in the positions in V will generate an occurrence of f as sub-picture,*
3. *Any tranformation $p_0 = p, p_1, \ldots, p_{d-1}, p_d = q$ is such that all intermediate pictures p_i, $i = 1, \ldots, d - 1$ are not f-free,*
4. *The occurrence of f in each p_i contains at least two positions in the set V.*

Proof.

1. : If $d < 2$ then sequence p, q is an f-free transformation from p to q.
2. : By contradiction, we could switch such position getting p' with $dist_\mathcal{H}(p', q) < d$ against minimality hypothesis.
3. : By contradiction, let p_r be f-free. We set $p_r = q'$ with $dist_\mathcal{H}(p, q') < d$ against minimality hypothesis.
4. : By contradiction, then q is not f-free.   □

Proposition 13. *Let $f \in \Sigma^{**}$. If f is bad then f has a 2-error overlap or a 1-error tl-overlap and a 1-error bl-overlap.*

Proof. Let $p, q \in \Sigma^{h,k}$ be two f-free pictures of minimal Hamming distance such that no f-free transformation from p to q does exist. Let $dist_\mathcal{H}(p, q) = d$. Since p and q are f-free, we have that $d \geq 2$. Let V be the set of the d positions in which p and q are different. We construct the sequence of pictures of a (non f-free) transformation $p_0 = p, p_1, \ldots, p_{d-1}, p_d = q$ as follows. Take $p_0 = p$, choose the position in V that is the most "high-and-left", say (i_1, j_1), and switch the symbol; this is the first picture p_1. By Lemma 12 we have that p_1 contains f as sub-picture, call it f^1, and inside f^1 there is at least another position in V. Choose one of such positions and switch the symbol to get picture p_2. Then repeat the procedure always choosing a position in V to be switched that belongs to the new occurrence of f we have just generated. Note that all the occurrences f^k of f we generate do overlap and then create a sort of "chain" of 1-error either tl- or bl- overlaps of f. After $d - 1$ steps, we get picture p_{d-1} where we just switched position (i_{d-1}, j_{d-1}) and that have an occurrence of f in it containing the last position to be switched (i_d, j_d). That is the occurrence of f, called f^{d-1}, in p_{d-1} contains positions (i_{d-1}, j_{d-1}) and (i_d, j_d). On the other hand if in p we directly switch the symbol in position (i_d, j_d) then, by Lemma 12, we get an occurrence of f, call it f', that should contain also at least another positions from V, say (i_r, j_r). Then we have two possibilities. If the occurrence f^r of f contains also position (i_d, j_d) then these two positions $((i_d, j_d)$ and $(i_r, j_r))$ lie in the overlap of these occurrences f' and f^r of f and therefore f has a 2-error overlap. If f^r does not contain (i_d, j_d), then this chain of 1-error overlaps of f contains a sort of loop and therefore there is at least one 1-error tl-overlap and at least one 1-error bl-overlap.   □

As an immediate consequence of Proposition 13, we can exhibit a family of good pictures on a binary alphabet.

Corollary 14. *Every picture over Σ where all the positions hold the same symbol is good.*

4   Index of Bad Pictures

In this last part of the paper we focus on bad pictures and bound the minimum size for which a bad picture is (h, k)-good. We introduce first a notation. Given two pairs of positive integers (h_1, k_1) and (h_2, k_2), we write $(h_1, k_1) \le (h_2, k_2)$ if $h_1 \le h_2$ and $k_1 \le k_2$; moreover, we write $(h_1, k_1) < (h_2, k_2)$ if $h_1 \le h_2$, $k_1 \le k_2$ and $(h_1, k_1) \ne (h_2, k_2)$. Note that there exist pairs such that neither $(h_1, k_1) \le (h_2, k_2)$ nor $(h_2, k_2) \le (h_1, k_1)$. In this case, we say that (h_1, k_1) and (h_2, k_2) are not comparable. Consider, as an example, the pairs (h_1, k_1), (h_2, k_2) with $h_1 \le h_2$ and $k_1 > k_2$.

Lemma 15. *If $f \in \Sigma^{m,n}$ is (h, k)-bad, then $(m, n) < (h, k)$.*

Proof. Trivially, m and n are such that $(m, n) \le (h, k)$. We show that $(m, n) \ne (h, k)$.

If f is (h, k)-bad, then there are two f-free pictures in $\Sigma^{h,k}$ for which no f-free transformation from one to the other exists. Let $p, q \in \Sigma^{h,k}$ be two pictures of minimal Hamming distance with this property, and $p_0, p_1, \cdots, p_l$ be a transformation of p in q of minimal distance l. If $(m, n) = (h, k)$, then some picture in the sequence is equal to f. Moreover, the minimality implies that $l = 2$, and that the transformation is p, f, q. In other words, p and q differ in two positions. Exchanging the steps of the transformation, we would obtain a f-free transformation form p to q, against the hypothesis. □

Lemma 16. *Let $f \in \Sigma^{m,n}$ be a picture. If f is (h, k)-bad, then f is $(h, k+1)$-bad and f is $(h + 1, k)$-bad.*

Proof. Let $p, q \in \Sigma^{h,k}$ be two f-free pictures such that no f-free transformation from p to q exists. If $f(1, n) = x$, then consider two picture $p', q' \in \Sigma^{h,k+1}$, obtained by adding a column of symbols $\bar{x}$ to the right of p and q. It is easy to prove that p' and q' are f-free. Moreover, since the positions where p' and q' differ are not in the last column, any transformation from p' to q' is in fact a transformation from p to q. Hence, it is not f-free.

An analogous reasoning shows that f is $(h + 1, k)$-bad, also. □

We have now all the ingredients to introduce the definition of *index* of a picture.

Definition 17. *Given a bad picture $f \in \Sigma^{m,n}$, a pair of positive integers (h, k) is an* index *of f if f is (h, k)-bad and f is not (h', k')-bad for any pair of positive integers $(h', k') < (h, k)$.*

Lemma 15, gives immediately the following bound for an index of a picture.

Proposition 18. *Let $f \in \Sigma^{m,n}$ be a bad picture. If (h, k) is an index of f, then $(h, k) > (m, n)$.*

Remark 19. Differently from the string case, a picture f could have more than one index. Indeed, it could exist two different, and not comparable pairs of positive integers, that are both indexes of f, as shown in the following example.

Example 20. Consider the following pictures over the alphabet $\Sigma = \{1, 0\}$:

$$f = \begin{array}{|c|c|c|}\hline 1&1&1\\\hline 0&0&1\\\hline 0&0&1\\\hline\end{array}\,,\quad p = \begin{array}{|c|c|c|c|}\hline 1&1&1&1\\\hline 0&0&0&1\\\hline 0&0&1&1\\\hline\end{array}\,,\quad q = \begin{array}{|c|c|c|c|}\hline 1&1&1&1\\\hline 0&0&1&1\\\hline 0&0&0&1\\\hline\end{array}\,,\quad p' = \begin{array}{|c|c|c|}\hline 1&1&1\\\hline 1&0&1\\\hline 0&0&1\\\hline 0&0&1\\\hline\end{array}\,,\ \text{and}\ q' = \begin{array}{|c|c|c|}\hline 1&1&1\\\hline 0&1&1\\\hline 0&0&1\\\hline 0&0&1\\\hline\end{array}\,.\ \text{One}$$

can check that p and q are f-free and no f-free transformation from p to q exists. Therefore, f is $(3,4)$-bad and, from Lemma 15, $(3,4)$ is an index of f. The analogous result holds for p' and q'. Hence, f has two different and not comparable indexes $(3,4)$ and $(4,3)$.

The following Proposition 21 characterizes bad pictures $f \in \Sigma^{m,n}$ with minimal index $(m, n+1)$. Note that an analogous characterization holds for bad pictures $f \in \Sigma^{m,n}$ with minimal index $(m+1, n)$.

Let $c \in \Sigma^{m,1}$ and denote by c^h the column concatenation of h copies of c.

Proposition 21. *Let $f \in \Sigma^{m,n}$ be a bad picture. The pair $(m, n+1)$ is an index of f if and only if either $f = c_1{}^h c_2{}^k c_3{}^t$, for some $h, k, t \geq 1$, $c_1, c_2, c_3 \in \Sigma^{m,1}$ with $dist_{\mathcal{H}}(c_1, c_2) = dist_{\mathcal{H}}(c_2, c_3) = 1$ or $f = c_1{}^h c_2{}^k$, for some $h, k \geq 1$, $c_1, c_2 \in \Sigma^{m,1}$ with $dist_{\mathcal{H}}(c_1, c_2) = 2$.*

Proof. If $(m, n+1)$ is an index of f, then there exists a pair of f-free pictures in $\Sigma^{m,n+1}$ for which no f-free transformation from one picture to the other one exists. Suppose that $p, q \in \Sigma^{m,n+1}$ are two f-free pictures of minimal Hamming distance such that no f-free transformation from p to q exists. Let $dist_{\mathcal{H}}(p, q) = d$ and let $V = \{(i_1, j_1), (i_2, j_2), \cdots, (i_d, j_d)\}$ be the set of all positions in which p and q are different. As noted in Lemma 12, we have $d \geq 2$ and for any position $(i, j) \in V$, if we switch $p(i, j)$, we obtain an occurrence of f in p. This implies that $d > 2$ is not possible, since p may contain only two different occurrences of f, for size reasons. More exactly, f can occur in p only at position $(1, 1)$ and at position $(1, 2)$. Therefore $V = \{(i_1, j_1), (i_2, j_2)\}$ and denote by $f_{(i_1, j_1)}$ ($f_{(i_2, j_2)}$, resp.) the occurrence of f in p that is obtained by switching $p(i_1, j_1)$ ($p(i_2, j_2)$, resp.). Note that both positions (i_1, j_1) and (i_2, j_2) are covered by both $f_{(i_1, j_1)}$ and $f_{(i_2, j_2)}$, because there is no f-free transformation from p to q. This implies that f has a 2-error h-overlap of size $(m, n-1)$. Now, if $j_1 \neq j_2$ and w.l.o.g. $j_1 < j_2$, then we have $f = c_1{}^h c_2{}^k c_3{}^t$, with $h = j_1$, $k = j_2 - j_1$, $t = n - j_2$, $c_1, c_2, c_3 \in \Sigma^{m,1}$ and $dist_{\mathcal{H}}(c_1, c_2) = dist_{\mathcal{H}}(c_2, c_3) = 1$. If instead $j_1 = j_2$ then we have $f = c_1{}^h c_2{}^k$, with $h = j_1$, $k = n - j_1$, $c_1, c_2 \in \Sigma^{m,1}$ and $dist_{\mathcal{H}}(c_1, c_2) = 2$.

Suppose now that either $f = c_1{}^h c_2{}^k c_3{}^t$, for some $h, k, t \geq 1$, $c_1, c_2, c_3 \in \Sigma^{m,1}$ with $dist_{\mathcal{H}}(c_1, c_2) =, dist_{\mathcal{H}}(c_2, c_3) = 1$, or $f = c_1{}^h c_2{}^k$, for some $h, k \geq 1$, with $c_1, c_2 \in \Sigma^{m,1}$ and $dist_{\mathcal{H}}(c_1, c_2) = 2$. It is easy to see that, in both cases, f has a 2-error h-overlap of size $(m, n-1)$. Then, following the construction in the proof of Proposition 8, we can obtain two f-free pictures α and β in $\Sigma^{m,n+1}$, for which no f-free transformation from α to β exists. Note that the 2-error h-overlap of f does not satisfy Condition (*), since $s = 1$ in this case. Then f is $(m, n+1)$-bad and $(m, n+1)$ is an index of f, applying Lemma 15. $\qquad\square$

We conclude with an example that exploits the above proposition.

Example 22. Consider the picture $f \in \Sigma^{3,3}$ in Example 20. The pair $(3,4)$ is an index of f. Then, following the previous Proposition 21, $f = c_1{}^2 c_2{}^1$ and

$$dist_\mathcal{H}(c_1, c_2) = 2 \text{ with } c_1 = \begin{array}{|c|}\hline 1 \\ \hline 0 \\ \hline 0 \\ \hline\end{array} \quad c_2 = \begin{array}{|c|}\hline 1 \\ \hline 1 \\ \hline 1 \\ \hline\end{array}.$$

References

1. Anselmo, M., Giammarresi, D., Madonia, M.: Unbordered pictures: properties and construction. In: Maletti, A. (ed.) CAI 2015. LNCS, vol. 9270, pp. 45–57. Springer, Cham (2015). https://doi.org/10.1007/978-3-319-23021-4_5
2. Anselmo, M., Giammarresi, D., Madonia, M.: Avoiding overlaps in pictures. In: Pighizzini, G., Câmpeanu, C. (eds.) DCFS 2017. LNCS, vol. 10316, pp. 16–32. Springer, Cham (2017). https://doi.org/10.1007/978-3-319-60252-3_2
3. Anselmo, M., Giammarresi, D., Madonia, M.: Non-expandable non-overlapping sets of pictures. Theor. Comput. Sci. **657**, 127–136 (2017)
4. Anselmo, M., Giammarresi, D., Madonia, M.: Sets of pictures avoiding overlaps. Int. J. Found. Comput. Sci. **30**(6–7), 875–898 (2019)
5. Gamard, G., Richomme, G.: Coverability in two dimensions. In: Dediu, A.-H., Formenti, E., Martín-Vide, C., Truthe, B. (eds.) LATA 2015. LNCS, vol. 8977, pp. 402–413. Springer, Cham (2015). https://doi.org/10.1007/978-3-319-15579-1_31
6. Giammarresi, D., Restivo, A.: Two-dimensional languages. In: Rozenberg, G., Salomaa, A. (eds.) Handbook of Formal Languages, pp. 215–268. Springer, Heidelberg (1997). https://doi.org/10.1007/978-3-642-59126-6_4
7. Ilic, A., Klavzar, S., Rho, Y.: The index of a binary word. Theor. Comput. Sci. **452**, 100–106 (2012)
8. Klavzar, S., Shpectorov, S.V.: Asymptotic number of isometric generalized Fibonacci cubes. Eur. J. Comb. **33**(2), 220–226 (2012)
9. Wei, J.: The structures of bad words. Eur. J. Comb. **59**, 204–214 (2017)
10. Wei, J., Yang, Y., Zhu, X.: A characterization of non-isometric binary words. Eur. J. Comb. **78**, 121–133 (2019)
11. Wei, J., Zhang, H.: Proofs of two conjectures on generalized Fibonacci cubes. Euro. J. Combinatorics **51**, 419–432 (2016). https://doi.org/10.1016/j.ejc.2015.07.018

Regular Expression Length via Arithmetic Formula Complexity

Ehud Cseresnyes[iD] and Hannes Seiwert[(✉)][iD]

Institute of Computer Science, Goethe University Frankfurt, Frankfurt, Germany
ehud@posteo.de, seiwert@em.uni-frankfurt.de

Abstract. We prove lower bounds on the length of regular expressions for finite languages by methods from arithmetic circuit complexity. First, we show a reduction from expression length to monotone arithmetic formula size. This yields lower bounds of $nk^{\Omega(\log k)}$ for the binomial language of all words with exactly k ones and $n - k$ zeros, and of $n^{\Omega(\log n)}$ for the language of all Dyck words of length $2n$. We also determine the blow-up of expression length when applying the operations intersection or shuffle to finite languages. Second, we adapt a lower bound method for multilinear arithmetic formulas by Hrubeš and Yehudayoff to regular expressions. With this method we give a tight lower bound of $\Omega(n^{-1}p^{\log(n/\log p)-2})$ for the language of all binary numbers with n bits that are divisible by a given odd integer p.

Keywords: Regular expression · Lower bound · Arithmetic formula · Arithmetic circuit complexity · Finite language

1 Introduction

Deriving lower bounds on the length of regular expressions is a fundamental problem in formal language theory [3–5,7,9,17,18]. Particularly interesting are language families that have small finite automata but require long regular expressions, since they reveal the gap between the descriptional complexity of these models. However, despite regular expressions being around for some decades, only few lower bounds are known so far. This is in sharp contrast to state complexity of finite automata which is understood quite well.

One has to distinguish between finite and infinite languages, as well as between alphabets of constant and growing size. Ehrenfeucht and Zeiger [3] gave an exponential lower bound for the infinite language of all walks in a complete graph over an alphabet of size n^2. This result was generalized by Gelade and Neven [5] for four-letter alphabets, and by Gruber and Holzer [7] for binary alphabets using concepts of star height and cycle rank; in particular, Gruber and Holzer showed that the length of every expression is exponential in the star

H. Seiwert—Partially supported by DFG grant JU 3105/1-2 (German Research Foundation).

G. Jirásková and G. Pighizzini (Eds.): DCFS 2020, LNCS 12442, pp. 26–38, 2020.
https://doi.org/10.1007/978-3-030-62536-8_3

height of its described language. In this paper, we focus on *finite* languages. Since star height of finite languages trivially is zero, this method is not applicable here. Instead, techniques from circuit complexity have proven useful.

Related Work. For a regular expression R we measure its *length* by the reverse polish length $\mathsf{rpn}(R)$, namely the number of nodes in its syntax tree. For a regular language L let $\mathsf{rpn}(L)$ be the length of a shortest expression describing L.

Jerrum and Snir [12] showed a lower bound of 2^n-2 on $\mathsf{rpn}(L)$ for the language L of all permutations over the alphabet $\Sigma = \{1,\ldots,n\}$ using a method for circuits over semirings, see [12, Sect. 5.4]. Recently, Molina Lovett and Shallit [17] improved this bound to $4^n n^{-(\log n)/4+\Theta(1)}$ by a custom method.

Hrubeš and Yehudayoff [11] (implicitly) showed a lower bound of $nk^{\Omega(\log k)}$ for the language $L_k = \{a_1 a_2 \cdots a_k : 1 \leq a_1 < a_2 < \cdots < a_k \leq n\}$ over $\Sigma = \{1,\ldots,n\}$ with $k \leq n/2$ by a method for multilinear arithmetic formulas.

Ellul, Krawetz, Shallit and Wang [4] gave a construction that transforms an expression R for a language $L \subseteq \{0,1\}^n$ into a boolean formula for its characteristic function $f_L : \{0,1\}^n \to \{0,1\}$ of size at most $\mathsf{rpn}(R)$. Thus, the length of an expression describing L is bounded from below by the *boolean formula complexity* of f_L: $\mathsf{rpn}(L) \geq \mathsf{Boolean}(f_L)$. Together with a result by Khrapchenko [15] on the formula complexity of the XOR function, they derived a lower bound of $\Omega(n^2)$ for the language $L_n^{\mathrm{xor}} = \{w \in \{0,1\}^n : |w|_1 \text{ is even}\}$.

A language $L \subseteq \{0,1\}^n$ is *monotone* if it is closed under replacing any number of zeros by ones. By methods from communication complexity, Gruber and Johannsen [9] gave a reduction of expression length for monotone languages L to the *monotone* boolean formula complexity of f_L: $\mathsf{rpn}(L) \geq \mathsf{Monotone\text{-}Boolean}(f_L)$. In particular, they showed that converting a DFA with n states for a finite language into an expression may cause a blow-up of $n^{\Omega(\log n)}$. Since DFAs (or NFAs) for finite languages can be simulated by expressions of length $n^{O(\log n)}$ (see [4, Cor. 22] or [9, Cor. 13]), this result is tight. In particular, expression length of finite languages with polynomial size NFAs is at most quasi-polynomial.

Our Contribution. The existing methods for finite languages work only for alphabets of growing size or rely on lower bounds on (monotone) boolean complexity which are rare and usually hard to obtain. Our goal in this paper is to improve the "boolean methods" [4,9] with regard to strength as well as to simplicity in application. We present two new methods, both working over binary alphabets, and demonstrate their application on several language families. As a byproduct, we determine blow-ups of language operations and improve the lower bound for converting DFAs in the case of finite languages.

The paper is organized as follows. In the next section we give basic definitions. In Sect. 3 we present our first method, the *arithmetic bound* (Theorem 2), which reduces expression length to monotone arithmetic formula complexity. In the succeeding subsections, we apply this method to uniform languages (Sect. 3.1), investigate the blow-up of operations (intersection and shuffle) for finite languages (Sect. 3.2) and address limitations (Sect. 3.3). In Sect. 4 we prove our second method, the *balance bound* (Theorem 10), and demonstrate its application on the language of all n-bit numbers that are divisible by a given number p in Sect. 4.1. Finally, we summarize the results in Sect. 5.

2   Preliminaries

Throughout let $\mathbb{N} = \{0, 1, 2, \ldots\}$ be the set of all nonnegative integers and $[n] = \{1, 2, \ldots, n\}$. In this paper, all logarithms have base 2.

For a word w over an alphabet Σ, its *length* $|w|$ is the number of its letters, and for a letter $a \in \Sigma$ we denote by $|w|_a$ its number of occurrences in w. To avoid trivialities, we assume throughout that our languages satisfy $L \neq \{\varepsilon\}, \emptyset$.

Regular expressions (or just *expressions*) over an alphabet Σ are defined recursively as follows: The empty word ε and every letter $a \in \Sigma$ is an expression. If R and R' are expressions, then so are R^*, $(R \cdot R')$ and $(R + R')$. Note that we do not allow the symbol $\emptyset$. Every expression R describes a regular language $L(R)$ in the usual way. Two expressions R and R' are *equivalent*, denoted by $R \equiv R'$, if they describe the same language. We identify every expression with its (unique) syntax tree. The expression defined by the subtree of a node u in the syntax tree of R is a *subexpression* of R and denoted by R_u. A language is *homogeneous* if all its words have same length, and an expression is homogeneous if every of its subexpressions describes a homogeneous language. We assume w.l.o.g. that expressions for finite languages do not contain star operations, and that expressions for homogeneous languages are homogeneous. For a language $L \subseteq \Sigma^*$ we call the homogeneous language $L_n := L \cap \Sigma^n$ its *n-slice*.

3   Reduction to Monotone Arithmetic Formula Size

In this section we reduce expression length to monotone arithmetic formula size. Let $L \subseteq \{0, 1\}^n$ be a language and R be a homogeneous expression describing L that does not contain any symbol ε. Ellul et al. [4, Lem. 24] gave a construction that transforms R into a boolean formula for the function $f_R \colon \{0, 1\}^n \to \{0, 1\}$ with $f_R(x) = 1$ iff $x \in L$. Namely, they assigned to each leaf of R a unique *position* i, such that its letter occurs as the i-th letter in all words in $L(R)$. For example, in the expression $(a+b)(cd+ce)$ the positions of the leaves holding the letters a, b, c, d, e are $1, 1, 2, 3, 3$, respectively. The construction is as follows: Replace each union by OR, each concatenation by AND, and each leaf at position i holding the letter 1 (resp. 0) by the literal x_i (resp. $\neg x_i$). We present a similar construction that transforms R into a monotone arithmetic formula.

A *monotone arithmetic formula* is a rooted tree with leaves holding either one of the variables $x_1, \ldots, x_n$ or a constant $c \in \mathbb{R}_{\geq 0}$. Every inner node (a *gate*) performs one of the operations $+$ (addition) or $\times$ (multiplication). The *size* of a formula is the total number of its nodes. Every formula computes a polynomial $p(x_1, \ldots, x_n) = \sum_{a \in A} \lambda_a \prod_{i=1}^n x_i^{a_i}$ over $\mathbb{R}_{\geq 0}$ in a natural manner, where $A \subseteq \mathbb{N}^n$

is its set of *exponent vectors* and λ_a are positive coefficients. Up to coefficients, the set A determines the polynomial. Let $\mathsf{Arith}(A)$ be the size of a smallest formula that computes a polynomial whose set of exponent vectors is A. We identify words $w = w_1 \cdots w_n$ with vectors $(w_1, \ldots, w_n)$.

The *arithmetic version of R* is the monotone arithmetic formula Φ_R that is constructed as follows: Replace each union node of R by an arithmetic addition gate and each concatenation node by an arithmetic multiplication gate. Replace each leaf of R holding the letter 0 by the constant 1 and replace each leaf holding the letter 1 at position i by the variable x_i. Note that in both cases a leaf holding a letter $\sigma \in \{0, 1\}$ at position i is replaced by x_i^σ. For example, the arithmetic version of the expression $011 + 100$ is the formula $x_2 x_3 + x_1$ which has $A = \{(0, 1, 1), (1, 0, 0)\}$ as its set of exponent vectors.

Lemma 1. *Let R be a homogeneous expression with $L(R) \subseteq \{0, 1\}^n$ and Φ_R be its arithmetic version. Then Φ_R has size at most $\mathsf{rpn}(R)$ and computes a polynomial p_R with $L(R)$ as its set of exponent vectors.*

That is, the formula Φ_R computes a polynomial $p_R(x) = \sum_{a \in A} \lambda_a \prod_{i=1}^n x_i^{a_i}$ with $A = L(R)$ and some coefficients $\lambda_a > 0$.

Proof. The proof is a simple induction on R, similar to the proof of [4, Lem. 24]. We omit it due to lack of space. $\square$

Lemma 1 directly yields the following theorem.

Theorem 2 (Arithmetic bound). *Let $L \subseteq \{0, 1\}^n$ be a homogeneous language. Then any regular expression describing L has length at least $\mathsf{rpn}(L) \geq \mathsf{Arith}(L)$.*

Informally stated, the following hierarchy for the different formula complexities holds:

$$\text{Monotone-Arithmetic} \geq \text{Monotone-Boolean} \geq \text{Boolean}$$

The gaps between these complexities can be exponentially large. So, Theorem 2 covers both boolean bounds mentioned in the introduction and can be exponentially stronger. Another advantage is that lower bounds for arithmetic formulas can be proven more easily than lower bounds for boolean formulas. In particular, there are already many strong bounds known, see for example [14]. For a survey on boolean complexity resp. arithmetic complexity see [13] resp. [19].

Remark 1 (Invariance under permutations). Since arithmetic operations $+$ and $\times$ are commutative, it does not matter at which position a variable occurs. So, reordering the variables $x_1, \ldots, x_n$ in a polynomial does not change its arithmetic complexity. For a language $L \subseteq \{0, 1\}^n$ and a permutation $\sigma : [n] \to [n]$ let $\sigma(L) := \{w_{\sigma(1)} \cdots w_{\sigma(n)} : w_1 \cdots w_n \in L\}$. Then all bounds shown with Theorem 2 for L also hold for the permuted language $\sigma(L)$. On the one hand, this fact strengthens the obtained bounds; on the other hand, it limits the possibilities for application. In Sect. 3.3 we address this issue in detail.

3.1 Bounds for Uniform Languages

A language $L \subseteq \{0,1\}^n$ is *uniform* if all words in L contain the same number of ones. The most basic uniform language is the *binomial language*

$$B_{n,k} = \{w \in \{0,1\}^n : |w|_1 = k\}$$

investigated by Ellul et al. [4]. They constructed an expression of length $n^{O(\log k)}$ and asked whether its length is optimal. Recently, Mousavi [18] showed the optimality for $k \leq 3$ by analyzing a linear program derived from the language. Using a lower bound shown by Hrubeš and Yehudayoff [11] for arithmetic formulas we show that the length is asymptotically optimal also for $k = n^{\Theta(1)}$.

Corollary 3 (Binomial language). *Let $k \leq n/2$. Then the binomial language $B_{n,k}$ requires regular expressions of length $\mathsf{rpn}(B_{n,k}) \geq nk^{\Omega(\log k)}$.*

Proof. The result follows as special case of the following corollary.   □

Corollary 4 (Uniform languages). *Let $k \leq n/2$ and $L \subseteq B_{n,k}$ be a uniform language. Then L requires expressions of length $\mathsf{rpn}(L) \geq nk^{\Omega(\log k)} \cdot |L|/\binom{n}{k}$.*

Proof. Assume $L \subseteq B_{n,k}$. Hrubeš and Yehudayoff [11, Prop. 7] showed that any polynomial f with a set $A_f \subseteq B_{n,k}$ of exponent vectors requires monotone arithmetic formulas of size $nk^{\Omega(\log k)}|A_f|/\binom{n}{k}$. Since each vector in A_f corresponds to a word in L, the claim follows by Theorem 2.   □

A *Dyck word* is a word $w \in \{0,1\}^*$ with the same number of zeros and ones, and such that every prefix of w contains not more ones than zeros. The language D of all Dyck words usually is interpreted as the language of all correctly nested sequences of brackets, with 0 representing opening and 1 representing closing brackets. We consider the *2n-slice* $D_{2n} := D \cap \{0,1\}^{2n}$.

Corollary 5 (Dyck language). *The language D_{2n} requires regular expressions of length $\mathsf{rpn}(D_{2n}) \geq n^{\Omega(\log n)}$.*

Proof. Clearly $D_{2n} \subseteq B_{2n,n}$ holds, since every word in D_{2n} contains the same number of zeros and ones. It is well known that D_{2n} contains exactly $\frac{1}{n+1}\binom{2n}{n}$ words – this number is known as the Catalan number – see for example [2] for an elegant proof. Thus, by Corollary 4, we have $\mathsf{rpn}(D_{2n}) \geq \frac{2n}{n+1} \cdot n^{\Omega(\log n)}$.   □

3.2 Blow-Up of Language Operations

By how much can the length of expressions increase when performing operations like complementation, intersection or shuffle? While the situation for *infinite* languages has been resolved by Gelade and Neven [5] and Gruber and Holzer [7,8], it is still open for finite languages.

The blow-up of intersection and shuffle for finite languages is at most $n^{O(\log n)}$, see the end of this subsection. We now give matching lower bounds. Recall the definition of the *shuffle* operation ⊔⊔ (also called *interleaving*): For two words v, w, their shuffle $v \sqcup\!\sqcup w$ is the set of all words of the form $v_1 w_1 v_2 w_2 \cdots v_k w_k$ where $k \in \mathbb{N}$, $v_i, w_i \in \Sigma^*$ for all i, $v_1 v_2 \cdots v_k = v$ and $w_1 w_2 \cdots w_k = w$. The shuffle of two languages is defined as $L_1 \sqcup\!\sqcup L_2 = \bigcup_{v \in L_1, w \in L_2} v \sqcup\!\sqcup w$.

Theorem 6 (Blow-up of intersection and shuffle). *There are finite languages L_1, L_2 with regular expressions of length $O(n)$, such that*

(a) $\mathsf{rpn}(L_1 \cap L_2) \geq n^{\Omega(\log n)}$,
(b) $\mathsf{rpn}(L_1 \sqcup L_2) \geq n^{\Omega(\log n)}$.

There is a regular language $L \subseteq \Sigma^*$ with an expression of length $O(n)$, such that

(c) $\mathsf{rpn}(L \cap \Sigma^n) \geq n^{\Omega(\log n)}$.

In particular, items (a) and (b) answer a question from [9], while item (c) answers a question from [4, Open Problem 5] asking for the blow-up of n-slices.

Proof.

(a) Consider the language $L_1 = (0+\varepsilon)^m (1(0+\varepsilon)^m)^m$ of all words with exactly m ones and not more than m zeros in a row, and let $L_2 = (0+1)^{2m}$. If we set $n = m^2$, then both L_1 and L_2 can be described by expressions of length $O(n)$. The intersection $L_1 \cap L_2$ is exactly the binomial language $B_{2m,m}$ and by Corollary 3 $\mathsf{rpn}(L_1 \cap L_2) = \mathsf{rpn}(B_{2m,m}) \geq m^{\Omega(\log m)} = n^{\Omega(\log n)}$ follows.

(b) Consider the languages $L_1 = 0^n$ and $L_2 = 1^n$ with expressions of length $O(n)$. Their shuffle $L_1 \sqcup L_2$ is exactly the binomial language $B_{2n,n}$, and Corollary 3 yields $\mathsf{rpn}(L_1 \sqcup L_2) \geq n^{\Omega(\log n)}$.

(c) Let $\Sigma = \{0,1\}$ and $L = 0^*(10^*)^{\lfloor n/2 \rfloor}$ be the language of all words with exactly $\lfloor n/2 \rfloor$ ones; hence, $\mathsf{rpn}(L) = O(n)$. Then $L \cap \Sigma^n = B_{n,\lfloor n/2 \rfloor}$ and Corollary 3 yields $\mathsf{rpn}(L \cap \Sigma^n) \geq n^{\Omega(\log n)}$. □

The matching *upper* bounds for intersection and shuffle can be obtained as follows: Given two expressions R_1 and R_2 of lengths m_1 resp. m_2, transform them into NFAs. Then build their corresponding (intersection or shuffle) product automaton by the standard construction. For both operations, this gives an NFA with $n = O(m_1 m_2)$ states. Finally, translate this NFA back into a regular expression. As its accepted language is finite, length $n^{O(\log n)} = (m_1 m_2)^{O(\log(m_1 m_2))}$ suffices according to [9, Cor. 13].

3.3 Limitations of the Arithmetic Bound

Let us address limitations of Theorem 2. We already mentioned in Remark 1 that arithmetic complexity ignores the *order* of variables. This prevents us from proving bounds for languages L that have a reordering σ such that $\sigma(L)$ has short expressions. Take for example the language $L = \{ww^{\text{reverse}} : w \in \{0,1\}^n\}$ of all palindromes of length $2n$ over $\{0,1\}$. With the fooling set method [1,6], one can easily show an exponential lower bound $\mathsf{rpn}(L) \geq \Omega(2^n)$. However, reordering the letters yields the language $L' := \{u_1 u_{2n} u_2 u_{2n-1} \cdots u_n u_{n+1} : u \in L\} = \{00,11\}^n$ with $\mathsf{rpn}(L') = O(n)$. According to Remark 1, lower bounds obtained by Theorem 2 are the same for $\mathsf{rpn}(L)$ and $\mathsf{rpn}(L')$, and so are at most linear. In other words, $\mathsf{Arith}(L) \leq O(n)$, but $\mathsf{rpn}(L) \geq \Omega(2^n)$. The same problem appears for the boolean methods, Gruber and Johannsen [9] actually presented the same example.

In the next section, we circumvent this issue by translating a lower bound method from arithmetic formula complexity *directly* to expression length.

4   Direct Lower Bounds

In the following, Σ is an arbitrary alphabet, R a homogeneous expression over Σ and $L = L(R)$. We adapt a lower bound technique by Hrubeš and Yehudayoff [11] for monotone (or even multilinear) arithmetic formulas by so-called "balanced polynomials" *directly* to regular expression length; see also [19, Sect. 3.6].

The high-level idea for lower bounding $\mathsf{rpn}(L)$ is roughly as follows. Transform R into a union $B_1 + \cdots + B_\ell$ of "balanced" expressions B_i, where $\ell \leq \mathsf{rpn}(R)$ and every balanced expression B_i can be factorized into several nontrivial factors $B_i \equiv F_1 F_2 \cdots F_m$. From L derive structural properties that any factor F_j must have. Finally, upper bound the number of words in any language with these properties to obtain an upper bound on $|L(B_i)|$.

Definition 7 (degree, balanced). *Let R be a homogeneous expression. The degree $\deg R$ of R is the length of its described words. R is balanced if either*

- $\deg R = 1$, *or*
- *if there are homogeneous expressions B, B' such that B is balanced itself, $\deg B \geq \deg B'$ and $R = BB'$ or $R = B'B$.*

In other words, any union of single letters is balanced, and if an expression B is balanced, then so are BB' and $B'B$ for any homogeneous expression B' with $\deg B' \leq \deg B$. Given a balanced expression B, we can construct a path from the root to a leaf by always continuing with the child whose subexpression is balanced and which has larger degree (i.e. B in Definition 7). We call this path the *canonical path* of B; note that all inner nodes on this path are concatenation nodes and that all their subexpressions are balanced.

The following proposition tells us that every balanced expression has a factorization where most factors have "sufficiently large" degree.

Proposition 8. *Let B be a balanced expression of degree $\deg B = n$ and let $\gamma \geq 1$. Then there exist $m \geq \log(1 + n/\gamma)$ and $2m$ homogeneous expressions $P_1, \ldots, P_m, S_1, \ldots, S_m$ such that $B \equiv P_1 P_2 \cdots P_m S_m S_{m-1} \cdots S_1$ and $\deg P_i + \deg S_i \geq \gamma$ holds for all $i \in [m-1]$, and $\deg P_m + \deg S_m \leq \gamma$.*

We call $P_1 \cdots P_m S_m \cdots S_1$ a γ-*factorization* and P_i and S_i *factors* of B. Note that for every factor F of B there are words x, y such that $L(xFy) \subseteq L(B)$.

Proof. We proceed by induction. For $n \leq \gamma$ the claim is trivial, so assume $n > \gamma$. To obtain a γ-factorization of B initialize $S = \varepsilon, P = \varepsilon$ and follow the canonical path downwards, starting at the root of B. For each node $v = x \cdot y$ passed by, update either P or S: if we went to the right child y, set $P := P \cdot B_x$, if we went to the left child x, set $S := B_y \cdot S$. By this procedure, the invariant $B \equiv PB_v S$

holds in each step, where v is the currently reached node. Eventually we arrive at some node u whose degree $n' := \deg B_u$ satisfies $(n - \gamma)/2 < n' \le n - \gamma$. This is the case just because the degree cannot drop more than by a factor of two at each step taken. Since B_u is balanced, by induction hypothesis there is a γ-factorization $B_u \equiv P_1 \cdots P_{m'} S_{m'} \cdots S_1$ with $m' \ge \log(1 + n'/\gamma)$. We claim that $PP_1 \cdots P_{m'} S_{m'} \cdots S_1 S$ is a γ-factorization of B with $2(m'+1)$ factors: since $n' \le n - \gamma$, we have $\deg P + \deg S = n - n' \ge \gamma$, and since $n' > (n - \gamma)/2$, we have $m := m' + 1 \ge \log(1 + n'/\gamma) + 1 > \log(1 + (n - \gamma)/2\gamma) + 1 = \log(1 + n/\gamma)$. $\square$

The following lemma is a straightforward adaption of Lemma 4 in [11].

Lemma 9. *Let $R \ne \varepsilon$ be a homogeneous expression. Then there exist $\ell \le \mathsf{rpn}(R)$ balanced expressions $B_1, \ldots, B_\ell$ such that $R \equiv B_1 + \cdots + B_\ell$.*

Proof. We proceed by induction on R. If R is a single letter, the claim is trivial. If $R = R_1 + R_2$ is a union, we can apply the induction hypothesis to both R_1 and R_2, and are finished. Finally, let $R = R_1 \cdot R_2$ be a concatenation. Assume $\deg R_1 \ge \deg R_2$, the other case is analogous. By induction hypothesis there are balanced expressions $B_1, \ldots, B_\ell$ such that $R_1 \equiv B_1 + \cdots + B_\ell$ for an $\ell \le \mathsf{rpn}(R_1)$. Since $\deg B_i = \deg R_1 \ge \deg R_2$ holds for all i, also every expression $B_i R_2$ is balanced. So, $R \equiv B_1 R_2 + \cdots + B_\ell R_2$ is a union of $\ell \le \mathsf{rpn}(R_1) \le \mathsf{rpn}(R)$ balanced expressions, as desired. $\square$

Remark 2. Lemma 9 still holds if we extend regular expressions by a *squaring operation* $(^2)$ with $L(R^2) := (L(R))^2$ as introduced in [16]; see also [10] for a more recent overview. To show this, proceed analogously to the case when R is a concatenation of two identical subexpressions $R = R' \cdot R'$.

From Lemma 9 our second lower bound method follows.

Theorem 10 (Balance bound). *Let $L \subseteq \Sigma^n$ be a homogeneous language and $h \in \mathbb{R}_{\ge 0}$. If $|L(B)| \le h$ holds for every balanced expression B with $L(B) \subseteq L$, then any expression for L has length at least $\mathsf{rpn}(L) \ge |L|/h$.*

In the next subsection we demonstrate how to apply Theorem 10.

4.1 The Divisibility Language

Let p be an odd integer. Ellul et al. [4] considered the language of all binary numbers that are divisible by p. This language has small DFAs with just p states, but it seems that regular expressions must be large. However, no lower bound is known so far. Here we consider the n-slice of this language. For a word $w \in \{0,1\}^n$ denote its interpretation as binary number by $\langle w \rangle_2$; we assume that the most significant bit is the leftmost letter, for example $\langle 0101 \rangle_2 = 5$, and for convenience let $\langle \varepsilon \rangle_2 = 0$. The *divisibility language*

$$L_{n,p}^{\mathrm{div}} = \left\{ w \in \{0,1\}^n : \langle w \rangle_2 \equiv_p 0 \right\}$$

consists of all binary numbers with n bits that are divisible by p. This language also has small DFAs with $O(np)$ states and regular expressions of length

$\mathsf{rpn}(L_{n,p}^{\mathrm{div}}) \le O(np \cdot p^{\log(n/\log p)})$ (see below). So, the following lower bound is tight apart from small polynomial factors.

Theorem 11 (Divisibility language). *Let $p > 2$ be odd. Then any expression describing the divisibility language has length at least*

$$\mathsf{rpn}(L_{n,p}^{\mathrm{div}}) \ge \Omega\big(n^{-1}p^{\log(n/\log p)-2}\big).$$

In particular, if p is constant, then $\Omega(n^{-1}p^{\log n}) \le \mathsf{rpn}(L_{n,p}^{\mathrm{div}}) \le O(np^{\log n})$.

Proof. Let $L = L_{n,p}^{\mathrm{div}}$ and B be any balanced expression with $L(B) \subseteq L$. We will show an upper bound $h = 2^n n \cdot p^{-\log(n/\log p)+1}$ on the number $|L(B)|$ of words in $L(B)$. Every p-th natural number (beginning with 0) is divisible by p, so there are $|L| \ge 2^n/p$ words in L. Hence, the bound $\mathsf{rpn}(L) \ge |L|/h \ge 2^n/p \cdot 2^{-n}n^{-1}p^{\log(n/\log p)-1} = \Omega(n^{-1}p^{\log(n/\log p)-2})$ will follow by Theorem 10.

For $\gamma := \log p$ let $P_1 \cdots P_m S_m \cdots S_1$ be a γ-factorization of B ensured by Proposition 8. To prove the bound on $|L(B)|$ we upper bound the number of words described by each factor. For $r \in \{0, 1, \ldots, p-1\}$ and $d \in \mathbb{N}$ let $L_{d,p}^r := \{w \in \{0,1\}^d : \langle w \rangle_2 \equiv_p r\}$ be the language of all d-bit numbers that have remainder r when divided by p, for example $L_{n,p}^0 = L_{n,p}^{\mathrm{div}}$. For a word w with $\langle w \rangle_2 \equiv_p r$ and a word x of length d with $\langle x \rangle_2 \equiv_p r'$, their concatenation satisfies $\langle wx \rangle_2 \equiv_p r \cdot 2^d + r'$. Since p is odd, the mapping $r \mapsto r \cdot 2^d$ is a bijection over $\{0, 1, \ldots, p-1\}$ for all d. Thus, if $\langle w \rangle_2 \not\equiv_p \langle v \rangle_2$ holds for two words w and v of same length, then also $\langle wx \rangle_2 \not\equiv_p \langle vx \rangle_2$ and $\langle xw \rangle_2 \not\equiv_p \langle xv \rangle_2$ hold for any word x.

Call a homogeneous expression T *pure*, if all words in $L(T)$ have the same remainder r when divided by p, that is, if $L(T) \subseteq L_{d,p}^r$ holds for some r and d.

Claim 1. *Every factor of B is pure.*

Proof of Claim 1. Assume to the contrary that some factor F of B is not pure, i. e. there are words $w, v \in L(F)$ with $\langle w \rangle_2 \not\equiv_p \langle v \rangle_2$. Since $L(B) \subseteq L$, there are words x, y such that $xwy, xvy \in L$. The observation above yields $\langle xwy \rangle_2 \not\equiv_p \langle xvy \rangle_2$. But all words in L have remainder $r = 0$, a contradiction. $\qquad\square$Claim 1

Let $F_i := P_i \cdot S_i$ and $d_i := \deg F_i = \deg P_i + \deg S_i$. The argument above also implies that concatenations of pure expressions are pure themselves, so every F_i is pure. For all d and all r we have $|L_{d,p}^r| \le \lceil 2^d/p \rceil \le 2^d/p + 1$, and since every expression F_i describes a subset of some language $L_{d_i,p}^r$, the inequality $|L(F_i)| \le 2^{d_i}/p + 1$ must hold. Proposition 8 ensures that for all $i \in [m-1]$ we have $d_i \ge \gamma = \log p$ and therefore $|L(F_i)| \le 2^{d_i}/p + 1 \le 2 \cdot 2^{d_i}/p$. Further, since our alphabet is binary, $|L(F_m)| \le 2^{d_m}$ trivially holds. Finally, recall that $\sum_{i=1}^m d_i = n$ and $m \ge \log(1 + n/\gamma) \ge \log(n/\log p)$. Hence,

$$|L(B)| = \prod_{i=1}^m |L(F_i)| \le 2^{d_m} \cdot \prod_{i=1}^{m-1} \frac{2 \cdot 2^{d_i}}{p} = 2^{\sum_{i=1}^m d_i} \cdot (2/p)^{m-1}$$

$$\le 2^n (2/p)^{\log(n/\log p)-1} \le 2^n n \cdot p^{-\log(n/\log p)+1} =: h.$$

$\square$

Upper Bound. To show that Theorem 11 is tight, we design an expression for $L_{n,p}^{\text{div}}$ of corresponding length. For simplicity assume that n is a power of 2. For each $r \in \{0, \ldots, p-1\}$ and $d \in \{n, n/2, n/4, \ldots\}$ define an expression $R_{d,p}^r$ for the language $L_{d,p}^r$ recursively by $R_{d,p}^r := \sum_{r_1, r_2} R_{d/2,p}^{r_1} \cdot R_{d/2,p}^{r_2}$, where the sum ranges over all p combinations (r_1, r_2) with $r_1 2^{d/2} + r_2 \equiv_p r$. If $d < \log p$, then $L_{d,p}^r$ contains at most a single word w, in this case let $R_{d,p}^r := w$. Finally, $R_{n,p}^0$ describes the language $L_{n,p}^0 = L_{n,p}^{\text{div}}$. This recursion has $2p$ branches in each step, depth at most $\lceil \log(n/\log p) \rceil$ and every base case has length at most $\log p$. Thus, length $\text{rpn}(L_{n,p}^{\text{div}}) \leq O(\log p \cdot (2p)^{\lceil \log(n/\log p) \rceil}) \leq O(np \cdot p^{\log(n/\log p)})$ suffices.

Blow-Up of DFA Conversion. Gruber and Johannsen [9] considered the blow-up of DFA conversion for finite languages. They showed that there are languages that can be accepted by DFAs with n^8 states, but require expressions of length $\Omega(n^{(\log n)/3})$. We now can improve on the constants in this gap.

Corollary 12. *There are finite languages that can be accepted by DFAs with n^2 states, but require expressions of length at least $n^{\log(n) - \Theta(\log\log n)}$.*

Proof. Consider the divisibility language $L_{n,p}^{\text{div}}$ and set $p = n$. The claim for DFA size is easy to see, the bound on expression length follows from Theorem 11. □

4.2 Utilizing Noncommutativity

In Sect. 3.3 we have discussed that the arithmetic bound (Theorem 2) is incapable of giving a nontrivial lower bound for the palindrome language $L = \{ww^{\text{reverse}} : w \in \{0,1\}^n\}$. With Theorem 10 we can give a (suboptimal but nevertheless exponential) lower bound.

One can show that any balanced expression B of degree $\deg B \geq 2$ can be written as balanced concatenation of *two* homogeneous expressions, i. e. one can write $B \equiv P \cdot S$ for homogeneous expressions P and S whose degrees satisfy $(1/3)\deg B \leq \deg P, \deg S \leq (2/3)\deg B$. We leave the proof to the reader. Let $n = 3k$ for a positive integer k. For an arbitrary balanced expression B with $L(B) \subseteq L$ consider a word $w = w_1 \cdots w_{2n}$ described by $B \equiv P \cdot S$. All letters $w_1, \ldots, w_{2k}$ lie in P and all letters $w_{4k+1}, \ldots, w_{6k}$ lie in S. By definition of L, we must have $w_i = w_{6k+1-i}$ for all $i \in [3k]$. Thus, all words in $L(P)$ have $w_{6k}w_{6k-1} \cdots w_{4k}$ as prefix and all words in $L(S)$ have $w_{2k}w_{2k-1} \cdots w_1$ as suffix. Hence, $|L(B)| = |L(P)| \cdot |L(S)| \leq 2^k \cdot 2^k =: h$, and Theorem 10 yields $\text{rpn}(L) \geq |L|/h \geq 2^{3k}/2^{2k} = 2^k = 2^{n/3}$.

5 Conclusion

We developed two lower bound methods for expression length of finite languages. With the *arithmetic bound* (Theorem 2) we reduced expression length of languages $L \subseteq \{0,1\}^n$ to monotone arithmetic formula complexity. This result naturally refines the existing methods of Ellul et al. [4] and Gruber and Johannsen [9] who gave reductions to boolean resp. monotone boolean formula complexity. With the *balance bound* (Theorem 10) we adapted a lower bound method for multilinear arithmetic formulas by Hrubeš and Yehudayoff [11]. This method provides a general framework that works for arbitrary alphabets, utilizes noncommutativity (see Sect. 4.2) and works even for expressions extended by a squaring operation (see Remark 2).

By these methods we obtained lower bounds for the binomial language $B_{n,k} = \{w \in \{0,1\}^n : |w|_1 = k\}$, the language D_{2n} of all length $2n$ Dyck words, and the divisibility language $L_{n,p}^{\mathrm{div}} = \{w \in \{0,1\}^n : \langle w \rangle_2 \equiv_p 0\}$. As a byproduct, we determined the blow-up of intersection and shuffle and improved the gap for DFA conversion, both for finite languages. We summarize these results in Table 1, together with upper bounds and state complexity for comparison.

Table 1. Results for languages and blow-ups for conversions of finite languages.

language	DFA size	rpn, upper bound	rpn, lower bound
$B_{n,k}$	$O(nk)$	$n^{O(\log k)}$	$nk^{\Omega(\log k)}$ [Corollary 3]
D_{2n}	$O(n^2)$	$n^{O(\log n)}$	$n^{\Omega(\log n)}$ [Corollary 5]
$L_{n,p}^{\mathrm{div}}$	$O(np)$	$O(np \cdot p^{\log(n/\log p)})$	$\Omega(n^{-1}p^{\log(n/\log p)-2})$ [Theorem 11]

conversion	upper bound	lower bound
$\mathrm{RE} \cap \mathrm{RE}$, $\mathrm{RE} \sqcup\!\!\sqcup \mathrm{RE}$ to RE	$n^{O(\log n)}$	$n^{\Omega(\log n)}$ [Theorem 6]
DFA, NFA to RE	$n^{\log(n)+O(1)}$ [4,9]	$n^{(\log n)/4-\Theta(\log \log n)}$ [Corollary 12]

We make two final remarks. The results in this paper were obtained only for finite languages. However, from them also bounds for *infinite* languages can be derived. This might be particularly useful for languages with *small star height* or languages whose star height is hard to determine. Gruber and Holzer showed that languages of star height h require expressions of length $2^{\Omega(h)}$ [7, Thm. 6]. Consider an infinite variant of the binomial language, namely $B'_{n,k} := \{w \in \{0,1\}^* : |w|_1 \geq k, |w|_0 \geq n-k\}$. This language has star height $h = 1$, so only a trivial bound follows from this theorem. In contrast, one can show that $\mathrm{rpn}(B'_{n,k}) \geq \mathrm{rpn}(B_{n,k})$ holds, and then $\mathrm{rpn}(B'_{n,k}) \geq nk^{\Omega(\log k)}$ follows from Corollary 3.

Finally, an open problem is to improve accuracy of the balance bound, particularly of Lemma 9. It seems that this lemma is loose by a factor of n (length of the words). For example, the language $L = \{w_1 \cdots w_n\}$ consisting of a single word w can be written as *one* balanced expression, but Lemma 9 only tells us, that $\mathrm{rpn}(L) = \Theta(n)$ balanced expressions suffice. This imprecision is a crucial weakness when dealing with languages having short polynomial size expressions.

Acknowledgments. We wish to thank Mario Holldack, Stasys Jukna and Georg Schnitger for inspiring discussions and thank the anonymous referees for their kind and useful comments.

References

1. Birget, J.-C.: Intersection and union of regular languages and state complexity. Inf. Process. Lett. **43**(4), 185–190 (1992). https://doi.org/10.1016/0020-0190(92)90198-5
2. Chen, Y.: The Chung-Feller theorem revisited. Discrete Mathematics **308**(7), 1328–1329 (2008). https://doi.org/10.1016/j.disc.2007.03.068
3. Ehrenfeucht, A., Zeiger, P.: Complexity measures for regular expressions. J. Comput. Syst. Sci. **12**(2), 134–146 (1976). https://doi.org/10.1016/S0022-0000(76)80034-7
4. Ellul, K., Krawetz, B., Shallit, J., Wang, M.-W.: Regular expressions: new results and open problems. J. Autom. Lang. Comb. **9**(2–3), 233–256 (2004). https://doi.org/10.25596/jalc-2004-233
5. Gelade, W., Neven, F.: Succinctness of the complement and intersection of regular expressions. ACM Trans. Comput. Logic (TOCL) **13**(1), 4 (2012). https://doi.org/10.1145/2071368.2071372
6. Glaister, I., Shallit, J.: A lower bound technique for the size of nondeterministic finite automata. Inf. Process. Lett. **59**(2), 75–77 (1996). https://doi.org/10.1016/0020-0190(96)00095-6
7. Gruber, H., Holzer, M.: Finite automata, digraph connectivity, and regular expression size. In: ICALP, pp. 39–50. Springer, Heidelberg (2008). https://doi.org/10.1007/978-3-540-70583-3_4
8. Gruber, H., Holzer, M.: Tight bounds on the descriptional complexity of regular expressions. In: Developments in Language Theory, pp. 276–287. Springer, Heidelberg (2009). https://doi.org/10.1007/978-3-642-02737-6_22
9. Gruber, H., Johannsen, J.: Optimal lower bounds on regular expression size using communication complexity. In: FoSSaCS, pp. 273–286. Springer, Heidelberg (2008). https://doi.org/10.1007/978-3-540-78499-9_20
10. Holzer, M., Kutrib, M.: The complexity of regular(-like) expressions. Int. J. Found. Comput. Sci. **22**(7), 1533–1548 (2011). https://doi.org/10.1142/S0129054111008866
11. Hrubeš, P., Yehudayoff, A.: Homogeneous formulas and symmetric polynomials. Comput. Complexity **20**(3), 559–578 (2011). https://doi.org/10.1007/s00037-011-0007-3
12. Jerrum, M., Snir, M.: Some exact complexity results for straight-line computations over semirings. J. ACM **29**(3), 874–897 (1982). https://doi.org/10.1145/322326.322341
13. Jukna, S.: Boolean Function Complexity: Advances and Frontiers, vol. 27. Springer, Heidelberg (2012). https://doi.org/10.1007/978-3-642-24508-4
14. Jukna, S.: Tropical complexity, sidon sets, and dynamic programming. SIAM J. Discrete Math. **30**, 2064–2085 (2016). https://doi.org/10.1137/16M1064738
15. Khrapchenko, V.M.: Method of determining lower bounds for the complexity of P-schemes. Math. Notes Acad. Sciences USSR **10**(1), 474–479 (1971)
16. Meyer, A.R., Stockmeyer, L.J.: The equivalence problem for regular expressions with squaring requires exponential space. In: 13th Annual Symposium on Switching and Automata Theory, pp. 125–129 (1972). https://doi.org/10.1109/SWAT.1972.29
17. Molina Lovett, A., Shallit, J.: Optimal regular expressions for permutations. In: ICALP, pp. 121:1–12 (2019). https://doi.org/10.4230/LIPIcs.ICALP.2019.121

18. Mousavi, H.: Lower bounds on regular expression size. CoRR abs/1712.00811 (2017). http://arxiv.org/abs/1712.00811
19. Shpilka, A., Yehudayoff, A.: Arithmetic circuits: a survey of recent results and open questions. Found. Trends Theor. Comput. Sci. 5(3–4), 207–388 (2010). https://doi.org/10.1561/0400000039

Crisp-Determinization of Weighted Tree Automata over Additively Locally Finite and Past-Finite Monotonic Strong Bimonoids Is Decidable

Manfred Droste[1], Zoltán Fülöp[2], Dávid Kószó[2(✉)], and Heiko Vogler[3]

[1] University of Leipzig, Leipzig, Germany
[2] University of Szeged, Szeged, Hungary
koszod@inf.u-szeged.hu
[3] Technische Universität Dresden, Dresden, Germany

Abstract. A weighted tree automaton is crisp-deterministic if it is deterministic and each of its transitions carries either the additive or multiplicative unit of the underlying weight algebra; weights different from these units may only appear at the root of the given input tree. A weighted tree automaton is crisp-determinizable if there exists an equivalent crisp-deterministic one. We prove that it is decidable whether weighted tree automata over additively locally finite and past-finite monotonic strong bimonoids are crisp-determinizable.

Keywords: Strong bimonoid · Semiring · Weighted tree automaton · Determinization · Decidability

1   Introduction

In the theory of automata, the determinization problem asks the following: for a given nondeterministic device of a given type, does there exist an equivalent deterministic device of the same type? This question was solved positively for finite-state (string or tree) automata by employing the powerset construction.

For the purpose of analysing quantitative properties, weighted string automata (wsa) were invented [37]. In a wsa, each transition carries a weight (quantity) and, in order to calculate with weights, an algebraic structure is needed such as, e.g., a semiring [3,12,17,29,36], lattice [35,39], strong bimonoid [9,15,16], valuation monoid [11,13], or multi-cost valuation structure [14]. In a similar way, finite-state tree automata have been extended to weighted tree automata (wta) over various algebraic structures [1,2,19,21–23].

Z. Fülöp—Research of this author was supported by grant TUDFO/47138-1/2019-ITM of the Ministry for Innovation and Technology, Hungary.
D. Kószó—Supported by the ÚNKP-19-3-SZTE-157 New National Excellence Program of the Ministry for Innovation and Technology.

© Springer Nature Switzerland AG 2020
G. Jirásková and G. Pighizzini (Eds.): DCFS 2020, LNCS 12442, pp. 39–51, 2020.
https://doi.org/10.1007/978-3-030-62536-8_4

For weighted automata the determinization problem is much more challenging [30], because there exist wta for which there does not exist an equivalent deterministic wta [7,32]. On the other side, there are particular classes of wsa for which the determinization problem can be solved positively: (a) wsa over locally finite semirings [26, p. 293] and [28], (b) trim unambiguous wsa over the tropical semiring having the twins property [32, Thm. 12], and (c) wsa over min-semirings having the twins property [26, Thm. 5]. Similar subclasses of wta were identified for which the determinization problem can be solved positively [7, Cor. 4.9 and Thm. 4.24], [23, Thm. 3.17], and [8, Thm. 5.2].

In this paper we investigate the *crisp-determinization problem* for wta: for a given wta over some strong bimonoid, does there exist an equivalent crisp-deterministic wta? Intuitively, strong bimonoids are semirings in which distributivity need not hold. We define the behavior of wta by using the run semantics. For a comparison with the initial algebra semantics we refer to [9,15,20].

A wta is *crisp-deterministic* if it is deterministic and each transition carries the additive or multiplicative unit element of the strong bimonoid as weight; thus, weights different from these units only occur as final weights (at the root of a tree). Clearly, for unweighted automata the notions of determinism and crisp-determinism coincide. The class of weighted tree languages recognized by crisp-deterministic wta is exactly the class of recognizable step mappings [20, Lm. 5.3] (cf. [15, Lm. 8 and Prop. 9] for the string case). A recognizable step mapping is the sum of finitely many weighted tree languages, each of which is constant over some recognizable tree language (called step language) and zero over the complement of that language. Hence the image of a recognizable step mapping is a finite set of elements of the strong bimonoid.

In [20, Thm. 8.5] it is shown that it is undecidable whether, for an arbitrary deterministic wta over some strong bimonoid, there is an equivalent crisp-deterministic wta. On the positive side, for each wsa $\mathcal{A}$ over the semiring $\mathbb{N}$ of natural numbers, the crisp-determinization problem is decidable by applying [15, Lm. 8 and Prop. 9] because (a) for each $n \in \mathbb{N}$ the preimage of n under the run semantics of $\mathcal{A}$ is a recognizable language [3, III. Cor. 2.5] (preimage property) and (b) it is shown to be decidable whether the image of the run semantics of $\mathcal{A}$ is finite [31, Cor. 5.2].

In this paper we follow this idea for decidability and extend it to wta over a new subclass of strong bimonoids. We define the class of monotonic strong bimonoids and prove that the crisp-determinization problem is decidable (1) for the class of all wta over additively locally finite and past-finite monotonic strong bimonoids with effective tests for 0 and 1 and (2) for the class of all unambiguous wta over past-finite monotonic strong bimonoids with effective tests for 0 and 1 (cf. Theorem 10). For the proof, we will generalize the preimage property [3, III. Cor. 2.5] to past-finite monotonic strong bimonoids (cf. Lemma 11). Moreover, for the proof that it is decidable whether the image of the run semantics of a wta is finite (cf. Theorem 13), we will employ a pumping lemma similar to [4, Lm. 5.5] (cf. Theorem 9). In particular, we will use this pumping lemma to construct an infinite sequence of values in the past-finite monotonic strong bimonoid. We note that in [5,38] a related concept, the cost-finiteness of wta was considered. In [5, Thm. 46] it was shown that cost-finiteness is decidable for an arbitrary wta over a monotonic and finitely factorizing semiring. In general, cost-finiteness of a wta does not imply that the image of its run semantics is finite, and the converse implication also fails. However, for wta over additively locally finite and past-finite monotonic strong bimonoids cost-finiteness and the finite image property coincide. Also we note that unambiguous wta form a larger class of wta than deterministic wta. For recent decidability results on wta with various degrees of unambiguity, we refer the reader to [33].

2 Preliminaries

2.1 General Notions and Notations

We denote by $\mathbb{N}$ the set of natural numbers $\{0, 1, 2, \ldots\}$ and by $\mathbb{N}_+$ the set $\mathbb{N} \setminus \{0\}$. For every $k \in \mathbb{N}$ we denote the set $\{i \in \mathbb{N} \mid 1 \leq i \leq k\}$ by $[k]$.

Let B be a set and $\preceq$ a binary relation on B. As usual, for every $a, b \in B$, we write $a \preceq b$ instead of $(a, b) \in \preceq$, and we write $a \prec b$ to denote that $a \preceq b$ and $a \neq b$. We say that $\preceq$ is a *partial ordering* if it is reflexive, antisymmetric, and transitive. For each $b \in B$, let $\text{past}(b) = \{a \in B \mid a \preceq b\}$. We call $(B, \preceq)$ *past-finite* if $\text{past}(b)$ is finite for each $b \in B$.

Let A be a set. Then $|A|$ denotes the cardinality of A, $\mathcal{P}_f(A)$ the set of finite subsets of A, A^* the *set of all strings over* A, and ε the empty string. For every $v, w \in A^*$, vw denotes the *concatenation of v and w*, $|v|$ the *length* of v, and $\text{prefix}(v)$ the set $\{w \in A^* \mid (\exists u \in A^*) : v = wu\}$.

2.2 Trees and Contexts

We suppose that the reader is familiar with the fundamental concepts and results of the theory of finite-state tree automata and tree languages [10,18,24]. Here we only recall some basic definitions.

A *ranked alphabet* is a tuple (Σ, rk) which consists of an alphabet Σ and mapping $\text{rk} : \Sigma \to \mathbb{N}$, called *rank mapping*, such that $\text{rk}^{-1}(0) \neq \emptyset$. For each $k \in \mathbb{N}$, we define $\Sigma^{(k)} = \{\sigma \in \Sigma \mid \text{rk}(\sigma) = k\}$. Sometimes we write $\sigma^{(k)}$ to mean that $\sigma \in \Sigma^{(k)}$. As usual, we abbreviate (Σ, rk) by Σ if rk is irrelevant or it is clear from the context.

Let Σ be a ranked alphabet and H be a set disjoint with Σ. The *set of Σ-trees over H*, denoted by $T_\Sigma(H)$, is defined in the standard way. We write T_Σ for $T_\Sigma(\emptyset)$. For every $\gamma \in \Sigma^{(1)}$ and $\alpha \in \Sigma^{(0)}$, we abbreviate the tree $\gamma(\ldots\gamma(\alpha)\ldots)$ with n occurrences of γ by $\gamma^n(\alpha)$ and write γ for γ^1. Any subset L of T_Σ is called *Σ-tree language*.

We define the *set of positions* of trees as a mapping $\text{pos} : T_\Sigma(H) \to \mathcal{P}_f(\mathbb{N}_+^*)$ such that (i) for each $\xi \in (\Sigma^{(0)} \cup H)$ let $\text{pos}(\xi) = \{\varepsilon\}$ and (ii) for every $\xi = \sigma(\xi_1, \ldots, \xi_k)$ with $k \in \mathbb{N}_+$, $\sigma \in \Sigma^{(k)}$, and $\xi_1, \ldots, \xi_k \in T_\Sigma(H)$, let $\text{pos}(\xi) = \{\varepsilon\} \cup \{iv \mid i \in [k], v \in \text{pos}(\xi_i)\}$. The *height* and the *size* of a tree $\xi \in T_\Sigma$ are $\text{height}(\xi) = \max\{|v| \mid v \in \text{pos}(\xi)\}$ and $\text{size}(\xi) = |\text{pos}(\xi)|$, respectively.

Let $\xi, \zeta \in T_\Sigma(H)$ and $v \in \text{pos}(\xi)$. In the standard way, the following notions are defined: label of ξ at v (denoted by $\xi(v)$), subtree of ξ at v (denoted by $\xi|_v$), and replacement of the subtree of ξ at v by ζ (denoted by $\xi[\zeta]_v$).

Let $\square$ be a new symbol such that $\square \notin \Sigma$. For each $\zeta \in T_\Sigma(\{\square\})$, we define $\text{pos}_\square(\zeta) = \{v \in \text{pos}(\zeta) \mid \zeta(v) = \square\}$ and for each $v \in \text{pos}(\zeta)$ we abbreviate by $\zeta|^v$ the tree $\zeta[\square]_v$. We denote by C_Σ the set $\{\zeta \in T_\Sigma(\{\square\}) \mid |\text{pos}_\square(\zeta)| = 1\}$ and call its elements *contexts over Σ* (for short: Σ-*contexts* or *contexts*).

Let $c \in C_\Sigma$ with $\{v\} = \text{pos}_\square(c)$ and $\zeta \in (T_\Sigma \cup C_\Sigma)$. Then we abbreviate $c[\zeta]_v$ by $c[\zeta]$. Obviously, if $\zeta \in C_\Sigma$, then also $c[\zeta] \in C_\Sigma$. Moreover, for each $n \in \mathbb{N}$, we define the *nth power of c*, denoted by c^n, by induction as follows: $c^0 = \square$ and $c^{n+1} = c[c^n]$.

In the rest of this paper, Σ will denote an arbitrary ranked alphabet if not specified otherwise.

2.3   Strong Bimonoids

A *strong bimonoid* [9,15,16] is an algebra $(B, \oplus, \otimes, \mathbb{0}, \mathbb{1})$ such that $(B, \oplus, \mathbb{0})$ is a commutative monoid, $(B, \otimes, \mathbb{1})$ is a monoid, $\mathbb{0} \neq \mathbb{1}$, and $\mathbb{0} \otimes b = b \otimes \mathbb{0} = \mathbb{0}$ for each $b \in B$. The strong bimonoid is called *commutative* if its multiplication $\otimes$ is commutative. We say that B is *additively locally finite* if, for each finite $A \subseteq B$, the submonoid of $(B, \oplus, \mathbb{0})$ generated by A is finite. If $\otimes$ is distributive with respect to $\oplus$ from both the left and the right, then B is called a *semiring*. For each $b \in B$, we let $b^0 = \mathbb{1}$ and for every $n \in \mathbb{N}$ we let $b^{n+1} = b \otimes b^n$. Moreover, for every $k \in \mathbb{N}$ and $b_1, \dots, b_k \in B$, we abbreviate $b_1 \otimes \cdots \otimes b_k$ by $\bigotimes_{i=1}^k b_i$.

In [5, Def. 12] the concept of *monotonic semiring* is defined. In the spirit of this definition, we define monotonic strong bimonoids as follows. Let $(B, \oplus, \otimes, \mathbb{0}, \mathbb{1})$ be a strong bimonoid and $\preceq$ a partial order on B. We say that $(B, \oplus, \otimes, \mathbb{0}, \mathbb{1}, \preceq)$ is *monotonic* if the following conditions hold:

(i) for every $a, b \in B : a \preceq a \oplus b$, and
(ii) for every $a, b, c \in B \setminus \{\mathbb{0}\}$ with $b \neq \mathbb{1}$ we have: $a \otimes c \prec a \otimes b \otimes c$.

We call $(B, \oplus, \otimes, \mathbb{0}, \mathbb{1}, \preceq)$ *past-finite* if $(B, \preceq)$ is past-finite.

We note that $\mathbb{0} \prec \mathbb{1} \prec b$ for each $b \in B \setminus \{\mathbb{0}, \mathbb{1}\}$ by [5, Lm. 14]. Also we note that the only finite monotonic strong bimonoid is the Boolean semiring $(\mathbb{B}, \sup, \inf, 0, 1)$ with its natural order, where $\mathbb{B} = \{0, 1\}$ [5, p. 122].

Example 1. We give six examples of past-finite monotonic semirings (cf. [5, p. 122]): (i) the semiring of natural numbers $(\mathbb{N}, +, \cdot, 0, 1, \leq)$; (ii) the arctic semiring $\text{ASR}_\mathbb{N} = (\mathbb{N}_{-\infty}, \max, +, -\infty, 0, \leq)$, where $\mathbb{N}_{-\infty} = \mathbb{N} \cup \{-\infty\}$; and (iii) the semiring $\text{Lcm} = (\mathbb{N}, \text{lcm}, \cdot, 0, 1, \leq)$, where $\text{lcm}(0, n) = n = \text{lcm}(n, 0)$ for each $n \in \mathbb{N}$ and otherwise lcm is the usual least common multiple; (iv) the semiring $\text{FSet}(\mathbb{N}) = (\mathcal{P}_f(\mathbb{N}), \cup, +, \emptyset, \{0\}, \preceq)$ where the addition on $\mathbb{N}$ is extended to sets as usual, and $\preceq$ is defined by $N_1 \preceq N_2$ if there is an injective mapping $f : N_1 \to N_2$ such that $n \leq f(n)$ for each $n \in N_1$; (v) for each $n \in \mathbb{N}_+$, the semiring $\text{Mat}_n(\mathbb{N}_+) = (\mathbb{N}_+^{n \times n} \cup \{\underline{0}, \underline{1}\}, +, \cdot, \underline{0}, \underline{1}, \leq)$ of square matrices over $\mathbb{N}_+$ with the common matrix addition and multiplication, where $\underline{0}$ is the $n \times n$ zero matrix and $\underline{1}$ is the $n \times n$ unit matrix; the partial order $\leq$ is defined by $M \leq M'$ if $M_{ij} \leq M'_{ij}$ for each $(i, j) \in [n] \times [n]$; (vi) the semiring $\mathrm{FLang}_\Sigma = (\mathcal{P}_f(\Sigma^*), \cup, \cdot, \emptyset, \{\varepsilon\}, \preceq)$ over the alphabet Σ with the operations of union and concatenation, and $\preceq$ is defined by $L_1 \preceq L_2$ if there is an injective mapping $f : L_1 \to L_2$ such that w is a subword of $f(w)$ for each $w \in L_1$. The semirings (i)–(iv) are commutative and (ii)–(iv), and (vi) are additively locally finite. $\qquad \square$

Also, there are examples of additively locally finite and past-finite monotonic strong bimonoids which are not semirings.

Example 2. We show a general method for generating past-finite monotonic strong bimonoids. Let $(B, \preceq)$ be a past-finite partially ordered set. Let $(B, +)$ be a commutative semigroup such that, for every $a, b \in B$, we have $a \preceq a + b$. Moreover, let $(B, \times)$ be a semigroup such that, for every $a, b, c \in B$, we have $a \prec a \times b$, $c \prec b \times c$, and $a \times c \prec a \times b \times c$. According to [16, Ex. 2.1(4)], we construct the *strong bimonoid induced by* $(B, +)$ *and* $(B, \times)$ to be the strong bimonoid $(B', \oplus, \otimes, 0, 1)$ defined as follows:

- $B' = B \cup \{0, 1\}$ where $0, 1 \notin B$;
- we define the operation $\oplus : B' \times B' \to B'$ such that $\oplus|_{B \times B} = +$ and for each $b \in B'$ we let $0 \oplus b = b = b \oplus 0$ and, if $b \neq 0$, then $1 \oplus b = b = b \oplus 1$;
- we define the operation $\otimes : B' \times B' \to B'$ such that $\otimes|_{B \times B} = \times$ and for each $b \in B'$ we let $0 \otimes b = 0 = b \otimes 0$, and $1 \otimes b = b = b \otimes 1$.

We define the partial ordering $\preceq'$ on B' such that $0 \prec' 1 \prec' b$ for each $b \in B$ and $\preceq' \cap (B \times B) = \preceq$. Then $(B', \oplus, \otimes, 0, 1, \preceq')$ is past-finite monotonic and is additively locally finite if, for each finite $A \subseteq B$, the subsemigroup of $(B, +)$ generated by A is finite. $\qquad \square$

In the rest of the paper, $(B, \oplus, \otimes, 0, 1)$ denotes an arbitrary strong bimonoid if not specified otherwise.

3   Weighted Tree Automata with Run Semantics

A (Σ, B)-*weighted tree language* (or: weighted tree language) is a mapping $r : T_\Sigma \to B$. The *image of* r is the set $\mathrm{im}(r) = \{r(\xi) \mid \xi \in T_\Sigma\}$, and for each $b \in B$, we denote by $r^{-1}(b)$ the set $\{\xi \in T_\Sigma \mid r(\xi) = b\}$.

We recall the concept of weighted tree automata over strong bimonoids from [34] (also cf., e.g., [20,23]). A (Σ, B)-*wta* is a tuple $\mathcal{A} = (Q, \delta, F)$, where Q is a finite nonempty set (*states*), $\delta = (\delta_k \mid k \in \mathbb{N})$ is a family of mappings $\delta_k : Q^k \times \Sigma^{(k)} \times Q \to B$ (*transition mappings*), and $F : Q \to B$ (*root weight mapping*). For each $q \in Q$, we abbreviate $F(q)$ by F_q. We say that $\mathcal{A}$ is *deterministic* (and *crisp-deterministic*) if, for every $k \in \mathbb{N}$, $w \in Q^k$, and $\sigma \in \Sigma^{(k)}$ there exists at most one $q \in Q$ such that $\delta_k(w, \sigma, q) \neq 0$ (respectively, there exists a $q \in Q$ such that $\delta_k(w, \sigma, q) = 1$, and $\delta_k(w, \sigma, q') = 0$ for each $q' \in Q \setminus \{q\}$). Clearly, crisp-determinism implies determinism.

Let $\mathcal{A} = (Q, \delta, F)$ be a (Σ, B)-wta, $\zeta \in T_\Sigma(\{\Box\})$, and $\rho : \mathrm{pos}(\zeta) \to Q$. We call ρ a *run of $\mathcal{A}$ on ζ* if, for every $v \in \mathrm{pos}(\zeta)$ with $\zeta(v) \in \Sigma$, we have $\delta_k(\rho(v1) \cdots \rho(vk), \sigma, \rho(v)) \neq \mathbb{0}$ where $\sigma = \zeta(v)$ and $k = \mathrm{rk}_\Sigma(\sigma)$. If $\rho(\varepsilon) = q$ for some $q \in Q$, then we say that ρ is a *q-run on ζ*. We denote by $\mathrm{R}_\mathcal{A}(q, \zeta)$ the set of all q-runs on ζ and we let $\mathrm{R}_\mathcal{A}(\zeta) = \bigcup_{q \in Q} \mathrm{R}_\mathcal{A}(q, \zeta)$. If $\mathcal{A}$ is deterministic, then $|\mathrm{R}_\mathcal{A}(\zeta)| \leq 1$. In particular, for $c \in C_\Sigma$ with $\mathrm{pos}_\Box(c) = \{v\}$, we call each $\rho \in \mathrm{R}_\mathcal{A}(q, c)$ a *$(q, \rho(v))$-run on c* and we denote the set of all (q, p)-runs on c by $\mathrm{R}_\mathcal{A}(q, c, p)$. We note that $\mathrm{R}_\mathcal{A}(q, c) = \bigcup_{p \in Q} \mathrm{R}_\mathcal{A}(q, c, p)$. Each element of $\mathrm{R}_\mathcal{A}(q, c, q)$ is called *loop*.

Let $\zeta \in T_\Sigma(\{\Box\})$, $\rho \in \mathrm{R}_\mathcal{A}(\zeta)$, and $v \in \mathrm{pos}(\zeta)$. We define the mapping $\rho|_v : \mathrm{pos}(\zeta|_v) \to Q$ such that, for each $v' \in \mathrm{pos}(\zeta|_v)$, we have $\rho|_v(v') = \rho(vv')$. Clearly, $\rho|_v \in \mathrm{R}_\mathcal{A}(\zeta|_v)$, and hence we call it the *run induced by ρ on $\zeta|_v$*.

Now we define the *weight of a run* $\rho \in \mathrm{R}_\mathcal{A}(\zeta)$ to be the element $\mathrm{wt}_\mathcal{A}(\zeta, \rho)$ of B by induction as follows: (i) if $\zeta = \Box$, then $\mathrm{wt}_\mathcal{A}(\zeta, \rho) = \mathbb{1}$ and (ii) if $\zeta = \sigma(\zeta_1, \ldots, \zeta_k)$ with $k \in \mathbb{N}$, then $\mathrm{wt}_\mathcal{A}(\zeta, \rho)$ is defined by

$$\mathrm{wt}_\mathcal{A}(\zeta, \rho) = \left(\bigotimes_{i=1}^k \mathrm{wt}_\mathcal{A}(\zeta_i, \rho|_i) \right) \otimes \delta_k(\rho(1) \cdots \rho(k), \sigma, \rho(\varepsilon)) \ . \tag{1}$$

If there is no confusion, then we drop the index $\mathcal{A}$ from $\mathrm{wt}_\mathcal{A}$ and write just $\mathrm{wt}(\zeta, \rho)$ for the weight of ρ. The *run semantics of $\mathcal{A}$* is the (Σ, B)-weighted tree language $[\![\mathcal{A}]\!] : T_\Sigma \to B$ defined, for each $\xi \in T_\Sigma$, by

$$[\![\mathcal{A}]\!](\xi) = \bigoplus_{\rho \in \mathrm{R}_\mathcal{A}(\xi)} \mathrm{wt}(\xi, \rho) \otimes F_{\rho(\varepsilon)} \ .$$

We say that $\mathcal{A}$ is *unambiguous* if, for each $\xi \in T_\Sigma$, there is at most one run $\rho \in \mathrm{R}_\mathcal{A}(\xi)$ with $F_{\rho(\varepsilon)} \neq \mathbb{0}$. In this case, for each $\xi \in T_\Sigma$ (a) for each $\rho \in \mathrm{R}_\mathcal{A}(\xi)$ we have $F_{\rho(\varepsilon)} = \mathbb{0}$ and thus $[\![\mathcal{A}]\!](\xi) = \mathbb{0}$ or (b) there is exactly one $\rho \in \mathrm{R}_\mathcal{A}(\xi)$ with $F_{\rho(\varepsilon)} \neq \mathbb{0}$ and $[\![\mathcal{A}]\!](\xi) = \mathrm{wt}(\xi, \rho) \otimes F_{\rho(\varepsilon)}$. Clearly, each deterministic wta is unambiguous, and there are easy examples of unambiguous wta A for which there does not exist a deterministic wta $\mathcal{A}'$ with $[\![\mathcal{A}]\!] = [\![\mathcal{A}']\!]$ [27]. A weighted tree language $r : T_\Sigma \to B$ is *run-recognizable* if there is a (Σ, B)-wta $\mathcal{A}$ such that $r = [\![\mathcal{A}]\!]$. The class of all run-recognizable (Σ, B)-weighted tree languages is denoted by $\mathrm{Rec}(\Sigma, B)$.

A *Σ-tree language* $L \subseteq T_\Sigma$ is *recognizable* if there is a $(\Sigma, \mathbb{B})$-wta $\mathcal{A}$ such that $L = [\![\mathcal{A}]\!]^{-1}(1)$ (recall that $(\mathbb{B}, \sup, \inf, 0, 1)$ is the Boolean semiring).

We note that also another semantics, called *initial algebra semantics*, can be defined for $\mathcal{A}$ [20,23,34]. In general, the two kinds of semantics are different [15], however, if B is a semiring or $\mathcal{A}$ is deterministic, then they coincide [15,20].

Example 3. Let $\Sigma = \{\gamma^{(1)}, \alpha^{(0)}\}$. We consider the $(\Sigma, \mathrm{ASR}_\mathbb{N})$-wta $\mathcal{A} = (\{q\}, \delta, F)$ with $\delta_0(\varepsilon, \alpha, q) = F_q = 0$ and $\delta_1(q, \gamma, q) = 1$. Clearly, $\mathcal{A}$ is deterministic and not crisp-deterministic (because 1 is not one of the unit elements of $\mathrm{ASR}_\mathbb{N}$). Moreover, $[\![\mathcal{A}]\!](\gamma^n(\alpha)) = n$ for each $n \in \mathbb{N}$. We note that $\mathrm{im}([\![\mathcal{A}]\!])$ is infinite. □

Lemma 4. (cf. [20, Lm. 5.3]) Let $r : T_\Sigma \to B$. Then the following statements are equivalent.

(i) There exists a crisp-deterministic (Σ, B)-wta $\mathcal{A}$ such that $r = [\![\mathcal{A}]\!]$.
(ii) $\mathrm{im}(r)$ is finite and for each $b \in B$ the Σ-tree language $r^{-1}(b)$ is recognizable.

Let $\mathcal{A} = (Q, \delta, F)$ be a (Σ, B)-wta. A state $p \in Q$ is *useful (in $\mathcal{A}$)* if there exist $\xi \in T_\Sigma$ and $\rho \in R_\mathcal{A}(\xi)$ such that $F_{\rho(\varepsilon)} \neq \mathbb{0}$ and $p \in \mathrm{im}(\rho)$. The (Σ, B)-wta $\mathcal{A}$ is *trim* if each of its states is useful.

Lemma 5. Let B have an effective test for $\mathbb{0}$ and $\mathcal{A}$ be a (Σ, B)-wta. If $\mathcal{A}$ contains a useful state, then we can effectively construct a (Σ, B)-wta $\mathcal{A}'$ such that $\mathcal{A}'$ is trim and $[\![\mathcal{A}']\!] = [\![\mathcal{A}]\!]$. If $\mathcal{A}$ is unambiguous, then $\mathcal{A}'$ is so.

In the rest of this paper, we let $\mathcal{A} = (Q, \delta, F)$ be an arbitrary (Σ, B)-wta.

4   Pumping Lemma

Pumping lemmas are used in order to achieve structural implications on small or particular large trees (cf. [24, Lm. 2.10.1] and [4]). Here we follow the idea of the pumping lemma [4, Lm. 5.5] and transfer it to our setting. On first glance, [4, Lm. 5.5] might not be appropriate, because it deals with deterministic wta and employs initial algebra semantics, whereas we deal with (arbitrary) wta and run semantics. However, we need a pumping lemma for a run of a wta on a tree and this situation is similar to [4, Lm. 5.5]. In order to spare the reader the transformation from Borchardt's setting to our one, we recall the relevant definitions and statements.

Let $c \in C_\Sigma$, $\zeta \in T_\Sigma$, $\{v\} = \mathrm{pos}_\Box(c)$, $q', q \in Q$, $\rho \in R_\mathcal{A}(q', c, q)$, and $\theta \in R_\mathcal{A}(q, \zeta)$. The *combination of ρ and θ*, denoted by $\rho[\theta]$, is the mapping $\rho[\theta] : \mathrm{pos}(c[\zeta]) \to Q$ defined for every $u \in \mathrm{pos}(c[\zeta])$ as follows: if $u = vw$ for some w, then we define $\rho[\theta](u) = \theta(w)$, otherwise we define $\rho[\theta](u) = \rho(u)$. Clearly, $\rho[\theta] \in R_\mathcal{A}(q', c[\zeta])$. For every $\xi \in T_\Sigma$, $\rho \in R_\mathcal{A}(\xi)$, and $v \in \mathrm{pos}(\xi)$, we define the run $\rho|^v$ on the context $\xi|^v$ such that for every $w \in \mathrm{pos}(\xi|^v)$ we set $\rho|^v(w) = \rho(w)$. If $\rho \in R_\mathcal{A}(\Box)$ with $\rho(\varepsilon) = q$ for some $q \in Q$, then sometimes we write $\widetilde{q}$ for ρ.

Let $c \in C_\Sigma$, $\{v\} = \mathrm{pos}_\Box(c)$, and $\rho \in R_\mathcal{A}(c)$. We define two mappings $l_{c,\rho} : \mathrm{prefix}(v) \to B$ and $r_{c,\rho} : \mathrm{prefix}(v) \to B$ inductively on the length of their arguments (cf. [4, p. 526] for deterministic wta). Intuitively, the product (1) which yields the element $\mathrm{wt}(c, \rho) \in B$, can be split into a left subproduct $l_{c,\rho}(\varepsilon)$ and a right subproduct $r_{c,\rho}(\varepsilon)$, where the border is given by the factor $\mathbb{1}$ coming from the weight of $\Box$. Formally, let $w \in \mathrm{prefix}(v)$. Then, assuming that $c(w) = \sigma$ and $\mathrm{rk}_\Sigma(\sigma) = k$, we let

$$l_{c,\rho}(w) = \begin{cases} \mathbb{1} & \text{if } w = v \\ \bigotimes_{j=1}^{i-1} \mathrm{wt}(c|_{wj}, \rho|_{wj}) \otimes l_{c,\rho}(wi) & \text{if } wi \in \mathrm{prefix}(v) \text{ for some } i \in \mathbb{N}_+ \end{cases}$$

$$r_{c,\rho}(w) = \begin{cases} \mathbb{1} & \text{if } w = v \\ r_{c,\rho}(wi) \otimes \bigotimes_{j=i+1}^{k} \text{wt}(c|_{wj}, \rho|_{wj}) \otimes \delta_k(\rho(w1)\cdots\rho(wk), \sigma, \rho(w)) \\ & \text{if } wi \in \text{prefix}(v) \text{ for some } i \in \mathbb{N}_+ \end{cases}.$$

In the sequel, we abbreviate $l_{c,\rho}(\varepsilon)$ and $r_{c,\rho}(\varepsilon)$ by $l_{c,\rho}$ and $r_{c,\rho}$, respectively.

Observation 6. Let $c \in C_\Sigma$ and $\rho \in R_{\mathcal{A}}(c)$. Then $\text{wt}(c, \rho) = l_{c,\rho} \otimes r_{c,\rho}$.

Lemma 7. (cf. [4, Lm. 5.1]) Let $c \in C_\Sigma$, $\zeta \in T_\Sigma$, $q', q \in Q$, $\rho \in R_{\mathcal{A}}(q', c, q)$, and $\theta \in R_{\mathcal{A}}(q, \zeta)$. Then $\text{wt}(c[\zeta], \rho[\theta]) = l_{c,\rho} \otimes \text{wt}(\zeta, \theta) \otimes r_{c,\rho}$.

Let $c \in C_\Sigma$, $q \in Q$, and $\rho \in R_{\mathcal{A}}(q, c, q)$ be a loop. For each $n \in \mathbb{N}$, the *nth power of ρ*, denoted by ρ^n, is the run on c^n defined by induction as follows: $\rho^0 = \tilde{q}$ (note that $c^0 = \square$) and $\rho^{n+1} = \rho[\rho^n]$. Next we apply the previous results to the weights of powers of loops.

Theorem 8. (cf. [4, Lm. 5.3]) Let $c', c \in C_\Sigma$ and $\zeta \in T_\Sigma$, $q', q \in Q$, $\rho' \in R_{\mathcal{A}}(q', c', q)$, $\rho \in R_{\mathcal{A}}(q, c, q)$, and $\theta \in R_{\mathcal{A}}(q, \zeta)$. Then, for each $n \in \mathbb{N}$,

$$\text{wt}(c'[c^n[\zeta]], \rho'[\rho^n[\theta]]) = l_{c',\rho'} \otimes (l_{c,\rho})^n \otimes \text{wt}(\zeta, \theta) \otimes (r_{c,\rho})^n \otimes r_{c',\rho'}.$$

Finally, we prove our pumping lemma for runs of $\mathcal{A}$ on trees in T_Σ which are large enough. We note that B need not be commutative.

Theorem 9. (cf. [4, Lm. 5.5]) Let $\xi \in T_\Sigma$, $q' \in Q$, $\kappa \in R_{\mathcal{A}}(q', \xi)$. If $\text{height}(\xi) \geq |Q|$, then there are $c', c \in C_\Sigma$, $\zeta \in T_\Sigma$, $q \in Q$, $\rho' \in R_{\mathcal{A}}(q', c', q)$, $\rho \in R_{\mathcal{A}}(q, c, q)$, and $\theta \in R_{\mathcal{A}}(q, \zeta)$ such that $\xi = c'[c[\zeta]]$, $\kappa = \rho'[\rho[\theta]]$, $\text{height}(c) > 0$, $\text{height}(c[\zeta]) < |Q|$, and, for each $n \in \mathbb{N}$,

$$\text{wt}(c'[c^n[\zeta]], \rho'[\rho^n[\theta]]) = l_{c',\rho'} \otimes (l_{c,\rho})^n \otimes \text{wt}(\zeta, \theta) \otimes (r_{c,\rho})^n \otimes r_{c',\rho'}.$$

Proof. Since $\text{height}(\xi) \geq |Q|$ there are $u, w \in \mathbb{N}_+^*$ such that $uw \in \text{pos}(\xi)$, $|w| > 0$, $\text{height}(\xi|_u) < |Q|$, and $\kappa(u) = \kappa(uw)$. Then we let $c' = \xi|^u$, $c = (\xi|_u)|^w$, $\zeta = \xi|_{uw}$. Clearly, $\xi = c'[c[\zeta]]$. Moreover, we set $\rho' = \kappa|^u$, $\rho = (\kappa|_u)|^w$ and $\theta = \kappa|_{uw}$. Then the statement follows from Theorem 8. $\qquad\square$

5   Main Result

A (Σ, B)-wta $\mathcal{A}$ is *crisp-determinizable (with respect to the run semantics)* if there exists a crisp-deterministic (Σ, B)-wta $\mathcal{C}$ such that $[\![\mathcal{A}]\!] = [\![\mathcal{C}]\!]$. We say that the strong bimonoid B *has effective tests for $\mathbb{0}$ and $\mathbb{1}$* if for each $b \in B$ we can decide whether $b = \mathbb{0}$ and whether $b = \mathbb{1}$. Then our main result is the following.

Theorem 10. *Let B be a past-finite monotonic strong bimonoid with effective tests for $\mathbb{0}$ and $\mathbb{1}$. Then the following two statements hold.*

1. *If B is additively locally finite, then it is decidable whether an arbitrary (Σ, B)-wta is crisp-determinizable.*

2. *It is decidable whether an arbitrary unambiguous (Σ, B)-wta is crisp-determinizable.*

The decidability problem addressed in Theorem 10 is meaningful, because in Example 3 we considered the additively locally finite and past-finite monotonic semiring $\text{ASR}_\mathbb{N}$ and a deterministic $(\Sigma, \text{ASR}_\mathbb{N})$-wta $\mathcal{A}$ which is not crisp-determinizable, due to Lemma 4 and the fact that $\text{im}(\llbracket \mathcal{A} \rrbracket)$ is infinite.

The blueprint for the proof of Theorem 10 is delivered by Lemma 4 and the fact that, for past-finite monotonic strong bimonoids, the preimage of each element is a recognizable tree language (cf. Lemma 11). Then it remains to show that the finiteness of $\text{im}(\llbracket \mathcal{A} \rrbracket)$ is decidable (cf. Corollary 14).

From now on, $(B, \oplus, \otimes, \mathbb{0}, \mathbb{1}, \preceq)$ is a monotonic strong bimonoid.

The following result is a generalization of [3, III. Cor. 2.5] from strings to trees and from the semiring $\mathbb{N}$ to any past-finite monotonic strong bimonoid B.

Lemma 11. *Let B be past-finite and $r \in \text{Rec}(\Sigma, B)$. Then $r^{-1}(b)$ is a recognizable Σ-tree language for each $b \in B$.*

Proof. Let $b \in B$ and put $C = B \setminus \text{past}(b) = \{a \in B \mid a \not\preceq b\}$. Moreover, let $\sim$ be the equivalence relation on the set B defined such that its classes are the singleton sets $\{a\}$ for each $a \in \text{past}(b)$ and the set C. We claim that $\sim$ is a congruence. To show that C is a congruence class, let $c, c' \in C$ and $d \in B$. Since B is monotonic, we have $c \preceq c \oplus d$, hence $c \oplus d \in C$ and similarly $c' \oplus d \in C$. Also, if $d \neq \mathbb{0}$, again we obtain $c \preceq c \otimes d$ and $c \preceq d \otimes c$, showing $c \otimes d, d \otimes c \in C$ and similarly $c' \otimes d, d \otimes c' \in C$. Hence C is a congruence class and the relation $\sim$ is a congruence relation on the strong bimonoid B. Then the quotient strong bimonoid $B/_\sim$ is finite. Let $h : B \to B/_\sim$ be the canonical strong bimonoid homomorphism. Then by a straightforward generalization of [6, Lm. 3] and [23, Thm. 3.9] (from semirings to strong bimonoids), $(h \circ r) \in \text{Rec}(\Sigma, B/_\sim)$. Moreover $r^{-1}(b) = (h \circ r)^{-1}(\{b\})$. Since the strong bimonoid $B/_\sim$ is finite, by [20, Cor. 7.5], there is a crisp-deterministic $(\Sigma, B/_\sim)$-wta $\mathcal{A}$ such that $\llbracket \mathcal{A} \rrbracket = h \circ r$. Then, by Lemma 4, the set $(h \circ r)^{-1}(\{b\})$ is a recognizable Σ-tree language. □

We say that *small loops of $\mathcal{A}$ have weight $\mathbb{1}$* if, for every $q \in Q$, $c \in C_\Sigma$, and loop $\rho \in R_\mathcal{A}(q, c, q)$, if $\text{height}(c) < |Q|$, then $\text{wt}(c, \rho) = \mathbb{1}$.

Lemma 12. *If small loops of $\mathcal{A}$ have weight $\mathbb{1}$, then, for every $\xi \in T_\Sigma$, $q' \in Q$, and $\kappa \in R_\mathcal{A}(q', \xi)$, there exist $\xi' \in T_\Sigma$ and $\kappa' \in R_\mathcal{A}(q', \xi')$ such that $\text{height}(\xi') < |Q|$ and $\text{wt}(\xi, \kappa) = \text{wt}(\xi', \kappa')$.*

Proof. Let $\xi \in T_\Sigma$, $q' \in Q$, $\kappa \in R_\mathcal{A}(q', \xi)$. We may assume that $\text{height}(\xi) \geq |Q|$. Applying Theorem 9 (for $n = 1$ and $n = 0$), there are $c, c' \in C_\Sigma$, $\zeta \in T_\Sigma$, $q \in Q$, $\rho' \in R_\mathcal{A}(q', c', q)$, $\rho \in R_\mathcal{A}(q, c, q)$, and $\theta \in R_\mathcal{A}(q, \zeta)$ such that $\xi = c'[c[\zeta]]$, $\kappa = \rho'[\rho[\theta]]$, $\text{height}(c) > 0$, $\text{height}(c[\zeta]) < |Q|$, and

$$\text{wt}(\xi, \kappa) = \text{wt}(c'[c[\zeta]], \rho'[\rho[\theta]]) = l_{c',\rho'} \otimes l_{c,\rho} \otimes \text{wt}(\zeta, \theta) \otimes r_{c,\rho} \otimes r_{c',\rho'} \ ,$$
$$\text{wt}(c'[\zeta], \rho'[\theta]) = l_{c',\rho'} \otimes \text{wt}(\zeta, \theta) \otimes r_{c',\rho'} \ .$$

By our assumption $\mathrm{wt}(c, \rho) = 1$, and by Observation 6 we have $\mathrm{wt}(c, \rho) = l_{c,\rho} \otimes r_{c,\rho}$. Thus $l_{c,\rho} = r_{c,\rho} = 1$ by monotonicity, and hence $\mathrm{wt}(\xi, \kappa) = \mathrm{wt}(c'[\zeta], \rho'[\theta])$.

Note that $\rho'[\theta] \in \mathrm{R}_{\mathcal{A}}(q', c'[\zeta])$ and $\mathrm{size}(c'[\zeta]) < \mathrm{size}(\xi)$. If $\mathrm{height}(c'[\zeta]) < |Q|$, then we are ready. Otherwise we continue with $c'[\zeta]$, q', and $\rho'[\theta]$ as before. After finitely many steps, we obtain $\xi' \in T_\Sigma$ and $\kappa' \in \mathrm{R}_{\mathcal{A}}(q', \xi')$ with $\mathrm{height}(\xi') < |Q|$ as required. $\qquad\square$

Theorem 13. *Let $\mathcal{A}$ be trim. Then the following two statements hold.*

1. *If B is past-finite and $\mathrm{im}(\llbracket \mathcal{A} \rrbracket)$ is finite, then small loops of $\mathcal{A}$ have weight 1.*
2. *If (a) small loops of $\mathcal{A}$ have weight 1 and (b) B is additively locally finite or $\mathcal{A}$ is unambiguous, then $\mathrm{im}(\llbracket \mathcal{A} \rrbracket)$ is finite.*

Proof. <u>Proof of 1:</u> We prove by contraposition. Suppose there are $q \in Q$, $c \in \mathrm{C}_\Sigma$, and $\rho \in \mathrm{R}_{\mathcal{A}}(q, c, q)$ such that $\mathrm{height}(c) < |Q|$ and $1 \prec \mathrm{wt}(c, \rho)$. Since $\mathcal{A}$ is trim, the state q is useful and thus there are $\xi \in T_\Sigma$, $\theta \in \mathrm{R}_{\mathcal{A}}(q, \xi)$ and $c' \in \mathrm{C}_\Sigma$, $q' \in Q$ with $F_{q'} \neq 0$, and $\rho' \in \mathrm{R}_{\mathcal{A}}(q', c', q)$. By Theorem 8, for each $n \in \mathbb{N}$, we have

$$\mathrm{wt}(c'[c^n[\xi]], \rho'[\rho^n[\theta]]) = l_{c',\rho'} \otimes (l_{c,\rho})^n \otimes \mathrm{wt}(\xi, \theta) \otimes (r_{c,\rho})^n \otimes r_{c',\rho'} \ .$$

Since $1 \prec \mathrm{wt}(c, \rho) = l_{c,\rho} \otimes r_{c,\rho}$, we have $1 \prec l_{c,\rho}$ or $1 \prec r_{c,\rho}$ and thus by monotonicity we obtain

$$\mathrm{wt}(c'[c^0[\xi]], \rho'[\rho^0[\theta]]) \prec \mathrm{wt}(c'[c^1[\xi]], \rho'[\rho^1[\theta]]) \prec \cdots \ . \tag{2}$$

We construct a sequence $\xi_1, \xi_2, \xi_3, \ldots$ of trees in T_Σ such that the elements $\llbracket \mathcal{A} \rrbracket(\xi_1)$, $\llbracket \mathcal{A} \rrbracket(\xi_2)$, $\llbracket \mathcal{A} \rrbracket(\xi_3)$, $\ldots$ are pairwise different as follows. We let $\xi_1 = c'[c[\xi]]$. Then $P_1 = \mathrm{past}(\llbracket \mathcal{A} \rrbracket(\xi_1))$ is finite. By (2) we choose n_2 such that $\mathrm{wt}(c'[c^{n_2}[\xi]], \rho'[\rho^{n_2}[\theta]]) \notin P_1$ and let $\xi_2 = c'[c^{n_2}[\xi]]$. Since $\rho'[\rho^{n_2}[\theta]] \in \mathrm{R}_{\mathcal{A}}(q', \xi_2)$ and B is monotonic, we have

$$\mathrm{wt}(\xi_2, \rho'[\rho^{n_2}[\theta]]) \preceq \mathrm{wt}(\xi_2, \rho'[\rho^{n_2}[\theta]]) \otimes F_{q'} \preceq \llbracket \mathcal{A} \rrbracket(\xi_2).$$

(Note that $F_{q'}$ may be 1.) Hence $\llbracket \mathcal{A} \rrbracket(\xi_2) \notin P_1$. Put $P_2 = \mathrm{past}(\llbracket \mathcal{A} \rrbracket(\xi_2))$. Then we choose $n_3 \in \mathbb{N}$ such that $\mathrm{wt}(c'[c^{n_3}[\xi]], \rho'[\rho^{n_3}[\theta]]) \notin P_1 \cup P_2$ and let $\xi_3 = c'[c^{n_3}[\xi]]$. As before, we have $\llbracket \mathcal{A} \rrbracket(\xi_3) \notin P_1 \cup P_2$. Continuing this process, we obtain the desired sequence of trees. It means $\mathrm{im}(\llbracket \mathcal{A} \rrbracket)$ is infinite.

<u>Proof of 2:</u> Let $\xi \in T_\Sigma$. We have $\llbracket \mathcal{A} \rrbracket(\xi) = \bigoplus_{\kappa \in \mathrm{R}_{\mathcal{A}}(\xi)} \mathrm{wt}(\xi, \kappa) \otimes F_{\kappa(\varepsilon)}$. By Assumption (a) and Lemma 12, for every $\kappa \in \mathrm{R}_{\mathcal{A}}(\xi)$ there are $\xi' \in T_\Sigma$ and $\kappa' \in \mathrm{R}_{\mathcal{A}}(\xi')$ such that $\mathrm{height}(\xi') < |Q|$, $\kappa(\varepsilon) = \kappa'(\varepsilon)$, and $\mathrm{wt}(\xi, \kappa) = \mathrm{wt}(\xi', \kappa')$.

Now we proceed by case analysis. Assume that B is additively locally finite. Then $\llbracket \mathcal{A} \rrbracket(\xi)$ is contained in the submonoid B' of $(B, \oplus, 0)$ generated by the finite set $H = \{\mathrm{wt}(\xi', \kappa') \otimes F_{q'} \mid q' \in Q, \xi' \in T_\Sigma, \mathrm{height}(\xi') < |Q|, \kappa' \in \mathrm{R}_{\mathcal{A}}(q', \xi')\}$. Since B is additively locally finite, the submonoid B' is finite. Since $\llbracket \mathcal{A} \rrbracket(\xi) \in B'$ for each $\xi \in T_\Sigma$ we have that $\mathrm{im}(\llbracket \mathcal{A} \rrbracket)$ is finite. Now assume that $\mathcal{A}$ is unambiguous. Then for each $\xi \in T_\Sigma$ we have (i) $\llbracket \mathcal{A} \rrbracket(\xi) = 0$ or (ii) there is a $\kappa \in \mathrm{R}_{\mathcal{A}}(\xi)$ with $F_{\kappa(\varepsilon)} \neq 0$ and $\llbracket \mathcal{A} \rrbracket(\xi) = \mathrm{wt}(\xi, \kappa) \otimes F_{\kappa(\varepsilon)}$. Hence $\mathrm{im}(\llbracket \mathcal{A} \rrbracket) \subseteq (H \cup \{0\})$. $\qquad\square$

Corollary 14. Let B be past-finite and have effective test for $\mathbb{1}$. Moreover, let $\mathcal{A}$ be trim. If B is additively locally finite or $\mathcal{A}$ is unambiguous, then it is decidable whether $\mathrm{im}(\llbracket \mathcal{A} \rrbracket)$ is finite.

Proof. By Theorem 13, $\mathrm{im}(\llbracket \mathcal{A} \rrbracket)$ is finite if and only if small loops of $\mathcal{A}$ have weight $\mathbb{1}$. The latter property is decidable because (a) there are only finitely many $c \in C_\Sigma$ such that $\mathrm{height}(c) < |Q|$, and (b) since B is monotonic, for all $c \in C_\Sigma$, $q \in Q$, and $\rho \in R_\mathcal{A}(q, c, q)$ we have $\mathrm{wt}(c, \rho) = \mathbb{1}$ if and only if for each $v \in \mathrm{pos}(c)$ we have $\delta_k(\rho(v1) \cdots \rho(vk), \sigma, \rho(v)) = \mathbb{1}$ where $\sigma = c(v)$ and $k = \mathrm{rk}_\Sigma(\sigma)$, and (c) this is decidable because B has effective test for $\mathbb{1}$. □

We note that from Corollary 14 we can formally derive the well-known result that the finiteness of context-free languages is decidable [25, Thm. 8.2.2].

Proof (of Theorem 10). Let $\mathcal{A}$ be an arbitrary (Σ, B)-wta and assume that B is additively locally finite or $\mathcal{A}$ is unambiguous. By Lemma 5, we can construct the trim (Σ, B)-wta $\mathcal{A}'$ such that $\llbracket \mathcal{A}' \rrbracket = \llbracket \mathcal{A} \rrbracket$. By Lemmas 4 and 11, $\mathcal{A}'$ is crisp-determinizable if and only if $\mathrm{im}(\llbracket \mathcal{A}' \rrbracket)$ is finite. By Corollary 14, it is decidable if $\mathrm{im}(\llbracket \mathcal{A}' \rrbracket)$ is finite. □

References

1. Alexandrakis, A., Bozapalidis, S.: Weighted grammars and Kleene's theorem. Inf. Process. Lett. **24**(1), 1–4 (1987)
2. Berstel, J., Reutenauer, C.: Recognizable formal power series on trees. Theor. Comput. Sci. **18**(2), 115–148 (1982)
3. Berstel, J., Reutenauer, C.: Rational Series and Their Languages. EATCS Monographs on Theoretical Computer Science, vol. 12. Springer, Heidelberg (1988)
4. Borchardt, B.: A pumping lemma and decidability problems for recognizable tree series. Acta Cybern. **16**(4), 509–544 (2004)
5. Borchardt, B., Fülöp, Z., Gazdag, Z., Maletti, A.: Bounds for tree automata with polynomial costs. J. Autom. Lang. Comb. **10**, 107–157 (2005)
6. Borchardt, B., Maletti, A., Šešelja, B., Tepavčevic, A., Vogler, H.: Cut sets as recognizable tree languages. Fuzzy Sets Syst. **157**, 1560–1571 (2006)
7. Borchardt, B., Vogler, H.: Determinization of finite state weighted tree automata. J. Autom. Lang. Comb. **8**(3), 417–463 (2003)
8. Büchse, M., May, J., Vogler, H.: Determinization of weighted tree automata using factorizations. J. Autom. Lang. Comb. **15**(3/4), 229–254 (2010)
9. Ćirić, M., Droste, M., Ignjatović, J., Vogler, H.: Determinization of weighted finite automata over strong bimonoids. Inf. Sci. **180**(18), 3479–3520 (2010)
10. Comon, H., et al.: Tree automata techniques and applications (2008). http://tata.gforge.inria.fr
11. Droste, M., Götze, D., Märcker, S., Meinecke, I.: Weighted tree automata over valuation monoids and their characterization by weighted logics. In: Kuich, W., Rahonis, G. (eds.) Algebraic Foundations in Computer Science. LNCS, vol. 7020, pp. 30–55. Springer, Heidelberg (2011). https://doi.org/10.1007/978-3-642-24897-9_2

12. Droste, M., Kuich, W., Vogler, H. (eds.): Handbook of Weighted Automata. EATCS Monographs in Theoretical Computer Science. Springer, Heidelberg (2009). https://doi.org/10.1007/978-3-642-01492-5

13. Droste, M., Meinecke, I.: Weighted automata and weighted MSO logics for average and long-time behaviors. Inf. Comput. **220–221**, 44–59 (2012)

14. Droste, M., Perevoshchikov, V.: Multi-weighted automata and MSO logic. Theory Comput. Syst. **59**, 231–261 (2016). https://doi.org/10.1007/s00224-015-9658-9

15. Droste, M., Stüber, T., Vogler, H.: Weighted finite automata over strong bimonoids. Inf. Sci. **180**(1), 156–166 (2010)

16. Droste, M., Vogler, H.: Weighted automata and multi-valued logics over arbitrary bounded lattices. Theor. Comput. Sci. **418**, 14–36 (2012)

17. Eilenberg, S.: Automata, Languages, and Machines - Volume A, Pure and Applied Mathematics, vol. 59. Academic Press, Cambridge (1974)

18. Engelfriet, J.: Tree automata and tree grammars. Technical report. DAIMI FN-10, Institute of Mathematics, University of Aarhus, Department of Computer Science, Denmark (1975). arXiv:1510.02036v1 [cs.FL], 7 October 2015

19. Ésik, Z., Liu, G.: Fuzzy tree automata. Fuzzy Sets Syst. **158**, 1450–1460 (2007)

20. Fülöp, Z., Kószó, D., Vogler, H.: Crisp-determinization of weighted tree automata over strong bimonoids (2019). arXiv:1912.02660v1 [cs.FL], 5 December 2019

21. Fülöp, Z., Maletti, A., Vogler, H.: A Kleene theorem for weighted tree automata over distributive multioperator monoids. Theory Comput. Syst. **44**, 455–499 (2009). https://doi.org/10.1007/s00224-007-9091-9

22. Fülöp, Z., Stüber, T., Vogler, H.: A Büchi-like theorem for weighted tree automata over multioperator monoids. Theory Comput. Syst. **50**(2), 241–278 (2012). https://doi.org/10.1007/s00224-010-9296-1

23. Fülöp, Z., Vogler, H.: Weighted tree automata and tree transducers. In: Droste, M., Kuich, W., Vogler, H. (eds.) Handbook of Weighted Automata. EATCS, pp. 313–403. Springer, Heidelberg (2009). https://doi.org/10.1007/978-3-642-01492-5_9

24. Gécseg, F., Steinby, M.: Tree Automata. Akadémiai Kiadó, Budapest (1984). arXiv:1509.06233v1 [cs.FL], 21 September 2015

25. Harrison, M.: Introduction to Formal Language Theory. Addison-Wesley, Boston (1978)

26. Kirsten, D., Mäurer, I.: On the determinization of weighted automata. J. Autom. Lang. Comb. **10**, 287–312 (2005)

27. Klimann, I., Lombardy, S., Mairesse, J., Prieur, C.: Deciding unambiguity and sequentiality from a finitely ambiguous max-plus automaton. Theor. Comput. Sci. **327**(3), 349–373 (2004)

28. Kostolányi, P.: On deterministic weighted automata. Inf. Process. Lett. **140**, 42–47 (2018)

29. Kuich, W., Salomaa, A.: Semirings, Automata, Languages. EATCS Monographs in Theoretical Computer Science, vol. 5. Springer, Heidelberg (1986). https://doi.org/10.1007/978-3-642-69959-7_4

30. Lombardy, S., Sakarovitch, J.: Sequential? Theor. Comput. Sci. **356**, 224–244 (2006)

31. Mandel, A., Simon, I.: On finite semigroups of matrices. Theor. Comput. Sci. **5**, 101–111 (1977)

32. Mohri, M.: Finite-state transducers in language and speech processing. Comput. Linguist. **23**(2), 269–311 (1997)

33. Paul, E.: Finite sequentiality of unambiguous max-plus tree automata. In: 36th International Symposium on Theoretical Aspects of Computer Science (STACS 2019). vol. 126, pp. 53:1–53:17. Schloss Dagstuhl – Leibniz-Zentrum für Informatik (2019)
34. Radovanović, D.: Weighted tree automata over strong bimonoids. Novi Sad J. Math. **40**(3), 89–108 (2010)
35. Rahonis, G.: Fuzzy languages. In: Droste, M., Kuich, W., Vogler, H. (eds.) Handbook of Weighted Automata. EATCS, pp. 481–517. Springer, Heidelberg (2009). https://doi.org/10.1007/978-3-642-01492-5_12
36. Sakarovitch, J.: Elements of Automata Theory. Cambridge University Press, Cambridge (2009)
37. Schützenberger, M.: On the definition of a family of automata. Inf. Control **4**, 245–270 (1961)
38. Seidl, H.: Finite tree automata with cost functions. Theor. Comput. Sci. **126**(1), 113–142 (1994)
39. Wechler, W.: The Concept of Fuzziness in Automata and Language Theory, 5th edn. Studien zur Algebra und ihre Anwendungen, Akademie-Verlag, Berlin (1978)

On the Power of Generalized Forbidding Insertion-Deletion Systems

Henning Fernau[1] , Lakshmanan Kuppusamy[2] ,
and Indhumathi Raman[3(✉)]

[1] Fachbereich 4 – Abteilung Informatikwissenschaften, CIRT, Universität Trier,
54286 Trier, Germany
fernau@uni-trier.de
[2] School of Computer Science and Engineering, VIT, Vellore 632 014, India
klakshma@vit.ac.in
[3] Department of Applied Mathematics and Computational Sciences,
PSG College of Technology, Coimbatore 641 004, India
ind.amcs@psgtech.ac.in

Abstract. We consider generalized forbidding insertion-deletion systems (GFID) where each insertion-deletion rule is associated with a set $\mathcal{F}$ of words and the rule can be applied to a string only if every word of $\mathcal{F}$ is not a subword of the string. The parameters in the size $(k; n, i', i''; m, j', j'')$ of a GFID system denote (from left to right) the maximum length of a word in $\mathcal{F}$, the maximal length of an insertion string, the maximal length of the left context for insertion, the maximal length of the right context for insertion; the last three parameters follow a similar pattern with respect to deletion. We show that GFID systems of sizes $(k; n, i', i''; m, j', j'')$, where $k = 2$ and $n + i' + i'' = m + j' + j'' = 2$, with $n, m > 0$ and $i', i'', j', j'' \in \{0, 1\}$, describe all recursively enumerable languages, by explaining algorithms that transform a given type-0 grammar in some normal form to a GFID system of the required size.

Keywords: Insertion-deletion · Semi-conditional · Forbidding grammars · Descriptional complexity · Special Geffert Normal Form

1 Introduction

Since the 1930s, many different formal models have been developed that turned out to be equivalent to Turing machines. We refer to [6,15] for descriptions of these (early) findings. From the viewpoint of Formal Languages, that means that there are many mechanisms that can describe the family of recursively enumerable languages, or RE for short.

Since the 1990s, there have been various attempts to create a formal basis of models for DNA computing; see [9,16]. One of the key observations here is that insertions and deletions play a central role in such formalisms. Research of formal systems based on these operations was initiated by Kari [8].

© Springer Nature Switzerland AG 2020
G. Jirásková and G. Pighizzini (Eds.): DCFS 2020, LNCS 12442, pp. 52–63, 2020.
https://doi.org/10.1007/978-3-030-62536-8_5

For the ease of possible implementations *in vitro*, quite from the early days of this area onwards, one of the main research questions was to look into the simplest possible models that can still achieve computational completeness, i.e., simulate arbitrary Turing machine computations. A tuple $(n, i', i''; m, j', j'')$ is associated with an insertion-deletion (ID) system to denote its size, where the six parameters are defined in Table 2. For instance, it is known that insertion-deletion systems of sizes $(1, 1, 1; 1, 1, 1)$, $(1, 1, 1; 2, 0, 0)$, $(2, 0, 0; 1, 1, 1)$, $(2, 0, 0; 3, 0, 0)$ or $(3, 0, 0; 2, 0, 0)$ are computationally complete (see [10,18]), while upon decreasing any of the non-zero size parameter bounds, we arrive at systems that are not capable to simulate every Turing machine; see [12].

For sizes that are too small to simulate Turing machines, a research line was followed that has been quite successful in a different context of Formal Languages, namely that of imposing further regulation strategies, as pioneered in the area of Regulated Rewriting, see [1]; there, mostly context-free rules (which are themselves too weak to simulate Turing machines) have been combined with various regulations (like graph-controlled, matrix, semi-conditional) to obtain computational completeness results. These regulated rewriting mechanisms are transferred to the insertion-deletion case; see [3,4,17]. In this paper, we follow this line of research for the case of forbidding context grammars, introduced by Meduna in [13] and further studied in [2,11,14].

Ivanov and Verlan initiated the study of semi-conditional ins-del (SCID) systems in [7]. An octuple $(i, j; n, i', i''; m, j', j'')$ is associated as size of a SCID system where the parameters denote (from left to right) the maximum length of a word in permitting set $\mathcal{P}$, the maximum length of a word in forbidding set $\mathcal{F}$, the rest of the parameters are defined in Table 2. The pair (i, j) is sometimes called degree. They proved that SCID systems with sizes $(2, 2; 1, 0, 0; 1, 0, 0)$ and $(1, 1; 2, 0, 0; 1, 1, 0)$ describe RE, however, SCID systems with size $(1, 1)$ and ID size $(1, 1, 0; 2, 0, 0)$ and $(1, 1, 0; m, 1, 1)$ are proved to be computationally incomplete. No computational (in)completeness results were obtained for SCID systems of other degrees in [7]. In [3], it was shown that *simple* SCID systems of sizes $(2, 1; 1 + i, i', i''; 1 + j, j', j'')$ describe RE for all $i + i' + i'' = 1 = j + j' + j''$. Is this situation the same even if the degree of (simple) SCID is changed from $(2, 1)$ to $(0, 2)$? This paper answers this question in the affirmative.

We call an SCID system of degree $(0, k)$ as a generalized forbidding insertion-deletion (GFID) system of degree k. Here, each insertion-deletion rule is associated with a set $\mathcal{F}$ of words and the rule can be applied to a string only if every word of $\mathcal{F}$ is not a subword of the string. We then show that GFID systems of sizes $(2; 1 + i, i', i''; 1 + j, j', j'')$ where $i + i' + i'' = j + j' + j'' = 1$ (with $i, i', i'', j, j', j'' \in \{0, 1\}$) are computationally complete; see Table 1 for clarity.

Note that in view of the mentioned computational incompleteness results of Ivanov and Verlan [7], we know that $\mathrm{GFID}(1; 1, 1, 0; x, y, z) \neq \mathrm{RE}$ for $(x, y, z) \in \{(2, 0, 0), (1, 1, 0), (1, 0, 1)\}$, so that in this sense, our computational completeness results cannot be further improved. Recall that insertion-deletion systems (without any regulations) of size $(2, 0, 0; 2, 0, 0)$ are computationally incomplete.

Table 1. Results of this paper

	Result	Reference
1.	$\mathrm{GFID}(2;2,0,0;2,0,0) = \mathrm{RE}$	Theorem 3
2.	$\mathrm{GFID}(2;1,1,0;2,0,0) = \mathrm{RE}$	Theorem 4
3.	$\mathrm{GFID}(2;1,1,0;1,1,0) = \mathrm{RE}$	Theorem 5
4.	$\mathrm{GFID}(2;1,1,0;1,0,1) = \mathrm{RE}$	Theorem 6
5.	$\mathrm{GFID}(2;2,0,0;1,1,0) = \mathrm{RE}$	Theorem 7

	Result	Reference
6.	$\mathrm{GFID}(2;1,0,1;2,0,0) = \mathrm{RE}$	Corollary 1
7.	$\mathrm{GFID}(2;1,0,1;1,0,1) = \mathrm{RE}$	Corollary 2
8.	$\mathrm{GFID}(2;1,0,1;1,1,0) = \mathrm{RE}$	Corollary 3
9.	$\mathrm{GFID}(2;2,0,0;1,0,1) = \mathrm{RE}$	Corollary 4

Our results are obtained by simulating so-called space separating special Geffert normal form grammars (or ssSGNF for short), a restriction of type-0 grammars introduced in [3]. All our results are constructive in the following sense: We describe algorithms how to transform a given ssSGNF grammar into a forbidding generalized insertion-deletion system and then prove the correctness of our algorithm. Incorporating the algorithmic transformations given in [3,5], we obtain an algorithm that transforms an input Turing machine (accepting a language L) into a GFID system (of the sizes specified above) that generates L.

2   Important Definitions

We assume some basic knowledge of formal languages on the side of the reader. We will also use standard notations from that area, for instance, T^* is the set of words over the alphabet T, including the empty word λ. For a word w, $sub(w)$ denotes the set of subwords (factors) of w and w^r denotes the reversal of w. From [3], we recall the following definition and theorem.

Definition 1. *A type-0 grammar $G = (N, T, P, S)$ is said to be in* Space Separating Special Geffert Normal Form, *or ssSGNF for short, if*

- *N decomposes as $N = N' \cup N''$, where $N'' = \{A, B, C, D, E, F\}$ and N' further decomposes as $N' = N_S \cup N_{S'}$ such that N_S contains at least the nonterminal S and $N_{S'}$ contains at least the nonterminal S',*
- *the only non-context-free rules are erasing: $AB \to \lambda$, $CD \to \lambda$ and $EF \to \lambda$,*
- *the non-erasing context-free rules are of the following forms:*
  $X \to Yb$ or $X \to b'Y (X \in N_S,\ Y \in N',\ X \neq Y,\ b \in T,\ b' \in \{A, C, E\})$, or
  $X \to Yb$ or $X \to b'Y (X, Y \in N_{S'},\ X \neq Y,\ b \in \{B, D, F\},\ b' \in \{A, C, E\})$;
- *G contains the erasing context-free rule $S' \to \lambda$ and also possibly $S \to \lambda$.*

We can restrict our attention to ssSGNF's whose derivations split into two phases; in the first phase, only context-free rules are applied and only strings in

$$\{EA, EC\}^* N_S T^* \cup \{EA, EC\}^* N_{S'} \{BF, DF\}^* T^* \cup \{EA, EC\}^* \{BF, DF\}^* T^*$$

are produced; in the second phase, only the said three non-context-free erasing rules are applied and strings from $\{EA, EC\}^* \{\lambda, EF\} \{BF, DF\}^* T^*$ only can be derived to terminal strings. This leads us to the following result.

Theorem 1. *For every recursively enumerable language, there exists a type-0 grammar in ssSGNF that describes it. Moreover, for any $w \in (N \cup T)^*$ such that $S \Rightarrow^* w$, $\{AA, BB, CC, DD, EE, FF\} \cap sub(w) = \emptyset$.* □

Notice that there is always a unique *central part* in a sentential form where derivations can actually happen, referring to a nonterminal from N' in the first phase, and to substrings AB, CD, EF in the second phase.

The core notion of this paper is the following one, see [7].

Definition 2. *[7] A generalized forbidding insertion-deletion system is a construct $\Pi = (V, T, A, R)$, where V is a finite alphabet, $T \subseteq V$ is the terminal alphabet, $A \subseteq V^*$ is a finite set of axioms , R is a finite set of rules of the form $[(u, s, v)_t, \mathcal{F}]$ where $u, v \in V^*$, $s \in V^+$, $t \in \{ins, del\}$, $\mathcal{F}$ is finite subset of V^*.*

An element $x \in A$ is called an *axiom*. For clarity, we often use unique labels for rules, even identifying a rule with its label, i.e., if $\ell \in R$ is a rule (label), then we write $\ell : [(u_\ell, s_\ell, v_\ell)_{t_\ell}, \mathcal{F}_\ell]$. The element u_ℓ is called the *left context* of s_ℓ and v_ℓ is called the *right context* of s_ℓ. If both contexts are empty for every insertion (deletion) rule, then the insertion (deletion) is called *context-free*. The set $\mathcal{F}_\ell$ is called the *forbidding* set. The maximum length of a word in $\mathcal{F}_\ell$, taken over all rules of $\ell \in R$, is denoted by k and is called the *degree* of the generalized forbidding ins-del system. We write $x \Rightarrow_\ell y$ if $\mathcal{F}_\ell \cap sub(x) = \emptyset$ and

1. $t_\ell = ins$ and $x = x_1 u_\ell v_\ell x_2$, $y = x_1 u_\ell s_\ell v_\ell x_2$, for some $x_1, x_2 \in V^*$; or
2. $t_\ell = del$ and $x = x_1 u_\ell s_\ell v_\ell x_2$, $y = x_1 u_\ell v_\ell x_2$, for some $x_1, x_2 \in V^*$.

The language generated by a GFID system Π is $L(\Pi) = \{w \in T^* \mid x \Rightarrow^* w$ for some $x \in A\}$, where $\Rightarrow^*$ is the reflexive and transitive closure of $\Rightarrow$.

The descriptional complexity of a GFID system is measured by its *size* $s = (k; n, i', i''; m, j', j'')$, where k is the degree of GFID and the other parameters represent resource bounds as given in Table 2. The families of languages generated by generalized forbidding insertion-deletion systems of size $(k; n, i', i''; m, j', j'')$ is denoted as GFID$(k; n, i', i''; m, j', j'')$.

Table 2. Parameters in the size of ins-del system.

$n = \max\{\lvert\eta\rvert : (u, \eta, v)_{ins} \in R\}$	$m = \max\{\lvert\delta\rvert : (u, \delta, v)_{del} \in R\}$
$i' = \max\{\lvert u\rvert : (u, \eta, v)_{ins} \in R\}$	$j' = \max\{\lvert u\rvert : (u, \delta, v)_{del} \in R\}$
$i'' = \max\{\lvert v\rvert : (u, \eta, v)_{ins} \in R\}$	$j'' = max\{\lvert v\rvert : (u, \delta, v)_{del} \in R\}$

3   Main Results

For theorems marked by $(*)$, proof details are omitted due to page constraint. However, at some places, we provide a proof sketch for easy understanding.

Theorem 2. (∗) *Let $\mathcal{L}$ be a language class that is closed under reversal. Then, for all non-negative integers $k, n, i', i'', m, j', j''$,*

1. $\mathrm{GFID}(k; n, i', i''; m, j', j'') = [\mathrm{GFID}(k; n, i'', i'; m, j'', j')]^r$.
2. $\mathcal{L} = \mathrm{GFID}(k; n, i', i''; m, j', j'')$ *iff* $\mathcal{L} = \mathrm{GFID}(k; n, i'', i'; m, j'', j')$.

An important special case of the above theorem will be $\mathcal{L} = \mathrm{RE}$, as RE is closed under reversal and we can use this for computational completeness results. Let $|P|$ be the number of rules in a type-0 grammar. We define some notations:

$$
\begin{aligned}
M &= \{m \mid m \in [1\ldots|P|]\}, & M' &= \{m' \mid m \in [1\ldots|P|]\}, \\
M'' &= \{m'' \mid m \in [1\ldots|P|]\}, & M''' &= \{m''' \mid m \in [1\ldots|P|]\}, \\
M^{iv} &= \{m^{iv} \mid m \in [1\ldots|P|]\}, & M^v &= \{m^v \mid m \in [1\ldots|P|]\}, \\
\mathcal{M}'' &= M \cup M' \cup M'', & \mathcal{M}''' &= M \cup M' \cup M'' \cup M''', \\
\mathcal{M}^{iv} &= \mathcal{M}''' \cup M^{iv}, & \mathcal{M}^v &= \mathcal{M}''' \cup M^{iv} \cup M^v,
\end{aligned}
$$

The general idea in our proofs is that we consider a type-0 grammar G in space-separating Special Geffert Normal form as described in Definition 1. We label the two types of context-free rules as follows: $p : X \to bY$ and $q : X \to Yb$ and label the non-context-free rules exemplarily as $f : AB \to \lambda$. Apart from the very end, a sentential form ξ of G corresponds to a string $\sigma\xi\sigma$ derivable in the simulating system Π, where σ is a new endmarker symbol. We also use

$$\Phi_1 = \{A, C, E, \sigma\}(\{B, D, F, \sigma\} \cup T) \cup T\{A, C, E\} \cup \{ZZ \mid Z \in \{A, B, C, D, E, F\}\}$$

to check if we are currently simulating phase 1 of the given ssSGNF grammar.

Remark 1. Notice that we are not making this explicit below, but there are malicious strings like Aa that might be derived in G (and hence in the simulating system Π) where we have to make sure that such strings can never derive anything useful within the simulating system Π. Therefore, we add the forbidden context Φ_1 to any context-free insertion rule. Similarly, if G derives A, then in Π we would derive $\sigma A\sigma$ in Π and get blocked.

Theorem 3. $\mathrm{GFID}(2; 2, 0, 0; 2, 0, 0) = \mathrm{RE}$.

Proof. Consider a type-0 grammar $G = (N, T, P, S)$ in ssSGNF as in Definition 1 whose rules are labelled uniquely by numbers $[1\ldots|P|]$. Construct a GFID system $\Pi = (V, T, \{\sigma S\sigma\}, R)$ of size $(2; 2, 0, 0; 2, 0, 0)$ as follows such that $L(\Pi) = L(G)$. Let $V = N \cup T \cup \{\sigma\} \cup \mathcal{M}^v$. The set of rules of R in Π is given next. (i) For every (context-free) rule of type $p : X \to bY$ in G, the set of simulating rules is stated in Fig. 1(a). (ii) For every rule of type $q : X \to Yb$ in G, the set of simulating rules is stated in Figure 1(b). (iii) Rules like $UV \to \lambda$, with $UV \in \{AB, CD, EF\}$, are simulated by the GFID rule $f_{UV} = [(\lambda, UV, \lambda)_{del}, N']$. (iv) The erasing rule $S' \to \lambda$ is simulated by $[(\lambda, S', \lambda)_{del}, \emptyset]$ (and possibly $S \to \lambda$ by by $[(\lambda, S, \lambda)_{del}, \emptyset]$). (v) To terminate, we include $[(\lambda, \sigma, \lambda)_{del}, V \setminus (T \cup \{\sigma\})]$.

$$p1 = [(\lambda, pp', \lambda)_{ins}, \quad \mathcal{M}^v \cup (N' \setminus \{X\}) \cup \Phi_1]$$
$$p2 = [(\lambda, p'X, \lambda)_{del}, \quad (\mathcal{M}^v \setminus \{p, p'\}) \cup (N' \setminus \{X\})]$$
$$p3 = [(\lambda, bp'', \lambda)_{ins}, \quad (\mathcal{M}^v \setminus \{p\}) \cup N' \cup \Phi_1]$$
$$p4 = [(\lambda, Yp''', \lambda)_{ins}, \quad (\mathcal{M}^v \setminus \{p, p''\}) \cup N' \cup \{p''Z \mid Z \in V \setminus \{p''\}\} \cup$$
$$\{Zp \mid Z \in V \setminus \{p''\}\} \cup \Phi_1]$$
$$p5 = [(\lambda, p^v p^{iv}, \lambda)_{ins}, \quad (\mathcal{M}^v \setminus \{p, p'', p'''\}) \cup (N' \setminus \{Y\}) \cup \{bp''\} \cup$$
$$\{Zp \mid Z \in V \setminus \{p''\}\} \cup \Phi_1]$$
$$p6 = [(\lambda, p^{iv} p''', \lambda)_{del}, \quad (\mathcal{M}^v \setminus \{p, p'', p''', p^{iv}, p^v\}) \cup (N' \setminus \{Y\}) \cup \{Yp''', bp''\} \cup$$
$$\{p'''Z \mid Z \in V \setminus \{p''\}\} \cup \{Zp \mid Z \in V \setminus \{p''\}\}]$$
$$p7 = [(\lambda, p'', \lambda)_{del}, \quad (\mathcal{M}^v \setminus \{p, p'', p^v\}) \cup (N' \setminus \{Y\}) \cup \{Yp'''\} \cup \{Zp \mid Z \in V \setminus \{p^v\}\}]$$
$$p8 = [(\lambda, p^v p, \lambda)_{del}, \quad (\mathcal{M}^v \setminus \{p^v, p\}) \cup (N' \setminus \{Y\})]$$

(a) Simulating $p : X \to bY$

$$q1 = [(\lambda, qq', \lambda)_{ins}, \quad \mathcal{M}^v \cup (N' \setminus \{X\}) \cup \Phi_1]$$
$$q2 = [(\lambda, q'X, \lambda)_{del}, \quad (\mathcal{M}^v \setminus \{q, q'\}) \cup (N' \setminus \{X\})]$$
$$q3 = [(\lambda, q''b, \lambda)_{ins}, \quad (\mathcal{M}^v \setminus \{q\}) \cup N' \cup \Phi_1]$$
$$q4 = [(\lambda, q'''Y, \lambda)_{ins}, \quad (\mathcal{M}^v \setminus \{q, q''\}) \cup N' \cup$$
$$\{Zq'' \mid Z \in V \setminus \{q\}\} \cup \{qZ \mid Z \in V \setminus \{q''\}\} \cup \Phi_1]$$
$$q5 = [(\lambda, q^{iv} q^v, \lambda)_{ins}, \quad (\mathcal{M}^v \setminus \{q, q'', q'''\}) \cup (N' \setminus \{Y\}) \cup \{q''b\} \cup$$
$$\{qZ \mid Z \in V \setminus \{q''\}\} \cup \Phi_1]$$
$$q6 = [(\lambda, q''' q^{iv}, \lambda)_{del}, \quad (\mathcal{M}^v \setminus \{q, q'', q''', q^{iv}, q^v\}) \cup (N' \setminus \{Y\}) \cup \{q'''Y, q''b\} \cup$$
$$\{Zq''' \mid Z \in V \setminus \{q''\}\} \cup \{qZ \mid Z \in V \setminus \{q''\}\}]$$
$$q7 = [(\lambda, q'', \lambda)_{del}, \quad (\mathcal{M}^v \setminus \{q, q'', q^v\}) \cup (N' \setminus \{Y\}) \cup \{q'''Y, q''b\} \cup$$
$$\{q''Z \mid Z \in V \setminus \{q^v\}\}]$$
$$q8 = [(\lambda, qq^v, \lambda)_{del}, \quad (\mathcal{M}^v \setminus \{q^v\}) \cup (N' \setminus \{Y\})]$$

(b) Simulating $q : X \to Yb$

Fig. 1. Simulating context-free rules of ssSGNF by $GFID(2; 2, 0, 0; 2, 0, 0)$.

Let $w, w' \in \{A, C, E\}^* N' \{B, D, F\}^* T^*$. Then, $w \Rightarrow_G w'$ if and only if $w \Rightarrow^+ w'$ in Π, not deriving a string from $\{A, C, E\}^* N' \{B, D, F\}^* T^*$ intermediately.[1] We now show the correctness of the working of the simulating rules of Figs. 1(a) and 1(b). Due to their similarities, we focus on the working of the p-rule simulation. Consider a sentential form $\alpha X \beta$ derivable in G, where $X \in N'$ and $\alpha \in \{A, C, E\}^*$, $\beta \in \{B, D, F\}^* T^*$. By induction, $\sigma \alpha X \beta \sigma$ can be derived in Π. The rules $p : X \to bY$ and $q : X \to Yb$ are correctly simulated as follows:

$$\alpha X \beta \Rightarrow_{p1} \alpha pp'X\beta \Rightarrow_{p2} \alpha p\beta \Rightarrow_{p3} \alpha bp''p\beta \Rightarrow_{p4} \alpha bY p'''p''p\beta \Rightarrow_{p5}$$
$$\alpha bY p^v p^{iv} p'''p''p\beta \Rightarrow_{p6} \alpha bY p^v p''p\beta \Rightarrow_{p7} \alpha bY p^v p\beta \Rightarrow_{p8} \alpha bY \beta.$$

$$\alpha X \beta \Rightarrow_{q1} \alpha qq'X\beta \Rightarrow_{q2} \alpha q\beta \Rightarrow_{q3} \alpha qq''b\beta \Rightarrow_{q4} \alpha qq''q'''Yb\beta \Rightarrow_{q5}$$
$$\alpha qq'' q''' q^{iv} q^v Yb\beta \Rightarrow_{q6} \alpha qq'' q^v Yb\beta \Rightarrow_{q7} \alpha qq^v Yb\beta \Rightarrow_{q8} \alpha Yb\beta.$$

Conversely, consider a sentential form $w_0 = \alpha X \beta$ derivable in Π, where $X \in N'$ and $\alpha \in \{A, C, E\}^*$, $\beta \in \{B, D, F\}^* T^*$. The only applicable rule is $p1$, since other insertion rules forbid the presence of a nonterminal of N', namely X. Hence, the resulting string w_1 is obtained from w_0 by inserting pp' anywhere in the string.

---

[1] Here and in the following, we mostly omit the delimiters σ for simplicity.

No rule from $p3$-$p8$ can be applied on w_1 due to the presence of $X \in N'$. Also, $p1$ cannot be re-applied due to the presence of marker nonterminals. So, rule $p2$ has to be applied. This also checks the position of the insertion of pp'. This means that $w_1 = \alpha pp' X \beta$ and the resulting next string $w_2 = \alpha p \beta$ is determined.

Observe that the presence of p (and absence of p') forbids us to apply the rules $p1, p2$. The absence of p'', p''' prevents the deletion rules from being applied. So, in principle, the insertion rules $p3$, $p4$ or $p5$ could be applied. However, $p4$ and $p5$ ask for p'' being to the left of the marker p, as something must be there, possibly σ. Therefore, $p3$ must be applied, yielding w_3 which is obtained from $w_2 = \alpha p \beta$ by inserting bp'' anywhere. Our previous reasoning already shows that in order to find any continuation (which must be by using the insertion rules $p4$ or $p5$), $w_3 = \alpha bp''p\beta$ is enforced. Due to the presence of p'', the rule $p3$ cannot be reapplied. Now, the substring bp'' in w_3 blocks $p5$ (and also $p7$) as a forbidden context. Hence, we have to apply $p4$, yielding w_4. Now, in order to enable any further derivations, the substring bp'' must be destroyed, which means that $w_4 = \alpha bYp'''p''p\beta$ is the only promising continuation. The substring Yp''' blocks $p6$ and $p7$, so that we must apply $p5$. To destroy the substring Yp''', the derivation continues with $w_5 = \alpha bYp^vp^{iv}p'''p''p\beta$.

Now, the three deletion rules $p6$, $p7$ and $p8$ should follow. However, the substring p^vp^{iv} blocks $p7$ and $p8$, so that $p6$ must be applied. Hence, $w_6 = \alpha bYp^vp''p\beta$. Now, the application of $p7$ is enforced, leading to $w_7 = \alpha bYp^v\beta$. The only rule that can deal with the presence of p^v in the absence of other marker nonterminals is $p8$, which yields $w_8 = \alpha bY\beta$ as intended.

With a similar argument, if we intend to apply some q-type rules, we need to start with $q1$ on $w_0 = \alpha X \beta$, and we have to continue with $q2$, so that the resulting string w_2 equals $\alpha q\beta$. Now observe that both the actions of deletions and insertions as well as the forbidden strings are mirror-symmetric to the situation when simulating a p-rule, as analyzed above, so that the intended derivation is enforced also for a q-rule. This mirror symmetry is also reflected in the middle part of the sentential forms; e.g., $bYp^vp^{iv}p'''p''p$ corresponds to $qq''q'''q^{iv}q^vYb$.

After a terminal string z is reached, one might be tempted to start (e.g.) the p simulation stated in Fig. 1(a), applying one of the four random insertion rules $p1, p3, p4$ or $p5$. If we start applying $p1$, then pp' is introduced into z at some random position. Though a sequence of rules, namely $p3, p4, p5, p6, p7, p8$, is applicable, the application of $p2$ is vital in order to get rid of p' again to derive a new terminal string z'. This is not possible since $p2$ says that p' could be deleted only along with a nonterminal X beside it. Hence, a yield of new terminal string z' from z is not possible. If we start with $p4, p5$, we introduce the substring $Yp^vp^{iv}p'''$ anywhere into the string. In order to produce a terminal string, the next rule to be applied is $p6$. However we cannot apply $p6$ on the substring $Yp^vp^{iv}p'''$, unless $p3$ was applied prior to the application of $p4, p5$ to obtain a substring $z' = bYp^vp^{iv}p'''p''$. In other words, we have applied $p3, p4, p5$ without applying $p1$ initially. On z', we could apply $p6, p7$, thereby deleting $p^{iv}p'''$ and p'' to obtain $z'' = bYp^v$. The marker p^v cannot be deleted by $p8$, since p does not occur in z'. As discussed earlier, starting with $p1$ makes it impossible to derive a new terminal string. Finally, starting with $p3$, we cannot apply $p7$ directly, as $p7$ requires nothing to the left of p'' but p^v, but after applying $p3$, the symbol b is to the left of p^v. Hence, we are forced into applying $p5$ after applying $p3$, and the deletion rules guarantee that inbetween, rule $p4$ has to be applied, which inevitably leads us into the analysis above.

$\square$

Theorem 4. $(*)$ GFID$(2; 1, 1, 0; 2, 0, 0)$ = RE.

We only sketch the construction, whose correctness proof is based on a case analysis similar to the previous proof.

Proof Sketch. The construction itself starts again from a type-0 grammar in ssSGNF. In particular, a context-free rule of type $p : X \to bY$ can be simulated by the set of rules presented in Fig. 2. The intended simulation is as follows:

$$\alpha X\beta \Rightarrow_{p1} \alpha Xp\beta \Rightarrow_{p2} \alpha p^v Xp\beta \Rightarrow_{p3} \alpha p\beta \Rightarrow_{p4} \alpha pp''\beta \Rightarrow_{p5}$$
$$\alpha pp'p''\beta \Rightarrow_{p6} \alpha pbp'p''\beta \Rightarrow_{p7} \alpha pbp^{iv}p'p''\beta \Rightarrow_{p8} \alpha pbp^{iv}p'Yp''\beta \Rightarrow_{p9}$$
$$\alpha pbp^{iv}p'Yp'''p''\beta \Rightarrow_{p10} \alpha pbp^{iv}p'Y\beta \Rightarrow_{p11} \alpha pbY\beta \Rightarrow_{p12} \alpha bY\beta.$$

The reader might wonder why twelve rules seem to be necessary for the simulation. The intuitive reason is that we have to fight possible malicious derivations. For instance, why is it not possible to simply insert p^v to the left of X (rule $p2$) and then delete X with rule $p3$? The reason is that we forbid something different from p to the right of the (unique) nonterminal X. As we assume σ to be present at the right end of the simulating string, this forbidding condition is equivalent to requiring that the marker symbol p must follow on X when applying $p3$. Hence, $p1$ has to be applied before. Also, the facts that $p1$ inserts the marker p to the right of X and that all further insertions rely on the presence of p render re-starts on terminal strings impossible.

Context-free rules of type $q : X \to Yb$ are treated in a mirrored fashion. As in the previous proof, the non-context-free deletion rules are trivial to simulate due to the deletion size of $(2, 0, 0)$.

$\square$

Combining the previous theorem with Theorem 2, we obtain:

Corollary 1. GFID$(2; 1, 0, 1; 2, 0, 0)$ = RE.

Theorem 5. $(*)$ GFID$(2; 1, 1, 0; 1, 1, 0)$ = RE.

Again, due to space constraints, we can only sketch our construction, starting out from a type-0 grammar in ssSGNF.

Proof Sketch. The context-free rules of type $p : X \to bY$ are simulated by eleven rules, as listed in Fig. 3. Their intended usage is as follows:

$$\alpha X\beta \Rightarrow_{p1} \alpha pX\beta \Rightarrow_{p2} \alpha pXp'\beta \Rightarrow_{p3} \alpha pp'\beta \Rightarrow_{p4} \alpha pp'p''\beta \Rightarrow_{p5} \alpha pp'p''p'''\beta \Rightarrow_{p6} \alpha p'p''p'''\beta$$
$$\Rightarrow_{p7} \alpha p'bp''p'''\beta \Rightarrow_{p8} \alpha p'bp''Yp'''\beta \Rightarrow_{p9} \alpha p'bp''Y\beta \Rightarrow_{p10} \alpha p'bY\beta \Rightarrow_{p11} \alpha bY\beta.$$

$$
\begin{aligned}
p1 &= [(X,p,\lambda)_{ins}, & \mathcal{M}^v \cup (N' \setminus \{X\}) \cup \Phi_1] \\
p2 &= [(\lambda,p^v,\lambda)_{ins}, & (\mathcal{M}^v \setminus \{p^v\}) \cup (N' \setminus \{X\}) \cup \{XZ \mid Z \in V \setminus \{p\}\} \cup \Phi_1] \\
p3 &= [(\lambda,p^vX,\lambda)_{del}, & (\mathcal{M}^v \setminus \{p,p^v\}) \cup (N' \setminus \{X\}) \cup \{XZ \mid Z \in V \setminus \{p\}\}] \\
p4 &= [(p,p'',\lambda)_{ins}, & (\mathcal{M}^v \setminus \{p,p^v\}) \cup N' \cup \Phi_1] \\
p5 &= [(p,p',\lambda)_{ins}, & (\mathcal{M}^v \setminus \{p,p'',p^v\}) \cup N' \cup \{pZ \mid Z \in V \setminus \{p''\}\} \cup \Phi_1] \\
p6 &= [(p,b,\lambda)_{ins}, & (\mathcal{M}^v \setminus \{p,p',p''\}) \cup N' \cup \{pZ \mid Z \in V \setminus \{p'\}\} \cup \Phi_1] \\
p7 &= [(b,p^{iv},\lambda)_{ins}, & (\mathcal{M}^v \setminus \{p,p',p'',p^{iv}\}) \cup N' \cup \{pZ \mid Z \in V \setminus \{b\}\} \cup \Phi_1] \\
p8 &= [(p',Y,\lambda)_{ins}, & (\mathcal{M}^v \setminus \{p,p',p'',p^{iv}\}) \cup N' \cup \{p'Z \mid Z \in V \setminus \{p''\}\} \cup \\
& & \{rp' \mid r \in V \setminus \{p^{iv}\}\} \cup \Phi_1] \\
p9 &= [(Y,p''',\lambda)_{ins}, & (\mathcal{M}^v \setminus \{p,p',p'',p^{iv},p'''\}) \cup (N' \setminus \{Y\}) \cup \{p''Z \mid Z \in V \setminus \{Y\}\} \cup \Phi_1] \\
p10 &= [(\lambda,p'''p'',\lambda)_{del}, & (\mathcal{M}^v \setminus \{p,p',p'',p^{iv},p'''\}) \cup \{pp'',pp'\} \cup (N' \setminus \{Y\})] \\
p11 &= [(\lambda,p^{iv}p',\lambda)_{del}, & \{p'',p'''\} \cup (N' \setminus \{Y\})] \\
p12 &= [(\lambda,p,\lambda)_{del}, & (\mathcal{M}^v \setminus \{p\}) \cup (N' \setminus \{Y\})]
\end{aligned}
$$

Fig. 2. Simulating $p : X \to bY$ with GFID rules of size $(2;1,1,0;2,0,0)$

Similar insertion and deletion rules are used to simulate q-type rules. Now, we also have to care about a non-trivial simulation of the non-context-free rules like $AB \to \lambda$. We refer to Fig. 4. In order to write the conditions concerning the central part in a more compact form, let $N''_\ell := \{A,C,E,\sigma\}$ and $N''_r := \{B,D,F,\sigma\}$.

$$
\alpha AB\beta t \Rightarrow_{f1} \alpha Af'B\beta t \Rightarrow_{f2} \alpha fAf'B\beta t \Rightarrow_{f3} \alpha fAf'Bf''\beta t \Rightarrow_{f4}
$$
$$
\alpha ff'Bf''\beta t \Rightarrow_{f5} \alpha ff'f''\beta t \Rightarrow_{f6} \alpha ff''\beta t \Rightarrow_{f7} \alpha f\beta t \Rightarrow_{f8} \alpha f\beta t
$$

Notice that the above simulation needs less resources than available, making it a good candidate for re-use in other simulations. We recall from Theorem 1 that strings of the form AA,BB,CC,DD do not occur in our strings. Hence the above derivation is the intended one.

$$
\begin{aligned}
p1 &= [(\lambda,p,\lambda)_{ins}, & \mathcal{M}''' \cup (N' \setminus \{X\}) \cup \Phi_1] \\
p2 &= [(X,p',\lambda)_{ins}, & (\mathcal{M}''' \setminus \{p\}) \cup (N' \setminus \{X\})] \\
p3 &= [(p,X,\lambda)_{del}, & (\mathcal{M}''' \setminus \{p,p'\}) \cup (N' \setminus \{X\}) \cup (\{X\gamma \mid \gamma \in V \setminus \{p'\}\}] \\
p4 &= [(p',p'',\lambda)_{ins}, & (\mathcal{M}''' \setminus \{p,p'\}) \cup N' \cup (\{pZ \mid Z \in V \setminus \{p'\}\})] \\
p5 &= [(p'',p''',\lambda)_{ins}, & (\mathcal{M}''' \setminus \{p,p',p''\}) \cup N' \cup (\{p'Z \mid Z \in V \setminus \{p''\}\})] \\
p6 &= [(\lambda,p,\lambda)_{del}, & (\mathcal{M}''' \setminus \{p,p',p'',p'''\}) \cup N' \cup \{p'Z \mid Z \in V \setminus \{p''\}\}] \\
p7 &= [(p',b,\lambda)_{ins}, & \{p'Z \mid Z \in V \setminus \{p''\}\} \cup \{p''Z \mid Z \in V \setminus \{p'''\}\} \cup N' \cup \{p\}] \\
p8 &= [(p'',Y,\lambda)_{ins}, & \{p'Z \mid Z \in V \setminus \{b\}\} \cup \{p''Z \mid Z \in V \setminus \{p'''\}\} \cup N' \cup \{p\}] \\
p9 &= [(Y,p''',\lambda)_{del}, & \{p,p'p'',p''p'''\} \cup (N' \setminus \{Y\})] \\
p10 &= [(b,p'',\lambda)_{del}, & \{p,p''',p'p''\} \cup (N' \setminus \{Y\})] \\
p11 &= [(\lambda,p',\lambda)_{del}, & \{p,p'',p'''\}]
\end{aligned}
$$

Fig. 3. Simulating $p : X \to bY$ by GFID rules of size $(2;1,1,0;1,1,0)$

$$f1 = [(\lambda, f', \lambda)_{ins}, \ N' \cup \mathcal{M}''' \cup (N''_\ell N''_r \setminus \{AB\})]$$
$$f2 = [(\lambda, f, \lambda)_{ins}, \ N' \cup (\mathcal{M}''' \setminus \{f'\}) \cup \{f'Z \mid Z \in V \setminus \{B\}\} \cup N''_\ell N''_r]$$
$$f3 = [(\lambda, f'', \lambda)_{ins}, \ N' \cup (\mathcal{M}''' \setminus \{f, f'\}) \cup \{f'Z \mid Z \in V \setminus \{B\}\} \cup$$
$$\{fZ \mid Z \in V \setminus \{A\}\} \cup N''_\ell N''_r]$$
$$f4 = [(f, A, \lambda)_{del}, \ N' \cup (\mathcal{M}''' \setminus \{f, f', f''\}) \cup \{f'Z \mid Z \in V \setminus \{B\}\} \cup$$
$$\{Zf'' \mid Z \in V \setminus \{B\}\} \cup N''_\ell N''_r]$$
$$f5 = [(f', B, \lambda)_{del}, \ N' \cup (\mathcal{M}''' \setminus \{f, f', f''\}) \cup \{fZ \mid Z \in V \setminus \{f'\}\} \cup$$
$$\{Zf'' \mid Z \in V \setminus \{B\}\} \cup N''_\ell N''_r]$$
$$f6 = [(f, f', \lambda)_{del}, \ N' \cup (\mathcal{M}''' \setminus \{f, f', f''\}) \cup \{f'Z \mid Z \in V \setminus \{f''\}\} \cup$$
$$\{Zf'' \mid Z \in V \setminus \{f'\}\} \cup N''_\ell N''_r]$$
$$f7 = [(f, f'', \lambda)_{del}, \ N' \cup (\mathcal{M}''' \setminus \{f, f''\}) \cup N''_\ell N''_r]$$
$$f8 = [(\lambda, f, \lambda)_{del}, \ \{f', f''\}]$$

Fig. 4. Simulating $AB \to \lambda$ by GFID rules of size $(2; 1, 0, 0; 1, 1, 0)$

$$p1 = [(X, p, \lambda)_{ins}, \mathcal{M}'' \cup (N' \setminus \{X\}) \cup \Phi_1]$$
$$p2 = [(\lambda, X, p)_{del}, (\mathcal{M}'' \setminus \{p\}) \cup (N' \setminus \{X\})]$$
$$p3 = [(p, Y, \lambda)_{ins}, (\mathcal{M}'' \setminus \{p\}) \cup N']$$
$$p4 = [(p, p', \lambda)_{ins}, (\mathcal{M}'' \setminus \{p\}) \cup (N' \setminus \{Y\}) \cup (\{pZ \mid Z \in V \setminus \{Y\}\})]$$
$$p5 = [(p', b, \lambda)_{ins}, (\mathcal{M}'' \setminus \{p, p'\}) \cup (N' \setminus \{Y\}) \cup (\{p'Z \mid Z \in V \setminus \{Y\}\})]$$
$$p6 = [(\lambda, p, p')_{del}, \{p'Y\}]$$
$$p7 = [(\lambda, p', \lambda)_{del}, \{p\}]$$

Fig. 5. Simulating $p : X \to bY$ by $\mathrm{GFID}(2; 1, 1, 0; 1, 0, 1)$

Combining the previous theorem with Theorem 2, we obtain:

Corollary 2. $\mathrm{GFID}(2; 1, 0, 1; 1, 0, 1) = \mathrm{RE}$.

Theorem 6. $(*)$ $\mathrm{GFID}(2; 1, 1, 0; 1, 0, 1) = \mathrm{RE}$.

As in all our constructions, we simulate a given type-0 grammar in ssSGNF.

Proof Sketch. The context-free rules of type p are simulated by the rules listed in Fig. 5. Its intended use amounts in the following derivation:

$$\alpha X \beta \Rightarrow_{p1} \alpha X p \beta \Rightarrow_{p2} \alpha p \beta \Rightarrow_{p3} \alpha p Y \beta \Rightarrow_{p4} \alpha p p' Y \beta \Rightarrow_{p5} \alpha p p' b Y \beta \Rightarrow_{p6} \alpha p' b Y \beta \Rightarrow_{p7} \alpha b Y \beta.$$

In this case, very few marker variants are needed, because the complimentary nature of insertion and deletion contexts allow for strong tests. The non-context-free erasing rules are simulated by a reversed (mirrored) version of the rules depicted in Fig. 4 to take the right context of deletion into consideration. □

Combining the previous theorem with Theorem 2, we obtain the following:

Corollary 3. $\mathrm{GFID}(2; 1, 0, 1; 1, 1, 0) = \mathrm{RE}$.

Theorem 7. $(*)$ $\mathrm{GFID}(2; 2, 0, 0; 1, 1, 0) = \mathrm{RE}$.

As in all our simulations, we start with a ssSGNF grammar. We can profit from the simulation of the non-context-free erasing rules as presented in Fig. 4.

Proof Sketch. The context-free rules need another tweak, as displayed in Fig. 6 for the p-type rules. The intended simulations of $p : X \to bY$ works as follows.

$$\alpha X\beta \Rightarrow_{p1} \alpha p X\beta \Rightarrow_{p2} \alpha p X p^{iv} p'''\beta \Rightarrow_{p3} \alpha p X p'''\beta \Rightarrow_{p4} \alpha p p'''\beta \Rightarrow_{p5} \alpha p p''' p' Y \beta$$
$$\Rightarrow_{p6} \alpha p p''' p' p'' b Y \beta \Rightarrow_{p7} \alpha p p''' p'' b Y \beta \Rightarrow_{p8} \alpha p p''' b Y \beta \Rightarrow_{p9} \alpha p b Y \beta \Rightarrow_{p10} \alpha b Y \beta$$

Every (context-free) rule of type $q : X \to Yb$ in G can be simulated by a set of simulating rules, very similar to those shown in Fig. 6. □

$$
\begin{aligned}
p1 &= [(\lambda, p, \lambda)_{ins}, & \mathcal{M}^{iv} \cup (N' \setminus \{X\})] \\
p2 &= [(\lambda, p^{iv}p''', \lambda)_{ins}, & (\mathcal{M}^{iv} \setminus \{p\}) \cup (N' \setminus \{X\})] \\
p3 &= [(X, p^{iv}, \lambda)_{del}, & (\mathcal{M}^{iv} \setminus \{p, p''', p^{iv}\}) \cup (N' \setminus \{X\})] \\
p4 &= [(p, X, \lambda)_{del}, & (\mathcal{M}^{iv} \setminus \{p, p'''\}) \cup (N' \setminus \{X\}) \cup \{XZ \mid Z \in V \setminus \{p'''\}\}] \\
p5 &= [(\lambda, p'Y, \lambda)_{ins}, & (\mathcal{M}^{iv} \setminus \{p, p'''\}) \cup N' \cup \{pZ \mid Z \in V \setminus \{p'''\}\}] \\
p6 &= [(\lambda, p''b, \lambda)_{ins}, & (\mathcal{M}^{iv} \setminus \{p, p', p'''\}) \cup (N' \setminus \{Y\}) \cup \\
 & & \{pZ \mid Z \in V \setminus \{p'''\}\} \cup \{Zp' \mid Z \in V \setminus \{p''\}\}] \\
p7 &= [(p''', p', \lambda)_{del}, & (\mathcal{M}^{iv} \setminus \{p, p', p'', p'''\}) \cup (N' \setminus \{Y\}) \cup \{ZY \mid Z \in V \setminus \{b\}\}] \\
p8 &= [(p'', p''', \lambda)_{del}, & (\mathcal{M}^{iv} \setminus \{p, p'', p'''\}) \cup (N' \setminus \{Y\})] \\
p9 &= [(p, p''', \lambda)_{del}, & (\mathcal{M}^{iv} \setminus \{p, p'''\}) \cup (N' \setminus \{Y\}) \cup \{p'''Z \mid Z \notin \{A, C, E\}\}] \\
p10 &= [(\lambda, p, \lambda)_{del}, & (\mathcal{M}^{iv} \setminus \{p\}) \cup (N' \setminus \{Y\})]
\end{aligned}
$$

Fig. 6. Simulating $p : X \to bY$ by GFID rules of size $(2; 2, 0, 0; 1, 1, 0)$

Combining the previous theorem with Theorem 2, we obtain:

Corollary 4. $\mathrm{GFID}(2; 2, 0, 0; 1, 0, 1) = \mathrm{RE}$.

4 Conclusions

We have seen that adding forbidden strings of length at most two to insertion-deletion rules as a kind of global control of derivation helps turn resources (sizes) of insertion-deletion systems that are too weak by themselves to simulate every Turing machine into devices that are computationally complete (refer Table 1). In this line of research, we propose the following for future investigations.

- We needed generalized forbidding insertion-deletion systems of degree two to prove our computational completeness results. But what happens if we allow degree one only? Can we still obtain computational completeness ?
- In our simulations, we were very generous with having quite large sets of forbidding words per rule. Would it be possible to delimit the number of forbidden strings per rule, without losing computational completeness?
- Another natural measure of descriptional complexity could be the number of forbidden strings of length two.

References

1. Dassow, J., Păun, G.: Regulated Rewriting in Formal Language Theory. EATCS Monographs in Theoretical Computer Science, vol. 18. Springer, Heidelberg (1989)
2. Fernau, H., Kuppusamy, L., Oladele, R.O., Raman, I.: Improved descriptional complexity results on generalized forbidding grammars. In: Pal, S.P., Vijayakumar, A. (eds.) CALDAM 2019. LNCS, vol. 11394, pp. 174–188. Springer, Cham (2019). https://doi.org/10.1007/978-3-030-11509-8_15
3. Fernau, H., Kuppusamy, L., Raman, I.: Computational completeness of simple semi-conditional insertion-deletion systems of degree (2, 1). Nat. Comput. **18**(3), 563–577 (2019). https://doi.org/10.1007/s11047-019-09742-w
4. Freund, R., Kogler, M., Rogozhin, Y., Verlan, S.: Graph-controlled insertion-deletion systems. In: McQuillan, I., Pighizzini, G. (eds.) Proceedings Twelfth Annual Workshop on Descriptional Complexity of Formal Systems, DCFS. EPTCS, vol. 31, pp. 88–98 (2010)
5. Geffert, V.: Normal forms for phrase-structure grammars. RAIRO Informatique théorique et Applications/Theor. Inform. Appl. **25**, 473–498 (1991)
6. Haussler, D.: Insertion languages. Inf. Sci. **31**(1), 77–89 (1983)
7. Ivanov, S., Verlan, S.: Random context and semi-conditional insertion-deletion systems. Fundamenta Informaticae **138**, 127–144 (2015)
8. Kari, L.: On insertions and deletions in formal languages. Ph.D. thesis, University of Turku, Finland (1991)
9. Kari, L., Păun, Gh., Thierrin, G., Yu, S.: At the crossroads of DNA computing and formal languages: characterizing recursively enumerable languages using insertion-deletion systems. In: Rubin, H., Wood, D.H. (eds.) DNA Based Computers III. DIMACS Series in Discrete Mathematics and Theoretical Computer Science, vol. 48, pp. 329–338 (1999)
10. Margenstern, M., Păun, Gh., Rogozhin, Y., Verlan, S.: Context-free insertion-deletion systems. Theor. Comput. Sci. **330**(2), 339–348 (2005)
11. Masopust, T., Meduna, A.: Descriptional complexity of generalized forbidding grammars. In: Descriptional Complexity of Formal Systems - 9th International Workshop, DCFS 2007, pp. 170–177, July 2007
12. Matveevici, A., Rogozhin, Y., Verlan, S.: Insertion-deletion systems with one-sided contexts. In: Durand-Lose, J., Margenstern, M. (eds.) MCU 2007. LNCS, vol. 4664, pp. 205–217. Springer, Heidelberg (2007). https://doi.org/10.1007/978-3-540-74593-8_18
13. Meduna, A.: Generalized forbidding grammars. Int. J. Comput. Math. **36**, 31–39 (1990)
14. Meduna, A., Svec, M.: Descriptional complexity of generalized forbidding grammars. Int. J. Comput. Math. **80**(1), 11–17 (2003)
15. Odifreddi, P.: Classical Recursion Theory. Studies in Logic and Foundations of Mathematics, vol. 125. North Holland, Amsterdam (1989)
16. Rozenberg, G., Salomaa, A.: DNA computing: new ideas and paradigms. In: Wiedermann, J., van Emde Boas, P., Nielsen, M. (eds.) ICALP 1999. LNCS, vol. 1644, pp. 106–118. Springer, Heidelberg (1998). https://doi.org/10.1007/3-540-48523-6_9
17. Petre, I., Verlan, S.: Matrix insertion-deletion systems. Theor. Comput. Sci. **456**, 80–88 (2012)
18. Takahara, A., Yokomori, T.: On the computational power of insertion-deletion systems. Nat. Comput. **2**(4), 321–336 (2003). https://doi.org/10.1023/B:NACO.0000006769.27984.23

State Complexity Bounds
for the Commutative Closure
of Group Languages

Stefan Hoffmann[✉]

Informatikwissenschaften, FB IV, Universität Trier,
Universitätsring 15, 54296 Trier, Germany
hoffmanns@informatik.uni-trier.de

Abstract. In this work we construct an automaton for the commutative closure of a given regular group language. The number of states of the resulting automaton is bounded by the number of states of the original automaton, raised to the power of the alphabet size, times the product of the order of the letters, viewed as permutations of the state set. This gives the asymptotic state bound $O((n \exp(\sqrt{n \ln n}))^{|\Sigma|})$, if the original regular language is accepted by an automaton with n states. Depending on the automaton in question, we label points of $\mathbb{N}_0^{|\Sigma|}$ by subsets of states and introduce unary automata which decompose the thus labelled grid. Based on these constructions, we give a general regularity condition, which is fulfilled for group languages.

Keywords: State complexity · Commutative closure · Group language · Permutation automaton

1   Introduction

The area of state complexity asks for sharp bounds on the size of resulting automata for regularity-preserving operations. This question goes back at least to work by Maslov [15], but, starting with the work [19], has revived at the end of the last millennium. The class of deterministic and complete automata is the most natural, or prototypical, class. But state complexity questions have also been explored for non-deterministic automata, or other automata models, see for example the surveys [5,12,13]. As the number of states of an accepting automaton could be interpreted as the memory required to describe the accepted language and is directly related to the runtime of algorithms employing regular languages, obtaining state complexity bounds is a natural question with applications in verification, natural language processing or software engineering [5,16,18]. So, nowadays, it is an active and important area of research under the broader theme of descriptional complexity of systems. We refer again to the survey [5] for an introduction and more information. It was shown in [6] that the commutative closure is regularity preserving on regular group languages. But the

© Springer Nature Switzerland AG 2020
G. Jirásková and G. Pighizzini (Eds.): DCFS 2020, LNCS 12442, pp. 64–77, 2020.
https://doi.org/10.1007/978-3-030-62536-8_6

method of proof was algebraic and used Ramsey-type arguments. The general form of an accepting automaton was still open, and in [14], a work that systematically studies the state complexity of several regularity preserving operations on group languages, it was, as an open problem, asked for a state complexity bound of the commutative closure. Here, we give methods to obtain an automaton for the commutative closure of regular group languages, and derive state bounds for this operation. The state complexity of the commutative closure on finite languages was investigated in [3,11,17].

2 Prerequisites

Let $\Sigma = \{a_1, \ldots, a_k\}$ be a finite set of symbols[1], called an alphabet. The set Σ^* denotes the set of all finite sequences, i.e., of all words. The finite sequence of length zero, or the empty word, is denoted by ε. For a given word w we denote by $|w|$ its length, and, for $a \in \Sigma$, by $|w|_a$ the number of occurrences of the symbol a in w. Subsets of Σ^* are called languages. With $\mathbb{N}_0 = \{0, 1, 2, \ldots\}$ we denote the set of natural numbers, including zero. A finite deterministic and complete automaton will be denoted by $\mathcal{A} = (\Sigma, S, \delta, s_0, F)$, with $\delta : S \times \Sigma \to S$ the state transition function, S a finite set of states, $s_0 \in S$ the start state and $F \subseteq S$ the set of final states. The properties of being deterministic and complete are implied by the definition of δ as a total function. The transition function $\delta : S \times \Sigma \to S$ could be extended to a transition function on words $\delta^* : S \times \Sigma^* \to S$, by setting $\delta^*(s, \varepsilon) := s$ and $\delta^*(s, wa) := \delta(\delta^*(s, w), a)$ for $s \in S$, $a \in \Sigma$ and $w \in \Sigma^*$. In the remainder we drop the distinction between both functions and will also denote this extension by δ. The language accepted by some automaton $\mathcal{A} = (\Sigma, S, \delta, s_0, F)$ is $L(\mathcal{A}) = \{w \in \Sigma^* \mid \delta(s_0, w) \in F\}$. A language $L \subseteq \Sigma^*$ is called regular if $L = L(\mathcal{A})$ for some finite automaton. The *state complexity* of a regular language is the size of a minimal automaton accepting this language. An automaton is called a *permutation automaton* if the transformation of the states induced by a letter is a permutation, i.e., a bijective function. A regular language is called a *group language* if it is accepted by some permutation automaton. The map $\psi : \Sigma^* \to \mathbb{N}_0^k$ given by $\psi(w) = (|w|_{a_1}, \ldots, |w|_{a_k})$ is called the *Parikh morphism*. For a given word $w \in \Sigma^*$ we define the *commutative closure* as $\mathrm{perm}(w) := \{u \in \Sigma^* : \psi(u) = \psi(w)\}$. For languages $L \subseteq \Sigma^*$ we set $\mathrm{perm}(L) := \bigcup_{w \in L} \mathrm{perm}(w)$. A language is called *commutative* if $\mathrm{perm}(L) = L$, i.e., with every word each permutation of this word is also in the language. Every function $f : X \to Y$ could be extended to subsets $S \subseteq X$ by setting $f(S) := \{f(x) : x \in S\}$, we will do this frequently without special mentioning. For $Z \subseteq X$ we denote by $f_{|Z} : Z \to Y$ the function obtained by restriction of the arguments to elements of Z. For a set X, we denote by $\mathcal{P}(X) = \{Y : Y \subseteq X\}$ the power set of X. If X, Y are sets, by $X \times Y$ we denote their cartesian product. By $\pi_1 : X \times Y \to X$ and $\pi_2 : X \times Y \to Y$ we denote the projection maps onto the first and second component, $\pi_1(x, y) = x$ and $\pi_2(x, y) = y$. If $a, b \in \mathbb{N}_0$ with

---

[1] If not otherwise stated we assume that our alphabet has the form $\Sigma = \{a_1, \ldots, a_k\}$, and k denotes the number of symbols.

$b > 0$, we denote by $a \bmod b$ the unique number $0 \leqslant r < b$ such that $a = bn + r$ for some $n \geqslant 0$. For $n \in \mathbb{N}_0$ we set $[n] := \{k \in \mathbb{N}_0 : 0 \leqslant k < n\}$. Let $M \subseteq \mathbb{N}_0$ be some *finite* set. By $\max M$ we denote the maximal element in M with respect to the usual order, and we set $\max \varnothing = 0$. Also for finite $M \subseteq \mathbb{N}_0 \setminus \{0\}$, i.e., M is finite without zero in it, by $\operatorname{lcm} M$ we denote the least common multiple of the numbers in M, and set $\operatorname{lcm} \varnothing = 0$.

2.1 Unary Languages

Let $\Sigma = \{a\}$ be a unary alphabet. In this section, we collect some results about unary languages. Suppose $L \subseteq \Sigma^*$ is regular with an accepting complete deterministic automaton $\mathcal{A} = (\Sigma, S, \delta, s_0, F)$. Then, by considering the sequence of states $\delta(s_0, a^1), \delta(s_0, a^2), \delta(s_0, a^3), \ldots$ we find numbers $i \geqslant 0, p > 0$ with i and p minimal such that $\delta(s_0, a^i) = \delta(s_0, a^{i+p})$. We call these numbers the index i and the period p of the automaton $\mathcal{A}$. Suppose $\mathcal{A}$ is initially connected, i.e., $\delta(s_0, \Sigma^*) = Q$. Then $i + p = |S|$, the states from $\{s_0, \delta(s_0, a), \ldots, \delta(s_0, a^{i-1})\}$ constitute the *tail*, and the states from $\{\delta(s_0, a^i), \delta(s_0, a^{i+1}), \ldots, \delta(s_0, a^{i+p-1})\}$ constitute the unique *cycle* of the automaton. If $\mathcal{A}$ is not initially connected, when we speak of the cycle or tail of that automaton, we nevertheless mean the above sets, despite the automaton graph might have more than one cycle, or more than one straight path.

3 Results

3.1 Intuition, Method of Proof and Main Results

We have two main results, first a general automaton construction for the commutative closure of a regular group language, and second a more general framework to derive this result, which entails a general regularity condition for commutative closures. The first result, in asymptotic form.

Theorem 1 (asymptotic version). *For a group language with state complexity n, the comm. closure is regular with state complexity in $O((ne^{\sqrt{n \ln n}})^{|\Sigma|})$.*

In Theorem 4, a more quantitative version in terms of the constructions will be given. But this result is more an application of a general scheme, which will be useful in future investigations as well. So, let us spend some time in explaining the basic idea. The constructions and definitions that follow in the next sections are rather involved and technical, but they are, I hope to convince the reader, the worked out formalisation of quite a natural idea. Imagine you have an operation that identifies certain words (in our case, we identify words if they are permutations of each other) and you apply this operation to a regular language. How could an (hitherto possibly infinite state) automaton for the result of this operation look? If you have two words u and v, which are identified and drive the original automaton into two states, say s and t, then in what state should an automaton end up for the resulting language after this identification? As it should not distinguish between both words, as they are identified, a possible state is $\{u, v\} \times \{s, t\}$, the set $\{u, v\}$ represents the read in word under identification, and $\{s, t\}$ represents the possible states of the original automaton. Applied to our situation, words are identified if they have the same Parikh image, i.e., the letter counts are equals. So, we start with *labelling the grid* $\mathbb{N}_0^k$ *with the states that are reachable by words whose Parikh image equals the point in question.* Hence, if the original automaton has state set Q, we can think of as constructing an (infinite) automaton with state set $\mathbb{N}_0^k \times \mathcal{P}(Q)$. We will not formally construct this automaton, but it is implicit in the constructions we give. This automaton could be used to accept the commutative closure, where a word is accepted if, after reading this word, the second component, the *state set label*, contains at least one final state, meaning for some word, which is equivalent to the read in word, we can reach a final state. For a regular language, this construction could also be viewed as a generalized Parikh map, where we not only label a point by the binary information if some word with that letter count is in the language or not, but we have the more rich information what states are reachable by all permutations of a given word. By only looking at the state labels containing a final state, we can recover the original Parikh map. We will adopt this viewpoint, which is sufficient for the results, in the formal treatment to follow. Also, note we have an intuitive correspondence to the power set construction, in the sense that in this construction, the states, as sets, save all possibilities to end up after reading a word. Here, our state labels serve the same purpose as saving all possibilities. So, intuitively and very roughly, the method could be thought of as both a refined Parikh map for regular languages and a power set construction for automata that incorporates the commutativity condition.

It turns out that the story does not end here, but that the "generalized Parikh map", or *state (label) map*, as we will call it in the following, admits a lot of structure that allows to derive a regularity criterion. First, let us state our regularity condition in intuitive terms, a more refined statement is given as Theorem 3 later.

Theorem 2 (intuitive form). *Suppose the grid $\mathbb{N}_0^k$ is labelled by the states of a given automaton. If we have a universal bound $N \geqslant 0$ and a period $P > 0$ such that, for $p = (p_1, \ldots, p_k) \in \mathbb{N}_0^K \setminus ([N] \times \ldots \times [N])$ and $j \in \{1, \ldots, k\}$, the labels at p and $(p_1, \ldots, p_{j-1}, p_j - P, p_{j+1}, \ldots, p_k)$ are equal, then the commutative closure of the language described by the original automaton is regular and could be accepted by an automaton of size at most N^k.*

The basic mechanism behind this theorem is a decomposition of the state labels into unary automata. I must confess, the form of these unary automata, formally stated in Definition 3, is rather involved and, to be honest, took me quite some time to come up with. The idea is to implement in these automata how the state labels are influenced by neighboring state labels. Imagine we are at a certain point, then we receive an input letter and go to the next point that corresponds to this additional input letter. What should the new state label look like? First, we should carry with us the state label from the previous point, but updated with the input letter. But, by the nature of the commutation relation, this input letter could also be read at a previous point up to permutational identification of words.

So, we also go back to our previous point and investigate all the state labels of its neighboring points from which we could reach this point. It turns out that it is enough to look at those points from which we could reach the current point in one step. Then, we took their state labels, update them for the input letter by going into the direction of this letter, but, after this, also take the state label thus obtained back to our target state label in correspondence with the letter from which we got from

$$
\begin{array}{ccc}
\vdots & \vdots & \\
b\uparrow & b\uparrow & \\
R \xrightarrow{\;a\;} \delta(R,a) \cup \delta(T,b) \xrightarrow{\;a\;} \cdots \\
b\uparrow & b\uparrow & \\
S \xrightarrow{\;\;a\;\;} T \xrightarrow{\;\;a\;\;} \cdots \\
(p_1-1,\,p_2) & (p_1,\,p_2) &
\end{array}
$$

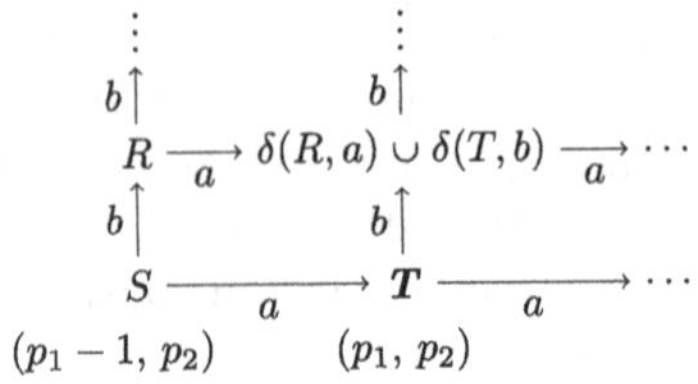

Fig. 1. Illustration of how state labels are updated if new input symbols are read. We are at (p_1, p_2) with state label T and read a b. So, we will end up at $(p_1, p_2 + 1)$. Then the state label at $(p_1, p_2 + 1)$ is made up out of the state label T, but also out of the neighboring state label R. Imagine as "going in both" ways, i.e., the path ab and ba, to compute the new state label.

the neighboring state to the starting state. We go around "both commuting" letters, please see Fig. 1 for the case of $\Sigma = \{a, b\}$. It will be shown that this operational scheme could be implemented into unary automata, which in this sense decompose the state labelling. So, let us take the journey and see how these ideas are actually implemented!

Outline: In Sect. 3.2, we first give a labelling of the grid $\mathbb{N}_0^k$ by states of a given automaton. This labelling is in some sense an abstract description of the commutative closure, which is more precisely stated in Corollary 1. We then construct unary automata for each letter. Very roughly, and intuitively, they read in letters parallel to the direction of this letter in $\mathbb{N}_0^k$, given by the Parikh map. We have one such automaton for each point on the hyperplane orthogonal to this direction. These unary automata are then used to describe the mentioned state labelling. In this sense, the state labelling is decomposed into these automata. This is made more precise in Proposition 2. If all the automata in this decomposition, for each letter, only have a bounded number of states, then the commutative closure is a regular language. By using the indices and periods, we give a state bound for the resulting automaton in Theorem 3. In Sect. 3.3, these results are applied to the case that the given automaton is a permutation automaton. It turns out, stated in Proposition 3 and Proposition 4, that the index and the period are always bounded, for a bound dependent on the input automaton, which is also stated in these Propositions. Intuitively, the main observations why this works is that 1) for permutations, the state labels cannot decrease as the unary automata read in symbols, and 2) we know when the state labels must become periodic. Finally, applying our general result, then gives that the commutative closure is regular, and also yields a state complexity bound.

3.2   A Regularity Condition by Decomposing into Unary Automata

As said in Sect. 2, we assume our alphabet has the form $\Sigma = \{a_1, \ldots, a_k\}$. First, we introduce the state label function.

Definition 1 (state label function). *Suppose $\mathcal{A} = (\Sigma, Q, \delta, s_0, F)$ is a finite automaton. The state label function, associated to the automaton, is the function $\sigma_{\mathcal{A}} : \mathbb{N}_0^{|\Sigma|} \to \mathcal{P}(Q)$ given by*

$$\sigma_{\mathcal{A}}(p) = \{\delta(s_0, u) : \psi(u) = p\}.$$

The value of the function $\sigma_{\mathcal{A}}$, for some fixed automaton $\mathcal{A} = (\Sigma, Q, \delta, s_0, F)$, will also be called the *state (set) label* of that point, or the *state set* corresponding to that point.

Example 1. Consider the minimal automaton of the language[2] $(a_1 a_2)^*$. The commutative closure of this language is not regular, as it is precisely the language of words with an equal number of both symbols.

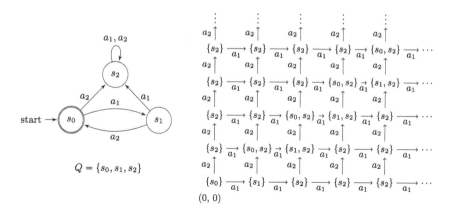

Fig. 2.   The minimal automaton of $(a_1 a_2)^*$ and a resulting state labelling in $\mathbb{N}_0^k$. Compare this to Example 3, where the labelling is given by a permutation automaton. The final state set is marked by a double circle. See Example 1 for an explanation.

The image of the Parikh morphism could be described by the state label function. In this sense, for a fixed regular language, it is a more finer notion of the Parikh image.

---

[2] Here the minimal automaton has the property that no word induces a non-trivial permutation on some subset of states. Languages which admit such automata are called aperiodic in the literature. In some sense these are contrary to group languages, the class considered in this paper.

Proposition 1 (connection with Parikh morphism). *Let $\psi : \Sigma^* \to \mathbb{N}_0^k$ be the Parikh morphism. Suppose $\mathcal{A} = (\Sigma, Q, \delta, s_0, F)$ is a finite automaton. Let $\sigma_{\mathcal{A}} : \mathbb{N}_0^k \to \mathcal{P}(Q)$ be the state label function. Then*

$$\psi(L(\mathcal{A})) = \sigma_{\mathcal{A}}^{-1}(\{S \subseteq Q \mid S \cap F \neq \varnothing\}).$$

As $\mathrm{perm}(L) = \psi^{-1}(\psi(L))$ for every language $L \subseteq \Sigma^*$, the next is implied.

Corollary 1. *Denote by $\psi : \Sigma^* \to \mathbb{N}_0^k$ the Parikh morphism. Suppose $\mathcal{A} = (\Sigma, Q, \delta, s_0, F)$ is a finite automaton. Let $\sigma_{\mathcal{A}} : \mathbb{N}_0^k \to \mathcal{P}(Q)$ be the state label function. Then*

$$\mathrm{perm}(L(\mathcal{A})) = \psi^{-1}(\sigma_{\mathcal{A}}^{-1}(\{S \subseteq Q \mid S \cap F \neq \varnothing\})).$$

Next, we introduce a notion for the hyperplanes that we will use in Definition 3.

Definition 2 (hyperplane aligned with letter). *Let $j \in \{1, \ldots, k\}$. We set*

$$H_j = \{(p_1, \ldots, p_k) \in \mathbb{N}_0^k \mid p_j = 0\}. \tag{1}$$

We will decompose the state label map into unary automata. For each letter a_j with $j \in \{1, \ldots, k\}$ and point $p \in H_j$, we construct unary automata $\mathcal{A}_p^{(j)}$. They are meant to read inputs in the direction $\psi(a_j)$, which is orthogonal to H_j. This will be stated more precisely in Proposition 2.

Definition 3 (unary aut. along letter $a_j \in \Sigma$). *Suppose $\mathcal{A} = (\Sigma, Q, \delta, s_0, F)$ is a finite automaton. Fix $j \in \{1, \ldots, k\}$ and $p \in H_j$. We define a unary automaton $\mathcal{A}_p^{(j)} = (\{a_j\}, Q_p^{(j)}, \delta_p^{(j)}, s_p^{(0,j)}, F_p^{(j)})$. But suppose, for points $q \in \mathbb{N}_0^k$ with $p = q + \psi(b)$ for some $b \in \Sigma$, the unary automata $\mathcal{A}_q^{(j)} = (\{a_j\}, Q_q^{(j)}, \delta_q^{(j)}, s_q^{(0,j)}, F_q^{(j)})$ are already defined. Set[3]*

$$\mathcal{R} = \{\mathcal{A}_q^{(j)} \mid p = q + \psi(b) \text{ for some } b \in \Sigma\}.$$

Let I and P be the maximal index and the least common multiple[4] of the periods of the unary automata in $\mathcal{R}$. Then set

$$Q_p^{(j)} = \mathcal{P}(Q) \times [I + P]$$

$$s_p^{(0,j)} = (\sigma_{\mathcal{A}}(p), 0) \tag{2}$$

$$\delta_p^{(j)}((S, i), a_j) = \begin{cases} (T, i+1) & \text{if } i+1 < I+P \\ (T, I) & \text{if } i+1 = I+P. \end{cases} \tag{3}$$

where

$$T = \delta(S, a_j) \cup \bigcup_{\substack{(q,b) \in \mathbb{N}_0^k \times \Sigma \\ p = q + \psi(b)}} \delta(\pi_1(\delta_q^{(j)}(s_q^{(0,j)}, a_j^{i+1})), b) \tag{4}$$

---

[3] Note, in the definition of $\mathcal{R}$, as $p \in H_j$, we have $b \neq a_j$ and $q \in H_j$. In general, points $q \in \mathbb{N}_0^k$ with $p = q + \psi(b)$, for some $b \in \Sigma$, are predecessor points in the grid $\mathbb{N}_0^k$.

[4] Note $\max \varnothing = 0$ and $\mathrm{lcm}\, \varnothing = 1$.

and $F_p^{(j)} = \{(S, i) \mid S \cap F \neq \varnothing\}$. For a state $(S, i) \in Q_p^{(j)}$, the set S will be called the state (set) label, or the state set associated with it.

See Example 2 for concrete constructions of the automata from Definition 3.

Example 2. In Fig. 3, we list the reachable part from the start state of the unary automata $\mathcal{A}_{(0,0)}^{(2)}$, $\mathcal{A}_{(1,0)}^{(2)}$, $\mathcal{A}_{(2,0)}^{(2)}$ and $\mathcal{A}_{(3,0)}^{(2)}$, corresponding to the automaton from Example 1, in order. Each automaton is constructed from previous ones according to Definition 3. Note that, for example for $\mathcal{A}_{(1,0)}^{(2)}$, the state label of the second state is the union of the action of a_2 on $\{s_1\}$, i.e, the set $\delta(\{s_1\}, a_2)$, but also of a_1 on the state label $\{s_2\}$ of the second state of the previous automaton $\mathcal{A}_{(0,0)}^{(2)}$. Note also that the second "counter" component is not enough to determine all states, as at the end some automata have equal values in this entry (this is essentially how these automata grow in size).

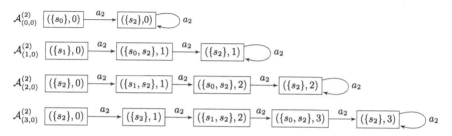

Fig. 3. The reachable part of the unary automata $\mathcal{A}_{(0,0)}^{(2)}$, $\mathcal{A}_{(1,0)}^{(2)}$, $\mathcal{A}_{(2,0)}^{(2)}$ and $\mathcal{A}_{(3,0)}^{(2)}$ from Definition 3, derived from the automaton from Example 1. In Example 1, these automata read in inputs in the up direction, but are drawn here horizontally to save space. See Example 2 for more explanation.

The next statement makes precise what we mean by decomposing the state label map along the hyperplanes into the automata $\mathcal{A}_p^{(j)} = (\{a_j\}, Q_p^{(j)}, \delta_p^{(j)}, s_p^{(0,j)}, F_p^{(j)})$ for $j \in \{1, \ldots, k\}$ and $p \in H_j$. Furthermore, it justifies calling the first component of any state $(S, i) \in Q_p^{(j)}$ also the state set label.

Proposition 2 (state label map decomposition). *Let* $p = (p_1, \ldots, p_k) \in \mathbb{N}_0^k$, $j \in \{1, \ldots, k\}$ *and* $\overline{p} = (p_1, \ldots, p_{j-1}, 0, p_{j+1}, \ldots, p_k) \in H_j$ *be the projection of* p *onto* H_j. *Then*

$$\sigma_{\mathcal{A}}(p) = \pi_1(\delta_{\overline{p}}^{(j)}(s_{\overline{p}}^{(0,j)}, a_j^{p_j}))$$

for the automata $\mathcal{A}_{\overline{p}}^{(j)} = (\{a_j\}, Q_{\overline{p}}^{(j)}, \delta_{\overline{p}}^{(j)}, s_{\overline{p}}^{(0,j)}, F_{\overline{p}}^{(j)})$ *from Definition 3.*

With this observation, in Theorem 3, we derive a sufficient condition when the commutative image of some regular language is itself regular. It also gives us a general bound on the size of a minimal automaton, in case the commutative language is regular.

Theorem 3. *Let $\mathcal{A} = (\Sigma, Q, \delta, s_0, F)$ be a finite automaton. Suppose, for every $j \in \{1, \ldots, k\}$ and $p \in H_j$, with H_j the hyperplane from Definition 2, the automata $\mathcal{A}_p^{(j)} = (\{a_j\}, Q_p^{(j)}, \delta_p^{(j)}, s_p^{(0,j)}, F_p^{(j)})$ from Definition 3 have a bounded number of states[5], i.e., $|Q_p^{(j)}| \leqslant N$ for some $N \geqslant 0$ independent of p and j. Then, the commutative closure $\mathrm{perm}(L(\mathcal{A}))$ is regular and could be accepted by an automaton of size*

$$\prod_{j=1}^{k} (I_j + P_j),$$

where I_j denotes the largest index among the unary automata $\{\mathcal{A}_p^{(j)} \mid p \in H_j\}$, and P_j the least common multiple of all the periods of these automata. In particular, by the relations of the index and period to the states from Sect. 2.1, the automaton size is bounded by N^k.

This gives us a general bound in case the commutative closure is regular. We will apply this to the case of group languages and permutation automata in Sect. 3.3. Theorem 3 has a close relation to Theorem 6.5 from [4], namely case (iii), as we could link the periodic languages introduced in this paper to unary automata, as was done in [9,10]. This linkage, in general, allows us to give more concrete bounds and constructions. For example, we can list all periodic languages inside the commutative closure, or we can even give concrete bounds on resulting automata. The proof in [4] used more abstract well-quasi order arguments that do not yield concrete automata, nor do they allow the arguments we employ in Sect. 3.3.

3.3   The Special Case of Group Languages

Here we apply Theorem 3 to derive state bounds for group languages. We need some basic observations about permutations, see for example [2]. Every permutation could be written in terms of disjoint cycles. For an element[6] of the permutation domain, by the *cycle length* of that element with respect to a given permutation, we mean the length of the cycle in which this element appears[7]. The *order* of a permutation is the smallest power such that the identity permutation results, which equals the least common multiple of all cycle lengths for all elements. Before stating our results, let us make some general assumptions and fix some notions, to make the statements more concise.

---

[5] Equivalently, the index and period is bounded, which is equivalent with just a finite number of distinct automata, up to (semi-automaton-)isomorphism. We call two automata (semi-automaton-)isomorphic if one automaton can be obtained from the other one by renaming states and alphabet symbols.

[6] In this context, the elements are also called points in the literature, but we will stick to the term elements or states.

[7] For a given element $m \in [n]$ and a permutation $\pi : [n] \to [n]$, this is the number $|\{\pi^i(m) \mid i \geqslant 0\}|$, in the literature also called the *orbit length* of m under the subgroup generated by π.

Assumption 1 (assumptions for this section). Let $\Sigma = \{a_1, \ldots, a_k\}$. Assume a permutation automaton $\mathcal{A} = (\Sigma, Q, \delta, s_0, F)$ is given with $j \in \{1, \ldots, k\}$ and a point $p \in H_j$, where H_j denotes the hyperplane from Definition 2. We denote by $\mathcal{A}_p^{(j)} = (\{a_j\}, Q_p^{(j)}, \delta_p^{(j)}, s_p^{(0,j)}, F_p^{(j)})$ the automata from Definition 3. By L_j we will denote the order of the permutation on Q induced by the letter a_j in $\mathcal{A}$, i.e., the least common multiple of the cycle lengths of all states. Also set[8] $\mathcal{R} = \{\mathcal{A}_q^{(j)} \mid p = q + \psi(b) \text{ for some } b \in \Sigma\}$. Denote by I the maximal index and by P the least common multiple of the periods of the unary automata in $\mathcal{R}$.

A crucial ingredient to our arguments will be the following observation.

Lemma 1. *Notation from Assumption 1. Then the state set labels of states from $\mathcal{A}_p^{(j)}$ will not decrease in cardinality as we read in symbols, and their cardinality will stay constant on the cycle of $\mathcal{A}_p^{(j)}$. More precisely, let $(S, x), (T, y) \in Q_p^{(j)}$ be any states. If $(T, y) = \delta_p^{(j)}((S, x), a_j^r)$ for some $r \geq 0$, then $|T| \geq |S|$. And if (S, x) and (T, y) are both on the cycle, i.e., $(S, x) = \delta_p^{(j)}((S, x), a_j^r)$ and $(T, y) = \delta_p^{(j)}(S, x), a_j^s)$ for some $r, s \geq 0$, then $|S| = |T|$.*

To give state bounds on a resulting automaton, using Theorem 3, we need bounds on the indices and periods of the unary automata from Definition 3. The following result gives us a criterion when we have reached the cycle in these automata, and will be used in deriving the mentioned bounds.

Lemma 2. *Choose the notation from Assumption 1. Suppose $S \subseteq Q$ and let $L_S = \operatorname{lcm}\{|\{\delta(s, a_j^i) : i \geq 0\}| : s \in S\}$ be the least common multiple of the cycle lengths of the elements in S with respect to the letter a_j, seen as a permutation of the states. Then for $m \geq I$ and the states $(S, x), (T, y) \in Q_p^{(j)}$ which fulfill*

$$(S, x) = \delta_p^{(j)}(s_p^{(0,j)}, a_j^m) \quad and \quad (T, y) = \delta_p^{(j)}(s_p^{(0,j)}, a_j^{m+\operatorname{lcm}(P, L_S)})$$

we have that if $|S| = |T|$, then $S = T$ and[9] $x = y$. This also implies that the period of $\mathcal{A}_p^{(j)}$ divides $\operatorname{lcm}(P, L_S)$.

The next results gives us a bound for the periods of the automata from Definition 3.

Proposition 3. *Choose the notation from Assumption 1. Let $p \in H_j$. Then the periods of all automata $\mathcal{A}_p^{(j)}$ divide L_j.*

The criterion for the cycle detection from Lemma 2 could be a little bit relaxed by the next result, which will be more useful for proving a bound on the index of the automata from Definition 3. Intuitively, it bounds the way in which the indices of the automata from Definition 3 can grow.

---

[8] For $p \in H_j$, the condition $p = q + \psi(b)$, for some $b \in \Sigma$, implies $q \in H_j$ and $b \neq a_j$.
[9] As we assume $m \geq I$, by Eq. (3) from Definition 3, we have $x \geq I$.

Corollary 2. *Notation from Assumption 1. For $(S, x), (T, y) \in Q_p^{(j)}$ with $x \geqslant I$ and $(T, y) = \delta_p^{(j)}((S, x), a_i^{L_j})$ we have that $|T| = |S|$ implies $T = S$ and $x = y$.*

Finally, we state a bound for the indices of the automata from Definition 3.

Proposition 4. *Choose the notation from Assumption 1. Then the index of any automaton $\mathcal{A}_p^{(j)}$ is bounded by $(|T| - 1) \cdot L_j$, where T is any state set label from a state on the cycle of $\mathcal{A}_p^{(j)}$.*

Combining everything gives our state complexity bound.

Theorem 4. *Choose the notation from Assumption 1. Then the commutative closure $\mathrm{perm}(L(\mathcal{A}))$ is regular and could be accepted by an automaton with at most*

$$\prod_{j=1}^{k}((|Q| - 1)L_j + L_j) = |Q|^k \left(\prod_{j=1}^{k} L_j \right) \tag{5}$$

states.

Proof. First note that Proposition 4 gives in particular that the indices of all automata are at most $(|Q| - 1)L_j$. Also Proposition 3 yields the bound L_j for the periods. So Theorem 3 gives the result.   □

Example 3. Let $\Sigma = \{a_1, a_2\}$ and consider the permutation automaton from Fig. 4. It is the same automaton as given in [6]. As an example for the group language case, we give its state labelling on $\mathbb{N}_0^k$ and an automaton for the commutative closure, constructed from the unary automata $\mathcal{A}_p^{(j)}$. Note that this is not the minimal automaton, which could be found in [6]. Also, note that, with the notational convention from Assumption 1, we have $L_1 = 3$ and $L_2 = 2$. Hence Theorem 4 gives the bound $3^2 \cdot 6 = 54$. The automaton constructed from the unary automaton $\mathcal{A}_p^{(j)}$ is much smaller here, as the indices stabilize much faster than given by the theoretical bound.

Example 4. Let $\Sigma = \{a_1, a_2\}$ and consider $\mathcal{A} = (\Sigma, Q, \delta, s_0, F)$ with $Q = [n]$ for some $n \geqslant 1$, s_0 and F arbitrary, and $\delta(0, a_1) = 1, \delta(1, a_1) = 0, \delta(x, a_1) = x$ for $x \in \{2, \ldots, n-1\}$, $\delta(x, a_2) = (x + 1) \bmod n$ for $x \in [n]$. Then $\mathrm{perm}(L(\mathcal{A}))$ could be accepted by an automaton of size $2n^3$.

As stated in [5], the maximal order of any permutation on a set of size n is given by Landau's function, which is asymptotically like $e^{\Theta(\sqrt{n \ln n})}$. Hence, Theorem 1, the asymptotic form of Theorem 4, is implied.

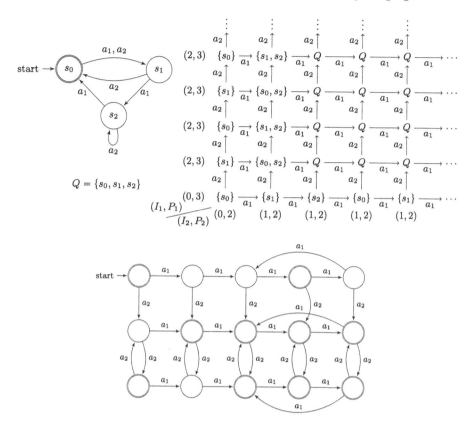

Fig. 4. The constructions from this paper for a permutation automaton, different from the one given in Fig. 2. In the state labelling of $\mathbb{N}_0^{|\Sigma|}$, the origin is in the bottom left corner, labeled by $\{s_0\}$. Also indicated, written beneath, or to the side of, the axes, are the indices and periods of the unary automata in the direction of $\varphi(a_j)$ from Definition 3. This is not the minimal automaton, see Example 3 for explanations.

4   Conclusion

We have shown that the commutative closure of regular group languages is regular, and have derived a bound on the size of the resulting automaton. The size is related to the least common multiples of the cycle lengths of the letters, viewed as permutations on the states, see Eq. (5). I do not know if the bound is sharp. I have not found a single example that has the property that the index of the constructed automata $\mathcal{A}_p^{(j)}$, for the letter a_j, has length $(|Q| - 1) \cdot L_j$, as would be necessary to reach the bound stated in Theorem 4. In fact, I believe that the cycles on individual elements of the state label are never "traversed" in its entirety before another element is added to the state label, or we reach the final cycle of the unary automata $\mathcal{A}_p^{(j)}$. So, I conjecture that for larger alphabets we can improve this bound, as the state labels grow faster in the index part of the automata $\mathcal{A}_p^{(j)}$, as more predecessor automata[10] add states of the original automaton to the state labels of $\mathcal{A}_p^{(j)}$, as inputs are read. This is somehow contrary to what usually happens in other existing state complexity results, namely that we need larger alphabets to reach the state bounds, see for example [1,7,8]. In our situation, I somehow conjecture that for larger alphabets (where surely, distinct letters have to be distinct permutations), indices of the unary automata $\mathcal{A}_p^{(j)}$ get smaller and smaller. Hence the overall state complexity bound reaches the product of the least common multiples of the cycle lengths for all letters, i.e., we have $\prod_{j=1}^{k} L_j$ as a bound in the limit for $k \to \infty$, with an alphabet of size k.

Acknowledgement. I thank my supervisor, Prof. Dr. Henning Fernau, for giving valuable feedback and remarks on the content of this article that improved its presentation. I also thank the anonymous reviewers for careful reading and suggestions for improvement.

References

1. Brzozowski, J., Jirásková, G., Liu, B., Rajasekaran, A., Szykuła, M.: On the state complexity of the shuffle of regular languages. In: Câmpeanu, C., Manea, F., Shallit, J. (eds.) DCFS 2016. LNCS, vol. 9777, pp. 73–86. Springer, Cham (2016). https://doi.org/10.1007/978-3-319-41114-9_6

2. Cameron, P.J.: Permutation Groups. London Mathematical Society Student Texts. Cambridge University Press, Cambridge (1999)

3. Cho, D., Goc, D., Han, Y., Ko, S., Palioudakis, A., Salomaa, K.: State complexity of permutation on finite languages over a binary alphabet. Theor. Comput. Sci. **682**, 67–78 (2017)

4. Ehrenfeucht, A., Haussler, D., Rozenberg, G.: On regularity of context-free languages. Theor. Comput. Sci. **27**, 311–332 (1983)

5. Gao, Y., Moreira, N., Reis, R., Yu, S.: A survey on operational state complexity. J. Automata Lang. Comb. **21**(4), 251–310 (2017)

6. Gómez, A.C., Guaiana, G., Pin, J.: Regular languages and partial commutations. Inf. Comput. **230**, 76–96 (2013)

7. Han, Y.-S., Salomaa, K.: State complexity of union and intersection of finite languages. In: Harju, T., Karhumäki, J., Lepistö, A. (eds.) DLT 2007. LNCS, vol. 4588, pp. 217–228. Springer, Heidelberg (2007). https://doi.org/10.1007/978-3-540-73208-2_22

8. Han, Y., Salomaa, K.: State complexity of union and intersection of finite languages. Int. J. Found. Comput. Sci. **19**(3), 581–595 (2008)

9. Hoffmann, S.: State complexity, properties and generalizations of commutative regular languages. Inf. Comput. (submitted)

10. Hoffmann, S.: Commutative regular languages - properties and state complexity. In: Ćirić, M., Droste, M., Pin, J.É. (eds.) CAI 2019. LNCS, vol. 11545, pp. 151–163. Springer, Cham (2019). https://doi.org/10.1007/978-3-030-21363-3_13

---

[10] For some automaton $\mathcal{A}_p^{(j)}$, with $p \in H_j$ and $j \in \{1, \ldots, k\}$, all automata $\mathcal{A}_q^{(j)}$ with $p = q + \psi(b)$, for some $b \in \Sigma$, are called *predecessor automata* of $\mathcal{A}_p^{(j)}$.

11. Hoffmann, S.: State complexity of permutation on finite languages. CoRR abs/2006.15178 (2020). https://arxiv.org/abs/2006.15178
12. Holzer, M., Kutrib, M.: Descriptional complexity - an introductory survey. In: Martín-Vide, C. (ed.) Scientific Applications of Language Methods, Mathematics, Computing, Language, and Life: Frontiers in Mathematical Linguistics and Language Theory, vol. 2, pp. 1–58. World Scientific/Imperial College Press (2010)
13. Holzer, M., Kutrib, M.: Descriptional and computational complexity of finite automata - a survey. Inf. Comput. **209**(3), 456–470 (2011)
14. Hospodár, M., Mlynárčik, P.: Operations on permutation automata. In: Jonoska, N., Savchuk, D. (eds.) DLT 2020. LNCS, vol. 12086, pp. 122–136. Springer, Cham (2020). https://doi.org/10.1007/978-3-030-48516-0_10
15. Maslov, A.N.: Estimates of the number of states of finite automata. Dokl. Akad. Nauk SSSR **194**(6), 1266–1268 (1970)
16. Mohri, M.: On some applications of finite-state automata theory to natural language processing. Nat. Lang. Eng. **2**(1), 61–80 (1996)
17. Palioudakis, A., Cho, D.-J., Goč, D., Han, Y.-S., Ko, S.-K., Salomaa, K.: The state complexity of permutations on finite languages over binary alphabets. In: Shallit, J., Okhotin, A. (eds.) DCFS 2015. LNCS, vol. 9118, pp. 220–230. Springer, Cham (2015). https://doi.org/10.1007/978-3-319-19225-3_19
18. Wang, J. (ed.): Handbook of Finite State Based Models and Applications. Chapman and Hall/CRC, Boca Raton (2012)
19. Yu, S., Zhuang, Q., Salomaa, K.: The state complexities of some basic operations on regular languages. Theor. Comput. Sci. **125**(2), 315–328 (1994)

Multiple Concatenation and State Complexity (Extended Abstract)

Jozef Jirásek[1] and Galina Jirásková[2(✉)]

[1] Institute of Computer Science, Faculty of Science, P. J. Šafárik University, Jesenná 5, 040 01 Košice, Slovakia
jozef.jirasek@upjs.sk
[2] Mathematical Institute, Slovak Academy of Sciences, Grešákova 6, 040 01, Košice, Slovakia
jiraskov@saske.sk

Abstract. We describe witnesses for the concatenation of k languages over an alphabet of $k + 1$ symbols with a significantly simpler proof then that from the literature. Then we use slightly modified Maslov's automata to get witnesses over a k-letter alphabet which solves an open problem stated by Caron et al. [2018, Fund. Inform. 160, 255–279]. We prove that for $k = 3$, the ternary alphabet is optimal. We also obtain lower bounds $n_1 - 1 + (1/2^{2k-2})2^{n_2+\cdots+n_k}$ and $(1/2^{2k-2})n_1 2^{n_2+\cdots+n_k}$ in the binary and ternary case, respectively. Finally, we show that an upper bound for unary cyclic languages is $n_1 n_k/d + n_1 + \cdots + n_k - k + 1 + d$ where $n_1 \leq \cdots \leq n_k$ and $d = \gcd(n_1, \ldots, n_k)$.

1 Introduction

The state complexity of a regular language is the smallest number of states in any deterministic finite automaton (DFA) recognizing this language. The state complexity of a regular operation is a function which assigns the maximal number of states in a DFA recognizing the resulting language to the sizes of DFAs recognizing the operands.

The first results on the state complexity of regular operations were obtained by Maslov [5]. In particular, he described binary witnesses meeting the upper bound $m2^n - 2^{n-1}$ on the state complexity of concatenation of two regular languages. Yu et al. [8] proved that this upper bound cannot be met if the first language is recognized by a DFA with more than one final state.

The concatenation of three and four regular languages was considered by Ésik et al. [2]. Here the witnesses for the concatenation of three language over a five-letter alphabet can be found. The rather complicated expression for the upper bounds for the concatenation of k languages, as well as witnesses over a $(2k - 1)$-letter alphabet were given by Gao and Yu [3].

J. Jirásek—Research supported by VEGA grant 1/0056/18 and grant APVV-15-0091.
G. Jirásková—Research supported by VEGA grant 2/0132/19 and grant APVV-15-0091.

G. Jirásková and G. Pighizzini (Eds.): DCFS 2020, LNCS 12442, pp. 78–90, 2020.
https://doi.org/10.1007/978-3-030-62536-8_7

Caron et al. [1] presented recursive formulas for the upper bounds, and described witnesses over a $(k+1)$-letter alphabet using Brzozowski's universal automata. They also showed that to meet the upper bound for the concatenation of two or three languages, the binary or ternary alphabet, respectively, is enough, and they conjectured that k symbols could be enough to describe witnesses for the concatenation of k languages.

In this paper, we study in detail the state complexity of multiple concatenation of k languages. We first describe witnesses over an alphabet consisting of $k+1$ symbols with significantly simpler proof than that in [1]. Our witness automata $A_1, \ldots, A_k$ are defined over the alphabet $\{a_1, \ldots, a_k\} \cup \{b\}$. Each a_i performs the big cycle in A_i and the identity in all the other automata. These k permutation symbols are used to get reachability of all so called valid states in a DFA for the concatenation. The symbol b performs a contraction in each A_i and gives the distinguishability of all valid states. Then we use modified Maslov's automata to get binary witnesses for the concatenation of two languages.

We combine our ideas used for the $(k+1)$-letter alphabet and those for binary Maslov's automata to describe witnesses for multiple concatenation over a k-letter alphabet which solves an open problem stated by Caron et al. [1]. In the case of $k=3$, we show that the ternary alphabet is optimal.

We also examine multiple concatenation on binary, ternary, and unary cyclic languages. While in the binary and ternary case, the lower bounds remain exponential in $n_2, \ldots, n_k$, in the case of unary cyclic languages, the upper bound is significantly smaller than that in the general case.

2   Preliminaries

We assume that the reader is familiar with basic notions in automata and formal languages theory, and for details, we refer to [4,7].

For a finite non-empty alphabet of symbols Σ, the set of all strings over Σ is denoted by Σ^*, and it includes the empty string ε. A language is any subset of Σ^*. The multiple concatenation of k languages $L_1, L_2 \ldots, L_k$ is the language $L_1 L_2 \cdots L_k = \{u_1 u_2 \cdots u_k \mid u_1 \in L_1, u_2 \in L_2, \ldots, u_k \in L_k\}$. The size of a finite set S is denoted by $|S|$, and the set of all its subsets by 2^S.

A *deterministic finite automaton* (DFA) is a quintuple $A = (Q, \Sigma, \cdot, s, F)$ where Q is a non-empty finite *set of states*, Σ is a non-empty finite *alphabet of input symbols*, $\cdot \colon Q \times \Sigma \to Q$ is the *transition function*, $s \in Q$ is the initial state, and $F \subseteq Q$ is the set of *final* (accepting) states. The transition function can be naturally extended to the domain $Q \times \Sigma^*$. The *language recognized (accepted)* by the DFA A is the set of strings $L(A) = \{w \in \Sigma^* \mid s \cdot w \in F\}$.

We usually omit $\cdot$, and write qa instead of $q \cdot a$. Next, for a subset S of Q, let $wS = \{q \mid qw \in S\}$. Each input symbol a induces a transformation on Q given by $q \mapsto qa$. We denote by $a \colon (q_1, q_2, \ldots, q_\ell)$ the transformation that maps q_i to q_{i+1} for $i = 1, \ldots, \ell - 1$, the state q_ℓ to q_1, and fixes any other state in Q. In particular, (q_1) denotes the identity. Next, we denote by $a \colon (q_1 \to q_2 \to \cdots \to q_\ell)$ the transformation that maps q_i to q_{i+1} for $i = 1, 2, \ldots, \ell - 1$ and fixes any other state. In particular, the map $(q_1 \to q_2)$ is a contraction that maps q_1 to q_2 and fixes any other state.

A DFA is *minimal* (with respect to the number of states) if all its states are reachable and pairwise distinguishable. The *state complexity* of a regular language L, $sc(L)$, is the number of states in the minimal DFA recognizing L. The state complexity of a k-ary regular operation f is a function from $\mathbb{N}^k$ to $\mathbb{N}$ given by $(n_1, \ldots, n_k) \mapsto \max\{sc(f(L_1, \ldots, L_k)) \mid sc(L_i) \le n_i \text{ for } i = 1, \ldots, k\}$.

A *nondeterministic finite automaton* (NFA) is a quintuple $N = (Q, \Sigma, \cdot, I, F)$ where Q, Σ, and F are the same as for a DFA, $I \subseteq Q$ is the *set of initial states*, and $\cdot : Q \times \Sigma \to 2^Q$ is the nondeterministic *transition function* which can be naturally extended to the domain $2^Q \times \Sigma^*$. The *language recognized* by the NFA N is the set of strings $L(N) = \{w \in \Sigma^* \mid Iw \cap F \ne \emptyset\}$.

We say that (p, a, q) is a *transition* in N if $q \in pa$. A state q of N is said to be a *dead state*, if no string is accepted by N from q.

The *subset automaton* of the NFA N is a deterministic finite automaton $\mathcal{D}(N) = (2^Q, \Sigma, \cdot, I, \{S \subseteq Q \mid S \cap F \ne \emptyset\})$; here $\cdot$ is the transition function of N extended to the domain $2^Q \times \Sigma$. We have $L(N) = L(\mathcal{D}(N))$.

The *reverse* of the NFA N is the NFA $N^R = (Q, \Sigma, \cdot^R, F, I)$ where the transition function is defined by $q \cdot^R a = \{p \in Q \mid q \in p \cdot a\}$.

A subset S of Q is *reachable* in N if there is a string w in Σ^* such that $S = Iw$, and it is *co-reachable* in N if it is reachable in the reverse N^R.

We use the following two simple observations to prove distinguishability of states in subset automata.

Lemma 1. *Let* $N = (Q, \Sigma, \cdot, I, F)$, $S, T \subseteq Q$, *and* $q \in S \setminus T$. *If the singleton set* $\{q\}$ *is co-reachable in* N, *then* S *and* T *are distinguishable in* $\mathcal{D}(N)$.

Proof. Since the set $\{q\}$ is co-reachable in N, there exists a string w which is accepted by N from and only from the state q. Then w is accepted by $\mathcal{D}(N)$ from S and rejected from T. □

Corollary 2. *If for each state* q *of an NFA* N, *the singleton set* $\{q\}$ *is co-reachable in* N, *then all states of the subset automaton* $\mathcal{D}(N)$ *are pairwise distinguishable.* □

3   Construction of NFAs for Multiple Concatenation

Let regular languages K and L be recognized by DFAs $A = (Q_A, \Sigma, \cdot_A, s_A, F_A)$ and $B = (Q_B, \Sigma, \cdot_B, s_B, F_B)$ with $Q_A \cap Q_B = \emptyset$. Then the concatenation KL is recognized by the NFA $N = (Q_A \cup Q_B, \Sigma, \cdot, I, F_B)$ with $I = \{s_A\}$ if $s_A \notin F_A$ and $I = \{s_A, s_B\}$ otherwise, and

$$q \cdot a = \begin{cases} \{q \cdot_A a\}, & \text{if } q \in Q_A \text{ and } q \cdot_A a \notin F_A; \\ \{q \cdot_A a\} \cup \{s_B\}, & \text{if } q \in Q_A \text{ and } q \cdot_A a \in F_A; \\ \{q \cdot_B a\}, & \text{if } q \in Q_B, \end{cases}$$

that is, the NFA N is obtained from the DFAs A and B by adding transitions (q, a, s_B) for each state q of A and each symbol a in Σ such that $q \cdot_A a \in F_A$, and by making appropriate states initial and final.

In the subset automaton $\mathcal{D}(N)$, every reachable state is of the form $\{q\} \cup S$ with $q \in Q_A$ and $S \subseteq Q_B$ since A is a complete DFA. We denote such a set by the pair (q, S), and with this notation, it is not necessary to have the state sets disjoint. Nevertheless, since we use properties of the NFA N, we still assume their disjointness, even if we have $Q_A = \{0, 1, \ldots, m-1\}$ and $Q_B = \{0, 1, \ldots, n-1\}$, and write 0_A or 0_B if necessary. We also denote all three transition functions by $\cdot$, and simply write (qa, S) or (q, Sb) or $(q, S)a$. The second important observation which follows from the construction of the NFA N is the following one: for each reachable state (q, S) of $\mathcal{D}(N)$ such that $q \in F_A$, we have $s_B \in S$.

The construction above can be generalized to get an NFA for the concatenation of k languages given by DFAs $A_i = (Q_i, \Sigma, \cdot, s_i, \{f_i\})$ with $s_i \neq f_i$ as follows. We construct an NFA N for $L(A_1)L(A_2) \cdots L(A_k)$ from DFAs $A_1, A_2, \ldots, A_k$ by adding the transitions (q, a, s_{i+1}) whenever $qa = f_i$ for $i = 1, 2, \ldots, k-1$. The initial state of N is s_1 and the final state of N is f_k. In the corresponding subset automaton $\mathcal{D}(N)$, every reachable state is of the form $(S_1, S_2, S_3, \ldots, S_k)$ with $S_i \subseteq Q_i$ for $i = 1, 2, \ldots, k$, and moreover, we have

(1) $|S_1| = 1$,
(2) if $S_i = \emptyset$ then $S_{i+1} = \emptyset$,
(3) if $f_i \in S_i$ then $s_{i+1} \in S_{i+1}$,

for $i = 1, 2, \ldots, k-1$. A state satisfying these three conditions is called a *valid state*. We usually write $(q, S_2, \ldots, S_k)$ instead of $(\{q\}, S_2, \ldots, S_k)$.

Proposition 3. *An upper bound on* $\mathrm{sc}(L(A_1)L(A_2) \cdots L(A_k))$ *is given by the number of valid states, which is maximal if each A_i has one final state.* $\square$

Proposition 4. ([3, **Theorems 5 and 6**]). *Let $k \geq 2$, $n_i \geq 2$ for $i = 1, 2, \ldots, k$, and A_i be an n_i-state DFA that has one final state. Then the number of valid states, $\#\tau_k$, is given by the expression*

$$\#\tau_k = n_1 2^{n_2 + \cdots + n_k} - D - \sum_{i=1}^{k-1} E_i, \quad where$$

$$D = n_1 \sum_{\ell=2}^{k-1} (2^{n_2-1} - 1)(2^{n_3-1} - 1) \cdots (2^{n_\ell-1} - 1)(2^{n_{\ell+1} n_{\ell+2} \cdots n_k} - 1);$$

$$E_1 = 1 + (2^{n_2-1} - 1)(1 + (2^{n_3} - 1)(1 + (2^{n_4} - 1) \cdots (1 + (2^{n_{k-1}} - 1)2^{n_k} \cdots));$$

$$E_i = ((n_1 - 1)(2^{n_2-1} - 1) \cdots 2^{n_i-1} + \cdots + 2^{n_2-2} \cdots 2^{n_i-2}).$$
$$\cdot (1 + (2^{n_{i+1}-1} - 1)(1 + (2^{n_{i+2}} - 1) \cdots (1 + (2^{n_{k-1}} - 1)2^{n_k}) \cdots))$$

for $i = 2, \ldots, k-1$. In the expression above, D counts the states with both $S_\ell = \emptyset$ and $S_{\ell+1} \neq \emptyset$ with $2 \leq \ell \leq k-1$, while E_i counts the states with both $f_i \in S_i$ and $s_i \notin S_i$ which are not in $E_1, E_2, \ldots, E_{i-1}$. $\square$

Every state $(S_1, S_2, \ldots, S_k)$ with $s_i \in S_i$ for $i = 2, 3, \ldots, k$ is a valid state, while every state $(S_1, S_2, \ldots, S_k)$ with $f_2 \in S_2$ and $s_3 \notin S_3$ is not valid. This gives the following inequalities for the number of valid states $\#\tau_k$.

Proposition 5. *We have* $\frac{1}{2^{k-1}} n_1 2^{n_2 + \cdots + n_k} \leq \#\tau_k \leq \frac{3}{4} n_1 2^{n_2 + \cdots + n_k}$.   □

4   Tightness for a $(k+1)$-letter Alphabet

In this section, we describe witnesses for multiple concatenation of k regular languages over an alphabet of $k + 1$ symbols with a significantly simpler proof than that in [1, Sect. 4, pp. 266–271]. We use k permutation symbols to get reachability of all valid states in the corresponding subset automaton, and one more symbol to guarantee their distinguishability. Then we use modified Maslov's automata to get binary witnesses for $L_1 L_2$. In the next section, we use all these results to get witnesses for the concatenation of k languages over a k-letter alphabet.

Let $\Sigma = \{a_i \mid 1 \leq i \leq k\} \cup \{b\}$ be an alphabet consisting of $k + 1$ symbols. Let $n_i \geq 3$ for $i = 1, 2, \ldots, k$, and define n_i-state DFA $A_i = (Q_i, \Sigma, \cdot, s_i, \{f_i\})$, where $Q_i = \{0, 1, \ldots, n_i - 1\}$, $s_i = 0$, $f_i = n_i - 1$, and $a_i: (0, 1, \ldots, n_i - 1)$, if $j \neq i$, then $a_j: (0)$, and $b: (0 \to 1)$, that is, the symbol a_i performs the circular permutation (big cycle) on Q_i, the symbol a_j with $j \neq i$ performs the identity, and the symbol b performs a contraction. The DFA A_i is shown in Fig. 1.

We first consider the concatenation $L(A_{i-1})L(A_i)$ with $2 \leq i \leq k$. We construct an NFA for this concatenation from DFAs A_{i-1} and A_i by adding the transitions $(f_{i-1} - 1, a_{i-1}, s_i)$ and (f_{i-1}, σ, s_i) with $\sigma \in \Sigma \setminus \{a_{i-1}\}$. The next observation shows that in the corresponding subset automaton each state $(\{0\}, S)$ is reachable from $(\{0\}, \{0\})$. Moreover, while reaching $(\{0\}, S)$ with $f_i \notin S$, the state f_i is never visited. This is a very important property since, later, we do not wish to influence the $(i+1)$th component of a valid state while setting its ith component.

Lemma 6. *Let* $2 \leq i \leq k$ *and consider the NFA* N_i *for* $L(A_{i-1})L(A_i)$ *described above. In the subset automaton* $\mathcal{D}(N_i)$, *for every non-empty subset* S *of* Q_i, *there exists a string* w_S *over* $\{a_{i-1}, a_i\}$ *such that*

(i) $(\{0\}, \{0\}) \cdot w_S = (\{0\}, S);$

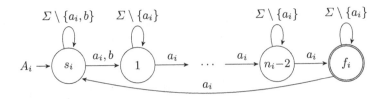

Fig. 1. The witness DFA A_i over $\Sigma = \{a_1, a_2, \ldots, a_k\} \cup \{b\}$; $s_i = 0$, $f_i = n_i - 1$.

(ii) if $f_i \notin S$ and $(\{0\}, \{0\}) \cdot u = (\{q\}, T)$ for a prefix u of w_S, then $f_i \notin T$.

Proof (Proof Idea). The proof of both (i) and (ii) is by induction on $|S|$. The state $(\{0\}, \{j\})$ is reached from $(\{0\}, \{0\})$ by a_i^j, and if $j < f_i$, then (ii) holds. Next, each state $(\{0\}, \{j_1, j_2, \ldots, j_\ell\})$ where $0 \le j_1 < j_2 < \cdots < j_\ell \le f_i$ is reached from $(\{0\}, \{j_2 - j_1, \ldots, j_\ell - j_1\})$ by $a_{i-1}^{n_i-1} a_i^{j_1}$, and (ii) holds as well. □

Now, construct the NFA N for $L(A_1)L(A_2)\cdots L(A_k)$ as described in Sect. 3, and consider its subset automaton $\mathcal{D}(N)$.

Lemma 7. *Each valid state $(\{j\}, S_2, S_3, \ldots, S_k)$ is reachable in the subset automaton $\mathcal{D}(N)$. These valid states are pairwise distinguishable.*

Proof. Each valid state $(\{j\}, \emptyset, \ldots, \emptyset)$ of $\mathcal{D}(N)$ is reached from the initial state $(\{0\}, \emptyset, \ldots, \emptyset)$ by the string a_1^j. Let $2 \le \ell \le k$ and $S_i \subseteq Q_i$ and $S_i \ne \emptyset$ for $i = 2, 3, \ldots, \ell$. Consider a valid state $(\{j\}, S_2, S_3, \ldots, S_\ell, \emptyset, \ldots, \emptyset)$.

Let w_{S_i} for $i = 2, 3, \ldots, \ell$ be the strings over $\{a_{i-1}, a_i\}$ given by Lemma 6; recall that $f_i \notin S_i$ implies that the state f_i is never visited while reaching S_i, which in turn implies that s_{i+1} is never added to the $(i + 1)$th component in such a case. If $f_i \in S_i$, then the state s_{i+1} is included in S_{i+1} since the state $(\{j\}, S_2, S_3, \ldots, S_\ell, \emptyset, \ldots, \emptyset)$ is a valid state, and moreover, there is a loop on both a_{i-1} and a_i in s_{i+1}. It follows that the state $(\{j\}, S_2, S_3, \ldots, S_\ell, \emptyset, \ldots, \emptyset)$ is reached from the initial state $(0, \emptyset, \ldots, \emptyset)$ by the string

$$(\prod_{i=1}^{\ell-1} a_i^{n_i})(\prod_{j=0}^{\ell-2} w_{S_{\ell-j}})a_1^j = a_1^{n_1} a_2^{n_2} \cdots a_{\ell-1}^{n_{\ell-1}} w_{S_\ell} w_{S_{\ell-1}} \cdots w_{S_3} w_{S_2} a_1^j$$

since we have

$(\{0\}, \quad \emptyset, \quad \emptyset, \quad \ldots, \quad \emptyset, \quad \emptyset, \quad \emptyset, \emptyset, \ldots, \emptyset) \xrightarrow{a_1^{n_1} a_2^{n_2} \cdots a_{\ell-1}^{n_{\ell-1}}}$

$(\{0\}, \{0\}, \{0\}, \ldots, \{0\}, \{0\}, \{0\}, \emptyset, \ldots, \emptyset) \xrightarrow{w_{S_\ell} \text{ over } \{a_{\ell-1}, a_\ell\}}$

$(\{0\}, \{0\}, \{0\}, \ldots, \{0\}, \{0\}, S_\ell, \emptyset, \ldots, \emptyset) \xrightarrow{w_{S_{\ell-1}} \text{ over } \{a_{\ell-2}, a_{\ell-1}\}}$

$(\{0\}, \{0\}, \{0\}, \ldots, \{0\}, S_{\ell-1}, S_\ell, \emptyset, \ldots, \emptyset) \xrightarrow{w_{S_{\ell-2}}} \cdots \xrightarrow{w_{S_3}}$

$\quad\quad\vdots$

$(\{0\}, \{0\}, S_3, \ldots, S_{\ell-2}, S_{\ell-1}, S_\ell, \emptyset, \ldots, \emptyset) \xrightarrow{w_{S_2} \text{ over } \{a_1, a_2\}}$

$(\{0\}, S_2, S_3, \ldots, S_{\ell-2}, S_{\ell-1}, S_\ell, \emptyset, \ldots, \emptyset) \xrightarrow{a_1^j}$

$(\{j\}, S_2, S_3, \ldots, S_{\ell-2}, S_{\ell-1}, S_\ell, \emptyset, \ldots, \emptyset)$.

In the reverse N^R, the initial set is $\{f_k\}$. Next, each singleton set $\{j\}$ such that $j \in Q_i$ $(1 \le i \le k)$ is reached from $\{f_i\}$ via a string in a_i^*. Finally, each $\{f_{i-1}\}$ $(2 \le i \le k)$ is reached from $\{s_i\}$ by b since $n_{i-1} \ge 3$. Thus, for every state q of N, the singleton set $\{q\}$ is co-reachable in N. By Corollary 2, all states of the subset automaton $\mathcal{D}(N)$ are pairwise distinguishable. □

As a corollary of Propositions 3 and 4 and the lemma above, we get our first result.

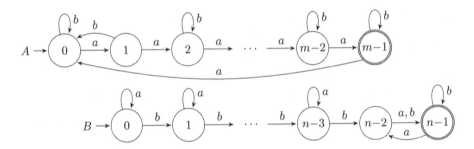

Fig. 2. Modified Maslov's [5] binary witnesses for concatenation of two languages.

Theorem 8. *Let $n_i \geq 3$ for $i = 1, 2, \ldots, k$. The DFAs A_i (1 $\leq i \leq k$) from Fig. 1 defined over the alphabet $\{a_1, a_2, \ldots, a_k\} \cup \{b\}$ are witnesses for multiple concatenation of k regular languages.* $\qquad\square$

In the next theorem, we use slightly modified Maslov's [5] automata to get binary witnesses for the concatenation of two regular languages. This shows that the $(k+1)$-letter alphabet used in the theorem above is not optimal.

Theorem 9. *Let $m, n \geq 3$ and A, B and N be automata from Figs. 2 and 3. Then all valid states are reachable and pairwise distinguishable in the subset automaton $\mathcal{D}(N)$ for $L(A)L(B)$.*

Proof. The proof of reachability of all valid states (i, S) is by induction on $|S|$. The basis, $|S| = 0$, holds true since each valid state $(i, \emptyset)$ is reached from the initial state $(0, \emptyset)$ by a^i. Let $1 \leq \ell \leq n$ and assume that our claim holds for each set of size $\ell - 1$. Let (i, S) be a valid state with $|S| = \ell$. Recall the we denote by wS the set of states $\{q \mid qw \in S\}$. Consider three cases:

(1) Let $i = m - 1$, and therefore $0 \in S$. Since a performs a permutation on the state set of B, the state $(m - 2, a(S \setminus \{0\}))$ is reachable by the induction hypothesis, and it is sent to $(m - 1, S)$ by a.

(2) Let $i = 0$. Since $a\{0\} = \{0\}$ in B, the state $(m - 1, a\{j - \min S \mid j \in S\})$ is reachable as shown in case (1), and it is sent to $(0, S)$ by $ab^{\min S}$.

(3) Let $1 \leq i \leq m - 2$. Then the state $(0, a^i S)$ is reachable as shown in case (2), and it is sent to (i, S) by a^i.

To prove distinguishability, notice that each singleton set is co-reachable in the NFA N via a string in $\varepsilon + ab^*a^*$ since we have $m, n \geq 3$. By Corollary 2, all states of the subset automaton $\mathcal{D}(N)$ are pairwise distinguishable. $\qquad\square$

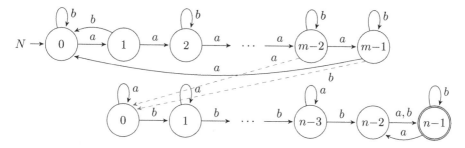

Fig. 3. An NFA N for $L(A)L(B)$ where A and B are DFAs from Fig. 2.

5 Tightness for a k-letter Alphabet

In this section, we use our previous results to describe witnesses for the concatenation of k languages over the k-letter alphabet $\{a_1, a_2, \ldots, a_{k-1}\} \cup \{b\}$. The idea is as follows. The transitions on input symbols $a_1, a_2, \ldots, a_{k-1}$ in automata $A_1, A_2, \ldots, A_{k-1}$ will be the same as in our $(k+1)$-letter witnesses from Theorem 8, while A_k over $\{a_{k-1}, b\}$ will be the same as the second Maslov's automaton from Theorem 9. The input symbol b performs the contraction $(1 \to 0)$ in each A_i except for A_k, and it is used to get reachability as well as distinguishability.

Let $k \geq 2$, $\Sigma = \{a_1, a_2, \ldots, a_{k-1}\} \cup \{b\}$, and $n_i \geq 3$ for $i = 1, 2, \ldots, k$. For $i = 1, 2, \ldots, k-1$, define an n_i-state DFA $A_i = (Q_i, \Sigma, \cdot, s_i, \{f_i\})$ where
$Q_i = \{0, 1, \ldots, n_i - 1\}$, $s_i = 0$, $f_i = n_i - 1$, and
$a_i: (0, 1, \ldots, n_i - 1)$,
$a_j: (0)$ if $j \neq i$,
$b: (1 \to 0)$.
Define an n_k-state DFA $A_k = (Q_k, \Sigma, \cdot, s_k, \{f_k\})$ where
$Q_k = \{0, 1, \ldots, n_k - 1\}$, $s_k = 0$, $f_k = n_k - 1$, and
$a_j: (0)$ if $j \neq k - 1$,
$a_j: (n_k - 2, n_k - 1)$ if $j = k - 1$,
$b: (0 \to 1 \to 2 \to \cdots \to n_k-2 \to n_k-1)$.
The DFAs A_i with $1 \leq i \leq k - 1$ and A_k are shown in Fig. 4.

Construct an NFA N for $L(A_1)L(A_2) \cdots L(A_k)$ from DFAs $A_1, A_2, \ldots, A_k$ by adding the transitions $(f_i - 1, a_i, s_{i+1})$, (f_i, a_j, s_{i+1}) for $j \neq i$, and (f_i, b, s_{i+1}) for $i = 1, \ldots, k-1$; the initial state of N is s_1, and the final state is f_k. The next theorem shows that all valid states are reachable and pairwise distinguishable in the corresponding subset automaton. The proof of reachability is based on our results concerning $(k+1)$-letter witnesses as well as Maslov's binary witnesses. The proof of distinguishability is not for free this time.

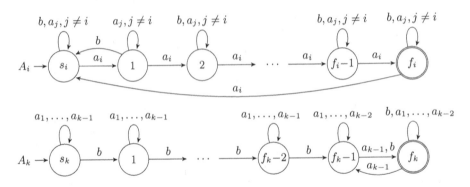

Fig. 4. Witness DFAs A_i for $i = 1, \ldots, k-1$ and A_k; $\Sigma = \{a_1, a_2, \ldots, a_{k-1}\} \cup \{b\}$.

Theorem 10. *Let* $k \geq 2$, $n_i \geq 3$ *for* $i = 1, 2, \ldots, k$. *Let* $A_1, A_2, \ldots, A_k$ *and* N *be automata over* $\{a_1, a_2, \ldots, a_{k-1}\} \cup \{b\}$ *described above. Then all valid states are reachable and pairwise distinguishable in the subset automaton* $\mathcal{D}(N)$.

Proof. Consider a valid state $(j, S_2, \ldots, S_{k-1}, S_k)$. First, let $S_k = \emptyset$. Notice that the transitions on $a_1, a_2, \ldots, a_{k-1}$ in $A_1, A_2, \ldots, A_{k-1}$ are the same as in automata in Lemma 7. Hence each valid state $(j, S_2, \ldots, S_{k-1}, \emptyset)$ is reachable exactly the same way as in the proof of Lemma 7.

Now let $S_k \neq \emptyset$. As shown in the proof of Theorem 9, for each S, there is a string v_S over $\{a_{k-1}, b\}$ such that in the subset automaton for $L(A_{k-1})L(A_k)$ we have $(\{0\}, \emptyset)v_S = (\{0\}, S)$. Since we have a loop on both a_{k-1} and b in the initial state of each A_i with $1 \leq i \leq k-2$, we get

$$(0, \emptyset, \ldots, \emptyset, \emptyset) \xrightarrow{a_1^{n_1} a_2^{n_2} \cdots a_{k-2}^{n_{k-2}}} (0, \{0\}, \ldots, \{0\}, \{0\}, \emptyset) \xrightarrow{v_S} (0, \{0\}, \ldots, \{0\}, \{0\}, S).$$

Next, let w_{S_i} for $i = 2, \ldots, k-1$ be the strings over $\{a_{i-1}, a_i\}$ given by Lemma 6; recall that $f_i \notin S_i$ implies that the state f_i is not visited while reading w_{S_i}. Let $u = w_{S_{k-1}} \cdots w_{S_3} w_{S_2}$. Then the state $(0, \{0\}, \ldots, \{0\}, uS_k)$ is reachable as shown above. Since each a_i performs a permutation on A_k, we finally get

$$(0, \{0\}, \ldots, \{0\}, uS_k) \xrightarrow{u} (0, S_2, \ldots, S_{k-1}, S_k) \xrightarrow{a_1^j} (j, S_2, \ldots, S_{k-1}, S_k).$$

To prove distinguishability, let $p = (S_1, S_2, \ldots, S_k)$ and $q = (T_1, T_2, \ldots, T_k)$ be two distinct valid states of $\mathcal{D}(N)$. For each state r in $Q_{k-1} \cup Q_k$, the singleton set $\{r\}$ is co-reachable in N via a string in $\varepsilon + a_{k-1}b^*a_{k-1}^*$. By Lemma 1, the states p and q are distinguishable if they differ in a state in $Q_{k-1} \cup Q_k$.

Let $S_i \neq T_i$ for some i with $1 \leq i \leq k-2$, while $S_j = T_j$ if $j > i$. Without loss of generality, let $\ell \in S_i \setminus T_i$. First, we read $a_i^{f_i - \ell}$ to reach the final state f_i of A_i from p and get states

$$(S_1', \ldots, S_{i-1}', \{f_i\} \cup S_i', \{0\} \cup S_{i+1}', S_{i+2}', \ldots, S_k') \text{ and}$$
$$(T_1', \ldots, T_{i-1}', \quad T_i', \quad\quad T_{i+1}' \quad T_{i+2}', \ldots, T_k')$$

with $f_i \notin T_i'$. Now, the string $(a_{i+1}b)^{n_{i+1}}$ sends all states in $(i+1)$th components to state 0, and it fixes each state of Q_i except for 1 that is sent to 0. Since $f_i \geq 2$, after reading $(a_{i+1}b)^{n_{i+1}}$, we get states

$$(S_1'', \ldots, S_{i-1}'', \{f_i\} \cup S_i'', \{0\}, S_{i+2}'', \ldots, S_k'') \text{ and}$$
$$(T_1'', \ldots, T_{i-1}'', \quad T_i'', \quad T_{i+1}'', T_{i+2}'', \ldots, T_k'')$$

with $f_i \notin T_i''$, and $T_{i+1}'' = \{0\}$ or $T_{i+1}'' = \emptyset$. Finally, we read a_{i+1} that performs the circular permutation on Q_{i+1} and the identity on Q_i to get states

$$(S_1''', \ldots, S_{i-1}''', \{f_i\} \cup S_i''', \{0,1\}, S_{i+2}''', \ldots, S_k''') \text{ and}$$
$$(T_1''', \ldots, T_{i-1}''', \quad T_i''', \quad T_{i+1}''', T_{i+2}''', \ldots, T_k''')$$

with $T_{i+1}''' = \{1\}$ or $T_{i+1}''' = \emptyset$. These states differ in the state 0 of Q_{i+1}. By induction, the states p and q can be sent to two states that differ in a state of Q_{k-1}, and therefore are distinguishable. □

We conjecture that k symbols are necessary for describing witnesses for concatenation of k languages. We are able to prove this for $k = 3$.

Theorem 11. *The ternary alphabet used to describe witnesses for the concatenation of three languages in Theorem 10 is optimal.*

Proof (Proof Idea). Let $A_i = (Q_i, \{a, b\}, \cdot, s_i, \{f_i\})$ for $i = 1, 2, 3$ be binary DFAs. To meet the upper bound for the concatenation of three languages, both A_2 and A_3 must have one permutation and one non-permutation symbol. To reach the state $(0, Q_2 \setminus \{f_2\}, \emptyset)$, automaton A_2 must have a symbol, say a, that maps the set $Q_2 \setminus \{f_2\}$ onto $Q_2 \setminus \{f_2\}$. Then f_2 is reached on b in A_2 and $f_2 b \neq f_2$. Then, depending on whether or not b performs a permutation on Q_2, we can show that both a and b perform permutations on Q_3, a contradiction. □

6 Binary and Ternary Languages

In this section, we examine the state complexity of multiple concatenation on binary and ternary languages. Our aim is to show that in the binary case, the resulting complexity is still exponential in $n_2, n_3, \ldots, n_k$, and in the ternary case, it is the same as in the general case, up to a multiplicative constant.

Theorem 12. *Let $k \geq 2$, $n_1 \geq 3$, $n_2 \geq 4$, and $n_i \geq 3$ for $i = 3, 4, \ldots, k$. Let $A_1, A_2, \ldots, A_k$ be the binary DFAs from Fig. 5. Every DFA for the concatenation $L(A_1)L(A_2) \cdots L(A_k)$ has at least $n_1 - 1 + (1/2^{2k-2}) 2^{n_2+n_3+\cdots+n_k}$ states.*

Proof (Proof Idea). Let s_i and f_i be the initial and final states of A_i, respectively. Construct an NFA for $L(A_1)L(A_2) \cdots L(A_k)$ from the DFAs $A_1, A_2, \ldots, A_k$ as described in Sect. 3. In this NFA, the states f_i and f_i+1 with $2 \leq i \leq k-1$, as well as the state $f_k + 1$ are dead, and we can omit them.

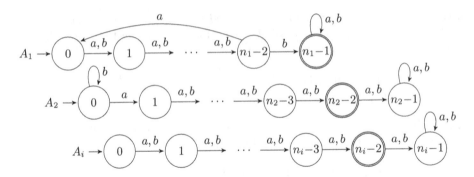

Fig. 5. Binary lower bound DFAs A_1, A_2, and A_i for $i = 3, 4, \ldots, k$ with
$\mathrm{sc}(L(A_1)L(A_2)\cdots L(A_k)) \geq n_1 - 1 + (1/2^{2k-2})\, 2^{n_2+n_3+\cdots+n_k}$.

In the subset automaton of the resulting NFA, each valid state $(j, \emptyset, \ldots, \emptyset)$
with $0 \leq j \leq n_1 - 1$ is reached from the initial state $(0, \emptyset, \ldots, \emptyset)$ by b^j, and the
state $(f_1, \{s_2\}, \emptyset, \ldots, \emptyset)$ is reached from $(f_1 - 1, \emptyset, \ldots, \emptyset)$ by b. Starting with the
state f_1, the NFA accepts all strings having an a in position $n_2 + n_3 \cdots + n_k - 2k + 2$ from the end, and we can show that every state $(f_1, \{s_2\} \cup S_2, S_3, \ldots, S_k)$
with $S_2 \subseteq \{1, 2, \ldots, n_2 - 3\}$, $S_i \subseteq \{0, 1, \ldots, n_i - 3\}$ for $i = 3, 4, \ldots, k - 1$
and $S_k \subseteq \{0, 1, \ldots, n_k - 2\}$ is reachable.

Next, each singleton set is co-reachable via a string in a^*, except for $\{q\}$
where q is a non-final state of A_1. By Lemma 1, the reachable states $(S_1, \ldots, S_k)$
and $(T_1, \ldots, T_k)$ are distinguishable if they differ in a state of A_i with $i \geq 2$ or
in f_1. Otherwise, the states $(i, \emptyset, \ldots, \emptyset)$ and $(j, \emptyset, \ldots, \emptyset)$ with $0 \leq i < j < f_1$ can
be sent to states that differ in f_1 by b^{f_1-j}.   □

Now, let us add the transitions on letter c to the binary automata from Fig. 5
as follows: $c: (0, 1, \ldots, n_1 - 1)$ in A_1, $c: (f_i \to f_i + 1)$ in A_i with $2 \leq i \leq k - 1$,
and $c: (0)$ in A_k. Denote the resulting DFAs by C_i $(1 \leq i \leq k)$. Then we can
prove the following result.

Theorem 13. *Let $k \geq 2$, $n_1 \geq 3$, $n_2 \geq 4$, and $n_i \geq 3$ for $i = 3, 4, \ldots, k$.*
Let $C_1, C_2, \ldots, C_k$ be the ternary automata described above. Then every DFA
for $L(C_1)L(C_2)\cdots L(C_k)$ has at least $(1/2^{2k-2})n_1 2^{n_2+n_3+\cdots+n_k}$ states.   □

The theorem above shows that the complexity of concatenation of k ternary
languages is the same as in the case of a general alphabet, up to a multiplicative
constant depending on k; cf. inequalities in Proposition 5 on page 4.

7   Unary Cyclic Languages

The state complexity of concatenation of two unary languages is $n_1 n_2$, and it
can be met by cyclic languages if $\gcd(n_1, n_2) = 1$ [8]. This gives a trivial upper
bound $n_1 n_2 \cdots n_k$ for concatenation of k unary languages. Here we show that a
tight upper bound for concatenation of k cyclic unary languages is much smaller.

Let $n_1, n_2, \ldots, n_k$ be positive integers with $\gcd(n_1, n_2, \ldots, n_k) = 1$.

Then $g(n_1, n_2, \ldots, n_k)$ denotes the Frobenius number, that is, the largest integer that cannot be expressed as $x_1 n_1 + x_2 n_2 + \cdots + x_k n_k$ for some non-negative integers $x_1, x_2, \ldots, x_k$. Denote $f(n_1, \ldots, n_k) = g(n_1, \ldots, n_k) + n_1 + \cdots + n_k$. Using this notation, we are able to prove the following result.

Theorem 14. *Let $A_1, \ldots, A_k$ be cyclic unary automata with $n_1, \ldots, n_k$ states, respectively. Let $d = \gcd(n_1, \ldots, n_k)$. Then $L(A_1) \cdots L(A_k)$ is recognized by a DFA with $d \cdot f(\frac{n_1}{d}, \ldots, \frac{n_k}{d}) - k + 1 + d$ states, and this bound is tight.*

Proof (Proof Idea). We show that $L(A_1) L(A_2) \cdots L(A_k)$ is recognized by a unary DFA with a tail of length $d \cdot f(\frac{n_1}{d}, \frac{n_2}{d}, \ldots, \frac{n_k}{d}) - k + 1$ and a cycle of size d. The proof follows almost line by line the proof of Theorem 8 in [6]. □

It is known that if $n_1 \leq \cdots \leq n_k$, then $g(n_1, n_2, \ldots, n_k) \leq n_1 n_k$. This gives an upper bound $n_1 n_k / d + n_1 + \cdots + n_k - k + 1 + d$ for concatenation of k cyclic languages where $n_1 \leq n_2 \leq \cdots \leq n_k$ and $d = \gcd(n_1, n_2, \ldots, n_k)$.

8   Conclusions

We examined in detail the state complexity of multiple concatenation of k languages. First, we described witness DFAs $A_1, A_2, \ldots, A_k$ over the $(k + 1)$-letter alphabet $\{a_1, a_2, \ldots, a_k\} \cup \{b\}$. Then we modified the first automaton of Maslov's [5] automata to get binary witnesses for the concatenation of two languages. Using our results concerning witnesses over a $(k + 1)$-letter alphabet as well as the results for modified Maslov's automata, we described witnesses for the concatenation of k languages over a k-letter alphabet. This solves an open problem stated in [1]. For $k = 3$, we proved that the ternary alphabet is optimal in the sense that the upper bound for the concatenation of three languages cannot be met by any binary languages. This provides a partial answer to the second open problem from [1].

We also considered multiple concatenation on binary and ternary languages, and obtained lower bounds $n_1 - 1 + (1/2^{2k-2}) 2^{n_2 + \cdots + n_k}$ and $(1/2^{2k-2}) n_1 2^{n_2 + \cdots + n_k}$, respectively. Finally, we investigated multiple concatenation on unary cyclic languages. We obtained a tight upper bound here, and we showed that for $k \geq 3$, it is much smaller than a trivial upper bound $n_1 n_2 \cdots n_k$, which is met by cyclic unary languages if $k = 2$ and $\gcd(n_2, n_2) = 1$ [8, Theorem 5.4].

Some problems remain open. If $n_2 = 1$, then the state complexity of the concatenation of two languages is n_1 [8, Theorem 2.4]. What is the state complexity of multiple concatenation if some languages may be equal to Σ^*? Next, we proved the optimality of a ternary alphabet for the concatenation of three languages. However, we cannot see any generalization of the proof. Is a k-letter alphabet for the concatenation of k languages optimal? Finally, we did not consider unary languages that are not cyclic.

References

1. Caron, P., Luque, J., Patrou, B.: State complexity of multiple catenations. Fund. Inform. **160**(3), 255–279 (2018). https://doi.org/10.3233/FI-2018-1683
2. Ésik, Z., Gao, Y., Liu, G., Yu, S.: Estimation of state complexity of combined operations. Theoret. Comput. Sci. **410**(35), 3272–3280 (2009). https://doi.org/10.1016/j.tcs.2009.03.026
3. Gao, Y., Yu, S.: State complexity approximation. In: Dassow, J., Pighizzini, G., Truthe, B. (eds.) DCFS 2009. EPTCS, vol. 3, pp. 121–130 (2009). https://doi.org/10.4204/EPTCS.3.11
4. Hopcroft, J.E., Ullman, J.D.: Introduction to Automata Theory, Languages and Computation. Addison-Wesley (1979)
5. Maslov, A.N.: Estimates of the number of states of finite automata. Soviet Math. Doklady **11**(5), 1373–1375 (1970)
6. Pighizzini, G., Shallit, J.O.: Unary language operations, state complexity and Jacobsthal's function. Internat. J. Found. Comput. Sci. **13**(1), 145–159 (2002). https://doi.org/10.1142/S012905410200100X
7. Sipser, M.: Introduction to the Theory of Computation. Cengage Learning (2012)
8. Yu, S., Zhuang, Q., Salomaa, K.: The state complexities of some basic operations on regular languages. Theoret. Comput. Sci. **125**(2), 315–328 (1994). https://doi.org/10.1016/0304-3975(92)00011-F

Combining Limited Parallelism and Nondeterminism in Alternating Finite Automata

Chris Keeler[(⊠)] and Kai Salomaa

School of Computing, Queen's University, Kingston, ON K7L 2N8, Canada
{keeler,ksalomaa}@cs.queensu.ca

Abstract. We introduce the existential width measure (respectively, the maximal existential width), which, roughly speaking, for an alternating finite automaton (AFA), counts the number of branches which do not need to be traversed in an accepting computation (respectively, the maximum number of branches which can be ignored in any computation tree of the AFA). We also define the combined width (respectively, the maximal combined width), by combining this new measure with an existing measure, the universal width (respectively, the maximal universal width), which counts the minimum number of branches of a computation tree which must be traversed for an AFA to accept a computation (respectively, the maximum number of branches which can be traversed in any computation tree of the AFA). We give a polynomial algorithm to decide whether the (maximal) combined width is bounded, and a construction showing that an AFA with finite combined width can be simulated by an NFA with only a polynomial blow-up in the number of states. We also improve the upper bound for deciding finiteness of an m-state NFA's tree width from $O(m^3)$ to $O(m^2)$.

1 Introduction

Deterministic and nondeterministic finite automata (DFA and NFA) are well understood models of computation for which a significant number of results are known. As an extension to nondeterminism, *alternation* was introduced by Chandra, Kozen, and Stockmeyer [1], and its presence in pushdown automata [1,9] and Turing machines [12] has been well-established. Alternation within the context of finite automata has subsequently been studied by King [8], Hromkovič [6], Geffert [2], and by Hospodár, Krajnáková, and Jirásková [4].

An automaton is said to *alternate* when it switches from an existential state to a universal state (or vice versa) [2]. A computation passing through a universal state must reach a final state across all nondeterministic branches, instead of at least one nondeterministic branch. The power of an AFA relies both on the presence of universal states, and the ability to alternate between universal and existential states. In the worst case, simulating an AFA with an NFA results in a doubly-exponential blow-up in the number of states required [1]. However,

© Springer Nature Switzerland AG 2020
G. Jirásková and G. Pighizzini (Eds.): DCFS 2020, LNCS 12442, pp. 91–103, 2020.
https://doi.org/10.1007/978-3-030-62536-8_8

there still exists an exponential state complexity blow-up simulating an AFA with at most k alternations using an AFA with at most $k - 1$ alternations [2]. The emptiness problem for AFAs was shown to be PSPACE-Complete even for unary alphabets [3], though it is polynomial for general alphabets under certain restrictions of an AFA's computation trees [7].

Restricted nondeterminism in automata has been measured in a number of different ways, likely the first being *ambiguity* [11,13]. Another "measure of nondeterminism" with a considerable number of results is the *tree width* [5,10]. There has also been a small amount of work done on restricted nondeterminism within the context of alternating machines [7]. However, little effort has been made towards examining the combination of restricted nondeterminism and alternation.

This paper is organized as follows. Section 2 gives the specifics for our model of alternating finite automata, introduces the notion of pruned computation trees, and fixes some notation used throughout the paper. Section 2.1 introduces the (maximal) universal width and (maximal) existential width, as well as several initial results concerning these new metrics. It also introduces the (maximal) combined width, which shows how these two metrics can measure the total amount of parallelism *and* nondeterminism present in a specific alternating computation. Section 3 presents several decision problems involving the new metrics which can be solved in polynomial time, including whether the maximal combined width of an AFA is bounded by a given constant, or whether the maximal existential width of an NFA is finite. It also shows that there is at most a polynomial blow-up in the number of states required by an NFA to simulate an AFA with bounded combined width, as compared to the general doubly-exponential bound [1]. As a corollary to these results, we improve the bound for deciding the finiteness of tree width for an m-state NFA from $O(m^3)$ [7] to $O(m^2)$. Section 4 gives a candidate structure for the greatest (maximal) existential width of any alternating machine.

2   Preliminaries

An AFA is a 6-tuple, $A = (Q_e, Q_u, \Sigma, \delta, q_0, F)$ where Q_e (the existential state set) and Q_u (the universal state set) are finite sets of states such that $Q_e \cap Q_u = \varnothing$, Σ is the input alphabet, $\delta : (Q_e \cup Q_u) \times \Sigma \rightarrow 2^{Q_e \cup Q_u}$ is the transition function, $q_0 \in Q_e \cup Q_u$ is the initial state, and $F \subseteq Q_e \cup Q_u$ is the set of final states. We use ε to mean the empty string, and A_q to mean A with a different specified starting state $q \in Q_e \cup Q_u$.

Remark 1. We note that the standard NFA model can be seen as an AFA where Q_e contains all of the states, and Q_u is the empty set.

We further define the *language* of an AFA, to account for the differences caused by universal states. We do so by defining them bottom-up with respect to their states.

Definition 1. *Let $A = (Q_e, Q_u, \Sigma, \delta, q_0, F)$ be an AFA, and A_q be a copy of the AFA with $q \in Q_e \cup Q_u$ as the initial state. We point out that $\varepsilon \in L(A_q)$ if $q \in F$. Consider $q \in Q_e \cup Q_u, a \in \Sigma$ where $\delta(q, a) = \{p_1, \ldots, p_n\}$. Then for $x \in \Sigma^*$, define:*

- *If $q \in Q_u$, then $ax \in L(A_q)$ if and only if $x \in L(A_{p_i})$ for all $1 \leqslant i \leqslant n$.*
- *If $q \in Q_e$, then $ax \in L(A_q)$ if and only if $x \in L(A_{p_i})$ for some $1 \leqslant i \leqslant n$.*

The language of A is defined as $L(A) = L(A_{q_0})$.

A *computation tree* of an AFA is a tree structure whose internal nodes are labeled by a tuple (p, a), for $p \in Q_e \cup Q_u, a \in \Sigma$ (i.e., each internal node is labeled by a state and character), and whose leaves are labeled by (q, ε) or the fail symbol $\bot$. We call a node of the computation tree T labeled by (p, a) a p-child of T, and the leaves of T labeled by (p, a) are called *state leaves*.

The computation tree of an AFA A on ε from $q \in Q_e \cup Q_u$, denoted $T_{A,q,\varepsilon}$ is the singleton node (q, ε). The computation tree of an AFA A on cv from q, denoted $T_{A,q,cv}$, such that $q \in Q_e \cup Q_u, c \in \Sigma, v \in \Sigma^*$ is defined inductively as the tree where:

- the root is labeled by (q, c), and
- the trees rooted at the children of (q, c) are
  - the computation trees $(T_{A,p_1,v}, \ldots, T_{A,p_n,v})$ if $\delta(q, c) = \{p_1, \ldots, p_n\}$, and
  - the failure node $\bot$ if $\delta(q, c) = \varnothing$ (that is, if $\delta(q, c)$ is undefined).

If a computation tree of an AFA A on a string x starts on the initial state of A, then we omit the state label, denoting it as $T_{A,x}$. If A is an NFA, this yields the computation trees as considered in [5].

For an AFA $A = (Q_e, Q_u, \Sigma, \delta, q_0, F)$ and a string cv, where $c \in \Sigma, v \in \Sigma^*$, a *pruned computation tree* of A on cv from $q \in Q_e \cup Q_u$ is obtained from $T_{A,q,cv}$, where $\delta(q, c) = \{p_1, \ldots, p_k\}$, as follows:

1. If q is an existential state, then replace $k-1$ of the children by a singleton tree consisting of a node labeled by a new symbol ψ (representing a pruning of the tree), and the final child $T_{A,p_i,v}$ by a pruned computation tree of $T_{A,p_i,v}$, for some $1 \leqslant i \leqslant k$.
2. If q is a universal state, then each child p_i, for all $1 \leqslant i \leqslant k$, is replaced by a pruned computation tree on $T_{A,p_i,v}$.

We note that each pruned computation tree represents one specific alternating computation in an AFA.

We use stateLeaves(T) to denote the set of all leaves in a tree T labeled by a state, and failLeaves(T) to denote the set of all leaves of a tree T labeled by the fail symbol $\bot$. We call leaves labeled by ψ *cut leaves*, and use cutLeaves(T) to denote the set of all cut leaves in a tree T.

The set of all pruned computation trees of a tree T is denoted $\bowtie(T)$. A pruned computation tree is accepting if all of its leaves labeled by states are labeled by accepting states, and no leaves are labeled by the fail symbol $\bot$. We denote the set of all accepting pruned computations on a tree T as $\bowtie^{acc}(T)$. A string x is accepted by an AFA A if and only if $\bowtie^{acc}(T_{A,x}) \neq \varnothing$.

2.1   Tree Width of Alternating Machines

The *tree width* [10] of an AFA A on a string x, denoted $\mathrm{tw}(A, x)$, is the number of state leaves and fail symbols in the computation tree $T_{A,x}$. Since there may be many pruned computation trees for a single alternating computation tree, we extend the notion of tree width to operate on pruned computation trees.

Definition 2. *For an AFA A and a pruned computation tree T^p of A, the universal width of T^p, denoted $\mathrm{uw}(T^p)$, is the number of leaves labeled in T^p by a state, and the maximal universal width, denoted $\mathrm{uw}^{\max}(T^p)$, is the number of leaves in T^p labeled by a state or by the fail symbol. Formally, these are:*

$$\mathrm{uw}(T^p) = |\mathrm{stateLeaves}(T^p)|, \ and$$

$$\mathrm{uw}^{\max}(T^p) = |\mathrm{stateLeaves}(T^p)| + |\mathrm{failLeaves}(T^p)|.$$

We extend the (maximal) universal width to be on strings:

Definition 3. *For an AFA A and a string $x \in \Sigma^*$, the universal width of A on x, denoted $\mathrm{uw}(A, x)$, is the smallest number of leaves labeled by a state in any accepting pruned computation tree of $T_{A,x}$, and the maximal universal width of A on x, denoted $\mathrm{uw}^{\max}(A, x)$, is the largest number of leaves labeled by a state or fail symbol in any pruned computation tree of $T_{A,x}$. Formally, these are:*

$$\mathrm{uw}(A, x) = \min\{\mathrm{uw}(T^p) \mid T^p \in {\succcurlyeq}^{\mathrm{acc}}(T_{A,x})\}, \ and$$
$$\mathrm{uw}^{\max}(A, x) = \max\{\mathrm{uw}^{\max}(T^p) \mid T^p \in {\succcurlyeq}(T_{A,x})\}.$$

By counting all of the leaves labeled by states across all pruned computation trees for a given string x, the universal width of an AFA A on x measures the universal parallelism in the "best" alternating computation, that is, the number of branches. Similarly, the maximal universal width of an AFA A on a string x measures the universal parallelism in the "worst" alternating computation, that is, the computation tree with the greatest number of branches needing to be checked to determine the membership of x in the language $L(A)$.

We can also measure the amount of nondeterminism present in an alternating computation.

Definition 4. *For an AFA A and a pruned computation tree T^p of A, the existential width of T^p, denoted $\mathrm{ew}(T^p)$ is the number of leaves labeled by the symbol ψ. Formally, this is:*

$$\mathrm{ew}(T^p) = |\mathrm{cutLeaves}(T^p)|.$$

Again, we extend the measure to be on strings:

Definition 5. *For an AFA A and a string $x \in \Sigma^*$, the existential width of A on x, denoted $\mathrm{ew}(A, x)$, is the smallest number of leaves labeled by the symbol ψ in any accepting pruned computation tree of $T_{A,x}$, and the maximal existential width of A on x, denoted $\mathrm{ew}^{\max}(A, x)$, is the largest number of leaves labeled by the symbol ψ in any pruned computation tree of $T_{A,x}$. Formally, these are:*

$$\mathrm{ew}(A, x) = \min\{\mathrm{ew}(T^p) \mid T^p \in {\succcurlyeq}^{\mathrm{acc}}(T_{A,x})\}, \ and$$
$$\mathrm{ew}^{\max}(A, x) = \max\{\mathrm{ew}(T^p) \mid T^p \in {\succcurlyeq}(T_{A,x})\}.$$

Intuitively, the existential width (respectively, the maximal existential width) of an AFA on a string x measures, roughly speaking, the smallest (respectively, the largest) number of nondeterministic branches that are not followed by a particular alternating computation on x.

We extend the tree width, (maximal) universal width, and (maximal) existential width functions as functions on the natural numbers and AFAs in the normal manner. For $f \in \{\text{tw}, \text{uw}, \text{ew}, \text{uw}^{\max}, \text{ew}^{\max}\}$:

$$f(A, \ell) = \max\{f(A, x) \mid x \in \Sigma^\ell\}, \text{ and } f(A) = \sup_{\ell \in \mathbb{N}}\{f(A, \ell)\}.$$

We can calculate the maximal existential width of an AFA through the following recursive definition on computation trees. For an AFA $A = (Q_e, Q_u, \Sigma, \delta, q_0, F)$, a state $q \in Q_e \cup Q_u$, and a string cv, such that $c \in \Sigma, v \in \Sigma^*$

- $\text{ew}^{\max}(A_q, \varepsilon) = 0$

- $\text{ew}^{\max}(A_q, cv) = \begin{cases} |\delta(q, c)| - 1 + \max\limits_{r \in \delta(q,c)} \{\text{ew}^{\max}(A_r, v)\} & \text{if } q \in Q_e, \text{ or} \\ \sum\limits_{r \in \delta(q,c)} \text{ew}^{\max}(A_r, v) & \text{if } q \in Q_u. \end{cases}$

We note that a similar recursive definition exists for calculating the existential width of an AFA, but that the conditions which cause the maximal existential width of an AFA to grow infinitely are insufficient in some cases to also cause the existential width of an AFA to grow infinitely. However, using this recursive definition for maximal existential width, Lemma 1 is proved similarly to how the conditions for infinite tree width are proved [10].

Lemma 1. *[10] Let $A = (Q_e, Q_u, \Sigma, \delta, q_0, F)$ be an AFA. Then $\text{ew}^{\max}(A)$ is infinite if and only if there exists a state $q \in Q_e$, a letter $c \in \Sigma$, and a string $v \in \Sigma^*$ such that $|\delta(q, c)| \geq 2$ and $q \in \delta(q, cv)$.*

That is, an AFA will have infinite maximal existential width if it has a nondeterministic state involved in a cycle.

We know that, for an m-state AFA A, if the tree width of A is finite, then $\text{tw}(A) \leq 2^{m-2}$ [10]. Since the tree width of an AFA is defined over *unpruned* computation trees, we get the following inequalities between the measures.

Corollary 1. *For any AFA A and string x:*

- $\text{uw}(A, x) \leq \text{uw}^{\max}(A, x) \leq \text{tw}(A, x)$, $\text{uw}(A) \leq \text{uw}^{\max}(A) \leq \text{tw}(A)$,
- $\text{ew}(A, x) \leq \text{ew}^{\max}(A, x) \leq \text{tw}(A, x)$, *and* $\text{ew}(A) \leq \text{ew}^{\max}(A) \leq \text{tw}(A)$.

In fact, since the maximal existential width and maximal universal width of an AFA A are always at most the tree width of A, we get the following corollary.

Corollary 2. *Let A be an AFA. Then $\text{tw}(A)$ is infinite if and only if $\text{ew}^{\max}(A)$ is infinite or $\text{uw}^{\max}(A)$ is infinite.*

And for NFAs, in the finite case we get an upper bound on the maximal existential width.

Theorem 1. *Let A be an m-state NFA such that $\mathrm{ew}^{\max}(A)$ is finite. Then*
$\mathrm{ew}^{\max}(A) \leqslant \frac{(m-2)(m-1)}{2}$.

Proof. Let $A_m = (Q, \Sigma, \delta, q_0, F)$ be the m-state unary NFA such that $\mathrm{ew}^{\max}(A)$ is finite and the greatest among all m-state unary NFAs.

Let $q \in Q$ be an arbitrary state such that $|\delta(q, a)| \geqslant 2$, that is, q has outgoing nondeterministic transitions. Then q cannot reach itself, since that would cause $\mathrm{ew}^{\max}(A)$ to be infinite. So then all $1 \leqslant k \leqslant m$ nondeterministic states are in a partial ordering of reachability, $p_1 \leqslant \ldots \leqslant p_k$. That is, there does not exist a string $x \in \Sigma^*$ such that $p_j \in \delta(p_i, x)$, for $1 \leqslant i \leqslant j \leqslant k$.

Let $d_1, \ldots, d_\ell$ be the deterministic states of Q. Assume there exists a d_h, for $1 \leqslant h \leqslant \ell$ such that $p_1 \leqslant \ldots \leqslant p_i \leqslant d_h \leqslant p_j$ That is, d_h is a deterministic state inbetween two nondeterministic states, p_i and p_j. But, p_j cannot be any of the states $p_1, \ldots, p_i$, as this would cause there to be a cycle on a nondeterministic state, and thus $\mathrm{ew}^{\max}(A)$ would not be finite.

So then d_h's transition must lead to some other state. However, if d_h transitions to *any* nondeterministic state p_j, then there are at least two states p_{j+1} and p_{j+2} such that $p_{j+1}, p_{j+2} \in \delta(p_j, a)$. This would mean that adding transitions from d_h to p_{j+1} and p_{j+2} would increase the maximal existential width, and thus $\mathrm{ew}^{\max}(A)$ is not maximal. So then d_h cannot lead to a nondeterministic state.

Therefore, the partial ordering of reachability must be $p_1 \leqslant \ldots \leqslant p_k \leqslant d_1 \leqslant \ldots \leqslant d_\ell$. There cannot be only one deterministic state, because then the only way to have $|\delta(p_k, a)| \geqslant 2$ is for p_k to lead to d_1 and one of the states $p_1, \ldots, p_k$, and this would cause infinite maximal existential width. So then there must be at least two deterministic states in the tail.

Since adding extra deterministic states at the end of a computation does not increase the maximal existential width, the number of deterministic states must be minimized. Therefore, the m-state NFA with the greatest maximal existential width consists of $m - 2$ nondeterministic states and 2 deterministic states, all maximally connected without forming a cycle.

We note additionally that adding non-unary transitions would not serve to increase the maximal existential width, and so this upper bound holds for NFAs of any alphabet size.

If none of the existential choices made during an alternating computation precede the universal branching, then the number of parallel branches is the same regardless of how the computation tree is pruned.

Lemma 2. *Let $A = (Q_e, Q_u, \Sigma, \delta, q_0, F)$, and $x \in \Sigma^*$ a string.*

(i) *If there exists a partial ordering on the nodes of $T_{A,x}$ such that no node labeled by a universal state occurs after a node labeled by a nondeterministic existential state, then $\mathrm{uw}(T_{A,x}) = \mathrm{uw}^{\max}(T_{A,x})$.*

(ii) *If there exists a partial ordering on the states such that no universal state occurs after a nondeterministic existential state, then the universal width and maximal universal width of A are equal. More formally: for all $q \in Q_u$, $p \in Q_e$, and $a \in \Sigma$, if $q \in \delta(p, a) \implies |\delta(p, a)| = 1$, then $\mathrm{uw}(A) = \mathrm{uw}^{\max}(A)$.*

For an AFA A, a string x, and a pruned computation tree $T^p \in \preccurlyeq(T_{A,x})$, the *combined width* of T^p is a pair of numbers (u, e), where u is the number of state leaves in T^p, and e is the number of cut leaves in T^p. Similarly, the *maximal combined width* of a pruned computation tree $T^p \in \preccurlyeq(T_{A,x})$ is a pair of numbers (u, e) where u is the number of state leaves and fail leaves in T^p, and e is the number of cut leaves in T^p. Formally:

$$\mathrm{cw}(T^p) = (\mathrm{uw}(T^p), \ \mathrm{ew}(T^p)), \ \text{and}$$

$$\mathrm{cw}^{\mathrm{max}}(T^p) = (\mathrm{uw}^{\mathrm{max}}(T^p), \ \mathrm{ew}(T^p)).$$

That is, the (maximal) combined width of a pruned computation tree measures both nondeterminism and universal parallelism in a specific alternating computation. Since, for a given AFA and string, there may be many pruned computation trees, we further specify the (maximal) combined width of AFAs on strings. The combined width of an AFA A on a string x, denoted $\mathrm{cw}(A, x)$, is the set of minimal elements from the set $\{\mathrm{cw}(T^p) \mid T^p \in \preccurlyeq^{\mathrm{acc}}(T_{A,x})\}$, where here "minimal" means a pair of natural numbers minimal with respect to the partial ordering $(a, b) \leqslant (c, d)$ if and only if $a \leqslant c$ and $b \leqslant d$. We define similarly the maximal combined width of an AFA A on a string x, denoted $\mathrm{cw}^{\mathrm{max}}(A, x)$, as the set of maximal elements from the set $\{\mathrm{cw}^{\mathrm{max}}(T^p) \mid T^p \in \preccurlyeq(T_{A,x})\}$.

For an AFA A and a string x, we say the (maximal) combined width of A on x is upper bounded by a pair (u, e) if the (maximal) universal width of A on x is at most u, and the (maximal) existential width of A on x is at most e.

Example 1. Let A be the AFA in Fig. 1. A has four possible pruned computation trees on strings of at least length 2:

For these four trees, we get $\mathrm{cw}(T_1) = (3, 1)$, $\mathrm{cw}(T_2) = (2, 2)$, $\mathrm{cw}(T_3) = \mathrm{cw}(T_4) = (1, 3)$. So then $\mathrm{uw}(A, aa) = 1$ and $\mathrm{ew}(A, aa) = 1$, but $\mathrm{cw}(A, aa)$ is not upper bounded by $(1, 1)$. Since none of the pairs are minimal or maximal with respect to the partial ordering, we get that $\mathrm{cw}(A, aa) = \mathrm{cw}^{\mathrm{max}}(A, aa) = \{(1, 3), (2, 2), (3, 1)\}$. Since $\mathrm{uw}^{\mathrm{max}}(A, aa) = 3$ and $\mathrm{ew}^{\mathrm{max}}(A, aa) = 3$, then $\mathrm{cw}(A, x)$ and $\mathrm{cw}^{\mathrm{max}}(A, x)$ are both upper bounded by the pair $(3, 3)$, even though there does not exist a tree T such that $\mathrm{cw}(T) = (3, 3)$ or $\mathrm{cw}^{\mathrm{max}}(T) = (3, 3)$.

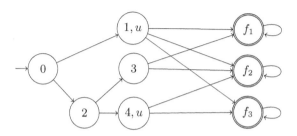

Fig. 1. AFA A where all transitions are on unary symbol a. Universal states are marked with an additional label 'u', and existential states are given as normal.

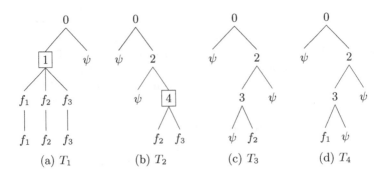

Fig. 2. Pruned computation trees of A. Universal states are denoted by squares.

We define the (maximal) combined width over natural numbers and on AFAs similarly to the (maximal) existential and (maximal) universal widths, except as sets of pairs. Formally, for $f \in \{cw, cw^{max}\}$: $f(A, \ell)$ is the set of maximal elements from the set $\{ \bigcup_{x \in \Sigma^\ell} f(A, x) \}$, and $f(A)$ is the set of supremal elements from the set $\{ \bigcup_{\ell \in \mathbb{N}} f(A, \ell) \}$. That is, $f(A)$ is the set of maximal elements across all strings of any length if there exists such a maximum, and is otherwise infinite. We say that the (maximal) combined width of A is upper bounded by a pair (u, e) if, for all strings $x \in \Sigma^*$ the (maximal) combined width of A on x is upper bounded by (u, e). If the (maximal) combined width of A is upper bounded by a pair (u, e), then we call A a finite (maximal) combined width AFA (Fig. 2).

Lemma 3. *Let A be an AFA, x be a string, $(u_1, e_1) \in cw(A, x)$, and $(u_2, e_2) \in cw^{max}(A, x)$. Then*

- *$uw(A, x) \leqslant u_1$ and $u_2 \leqslant uw^{max}(A, x)$, and*
- *$ew(A, x) \leqslant e_1$ and $e_2 \leqslant ew^{max}(A, x)$.*

Remark 2. Let A be an AFA and x an arbitrary string. If A is a DFA, then the (maximal) combined width of A on x is $\{(1, 0)\}$. If A is an NFA, then the (maximal) combined width of A on x is a set of pairs of the form $(1, e)$, for $e \in \mathbb{N}$. If A is a UFA (that is, all states are universal), or if all existential states of A are deterministic, then the (maximal) combined width of A on x is a set of pairs of the form $(u, 0)$, for $u \in \mathbb{N}$.

3   Decision Problems

Theorem 2. *Let A be an m-state AFA, and u, e be constants. Then we can decide whether or not $cw^{max}(A) \leqslant (u, e)$ in $O(m^u \cdot e)$ time.*

Proof. Let $A = (Q_u, Q_e, \Sigma, \delta, q_0, F)$ be an m-state AFA, and let $u, e \in \mathbb{N}$. We construct NFA B such that $L(B) \neq \varnothing$ if and only if $cw^{max}(A) \leqslant (u, e)$ does not hold. That is, $L(B) \neq \varnothing$ if and only if there exists a string x such that $uw(A, x) > u$ or $ew(A, x) > e$.

– States of B are $(u+1)$-tuples of states of A. That is, a state $(p_1, \ldots, p_u, g)$ where $p_h \in Q_e \cup Q_u \cup \{\#\}$, $1 \leqslant h \leqslant u$, $0 \leqslant g \leqslant e$, and $\#$ is a "dummy symbol". B nondeterministically simulates the steps of A, and g is a counter which keeps track of the number of ψ leaves.

– The start state of B is $(q_0, \#, \ldots, \#, 0)$.

– Transitions of B simulate transitions of A on all components of the tuple. For each state $b = (e_1, \ldots, e_y, u_1, \ldots, u_z, \#, \ldots, \#, g)$ of B where $\{e_1, \ldots, e_y\} \subseteq Q_e$, $\{u_1, \ldots, u_z\} \subseteq Q_u$ and each character $a \in \Sigma$:

  • Let $\delta(e_i, a) = \{s_{i,1}, \ldots, s_{i,k_i}\}$ for $1 \leqslant i \leqslant y$ and $1 \leqslant k_i$.
  • Let $\delta(u_j, a) = \{t_{j,1}, \ldots, t_{j,\ell_j}\}$ for $1 \leqslant j \leqslant z$ and $1 \leqslant \ell_j$.
  • If state b has at least $\sum_{j=1}^{z}(\ell_j - 1)$ remaining dummy symbols, then for
    $s_i \in \delta(e_i, a)$, $1 \leqslant i \leqslant y$, b will have outgoing nondeterministic transitions to all states

$$(s_1, \ldots, s_y, t_{1,1} \ldots, t_{1,\ell_1}, \ldots, t_{z,1}, \ldots t_{z,\ell_z}, \#, \ldots, \#, g'),$$

    such that $g' = g - y + \sum_{i=1}^{y} |\delta(e_i, a)|$.

    That is, for each universal state u_j, u_j and $\ell_j - 1$ dummy symbols are replaced in the tuple by $t_{j,1}, \ldots, t_{j,\ell_j}$, each existential state e_i is replaced by one of its successors in $\delta(e_i, a)$, and the cut symbol count is increased by the number of existential branches removed by taking these specific existential transitions.

  • If b has fewer than $\sum_{j=1}^{z}(\ell_j - 1)$ remaining dummy symbols, or if $g > e$,
    then the transition on a from b instead leads to the sink state.

– We note that a tuple with no remaining dummy symbols can only continue its simulation further if its transitions do not try to add any more components, and a tuple whose count value is already e can only continue its simulation if its transitions are deterministic.

– The only accepting state in B is the sink state, meaning that $L(B) \neq \varnothing$ exactly when some pruned computation tree has at least $u + 1$ branches, or if the "count" of pruned branches exceeds e.

– The language of B is then non-empty if and only if the maximal combined width of A is not bounded by (u, e).

Since B has at most $(m+1)^u \cdot e$ states, this gives a polynomial time algorithm to decide whether the maximal combined width is bounded by (u, e).   □

We note that if the existential width of an AFA A is at most polynomially larger than the number of states of A, then the Theorem 2's complexity remains polynomial. In particular, since by Theorem 1 the maximal existential width of an NFA is at most polynomially larger than the number of states, then we can decide whether the maximal existential width of an NFA is bounded by a specific constant, or even whether it is finite.

Corollary 3. *Let A be an m-state NFA. Then we can decide whether or not* $\mathrm{ew}^{\max}(A)$ *is finite in* $O(m^2)$ *time.*

And since by Corollary 2, the tree width of an *NFA* is infinite if and only if the maximal existential width is infinite, then we also improve the known bound for deciding the finiteness of an NFA's tree width. Previously, the best-known upper bound for deciding finiteness of an m-state NFA's tree width was $O(m^3)$ [7].

Corollary 4. *Let A be an m-state NFA. Then we can decide whether or not* $\mathrm{tw}(A)$ *is finite in* $O(m^2)$ *time.*

We use a similar construction as in Theorem 2 to efficiently simulate finite combined width AFAs with NFAs. This is in contrast to the general simulation of an m-state AFA by an NFA, which can require as many as 2^{2^m} states [1].

Theorem 3. *Let A be an m-state AFA, such that, for some constants u and e, every string* $w \in L(A)$ *has a pruned computation tree* T^p *such that* $\mathrm{cw}(T^p) \leqslant (u, e)$. *Then* $(m + 1)^u \cdot (e + 1)$ *states are sufficient for an NFA to simulate A.*

We can also decide whether or not an AFA's combined width is bounded by a specific pair of natural numbers.

Theorem 4. *Let A be an AFA, and* $u, e \in \mathbb{N}$. *Then it is decidable whether, for all strings* $w \in L(A)$, *there exists an accepting pruned computation tree* $T^p_{A,w}$, *such that* $\mathrm{cw}(T^p_{A,w}) \leqslant (u, e)$.

We know that, if the maximal universal width of an m-state AFA is finite, then it is at most 2^{m-2} [7]. Under the assumption that the maximal universal width of an m-state AFA is finite, then we can use the construction from Theorem 4, with 2^{m-2} as our u value, and decide whether the existential width of that AFA is bounded by some value e.

Corollary 5. *For an AFA with finite universal width, it is decidable whether the existential width of A is bounded by* $e \in \mathbb{N}$.

We also know, by Corollary 1, that the (maximal) existential width of any AFA A is at most the tree width of A. So then we can also decide, for an m-state AFA with finite tree width, whether the combined width is also bounded, by using the construction from Theorem 4 with 2^{m-2} as our u and e values.

Corollary 6. *Let A be an AFA with finite tree width. Then it is decidable whether the existential width, or, the combined width of A is bounded.*

If the construction does not involve the universal width, it is possible that there is a more efficient way to decide whether the existential width is bounded.

Question 1. For a given AFA A, does there exist a polynomial algorithm to decide whether A has bounded existential width?

4 Width Measure Bounds

If an AFA is acyclic, then there exists a "largest" computation tree for that AFA, where, by largest we mean a tree with the greatest number of internal and leaf nodes, where an "internal" node is a node with at least one child node not labeled by the fail symbol $\perp$.

Lemma 4. *Let A be an m-state unary acyclic AFA. Then the computation tree $T_{A,a^{m-1}}$ has:*

(i) the great est number of leaves for any computation tree on A, and
(ii) the greatest number of internal nodes for any computation tree on A.

We note that we avoid double-counting the nodes leading to fail nodes $\perp$ by not considering them as leaves or internal nodes.

If an AFA's cycles are all on sink states, then its computation trees still have a bounded number of leaf nodes.

Lemma 5. *Let A be an m-state unary AFA whose only cycles appear on sink states. Then the computation tree $T_{A,a^{m-1}}$ has the greatest number of leaves for any computation tree on A.*

We know that there exists an m-state acyclic AFA whose (maximal) universal width is 2^{m-2} [7]. We use this, in part, to get the following result on the maximal number of internal nodes for an acyclic AFA.

Lemma 6. *Let A be an m-state acyclic unary AFA. Then T_{A,a^ℓ} has at most 2^{m-1} internal and leaf nodes, for any $\ell \geqslant 1$.*

We note that, since the AFAs A_m given in Lemma 6 contain only universal states, then no nodes are removed from the computation tree during a pruning.

Lemma 7. *For $|Q_e| \geqslant 3$ and $|Q_u| \geqslant 1$, there exists an AFA $A = (Q_e, Q_u, \Sigma, \delta, q_0, F)$ such that*

$$\mathrm{ew}(A) = 2^{|Q_u|-1} \cdot \binom{|Q_e|-1}{2}, \quad \text{and } \mathrm{ew}^{\max}(A) = 2^{|Q_u|-1} \cdot \binom{|Q_e|}{3}.$$

Taking an m-state AFA of the form given in Fig. 3, the existential width (respectively, the maximal existential width) is maximized when there are 4 or 5 existential states (respectively, 5 or 6 existential states), and the remaining state(s) are universal.

Theorem 5. *There exists an m-state AFA A and an m-state AFA A' such that*

$$\mathrm{ew}(A) = 3 \cdot 2^{m-5}, \qquad \mathrm{ew}^{\max}(A') = 5 \cdot 2^{m-5},$$

$$\mathrm{cw}(A) = (2^{m-5}, \ 3 \cdot 2^{m-5}), \ \text{and } \mathrm{cw}^{\max}(A') = (2^{m-7}, \ 5 \cdot 2^{m-5}).$$

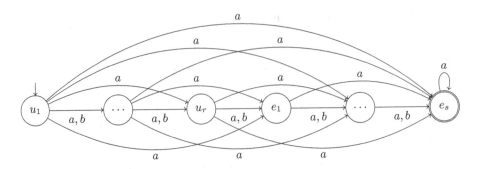

Fig. 3. An AFA with r universal states, s existential states, an existential width of $2^{r-1} \cdot \binom{s-1}{2}$, and a maximal existential width of $2^{r-1} \cdot \binom{s}{3}$.

Acknowledgements. Research supported by NSERC grant OGP0147224.

References

1. Chandra, A.K., Kozen, D.C., Stockmeyer, L.J.: Alternation. J. ACM **28**(1), 114–133 (1981)
2. Geffert, V.: An alternating hierarchy for finite automata. Theor. Comput. Sci. **445**, 1–24 (2012)
3. Holzer, M.: On emptiness and counting for alternating finite automata. In: Developments in Language Theory II, At the Crossroads of Mathematics, Computer Science and Biology, Magdeburg, Germany, 17–21 July 1995, pp. 88–97 (1995)
4. Hospodár, M., Jirásková, G., Krajňáková, I.: Operations on Boolean and alternating finite automata. In: Fomin, F.V., Podolskii, V.V. (eds.) CSR 2018. LNCS, vol. 10846, pp. 181–193. Springer, Cham (2018). https://doi.org/10.1007/978-3-319-90530-3_16
5. Hromkovič, J., Seibert, S., Karhumäki, J., Klauck, H., Schnitger, G.: Communication complexity method for measuring nondeterminism in finite automata. Inform. Comput **172**(2), 202–217 (2002)
6. Hromkovic, J.: On the power of alternation in automata theory. J. Comput. Syst. Sci. **31**(1), 28–39 (1985)
7. Keeler, C., Salomaa, K.: Alternating finite automata with limited universal branching. In: Leporati, A., Martín-Vide, C., Shapira, D., Zandron, C. (eds.) LATA 2020. LNCS, vol. 12038, pp. 196–207. Springer, Cham (2020). https://doi.org/10.1007/978-3-030-40608-0_13
8. King, K.N.: Alternating multihead finite automata (extended abstract). In: Automata, Languages and Programming, 8th Colloquium, Acre (Akko), Israel, July 13–17, 1981, Proceedings, pp. 506–520 (1981)
9. Moriya, E.: A grammatical characterization of alternating pushdown automata. Theor. Comput. Sci. **67**(1), 75–85 (1989)
10. Palioudakis, A., Salomaa, K., Akl, S.G.: State complexity of finite tree width NFAs. J. Autom. Lang. Comb. **17**(2–4), 245–264 (2012)
11. Ravikumar, B., Ibarra, O.H.: Relating the type of ambiguity of finite automata to the succinctness of their representation. SIAM J. Comput. **18**(6), 1263–1282 (1989)

12. Ruzzo, W.L.: Tree-size bounded alternation. J. Comput. Syst. Sci. **21**(2), 218–235 (1980)
13. Weber, A., Seidl, H.: On the degree of ambiguity of finite automata. Theoret. Comput. Sci. **88**(2), 325–349 (1991)

Longer Shortest Strings in Two-Way Finite Automata

Stanislav Krymski and Alexander Okhotin[(✉)] [iD]

Department of Mathematics and Computer Science, St. Petersburg State University,
7/9 Universitetskaya nab, 199034 Saint Petersburg, Russia
krymskiy.stas@yandex.ru, alexander.okhotin@spbu.ru

Abstract. In a recent paper, Dobronravov et al. ("On the length of of shortest strings accepted by two-way finite automata", DLT 2019) prove that the shortest string in a language recognized by an n-state two-way finite automaton (2DFA) can be at least $7^{n/5} - 1$ symbols long, improved to $10^{n/5} - 1 = \Omega(1.584^n)$ in their latest contribution. The lower bound was obtained using "direction-determinate" 2DFA, which always remember their direction of motion at the last step, and used an alphabet of size $\Theta(n)$. In this paper, the method of Dobronravov et al. is extended to a new, more general class: the semi-direction-determinate 2DFA. This yields n-state 2DFA with shortest strings of length $7^{n/4} - 1 = \Omega(1.626^n)$. Furthermore, the construction is adapted to use a fixed alphabet, resulting in shortest strings of length $\Omega(1.275^n)$. It is also shown that an n-state semi-direction-determinate 2DFA can be transformed to a one-way NFA with $O(\frac{1}{\sqrt{n}}3^n)$ states.

1 Introduction

The length of the shortest string in a language is a natural descriptional complexity measure. For one-way nondeterministic finite automata (1NFA) with n states, this length is at most $n - 1$, as the length of the shortest part to an accepting state. For other models, the same question turns out to be much more interesting. The length of shortest strings *not* accepted by an n-state 1NFA was studied by Ellul et al. [5]; Alpoge et al. [1] studied shortest strings in intersections of deterministic one-way automata (1DFA); Chistikov et al. [2] investigated the same question for counter automata. The length of shortest strings in formal grammars was estimated by Pierre [11].

For deterministic two-way finite automata (2DFA) with n states, it is no surprise that the shortest string can be of length exponential in n: the well-known result by Kozen [9] on the PSPACE-completeness of their emptiness problem implicitly relies on this fact. At the same time, an exponential upper bound on this length is given by transforming a 2DFA to a one-way nondeterministic automaton (1NFA) by the method of Kapoutsis [7], which yields $\binom{2n}{n+1} = \Theta(\frac{1}{\sqrt{n}}4^n)$ states. Therefore, the length of the shortest string is less

Research supported by Russian Science Foundation, project 18-11-00100.

G. Jirásková and G. Pighizzini (Eds.): DCFS 2020, LNCS 12442, pp. 104–116, 2020.
https://doi.org/10.1007/978-3-030-62536-8_9

than 4^n. Overall, the longest length of a shortest string is of the order $\Theta(1)^n$, with the base of exponentiation bounded by 4. The question is, what is the exact base?

This question was first addressed in a recent paper by Dobronravov et al. [3], who proposed a method for constructing 2DFA with long shortest strings. Their method is based on taking a small base 2DFA with k states and a shortest string of length $\ell - 1$, and then constructing n-state 2DFA that simulate the base automaton on multiple levels for different subsets of the alphabet, ultimately obtaining a shortest string of length $\Omega((\sqrt[k]{\ell})^n)$. The base 2DFA must belong to a subclass of *direction-determinate 2DFA*; these are automata that remember the direction of the last transition in their state. Dobronravov et al. [3,4] presented a base 2DFA with 5 states and with a shortest string of length 9, leading to n-state 2DFA with shortest strings of length $\Omega((\sqrt[5]{10})^n) \geqslant \Omega(1.584^n)$.

The method of Dobronravov et al. [3] relies on finding sophisticated small automata, and the direction-determinance requirement makes it complicated. Furthermore, the n-state 2DFA constructed are also direction-determinate, and since it is known that every n-state automaton from this class can be transformed to an equivalent 1NFA with only $\binom{n}{\lfloor n/2 \rfloor} = \Theta(\frac{1}{\sqrt{n}}2^n)$ states [6], this method cannot possibly provide shortest strings of length 2^n or more.

This paper presents an improvement to the method of Dobronravov et al. [3], based on relaxing the condition of direction-determinacy. A more general class of *semi-direction-determinate two-way automata* is introduced, and it is shown that small examples from this class can be used to construct n-state 2DFA with shortest accepted strings of exponential length. An example of a 3-state semi-direction-determinate 2DFA with a shortest string of length 3 is presented in Sect. 3: to compare, a 3-state direction-determinate 2DFA cannot have shortest string longer than 2 symbols. In Sect. 4, the construction of Dobronravov et al. [3] is generalized to support semi-direction-determinate automata.

The original construction uses an alphabet of size linear in n, the new construction may use exponentially many symbols. In Sect. 5, the construction is improved to use a fixed alphabet independent of n, at the expense of obtaining shorter longest strings.

The resulting new lower bounds on the length of shortest strings are presented in Sect. 6. The constructions are based on a provided example of a 4-state semi-direction-determinate 2DFA with a shortest string of length 6. This leads to n-state 2DFA over a growing alphabet with shortest strings of length $\Omega(1.626^n)$ and 2DFA over a fixed alphabet with shortest strings of length $\Omega(1.275^n)$.

The last result of this paper is a transformation of n-state semi-direction-determinate 2DFA to 1NFA with $O(\frac{1}{\sqrt{n}}3^n)$ states.

2   Definitions

Definition 1. *A* nondeterministic two-way finite automaton *(2NFA) is a quintuple* $\mathcal{A} = (\Sigma, Q, Q_0, \delta, F)$, *in which:*

- Σ is a finite alphabet, the tape is bounded by a left end-marker $\vdash \notin \Sigma$, and a right end-marker $\dashv \notin \Sigma$;
- Q is a finite set of states;
- $Q_0 \subseteq Q$ is the set of initial states;
- $\delta \colon Q \times (\Sigma \cup \{\vdash, \dashv\}) \to 2^{Q \times \{-1,+1\}}$ is the transition function, which specifies all possible transitions in a certain state while observing a certain tape symbol;
- $F \subseteq Q$ is the set of accepting states, effective at the right end-marker $\dashv$.

On an input string $w \in \Sigma^*$, a 2NFA operates on a read-only tape containing this string enclosed within end-markers $(\vdash w \dashv)$. It begins its computation in any initial state at the left end-marker $(\vdash)$. At every step, when $\mathcal{A}$ is in a state $q \in Q$ and observes a symbol $a \in \Sigma \cup \{\vdash, \dashv\}$, the transition function $\delta(q, a)$ provides a set of pairs (q', d) of the next state q' and the direction of head's motion, $d \in \{-1, +1\}$. If any sequence of nondeterministic choices leads the automaton to an accepting state while at the right end-marker $(\dashv)$, then the string is said to be accepted.

The set of all accepted strings, denoted by $L(\mathcal{A})$, is the language recognized by the 2NFA.

Other types of finite automata are obtained by restricting 2NFA. An automaton is *deterministic* (2DFA), if $|Q_0| = 1$ and $|\delta(q, a)| \leqslant 1$ for all q and a. An automaton is *direction-determinate* [10], if, for every state $q \in Q$, all transitions to q move the head in the same direction $d(q) \in \{-1, +1\}$.

In a *one-way* automaton (1DFA or 1NFA), all transitions move its head to the right, so that the automaton makes a single left-to-right pass, accepting or rejecting in the end. End-markers are of no use in one-way automata, and are usually omitted from the definition.

Theorem A (Kapoutsis [7]). *For every n-state 2NFA, there exists a 1NFA with $\binom{2n}{n+1} = \Theta(\frac{1}{\sqrt{n}} 4^n)$ states, which recognizes the same language.*

Since a k-state 1NFA cannot have a shortest accepted string of length greater than $k - 1$, this has the following implication.

Corollary B *For every n-state 2NFA, the length of the shortest string it accepts is at most $\binom{2n}{n+1} - 1$.*

For direction-determinate automata, the bound in Theorem A is reduced by adapting the method of Kapoutsis [7] to produce fewer states. Accordingly, the length of their shortest strings cannot exceed the following bound.

Theorem C (Geffert and Okhotin [6]). *For every n-state direction-determinate 2NFA, there is a 1NFA with $\binom{n}{\lfloor n/2 \rfloor} = \Theta(\frac{1}{\sqrt{n}} 2^n)$ states that recognizes the same language.*

As far as shortest strings are concerned, 2DFA have the same power as 2NFA.

Theorem D (Dobronravov et al. [3]). *For every n-state 2NFA, there exists an n-state 2DFA with the shortest string of the same length.*

The construction increases the size of the alphabet by a factor of n^n.

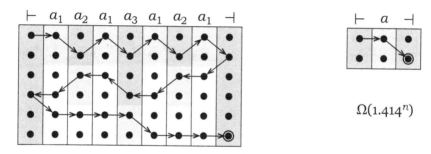

$$\Omega(1.414^n)$$

Fig. 1. (left) A 3-pass 2DFA with $2 \cdot 3$ states and with a shortest string of length $2^3 - 1$; (right) the base automaton.

3   Shortest Strings in 2DFA

Two-way automata with n states and with the shortest string of length exponential in n can be constructed by the following simple method.

Example E *([3]). Assume that $n = 2k$, with k odd, and let the alphabet be $\Sigma_k = \{a_1, \ldots, a_k\}$. Consider a 2DFA that makes k passes over the string. At the first pass, the automaton regards all symbols $a_2, \ldots, a_k$ as separators, and verifies that there is at least one symbol a_1 between every two separators. Similarly, at each i-th pass, the symbols $a_{i+1}, \ldots, a_k$ are regarded as separators, and the automaton checks that there is at least one symbol a_i between every two separators. Each pass uses two states, and the shortest accepted string is of length $2^k - 1$.*

For $k = 3$, the computation of the resulting 6-state automaton is illustrated in Fig. 1(left).

This yields automata with shortest strings of length $2^{n/2} - 1$. Together with Corollary B, this example shows that the longest length of the shortest string accepted by an n-state 2DFA is of the order $\Theta(1)^n$, where the base is between 1.414 and 4. The question is, what is the exact base?

The method of constructing 2DFA with longer shortest accepted strings, invented by Dobronravov et al. [3], begins with the following interpretation of Example E. At each i-th pass, counting up to two can be regarded as a simulation of a 1DFA presented in Fig. 1(right) on the symbols a_i. Any symbols $\{a_1, \ldots, a_{i-1}\}$ encountered are ignored, that is, the 2DFA continues moving without changing its state. For any separator from $\{a_{i+1}, \ldots, a_k, \vdash, \dashv\}$, the 2DFA checks that the currently simulated instance of the 1DFA is in an accepting state, and restarts the simulation in anticipation of the next substring enclosed between two separators.

Dobronravov et al. [3] extended this idea to use a direction-determinate 2DFA as a base automaton. Direction-determinance is essential for the following reason: when the constructed automaton is at an i-th pass simulating the original automaton's being in a state q, and it scans one of the symbols $a_1, \ldots, a_{i-1}$ that it is expected to skip, it knows that the state q is reachable only from the

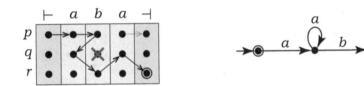

Fig. 2. (left) A 3-state 2DFA with a shortest string of length 3; (right) the equivalent 1DFA.

direction $d(q)$, and therefore can determine the direction in which to proceed: it will be $d(q)$ for i odd and $-d(q)$ for i even.

The other component of the proof of Dobronravov et al. [3] is a single example of a 5-state direction-determinate 2DFA with a shortest string of length 9. Iterating it in the same way as in Example E yields a family of n-state 2DFA with shortest accepted strings of length $10^{n/5} - 1 = \Omega(1.584^n)$ [3].

This paper extends the method of Example E beyond direction-determinate base automata. The new, less restrictive family of base automata is best illustrated by the following small specimen.

Example 1. Let $\mathcal{A}$ be a 2DFA over the alphabet $\Sigma = \{a, b\}$, with the states $Q = \{p, q, r\}$, where p is initial and r is accepting, and with the following transitions:

$$\delta(p, \vdash) = (p, +1),$$
$$\delta(p, a) = (p, +1), \quad \delta(q, a) = (r, +1),$$
$$\delta(p, b) = (q, -1), \quad \delta(r, b) = (q, +1).$$

The shortest string accepted by $\mathcal{A}$ is $w = aba$, as illustrated in Fig. 2(left). To see that w is indeed the shortest string accepted by $\mathcal{A}$, it is sufficient to transform this automaton to the minimal equivalent partial 1DFA, which is presented in Fig. 2(right). The shortest string is clearly visible in the figure.

The above automaton is not direction-determinate, since the state q is enterable both from the left and from the right. The new notion of *semi-direction-determinate automata* allows such states, but imposes special restrictions on each of them. This new type of automata, which generalizes direction-determinate automata, is defined as follows.

Definition 2. *A 2DFA $(\Sigma, Q, q_0, \delta, F)$ is called* semi-direction-determinate, *if there exists a partial function $d: Q \to \{-1, +1\}$, such that:*

1. *every transition $\delta(p, a) = (q, d)$ leading to a state q with $d(q)$ defined moves the head in the prescribed direction $d = d(q)$;*
2. *whenever a transition $\delta(p, a) = (q, d)$ leads to a state q with $d(q)$ undefined, the transition $\delta(q, a)$ may either proceed to (q, d), or be undefined.*

The 2DFA in Example 1 is semi-direction-determinate, with $d(p) = d(r) = +1$ and $d(q)$ undefined. Transitions leading to q are $\delta(p, b) = (q, -1)$, and $\delta(r, b) = (q, +1)$; since $\delta(q, b)$ is undefined, these transitions are allowed.

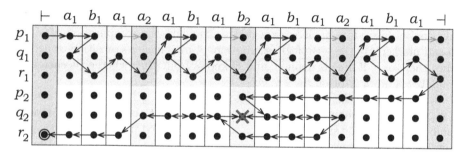

Fig. 3. A 2NFA obtained by iterating the semi-direction-determinate 2DFA in Example 1 twice, as it accepts its shortest string.

It turns out that the condition of semi-direction-determinance is sufficient to iterate the example in generally the same way as in Fig. 1, and thus to obtain longer shortest strings than presented by Dobronravov et al. [3].

4   Iterating Semi-direction-determinate Automata

The proposed new construction of two-way finite automata, given below, actually produces a nondeterministic automaton, which is then processed by Theorem D. A 2NFA obtained in this way, along with its shortest string, is illustrated in Fig. 3.

Lemma 1. *Let $\mathcal{A} = (\Sigma, Q, q^{init}, \delta, F)$ be a semi-direction-determinate 2DFA with k states, which satisfies a further technical condition: for every state $q \in Q$, if $\delta(q, \vdash)$ is defined, then $d(q) = -1$, and if $\delta(q, \dashv)$ is defined or $q \in F$, then $d(q) = +1$. Let $\ell - 1$ be the length of the shortest string accepted by $\mathcal{A}$. Then, for every odd number $m \geqslant 3$, there exists a km-state 2NFA $\mathcal{B}_m$, defined over an alphabet of size $m \cdot |\Sigma|$, with the shortest accepted string of length $\ell^m - 1$.*

Proof. Let $Q = Q_{+1} \cup Q_{-1} \cup Q_?$ be $\mathcal{A}$'s set of states, where $Q_{+1} = \{ q \mid d(q) = +1 \}$, $Q_{-1} = \{ q \mid d(q) = -1 \}$ and $Q_? = \{ q \mid d(q) \text{ is not defined} \}$. The new 2NFA $\mathcal{B}_m$ is defined over the alphabet $\Omega = \bigcup_{i=1}^{m} \Sigma_i$, where $\Sigma_i = \{ a_i \mid a \in \Sigma \}$. It makes m passes over the input. At an i-th pass, with $i \in \{1, \ldots, m\}$, it sees its tape as $\vdash u_0 \#_1 u_1 \#_2 \ldots \#_n u_n \dashv$, where $\#_1, \ldots, \#_n \in \{a_{i+1}, \ldots, a_m\}$ are separators and $u_0, \ldots, u_n \in (\Sigma_1 \cup \ldots \cup \Sigma_i)^*$ are the substrings they separate.

The substrings are processed one by one, from left to right for odd i, and from right to left for even i. For each string u_j, the automaton $\mathcal{B}_m$ simulates the computation of $\mathcal{A}$ on that string (if i is odd) or on its reverse (if i is even), taking into account only symbols a_i, with $a \in \Sigma$. All other symbols a_j, with $j < i$ and $a \in \Sigma$, are ignored by passing over them without changing the state: for states q with $d(q)$ defined, the new automaton knows in which direction to proceed; and if $d(q)$ is undefined, then the automaton moves nondeterministically in either direction.

Each symbol $\#_t$ separates u_{t-1} from u_t, and when the automaton $\mathcal{B}_m$ reaches this symbol in a state q_i, it is expected to simulate the computation of $\mathcal{A}$ on an end-marker. By the technical assumption, $\mathcal{A}$ may have a transition or acceptance there only if $d(q)$ is defined, and $\mathcal{B}$ knows from $d(q)$, whether it currently simulates $\mathcal{A}$ on u_{i-1} or on u_t.

The automaton $\mathcal{B}_m$ uses the set of states $Q_m = \{ q_i \mid q \in Q, i \in \{1, \ldots, m\} \}$. A state q_i means simulating $\mathcal{A}$ in the state $q \in Q$ at the i-th pass. At odd-numbered passes, the substrings $u_0, \ldots, u_n$ are processed from left to right, and from right to left at even-numbered passes. Let $d(i)$ be the general direction of traversal at the i-th pass: $d(i) = +1$ for odd i and $d(i) = -1$ for even i.

The automaton $\mathcal{B}_m$ is constructed as semi-direction-determinate, with $d(q_i) = d(q) \cdot d(i)$ if $d(q)$ is defined, and $d(q_i)$ undefined if so is $d(q)$.

Let the initial transition of $\mathcal{A}$ be $\delta(q^{init}, \vdash) = r$. Then, the initial state of $\mathcal{B}_m$ is q_1^{init}, with the following initial transition.

$$\delta'(q_1^{init}, \vdash) = (r_1, +1) \tag{1a}$$

At every i-th pass, with $i \in \{1, \ldots, m\}$, each $\mathcal{A}$'s transition $\delta(q, a) = (r, d)$, with $a \in \Sigma$ and $q, r \in Q$, is implemented in $\mathcal{B}_m$ by the following transition on the symbol a_i with a matching subscript.

$$\delta'(q_i, a_i) = (r_i, d \cdot d(i)) \tag{1b}$$

Each lesser symbol a_j, with $j < i$ and $a \in \Sigma$, is ignored by continuing in the same direction. Whenever $\mathcal{B}_m$ simulates $\mathcal{A}$ in a state q with the direction $d(q)$ defined, it knows in which direction to proceed.

$$\delta'(q_i, a_j) = (q_i, d(q) \cdot d(i)), \quad \text{for } q \in Q, d(q) \text{ is defined}, j < i, a \in \Sigma \tag{1c}$$

If $d(q)$ is undefined, the automaton $\mathcal{B}_m$ can move in either direction nondeterministically (and this is the only place where $\mathcal{B}_m$ uses its nondeterminism).

$$\delta'(q_i, a_j) = \{(q_i, +1), (q_i, -1)\}, \quad \text{for } q \in Q, d(q) \text{ undefined}, j < i, a \in \Sigma \tag{1d}$$

Following these transitions, the automaton can freely move over a substring $x \in (\Sigma_1 \cup \ldots \cup \Sigma_{i-1})^*$ in a state q_i. If $\mathcal{B}_m$ ever crosses this substring, then it correctly simulates one transition of $\mathcal{A}$. If it returns to the symbol a_i from which it entered x, then, by the definition of semi-direction-determinacy, it cannot proceed anywhere else except back into x in the same state q_i. For this reason, regardless of the nondeterministic choices it makes, $\mathcal{B}_m$ can either continue simulating $\mathcal{A}$, or loop.

Next, let $\mathcal{c}_i$ and $\$_i$ be the end-markers at which the i-th pass begins and ends, respectively ($\mathcal{c}_i = \vdash$ and $\$_i = \dashv$ for i odd, and vice versa for i even). For each $\mathcal{A}$'s transition $\delta(q, \vdash) = (r, +1)$ for turning at the left end-marker, with $q \neq q^{init}$, the new automaton executes the same turn on any separator symbols.

$$\delta'(q_i, s) = (r_i, d(i)), \quad \text{for } s \in \{\mathcal{c}_i\} \cup \Sigma_{i+1} \cup \ldots \cup \Sigma_m \tag{1e}$$

Each turn at the right end-marker, $\delta(q, \dashv) = (r, -1)$, is implemented similarly.

$$\delta'(q_i, s) = (r_i, -d(i)), \qquad \text{for } s \in \{\$_i\} \cup \Sigma_{i+1} \cup \ldots \cup \Sigma_m \qquad (1\text{f})$$

If $q \in F$ is an accepting state of $\mathcal{A}$, effective at the right end-marker $(\dashv)$, then $\mathcal{B}_m$ moves on to the next block through a separator symbol: if the initial transition is $\delta(q^{init}, \vdash) = (r, +1)$, it goes through the separator in the state r, thus simulating the end of one computation and the beginning of another.

$$\delta'(q_i, s) = (r_i, d(i)), \qquad \text{for } s \in \Sigma_{i+1} \cup \ldots \cup \Sigma_m \qquad (1\text{g})$$

When $\mathcal{B}_m$ finishes processing the last block at its i-th pass, it proceeds to the next pass.

$$\delta'(q_i, \$_i) = (r_{i+1}, d(i+1)) \qquad (i < m) \qquad (1\text{h})$$

For $i = m$, the automaton $\mathcal{B}_m$ accepts; accordingly, its set of accepting states is $F' = \{q_m\}$.

Note that, by the technical assumption, case (1e) is possible only for $d(q) = -1$, whereas cases (1f–1h) require $d(q) = +1$ and are mutually exclusive. Hence, at most one of these transitions may be defined.

The language recognized by this automaton is expressed as follows. For each $i \in \{0, 1, \ldots, m\}$, let $L_i \subseteq (\Sigma_1 \cup \ldots \cup \Sigma_i)^*$ be the language representing all substrings, on which the computation of $\mathcal{A}$ is successfully simulated at the i-th pass. Then, $L_0 = \{\varepsilon\}$, $L_i = \bigcup_{a^{(1)}\ldots a^{(n)} \in L(\mathcal{A})} L_{i-1} a_i^{(1)} L_{i-1} a_i^{(2)} L_{i-1} \ldots a_i^{(n)} L_{i-1}$ for odd i, and symmetrically for even i. The automaton $\mathcal{B}_m$ recognizes exactly L_m, and the length of the shortest string therein is $\ell^m - 1$. The proof is omitted due to space constraints. □

It is also worth note that, once the transformation in Theorem D is applied to the 2NFA produced by Lemma 1, the resulting 2DFA is semi-direction-determinate.

For the 3-state base automaton in Example 1, with a shortest string of length 3, Lemma 1 yields a lower bound $\Omega(4^{n/3}) = \Omega(1.587^n)$ for a growing alphabet. This already improves over the previously known result.

5   Encoding in a Fixed Alphabet

Example E, as well as all other constructions of DFA with exponentially long shortest accepted strings known to date, essentially rely on using an alphabet that grows with n. The construction by Dobronravov et al. [3] uses an alphabet of size $\Theta(n)$; the new construction in Lemma 1 provides a 2NFA using $\Theta(n)$ symbols, which is then turned to a 2DFA with exponentially many symbols.

For a fixed alphabet, no results on the length of shortest accepted strings are known yet. The first such result shall now be presented. This is an adaptation of the construction in Lemma 1, in which every symbol a_j is replaced by an encoding over a fixed alphabet; a new 2DFA carries out a computation simular to the one in Lemma 1. It uses twice as many states as in the original version, resulting in a weaker lower bound.

Lemma 2. *Let $\mathcal{A} = (\Sigma, Q, q^{init}, \delta, F)$ be a k-state semi-direction-determinate 2DFA that satisfies the conditions of Lemma 1. Let $\ell - 1$ be the length of its shortest string. Then, for every even number $m \geqslant 2$, there exists a $(2(m-1)k + \frac{3}{2}m - 1)$-state 2NFA C_m, defined over an alphabet with $2|\Sigma| + 1$ symbols, with the shortest accepted string of length at least ℓ^m.*

Proof (a sketch). Given a base semi-direction-determinate 2DFA over an alphabet Σ, the new 2NFA uses the alphabet $\Omega = \Sigma_{\pm 1} \cup \{s\}$, where $\Sigma_{\pm 1} = \{\, a_d \mid a \in \Sigma,\ d \in \{-1, +1\}\,\}$. The strings in the original construction shall be encoded by a homomorphism h, with $h(a_{2j+1}) = s^j a_{+1} s^{m-2-j}$ for odd-numbered symbols, and $h(a_{2j+2}) = s^j a_{-1} s^{m-2-j}$ for even-numbered symbols.

The new 2DFA shall first check that the input string is a well-formed image of some string, and then proceed with an m-pass simulation, using $2(m-1)|Q|$ states, cf. $m|Q|$ states in Lemma 1. After the last pass, one more state is used to move the head to the right end-marker.

Checking that an input string is an image under h takes a partial DFA with $\frac{3}{2}m - 2$ states; the construction is easy. For the simulation, the 2DFA shall use states of the form $q_{i,d}$, where $q \in Q$, $-(\frac{m}{2}-1) \leqslant i \leqslant \frac{m}{2}-1$ and $d \in \{-1, +1\}$. The subscript d indicates the general direction of the current pass, that is, $d = +1$ for the first pass, $d = -1$ for the second pass, etc. The subscript i reflects the number of the current pass whenever the automaton is at the first symbol of the image of some symbol; as the automaton moves over the image, the subscript i is in constant rotation: the automaton increments i whenever it moves to the left, and decrements it when it moves to the right. Once i exceeds $\frac{m}{2} - 1$, the counting is wrapped to $-(\frac{m}{2} - 1)$, and the other way around. This allows the automaton to compare the number of the current pass to the number of the encoded symbol.

The computation involves keeping track of several directions, and it order to explain it more clearly, it shall be described for the case of a left-to-right pass in a right-moving state. Having entered an image $h(a_{2j+1}) = s^j a_{+1} s^{m-2-j}$ in a state $q_{-i,+1}$ with $d(q) = +1$, the automaton moves to the right while inrementing i at every step, and arrives to the symbol a_{+1} in the state $q_{j-i,+1}$. If $j - i < 0$, this means that this symbol must be ignored, and the automaton proceeds further to the right while incrementing i, entering the next image in the same state $q_{-i,+1}$.

If $j - i = 0$, the automaton simulates the transition on a. If the original automaton's transition was $\delta(q, a) = (r, d(r))$, then the new automaton moves in the direction $d(r)$ in the state $r_{0+d(r),+1}$, and eventually moves out of the image in the direction $d(r)$ in the state $r_{-i,+1}$.

If $j - i > 0$, the automaton treats this symbol as an end-marker and takes the appropriate action. Since the automaton is now in a state $q_{j-i,+1}$ with $d(q) = +1$, this must be a right end-marker. If the original automaton had a transition $\delta(q, \dashv) = (r, -1)$, then the new automaton moves in the direction -1 in the state $r_{j-i-1,+1}$, and later reaches the first symbol of the image in the state $r_{-i,+1}$, leaving the image to the left. If the original automaton accepts in q, the new automaton should proceed to the next substring to the right; accordingly, if the initial transition is $\delta(q^{init}, \dashv) = (r, +1)$, the new automaton moves to the right in the state $r_{j-i+1,+1}$ and eventually leaves the image in the direction $+1$ in the state $r_{-i,+1}$.

The full list of transitions is omitted due to space constraints.   □

An immediate application of Lemma 2 yields the following result.

Theorem 1. *Let* $\mathcal{A} = (\Sigma, Q, q_0, \delta, F)$ *be a* k-*state semi-direction-determinate 2DFA with a shortest string of length* $\ell - 1$, *which satisfies the conditions of Lemma 1. Then, there exists a fixed alphabet* Γ, *such that for every* n, *there exists an* n-*state semi-direction-determinate 2DFA over* Γ *with a shortest string of length at leas* $\Omega((\sqrt[2k+\frac{3}{2}]{\ell})^n)$.

For instance, the automaton in Example 1 has $k = 3$ and $\ell = 4$, and Lemma 2 provides automata with $\frac{15}{2}m - 7$ states and with a shortest string of length ℓ^m. For an n-state base automaton, the length of the shortest string is then of the order $\Omega((4^{2/15})^n) = \Omega(1.203^n)$.

This can be improved by first iterating the base automaton using Lemma 1, obtaining a larger base automaton, and only then applying Lemma 2.

Theorem 2. *Let* $\mathcal{A} = (\Sigma, Q, q_0, \delta, F)$ *be a* k-*state semi-direction-determinate 2DFA with a shortest string of length* $\ell - 1$, *which satisfies the conditions of Lemma 1. Then, for every* $\varepsilon > 0$, *there exists an alphabet* Γ, *such that for every* n, *there exists an* n-*state semi-direction-determinate 2DFA over* Γ *with a shortest string of length at least* $\Omega((\sqrt[k]{\ell} - \varepsilon)^n)$.

With this improvement, the base automaton in Example 1 provides shortest strings of length $\Omega((\sqrt[6]{4} - \varepsilon)^n) = \Omega(1.259^n)$ over a fixed alphabet.

6   Automata with Longer Shortest Strings

The efficiency of the proposed method relies on finding small examples of semi-direction-determinate 2DFA with long shortest accepting strings. Using a better base example given below leads to further improvement.

Example 2. Let $\mathcal{A}$ be a 2DFA over the alphabet $\Sigma = \{a, b, c, d\}$, with the states $Q = \{p, q, r, s\}$, where p is initial and s is accepting, and with transitions illustrated in Fig. 4. It is semi-direction-determinate with $d(p) = d(q) = d(s) = +1$ and $d(r)$ undefined. The shortest string accepted by $\mathcal{A}$ is $w = abcdbc$, this can be verified by transforming it to a 1DFA.

Corollary 1. *For every* n, *there exists a semi-direction-determinate 2DFA over an alphabet of size exponential in* n, *with a shortest string of length at least* $\Omega(7^{n/4}) = \Omega(1.626^n)$.

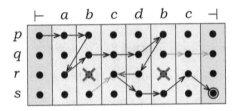

Fig. 4. A 4-state 2DFA with a shortest string of length 6.

Corollary 2. *For every n, there exists a semi-direction-determinate 2DFA over a fixed alphabet, with a shortest string of length at least $\Omega((\sqrt[8]{7} - \varepsilon)^n) = \Omega(1.275^n)$.*

7 Transforming Semi-direction-determinate to One-Way

The method of Donbronravov et al. [3] can potentially provide automata with shortest strings of length up to at most $O(\frac{1}{\sqrt{n}}2^n)$, since direction-determinate 2DFA can be transformed to 1NFA with this number of states. Although the proposed new method is not subject to this limitation, it has its own limitations, revealed by the following result.

Theorem 3. *For every n-state semi-direction-determinate 2DFA there exists a 1NFA with $\sum_{k=0}^{n-1} \binom{n}{k}\binom{n-k}{k+1} = \Theta(\frac{1}{\sqrt{n}}3^n)$ states, which recognizes the same language.*

The construction is based on the known transformation of an arbitrary 2DFA to an 1NFA by Kapoutsis [7], Upon reading a prefix u of an input string, the 1NFA remembers the states in which the 2DFA crosses the border between the last symbol of u and the next symbol to the right. This is represented by a pair (P, R), with $P, R \subseteq Q$ and $|P| = |R| + 1$. It turns out that for a semi-direction-determinate automaton, pairs (P, R) with $P \cap R \neq \varnothing$ are useless and can be omitted. The number of remaining pairs is $\binom{n}{k}\binom{n-k}{k+1}$ for a fixed cardinality $|P| = k$, and summation over all k yields the desired formula. This is a known integer sequence, OEIS A005717 [12], and it is of the order $\Theta(\frac{1}{\sqrt{n}}3^n)$.

8 Conclusion

This paper has made a new addition to the zoo of different variants of two-way finite automata, such as sweeping, direction-determinate, halting, reversible, nondeterministic, alternating, pebble, etc. Understanding the difference between these variants is an important research subject; in particular, the relative size of 2NFA and 2DFA appears to be the key to solving the L *vs. NL* problem in the complexity theory [8]. The length of the shortest string is a natural complexity measure that may be useful to compare some of these models.

Table 1. The known bounds on the length of shortest strings for subfamilies of 2DFA.

Family	Lower bound	Upper bound
Sweeping	$\Omega((\sqrt[3]{3})^n) = \Omega(1.442^n)$	$\binom{n}{\lfloor n/2 \rfloor} = \Theta(\frac{1}{\sqrt{n}}2^n)$
Direction-determinate	$\Omega((\sqrt[5]{10})^n) = \Omega(1.584^n)$	$\binom{n}{\lfloor n/2 \rfloor} = \Theta(\frac{1}{\sqrt{n}}2^n)$
Semi-direction-determinate	$\Omega((\sqrt[4]{7})^n) = \Omega(1.626^n)$	$O(\frac{1}{\sqrt{n}}3^n)$
All 2DFA, and also 2NFA	$\Omega((\sqrt[4]{7})^n) = \Omega(1.626^n)$	$\binom{2n}{n+1} = \Theta(\frac{1}{\sqrt{n}}4^n)$

The known lower and upper bounds on the length of shortest accepted strings in n-state 2DFA from different subclasses are presented in Table 1. There is still a long way to go to any precise answers.

Acknowledgement. The authors are grateful to the anonymous reviewers for careful reading and for pertinent remarks.

References

1. Alpoge, L., Ang, T., Schaeffer, L., Shallit, J.: Decidability and shortest strings in formal languages. In: Holzer, M., Kutrib, M., Pighizzini, G. (eds.) DCFS 2011. LNCS, vol. 6808, pp. 55–67. Springer, Heidelberg (2011). https://doi.org/10.1007/978-3-642-22600-7_5
2. Chistikov, D., Czerwiński, W., Hofman, P., Pilipczuk, M., Wehar, M.: Shortest paths in one-counter systems. In: Jacobs, B., Löding, C. (eds.) FoSSaCS 2016. LNCS, vol. 9634, pp. 462–478. Springer, Heidelberg (2016). https://doi.org/10.1007/978-3-662-49630-5_27
3. Dobronravov, E., Dobronravov, N., Okhotin, A.: On the length of shortest strings accepted by two-way finite automata. In: Hofman, P., Skrzypczak, M. (eds.) DLT 2019. LNCS, vol. 11647, pp. 88–99. Springer, Cham (2019). https://doi.org/10.1007/978-3-030-24886-4_6
4. Dobronravov, E., Dobronravov, N., Okhotin, A.: On the length of shortest strings accepted by two-way finite automata, revised full version, submitted
5. Ellul, K., Krawetz, B., Shallit, J., Wang, M.-W.: Regular expressions: new results and open problems. J. Automata Lang. Comb. **10**(4), 407–437 (2005)
6. Geffert, V., Okhotin, A.: One-way simulation of two-way finite automata over small alphabets. In: NCMA 2013 (Umeå, vol. 13–14, Sweden, August 2013
7. Kapoutsis, C.: Removing bidirectionality from nondeterministic finite automata. In: Jędrzejowicz, J., Szepietowski, A. (eds.) MFCS 2005. LNCS, vol. 3618, pp. 544–555. Springer, Heidelberg (2005). https://doi.org/10.1007/11549345_47
8. Kapoutsis, C.A.: Two-way automata versus logarithmic space. Theory Comput. Syst. **55**(2), 421–447 (2014)
9. Kozen, D.: Lower bounds for natural proof systems. In: FOCS 1977, pp. 254–266 (1977). http://dx.doi.org/10.1109/SFCS.1977.16
10. Kunc, M., Okhotin, A.: Reversibility of computations in graph-walking automata. In: Chatterjee, K., Sgall, J. (eds.) MFCS 2013. LNCS, vol. 8087, pp. 595–606. Springer, Heidelberg (2013). https://doi.org/10.1007/978-3-642-40313-2_53

11. Pierre, L.: Rational indexes of generators of the cone of context-free languages. Theor. Comput. Sci. **95**(2), 279–305 (1992). https://doi.org/10.1016/0304-3975(92)90269-L
12. Sloane, N.J.A. (ed.): The On-Line Encyclopedia of Integer Sequences, published electronically at https://oeis.org

Iterated Uniform Finite-State Transducers: Descriptional Complexity of Nondeterminism and Two-Way Motion

Martin Kutrib[1], Andreas Malcher[1], Carlo Mereghetti[2(✉)], and Beatrice Palano[3]

[1] Institut Für Informatik, Universität Giessen, Arndtstr. 2, 35392 Giessen, Germany
{kutrib,andreas.malcher}@informatik.uni-giessen.de
[2] Dipartimento di Fisica "Aldo Pontremoli", Università degli Studi di Milano via Celoria 16, 20133 Milano, Italy
carlo.mereghetti@unimi.it
[3] Dipartimento di Informatica "G. degli Antoni", Università degli Studi di Milano via Celoria 18, 20133 Milano, Italy
palano@unimi.i

Abstract. An *iterated uniform finite-state transducer* executes the same length-preserving transduction in iterative sweeps. The first sweep occurs on the input string, while any subsequent sweep works on the output of the previous one. We consider devices with one-way motion and two-way motion, i.e., sweeps are either from left to right only, or alternate from left to right and from right to left. In addition, devices may work deterministically or nondeterministically. Here, we restrict to study devices performing a constant number of sweeps, which are known to characterize exactly the regular languages. We determine the descriptional costs of removing two-way motion, nondeterminism, and sweeps, and, in particular, the costs for the conversion to deterministic or nondeterministic finite automata. Finally, the special case of unary languages is investigated, and a language family is presented that is immune to the resources of nondeterminism and two-way motion, in the sense that both resources can neither reduce the number of states nor the number of sweeps.

Keywords: Iterated transducers · Nondeterminism · Two-way motion

1 Introduction

The notion of an iterated uniform finite-state transducer (IUFST) has been introduced in [12]. Basically, it consists of a length-preserving finite-state transducer that works in iterative sweeps from left to right on its input tape. In the first sweep the input string is processed, while any further sweep operates on the output of the previous sweep. The model is uniform in the sense that every sweep always starts in the initial state of the transducer. An input string is accepted whenever the transducer halts in an accepting state at the end of a sweep.

G. Jirásková and G. Pighizzini (Eds.): DCFS 2020, LNCS 12442, pp. 117–129, 2020.
https://doi.org/10.1007/978-3-030-62536-8_10

A theoretical investigation of IUFSTs is motivated by the fact that iterated or cascade transductions show up in several fields of computer science. For example, in the context of natural language processing, cascades of finite-state transducers are used in [8] to extract information from natural language texts. In compiler design, the lexical analysis is often done by a finite-state transducer whose output is subsequently processed by a pushdown transducer implementing the syntactical analysis. Again, from a theoretical perspective, the Krohn-Rhodes decomposition theorem states that every regular language can be represented as a cascade of several finite-state transducers with a simple algebraic structure [9,11]. Finally, cascades of deterministic pushdown transducers as language accepting devices have been studied in [7]. Yet, in [6,16], iterated finite-state transducers as language generating devices have been proposed. It might be worth noticing that only this latter contribution introduces a notion of "uniformity" on iterated transduction, in the sense that always the same transducer is iteratively applied.

Deterministic and nondeterministic IUFSTs have been investigated in [12,13]. For a constant number of sweeps, IUFSTs characterize the class of regular languages. So, in both papers, a detailed investigation of constant sweep bounded IUFSTs descriptional power has been carried on, tackling classical problems such as the state cost of: removing nondeterminism (see, e.g., [2]) and sweeps (see, e.g., [15]), and of implementing language operations (see, e.g., [1,3]). The computational complexity of typical decidability questions (see, e.g., [14]) have also been studied. In case of a non-constant number of sweeps, non-regular languages can be accepted as soon as at least a logarithmic number of sweeps is provided. Moreover, all commonly studied decidability questions are undecidable.

In this paper, we enhance both deterministic and nondeterministic IUFSTs with two-way motion. More precisely, differently from the already studied models where sweeps always go from left to right starting in the initial state, now sweeps alternate from left to right and from right to left, always starting in the initial state. We focus on constant sweep bounded devices, still accepting all and only regular languages, and study their descriptional power with respect to that of classical finite state automata. Moreover, we emphasize how two-way motion affects the descriptional power of deterministic and nondeterministic iterated transduction, and highlight situations where adding both nondeterminism and two-way motion cannot help in reducing the size of IUFSTs.

In Sect. 2, we define the models of two-way deterministic and nondeterministic IUFSTs (2IUFSTs), providing an illustrative example of their way of processing languages. In Sect. 3, we study the state costs of turning nondeterministic IUFSTs and 2IUFSTs into equivalent NFAs. We show that both nondeterministic IUFSTs and 2IUFSTs operating with k sweeps and n states can be turned to equivalent NFAs with $2n^k$ states. Moreover, since our conversion algorithm preserves determinism, we get that a deterministic IUFST with k sweeps and n states can be converted into an equivalent DFA with $2n^k$ states as well. In Sect. 4, we study in more detail the conversions of deterministic devices and present upper and lower bounds on the state cost for the conversions of deterministic IUFSTs and

2IUFSTs to equivalent DFAs, for the conversion of deterministic 2IUFSTs to equivalent deterministic IUFSTs (two-way motion removal), and for the conversion of nondeterministic 2IUFSTs to deterministic 2IUFSTs (nondeterminism removal). In all cases, the upper and lower bounds on the state cost for the conversions turn out to be exponential. Finally, in Sect. 5, we discuss the special case of *unary languages* (see, e.g., [4,5]). We define a family $L_{\Pi(p)}$ of unary languages accepted by deterministic IUFSTs with p states and $\pi(p)$ sweeps, with $\pi(p)$ the number of primes not exceeding p, and such that any equivalent deterministic or nondeterministic IUFST or 2IUFST needs at least p states and cannot have $o(\pi(p))$ sweeps. Hence, accepting $L_{\Pi(p)}$ represents a task where the size of IUFSTs cannot benefit from the additional resources of nondeterminism and two-way motion.

2 Definitions and Preliminaries

We denote the set of positive integers and zero by $\mathbb{N}$. Given a set S, we write 2^S for its power set and $|S|$ for its cardinality. Let Σ^* denote the set of all words over the finite alphabet Σ. The length of a word w is denoted by $|w|$.

Roughly speaking, an iterated uniform finite-state transducer is a finite-state transducer which processes the input in multiple passes (also sweeps). In the first pass, it reads the input word enclosed between endmarkers and emits an output word. In any of the following passes, it reads the output word of the previous pass and a new word is output. The number of passes taken, the *sweep complexity*, is given as a function of the length of the input. We will consider length-preserving finite-state transducers, also known as Mealy machines [17], to be iterated.

Formally, we define a *nondeterministic iterated uniform finite-state transducer* (NIUFST) as a system $T = \langle Q, \Sigma, \Delta, q_0, \rhd, \lhd, \delta, F \rangle$, where Q is the set of *internal states*, Σ is the set of *input symbols*, Δ is the set of *output symbols*, $q_0 \in Q$ is the initial state, $\rhd \in \Delta \setminus \Sigma$ and $\lhd \in \Delta \setminus \Sigma$ are *left and right endmarkers*, respectively, $F \subseteq Q$ is the set of *accepting states*, and $\delta \colon Q \times (\Sigma \cup \Delta) \to 2^{Q \times \Delta}$ is the partial *transition function*. The NIUFST T *halts* whenever the transition function is undefined or T enters an accepting state at the end of a sweep. Since the transduction is applied in multiple passes, that is, in any but the initial pass it operates on an output of the previous pass, the transition function depends on input symbols from $\Sigma \cup \Delta$. We denote by $T(w)$ the set of possible outputs produced by T in a complete sweep on input $w \in (\Sigma \cup \Delta)^*$.

We distinguish between *one-way* and *two-way* computations. In a one-way computation all sweeps are from left to right, whereas in a two-way computation the sweeps are alternating from left to right and from right to left. So, a *computation* of the NIUFST T on input $w \in \Sigma^*$ consists of a sequence of words $w_1, \ldots, w_i, w_{i+1}, \ldots \in (\Sigma \cup \Delta)^*$. If the computation is one-way then $w_1 \in T(\rhd w \lhd)$ and $w_{i+1} \in T(w_i)$ for $i \geq 1$. If the computation is two-way then $w_1 \in T(\rhd w \lhd)$ and $w_{i+1} \in T(w_i)$ for even $i \geq 2$, and $w_{i+1}^R \in T(w_i^R)$ for odd $i \geq 1$. We denote an iterated uniform finite-state transducer operating in one-way (resp., two-way) mode by NIUFST (resp., 2NIUFST).

An iterated uniform finite-state transducer is said to be *deterministic* (IUFST, 2IUFST) if and only if $|\delta(p, x)| \leq 1$, for all $p \in Q$ and $x \in (\Sigma \cup \Delta)$. In this case, we simply write $\delta(p, x) = (q, y)$ instead of $\delta(p, x) = \{(q, y)\}$ assuming that the transition function is a mapping $\delta \colon Q \times (\Sigma \cup \Delta) \to Q \times \Delta$.

Now we turn to language acceptance. For nondeterministic computations and some complexity bound, several acceptance modes can be considered. For instance, a machine accepts a language $L \subseteq \Sigma^*$ in the *weak mode* if for any $w \in L$ an accepting computation exists obeying the complexity bound. Instead, L is accepted in the *strong mode* if the machine obeys the complexity bound for all computations (accepting or not) on every $w \in \Sigma^*$. Here we deal with the number of sweeps as (computational) complexity measure. The weak mode seems too optimistic for this measure, while the strong mode seems too restrictive. Therefore, we consider an intermediate mode, the so-called *accept mode*. A language is accepted in the *accept mode* if all accepting computations obey the complexity bound (see [18] for separation of these modes with respect to space complexity).

A computation is halting if there exists an $r \geq 1$ such that T halts on w_r, thus performing r sweeps. The input word $w \in \Sigma^*$ is *accepted* by T if at least one computation on w halts at the end of a sweep in an accepting state. Otherwise it is *rejected*. Indeed, the output of the last sweep is not used. The language accepted by T is the set $L(T) \subseteq \Sigma^*$ defined as $L(T) = \{\, w \in \Sigma^* \mid w \text{ is accepted by } T \,\}$.

Given a function $s \colon \mathbb{N} \to \mathbb{N}$, an iterated uniform finite-state transducer T is said to be of *sweep complexity* $s(n)$ if for all $w \in L(T)$ all accepting computations on w halt after at most $s(|w|)$ sweeps. In this case, we add the prefix $s(n)$- to the notation of the device. It is easy to see that 1-IUFSTs as well as 1-2IUFSTs (resp., 1-NIUFSTs as well as 1-2NIUFSTs) are actually deterministic (resp., nondeterministic) finite automata (DFAs and NFAs, respectively).

Example 1. For any $n, k > 0$, the unary language $L_{n,k} = \{\, a^{c \cdot n^k} \mid c \geq 0 \,\}$ is accepted by the n-state k-2IUFST $T = \langle Q, \Sigma, \Delta, q_0, \rhd_0, \lhd_0, \delta, F \rangle$, with $\Sigma = \{a\}$, $Q = \{q_0, \dots, q_{n-1}\}$, $\Delta = \{a, \sqcup, \#, \rhd_0, \dots, \rhd_{k-1}, \lhd_0, \dots, \lhd_{k-1}\}$, $F = \{q_0\}$. To explain the definition of the transition function δ, we first implement the behavior of T on the endmarkers. In general, the sweep number is identified by the indexes of the endmarkers. Since q_0 is the accepting state, the last step of all but the last sweep sends T into state q_1 to avoid to accept accidentally:

(1) $\delta(q_0, \rhd_i) = (q_0, \rhd_{i+1})$ (2) $\delta(q_0, \lhd_i) = (q_1, \lhd_{i+1})$ for even $0 \leq i \leq k - 2$,

(3) $\delta(q_0, \lhd_i) = (q_0, \lhd_{i+1})$ (4) $\delta(q_0, \rhd_i) = (q_1, \rhd_{i+1})$ for odd $1 \leq i \leq k - 2$.

In the first sweep, T verifies that the length of the input is divisible by n and rewrites the input as a sequence of consecutive blocks of the form $\#\sqcup^{n-1}$:

(5) $\delta(q_0, a) = (q_1, \#)$,   (6) $\delta(q_i, a) = (q_{i+1}, \sqcup)$ for $1 \leq i \leq n - 2$,

(7) $\delta(q_{n-1}, a) = (q_0, \sqcup)$.

In the following $k - 1$ sweeps, T verifies that the number of $\#$ symbols is divisible by n and, from each n symbols $\#$, one remains and $n - 1$ are replaced by $\sqcup$:

(8) $\delta(q_i, \sqcup) = (q_i, \sqcup)$ for $0 \leq i \leq n - 1$,

(9) $\delta(q_i, \#) = (q_{i+1}, \sqcup)$ for $0 \leq i \leq n - 2$,   (10) $\delta(q_{n-1}, \#) = (q_0, \#)$.

In the last sweep, the endmarkers do not have to be rewritten. If the divisibility check is positive, the last step sends T into state q_0 and, thus T halts accepting:

(11) $\delta(q_0, \rhd_{k-1}) = (q_0, \rhd_{k-1})$,   (12) $\delta(q_0, \lhd_{k-1}) = (q_0, \lhd_{k-1})$.

By construction, T accepts if all divisibility checks are positive. Let m be the length of an input from language $L_{n,k}$. After the first sweep all blocks have length n, thus, there are m/n symbols # in the output. After the ith sweep there are m/n^i symbols # in the output. So, after the kth sweep it is verified the length of the input is a multiple of n^k. On the other hand, the sole accepting state q_0 is never entered at the end of the first $k-1$ sweeps. So, accepting is only possible after the last sweep. To see that no input of incorrect length is accepted it is sufficient to look at the states reached at the end of a sweep. If it turns out that the length of the input is not divisible by n (first sweep) or the number of # symbols is not divisible by n (remaining sweeps), the sweep ends in some state unequal to q_0 on the endmarker. However, the transition function is undefined for such situations and T halts in a non-accepting state. ∎

3   Complexity of Mutual Nondeterministic Simulations

We study the simulation of 2NIUFSTs by NFAs, thus restricting to a constant number of sweeps. The underlying idea of this simulation combines the reverse guessing and verifying of sweeps with merging several sweeps into one.

Theorem 2. *Let $k \geq 1$ be an integer. Every n-state k-2NIUFST can be converted to an equivalent NFA with at most $2n^k$ states.*

Proof. Let $T = \langle Q, \Sigma, \Delta, q_0, \triangleright, \triangleleft, \delta, F \rangle$ be a k-2NIUFST with $|Q| = n$. The NFA N equivalent to T we are going to construct simulates in its states the k sweeps of T in parallel, where odd sweeps are simulated directly and even sweeps (which T performs right to left) are guessed and verified. One problem to cope with is that T may get stuck in some sweep $j \leq k$ but an earlier sweep $1 \leq i < j$ ends accepting. To manage this situation the NFA N has to continue the simulation of all sweeps $1 \leq i < j$ and, at the same time, has to remember that the results of all sweeps after i are irrelevant. Moreover, N has to overcome the problem to verify an accepting right-to-left sweep of T and to keep the information that the sweep is initially guessed to be accepting during the simulation. The latter problem is coped with as follows. If in the first step some even sweep i is guessed to be accepting then the simulation does not need to care about subsequent sweeps. Either the guess can be verified and the input would be accepted in the ith sweep or the guess was wrong and the simulation of all subsequent sweeps ends non-accepting. So, if in the first step some even sweep i is guessed to be accepting, all later sweeps are performed by some dummy state d. This means that at most one simulated right-to-left sweep is initially guessed to be accepting. Moreover, whenever initially no right-to-left sweep is guessed to be accepting then the last sweep can be performed by the dummy state if k is even. In particular we have the following situation. If N is currently simulating an even number of non-dummy sweeps, the last one is guessed to be accepting and it is the only right-to-left sweep with this property. If N is currently simulating an odd number of non-dummy sweeps, there is no possibly accepting right-to-left sweep. This situation can be kept when a simulated sweep gets stuck. If it is an even sweep it can be turned into a dummy sweep and the number of non-dummy sweeps becomes odd. If it is an odd sweep it can be turned into a dummy sweep together with its predecessor sweep and the number of non-dummy sweeps remains odd.

Formally, the state set of N is defined as $Q' = \bigcup_{i=0}^{k} Q^i \times \{d\}^{k-i}$, where d is a new state not in Q. The initial state $q_0' \in Q'$ is $(q_0, q_0, \ldots, q_0)$. The transition function $\delta' \colon Q' \times \Sigma \to 2^{Q'}$ is defined by a procedure that determines the successor states. For the initial step, we define $(r_1, r_2, \ldots, r_k) \in \delta'((q_0, q_0, \ldots, q_0), \triangleright)$ as:

```
 1: r₀ := q₀;   y₀ := ▷;   dummynow := false;
 2: for i = 1 to k do
 3:     if dummynow then
 4:         (rᵢ, yᵢ) := (d, yᵢ₋₁);
 5:     else if i is odd then
 6:         S := δ(q₀, yᵢ₋₁);
 7:         if S ≠ ∅ then guess (rᵢ, yᵢ) ∈ S;
 8:         else
 9:             (rᵢ, yᵢ) := (d, yᵢ₋₁);   (rᵢ₋₁, yᵢ₋₁) := (d, yᵢ₋₁);
10:             dummynow := true;
11:         end if
12:     else if i is even then
13:         S := { (p, y) | (q, y) ∈ δ(p, yᵢ₋₁) };
14:         if S ≠ ∅ then guess (rᵢ, yᵢ) ∈ S;
15:             if δ(rᵢ, yᵢ₋₁) yields some accepting state then
16:                 dummynow := true;
17:             end if
18:         else   (rᵢ, yᵢ) := (d, yᵢ₋₁);   dummynow := true;
19:         end if
20:     end if
21: end for
```

Further steps are similar but not identical. In particular, the guessed reverse right-to-left sweeps have to be verified step by step. So, for $x \in \Sigma \cup \{\triangleleft\}$ we obtain $(r_1, r_2, \ldots, r_k) \in \delta'((s_1, s_2, \ldots, s_k), x)$ as:

```
 1: r₀ := q₀;   y₀ := x;   dummynow := false;
 2: for i = 1 to k do
 3:     if dummynow or sᵢ = d then
 4:         (rᵢ, yᵢ) := (d, yᵢ₋₁);
 5:     else if i is odd then
 6:         S := δ(sᵢ, yᵢ₋₁);
 7:         if S ≠ ∅ then guess (rᵢ, yᵢ) ∈ S;
 8:         else
 9:             (rᵢ, yᵢ) := (d, yᵢ₋₁);   (rᵢ₋₁, yᵢ₋₁) := (d, yᵢ₋₁);
10:             dummynow := true;
11:         end if
12:     else if i is even then
13:         S := { (p, y) | (sᵢ, y) ∈ δ(p, yᵢ₋₁) };
14:         if S ≠ ∅ then guess (rᵢ, yᵢ) ∈ S;
15:         else   (rᵢ, yᵢ) := (d, yᵢ₋₁);   dummynow := true;
16:         end if
17:     end if
18: end for
```

To define the set of accepting states of N, we notice that δ' is well defined even on the symbol $\lhd$. If T accepts (for the first time) at the end of a sweep i, the NFA N can simulate T at least up to that sweep successfully. So, for odd i, any state $(r_1, r_2, \ldots, r_k) \in Q'$ with an $r_i \in F$ is accepting for N. For even i, the NFA has simulated exactly i sweeps of T and $r_{i+1} = r_{i+2} = \cdots = r_k = d$. Moreover, the initially guessed accepting sweep i can be verified, that is, state r_i is the initial state q_0 of T. So, any state $(r_1, r_2, \ldots, r_i, d, d, \ldots, d) \in Q'$ with an $r_i = q_0$ is accepting for N. Finally, for $n \geq 2$, $|Q'| = \sum_{i=0}^{k} n^i = \frac{n^{k+1}-1}{n-1} \leq 2n^k$.   □

A direct construction yields the same upper bound for the conversion of a one-way n-state k-NIUFST to an equivalent NFA as for the two-way to NFA conversion. In fact, a simplified version of the proof of Theorem 2 can be applied, where only left-to-right sweeps have to be simulated. This can be done in parallel but directly. Moreover, the construction preserves determinism.

Theorem 3. *Let $k \geq 1$ be an integer. Every n-state k-NIUFST (k-IUFST) can be converted to an equivalent NFA (DFA) with at most $2n^k$ states.*

4 Costs of Simulations Involving Deterministic Devices

The mutual simulations of nondeterministic iterated uniform finite state transducers revealed that the ability to perform sweeps in the two-way mode helps only a little to save states compared with the one-way mode and vice versa. The situation changes drastically in the deterministic case.

We first define a language that witnesses the descriptional power of two-way sweeping in the deterministic case. Namely, for any integers $n, k \geq 1$, we let

$$E_{n,k} = \{\, w \mid w \in \{a,b\}^* b \{a,b\}^{n^k-1} \,\}.$$

Lemma 4. *(i) For any $n \geq 2$ and even $k \geq 2$, the language $E_{n,k}$ can be accepted by a k-2IUFST with $n^2 + 1$ states. (ii) For any $n \geq 2$ and odd $k \geq 3$, the language $E_{n,k}$ can be accepted by a $(k+1)$-2IUFST with n^2 states.*

Since any DFA accepting language $E_{n,k}$ has at least 2^{n^k} states, Lemma 4 yields a lower bound for the conversion of a k-2IUFST to a DFA.

Theorem 5. *Let $n \geq 2$ and $k \geq 2$. If k is even (resp., odd), at least $2^{(n-1)^{k/2}}$ (resp., $2^{n^{(k-1)/2}}$) states are necessary in the worst case for a DFA to accept the language of an n-state k-2IUFST.*

A size upper bound for turning k-2IUFSTs to DFAs is derived in the following

Theorem 6. *Let $k \geq 1$ be an integer. Every n-state k-2IUFST can be converted to an equivalent DFA with at most 2^{2n^k} states.*

Proof. A given n-state k-2IUFST is in particular an n-state k-2NIUFST which in turn can be converted to an equivalent NFA with at most $2n^k$ states by Theorem 2. Determinization of the NFA gives a DFA with at most 2^{2n^k} states.   □

Next we turn to discuss the descriptional capacity gained in two-way sweeping compared with one-way sweeping. In the nondeterministic case it was sufficient to double the number of states to make two-way sweeping one-way and vice versa. Theorem 6 gives the upper bound of 2^{2n^k} states for the two-way to one-way conversion in the deterministic case. This upper bound includes the sweep reduction to one. However, we also derive a lower bound that is much more costly than in the nondeterministic case.

Theorem 7. *Let $n \geq 2$ and $k \geq 2$. (i) Every n-state k-2IUFST can be converted to an equivalent k-IUFST with at most 2^{2n^k} states. (ii) If k is even (resp., odd), at least $2^{((n-1)^{\frac{k}{2}}-1)/k}$ (resp., $2^{(n^{\frac{k-1}{2}}-1)/k-1}$) states are necessary in the worst case for a k-IUFST to accept the language of an n-state k-2IUFST.*

Proof. It suffices to prove the lower bound. Let k be even. By Lemma 4, the language $E_{n,k}$ is accepted by a k-2IUFST T' with $n' = n^2 + 1$ states. Assume T' can be turned to a k-IUFST T with strictly less than $2^{\frac{(n'-1)^{\frac{k}{2}}-1}{k}} = 2^{\frac{n^k-1}{k}}$ states. By Theorem 3, T transforms to an equivalent DFA with strictly less than 2^{n^k} states, a contradiction since each DFA accepting $E_{n,k}$ has at least 2^{n^k} states. Similarly, we derive a contradiction for odd k. By Theorem 3, the language $E_{n,k}$ is accepted by a k'-2IUFST T' with $k' = k+1$ sweeps and $n' = n^2$ states. Assume T' can be turned to a k-IUFST T with strictly less than $2^{\frac{n'^{\frac{k'-1}{2}}-1}{k'-1}} = 2^{\frac{n^k-1}{k}}$ states. As in the even case, this would result in a DFA accepting $E_{n,k}$ with strictly less than 2^{n^k} states, a contradiction. □

The next result shows that making one-way sweeping two-way is much cheaper than the converse, in sharp contrast to the nondeterministic case.

Theorem 8. *Let $n \geq 2$ and $k \geq 2$. Every n-state k-IUFST can be converted to an equivalent k-2IUFST with at most n^2 states.*

Finally we turn to discuss the descriptional complexity of determinization. An upper bound for the determinization of a k-NIUFST can be derived with the help of Theorem 3, where it is shown that every n-state k-NIUFST can be converted to an equivalent NFA with at most $2n^k$ states. By the usual powerset construction one obtains an equivalent DFA with at most 2^{2n^k} states. A lower bound has been shown for the witness language $\{ vbw \mid v, w \in \{a,b\}^*, |w| = c \cdot n^k \text{ for } c > 0 \}$ that is accepted by some $(n + 1)$-state k-NIUFST [13]. On the other hand, any equivalent DFA needs at least 2^{n^k+1} states.

Theorem 9. *Let $n \geq 2$ and $k \geq 1$. (i) Every n-state k-NIUFST can be turned to an equivalent DFA with at most 2^{2n^k} states. (ii) At least $2^{(n-1)^k+1}$ states are necessary in the worst case for a DFA to accept the language of an n-state k-NIUFST.*

Since the costs for converting between one-way and two-way mode for nondeterministic devices are cheap, a similar result can be derived for the conversion from k-2NIUFST to DFA. However, since this conversion not only determinizes the device but also reduces the number of sweeps to its minimum, and since the conversion from two-way to one-way is expensive for deterministic devices, it is not clear where the expensive costs appear when a k-2NIUFST is converted to a DFA. So, we consider next the determinization from k-2NIUFST to k-2IUFST. To this end, for $n, k \geq 2$, we consider the language

$$S_{n,k} = \{\, u_1 \$ u_2 \$ \cdots \$ u_r \# v_1 \$ v_2 \$ \cdots \$ v_s \mid r, s \geq 0,$$

$$u_i, v_i \in \{a, b\}^{k \lfloor \log n \rfloor}, \{u_1, u_2, \ldots, u_r\} \neq \{v_1, v_2, \ldots, v_s\} \,\},$$

for which an $O(n \log n)$-state k-2NIUFST T can be constructed.

Lemma 10. *Let $k \geq 2$ and $n = 2^i$ for some $i \geq 1$. Any k-2IUFST for $S_{n,k}$ has at least $2^{(n^k - 1)/k}$ states.*

Proof. Let $T = \langle Q, \Sigma, \Delta, q_0, \triangleright, \triangleleft, \delta, F \rangle$ be a k-2IUFST accepting $S_{n,k}$. For subsets $\{u_1, u_2, \ldots, u_r\}$ of $\{a, b\}^{k \log n}$, we consider computations on inputs of the form $u \# u$, where $u = u_1 \$ u_2 \$ \cdots \$ u_r$. In particular, we consider the states in which T enters the $\#$ symbol during left-to-right sweeps and in which T leaves the $\#$ symbol during right-to-left sweeps. Since T may perform up to k sweeps, depending on u this sequence of states has a length of at most k.

Assume that for two different subsets $\{u_1, u_2, \ldots, u_r\}$ and $\{v_1, v_2, \ldots, v_s\}$ the sequences of states coincide. Since neither $u \# u$ nor $v \# v$ belongs to $S_{n,k}$, both inputs are not accepted. Now we consider the computation of T on input $u \# v$. Since the state sequences are identical, the behavior of T on the prefix u is the same as on the prefix u in the computation on $u \# u$. Similarly, the behavior of T on the suffix $\# v$ is the same as on the suffix $\# v$ in the computation on $v \# v$. Therefore, the input $u \# v$ is not accepted by T. However, since u and v are based on different subsets the word $u \# v$ belongs to $S_{n,k}$. From the contradiction we conclude that the sequence of states is different for all subsets of $\{a, b\}^{k \log n}$.

Let $m = |Q|$. Then there are at most $\sum_{i=0}^{k} m^i = \frac{m^{k+1} - 1}{m - 1} \leq 2m^k$ different state sequences up to length k. On the other hand, $|\{a, b\}^{k \log n}| = n^k$ and, thus, there are 2^{n^k} different subsets. From $2m^k \geq 2^{n^k}$ we derive $m \geq 2^{(n^k - 1)/k}$. $\qquad\square$

By the upper bound from previous results and the lower bound of Lemma 10, the size cost of determinizing k-2NIUFST is stated in the following

Theorem 11. *Let $k \geq 2$. (i) For $n \geq 1$, every n-state k-2NIUFST can be converted to an equivalent DFA (and, thus, to a k-2IUFST) with at most 2^{2n^k} states. (ii) For $n = 2^i$ with $i \geq 1$, at least $2^{(n^k - 1)/k}$ states are necessary in the worst case for a k-2IUFST to accept the language of an $O(n \log n)$-state k-2NIUFST.*

5   Iterated Transduction on Unary Languages

In this section, we single out a family of unary languages whose acceptance by iterated transduction is particularly hard from a size complexity point of view.

In fact, we prove that the size of iterated transducers for such family cannot be lowered by the use of both nondeterminism and two-way motion. On the other hand, accepting this family by iterated transduction leads to extremely small devices if compared with equivalent classical finite automata.

To cleverly cope with unary languages, we need to briefly recall some basic results in Number Theory concerning the distribution of primes (see, e.g.., [10]). In what follows, by ln we denote the natural logarithm. For any real number x, let $\mathbb{P}(x) = \{p \in \mathbb{N} \mid p\} \leq x$ and p prime be the set of prime numbers not exceeding x. By the well-known Prime Number Theorem, the cardinality $\pi(x)$ of $\mathbb{P}(x)$ satisfies $\pi(x) \sim x/\ln x$ (i.e., $\lim_{x \to +\infty} \frac{\pi(x)}{x/\ln x} = 1$). Closely related to $\pi(x)$, the Chebyshev function $\vartheta(x) = \sum_{p \in \mathbb{P}(x)} \ln p$ is deeply investigated, for which $\vartheta(x) \sim x$ holds true. From this latter result, one may easily see that the primorial function $\Pi(x) = \prod_{p \in \mathbb{P}(x)} p$ has an asymptotic behavior as $\Pi(x) \sim \mathrm{e}^x$. By iterating sum instead of product, the function $\Sigma(x) = \sum_{p \in \mathbb{P}(x)} p$ can be defined, whose asymptotic behavior turns out to be $\Sigma(x) \sim x^2/(2\ln x)$.

We are now ready to define our family of unary regular languages, and design succinct IUFSTs for their acceptance. Given a prime number p, we let

$$L_{\Pi(p)} = \{\, 0^{c \cdot \Pi(p)} \mid c \geq 0 \,\}.$$

Theorem 12. *The language $L_{\Pi(p)}$ can be accepted by a p-state $\pi(p)$-IUFST.*

Let us now turn to compare the size of the p-state $\pi(p)$-IUFST T for $L_{\Pi(p)}$ presented in Theorem 12 with that of equivalent DFAs and NFAs: (i) By pumping arguments, it is not hard to see that $\Pi(p)$ states are necessary and sufficient for DFAs and NFAs to accept $L_{\Pi(p)}$. (ii) As recalled at the beginning of this section, we have $\Pi(p) \sim e^p$. Thus, for large primes p, our p-state IUFST T for $L_{\Pi(p)}$ turns out to be exponentially smaller than any equivalent DFA and NFA.

We can prove that this exponential gap cannot be further enlarged by showing that T simultaneously uses the minimum possible amount of states and sweeps. The minimality of T in terms of states is provided in the following theorem.

Theorem 13. *Any IUFST accepting $L_{\Pi(p)}$ must use at least p states, regardless the number of performed sweeps.*

Proof. In [12, Thm. 3], it is proved that, for any given prime p, the language $L_p = \{\, 0^{c \cdot p} \mid c \geq 0 \,\}$ cannot be accepted by any IUFST with less than p states. The proof goes by contradiction, assuming the existence of a IUFST T for L_p with less than p states. A string $0^{c \cdot p} \in L_p$, for c large enough, is then taken. By a fooling argument, it is shown that T accepts $0^{c \cdot p}$ if and only if it accepts the string $0^{c \cdot p - \alpha}$ as well, α being a product of numbers all strictly less than p. This contradicts the fact that $0^{c \cdot p - \alpha}$ does not belong to L_p, whence the result.

This approach adapts to $L_{\Pi(p)}$ as follows. We suppose, by contradiction, the existence of a IUFST T for $L_{\Pi(p)}$ with less than p states, and now take $0^{c \cdot p}$, for c being a large enough multiple of $\Pi(p)/p$, as a fooling string. Clearly, $0^{c \cdot p}$ belongs to $L_{\Pi(p)}$ and, as above, it is proved to be accepted by T if and only if the string

$0^{c \cdot p - \alpha}$ is accepted as well, α being a product of numbers all strictly less than p. However, $0^{c \cdot p - \alpha}$ does not belong to $L_{\Pi(p)}$, and hence we get the result. $\square$

Instead, the next theorem states the minimality of our T in terms of sweeps.

Theorem 14. *For large primes p, any p-state IUFST accepting $L_{\Pi(p)}$ cannot use a number of sweeps which is $o(\pi(p))$.*

Proof. According to Theorem 3, from any given p-state k-IUFST for $L_{\Pi(p)}$, we can obtain an equivalent $2p^k$-state DFA. By recalling (i) above, we have that the minimal DFA for $L_{\Pi(p)}$ has $\Pi(p)$ states. So, we must have $2p^k \geq \Pi(p)$, or equivalently, $k \geq \ln \frac{\Pi(p)}{2} / \ln p$. For large primes p, we have that $\Pi(p) \sim e^p$ and $\pi(p) \sim p / \ln p$. So, $k \notin o((\ln e^p - \ln 2)/\ln p) \Rightarrow k \notin o(p/\ln p) \Rightarrow k \notin o(\pi(p))$. $\square$

Even using nondeterministic iterated transduction for accepting $L_{\Pi(p)}$ does not lead to smaller devices. In fact, we obtain similar minimality results on the number of states and sweeps for NIUFSTs accepting the language $L_{\Pi(p)}$:

Theorem 15. *(i) The language $L_{\Pi(p)}$ can be accepted by a p-state $\pi(p)$-NIUFST. (ii) Any NIUFST accepting $L_{\Pi(p)}$ must use at least p states, regardless the number of performed sweeps. (iii) For large primes p, any p-state NIUFST accepting $L_{\Pi(p)}$ cannot use a number of sweeps which is $o(\pi(p))$.*

Proof. (i) Clearly, the p-state $\pi(p)$-IUFST provided in Theorem 12 for $L_{\Pi(p)}$ can be seen as a NIUFST. (ii) We can use the pumping argument in Theorem 13. Here, we fool any NIUFST with less than p states by focusing on an accepting computation for a string $0^{c \cdot p} \in L_{\Pi(p)}$, for c being a large enough multiple of $\Pi(p)/p$. (iii) By Theorem 3, any given p-state k-NIUFST for $L_{\Pi(p)}$ can be turned into an equivalent $2p^k$-state NFA. By (i) before Theorem 13, a minimal NFA for $L_{\Pi(p)}$ has $\Pi(p)$ states. So, $2p^k \geq \Pi(p)$, or equivalently, $k \geq \ln \frac{\Pi(p)}{2} / \ln p$. The result follows since, for large primes p, we have that $\Pi(p) \sim e^p$. $\square$

Let us add more features to our IUFSTs, in the attempt of shrinking the hardware to accept $L_{\Pi(p)}$. So, together with nondeterminism, we also allow two-way motion. The next theorem shows that even this enhancement does not help.

Theorem 16. *(i) The language $L_{\Pi(p)}$ can be accepted by a p-state $\pi(p)$-2IUFST. (ii) Any 2NIUFST accepting $L_{\Pi(p)}$ must use at least p states, regardless the number of performed sweeps. (iii) For large primes p, any p-state 2NIUFST accepting $L_{\Pi(p)}$ cannot use a number of sweeps which is $o(\pi(p))$.*

We conclude by comparing the size of the p-state $\pi(p)$-IUFST for $L_{\Pi(p)}$ presented in Theorem 12 with that of equivalent one-way isolated cut point probabilistic automata (PFAs) [19,21], two-way DFAs (2DFAs), and two-way NFAs (2NFAs): (i) By [19, Thm. 2.8], we get that $\Sigma(p)$ states are necessary and sufficient for PFAs to accept $L_{\Pi(p)}$. By [20, Thm. 9], this size complexity result extends to 2DFAs and 2NFAs as well. (ii) As noted at the beginning of this section, we have $\Sigma(p) \sim p^2/(2 \ln p)$. So, for large primes p, our p-state IUFST for $L_{\Pi(p)}$ turns out to be almost quadratically smaller than any equivalent PFA, 2DFA, and 2NFA.

Acknowledgement. The authors wish to thank the anonymous referees for their kind comments.

References

1. Bednárová, Z., Geffert, V., Mereghetti, C., Palano, B.: The size-cost of Boolean operations on constant height deterministic pushdown automata. Thoer. Comput. Sci. **449**, 23–36 (2012)
2. Bednárová, Z., Geffert, V., Mereghetti, C., Palano, B.: Removing nondeterminism in constant height pushdown automata. Inf. Comput. **237**, 257–267 (2014)
3. Bertoni, A., Mereghetti, C., Palano, B.: Trace monoids with idempotent generators and measure only quantum automata. Natl. Comput. **9**, 383–395 (2010)
4. Bianchi, M.P., Mereghetti, C., Palano, B.: Complexity of promise problems on classical and quantum automata. In: Calude, C.S., Freivalds, R., Kazuo, I. (eds.) Computing with New Resources. LNCS, vol. 8808, pp. 161–175. Springer, Cham (2014). https://doi.org/10.1007/978-3-319-13350-8_12
5. Bianchi, M.P., Palano, B.: Behaviours of unary quantum automata. Fund. Inf. **104**, 1–15 (2010)
6. Bordihn, H., Fernau, H., Holzer, M., Manca, V., Martín-Vide, C.: Iterated sequential transducers as language generating devices. Theor. Comput. Sci. **369**, 67–81 (2006)
7. Citrini, C., Crespi-Reghizzi, S., Mandrioli, D.: On deterministic multi-pass analysis. SIAM J. Comput. **15**, 668–693 (1986)
8. Friburger, N., Maurel, D.: Finite-state transducer cascades to extract named entities in texts. Theor. Comput. Sci. **313**, 93–104 (2004)
9. Ginzburg, A.: Algebraic Theory of Automata. Academic Press, New York (1968)
10. Hardy, G., Wright, E.: An Introduction to the Theory of Numbers, 5th edn. Oxford University Press, Oxford (1979)
11. Hartmanis, J., Stearns, R.E.: Algebraic Structure Theory of Sequential Machines. Prentice-Hall, Englewood Cliffs (1966)
12. Kutrib, M., Malcher, A., Mereghetti, C., Palano, B.: Descriptional complexity of iterated uniform finite-state transducers. In: Hospodár, M., Jirásková, G., Konstantinidis, S. (eds.) DCFS 2019. LNCS, vol. 11612, pp. 223–234. Springer, Cham (2019). https://doi.org/10.1007/978-3-030-23247-4_17
13. Kutrib, M., Malcher, A., Mereghetti, C., Palano, B.: Deterministic and nondeterministic iterated uniform finite-state transducers: computational and descriptional power. In: Anselmo, M., Della Vedova, G., Manea, F., Pauly, A. (eds.) CiE 2020. LNCS, vol. 12098, pp. 87–99. Springer, Cham (2020). https://doi.org/10.1007/978-3-030-51466-2_8
14. Kutrib, M., Malcher, A., Mereghetti, C., Palano, B., Wendlandt, M.: Deterministic input-driven queue automata: finite turns, decidability, and closure properties. Theor. Comput. Sci. **578**, 58–71 (2015)
15. Malcher, A., Mereghetti, C., Palano, B.: Descriptional complexity of two-way pushdown automata with restricted head reversals. Theor. Comput. Sci. **449**, 119–133 (2012)
16. Manca, V.: On the generative power of iterated transductions. In: Words, Semigroups, and Transductions - Festschrift in Honor of Gabriel Thierrin, pp. 315–327. World Scientific (2001)
17. Mealy, G.H.: A method for synthesizing sequential circuits. Bell Syst. Tech. J. **34**, 1045–1079 (1955)

18. Mereghetti, C.: Testing the descriptional power of small Turing machines on non-regular language acceptance. Int. J. Found. Comput. Sci. **19**, 827–843 (2008)
19. Mereghetti, C., Palano, B., Pighizzini, G.: Note on the succinctness of deterministic, nondeterministic, probabilistic and quantum finite automata. Theor. Inf. Appl. **35**, 477–490 (2001)
20. Mereghetti, C., Pighizzini, G.: Two-way automata simulations and unary languages. J. Autom. Lang. Comb. **5**, 287–300 (2000)
21. Rabin, M.O.: Probabilistic automata. Inf. Control **6**, 230–245 (1963)

Descriptional Complexity of Winning Sets of Regular Languages

Pierre Marcus[1] and Ilkka Törmä[2(✉)] ⓘ

[1] M2 Informatique Fondamentale, École Normale Supérieure de Lyon, Lyon, France
pierre.marcus@ens-lyon.fr
[2] Department of Mathematics and Statistics, University of Turku, Turku, Finland
iatorm@utu.fi

Abstract. We investigate certain word-construction games with variable turn orders. In these games, Alice and Bob take turns on choosing consecutive letters of a word of fixed length, with Alice winning if the result lies in a predetermined target language. The turn orders that result in a win for Alice form a binary language that is regular whenever the target language is, and we prove some upper and lower bounds for its state complexity based on that of the target language.

Keywords: State complexity · Regular languages · Winning sets

1 Introduction

Let us define a word-construction game of two players, Alice and Bob, as follows. Choose a set of binary words $L \subseteq \{0,1\}^*$ called the *target set*, a length $n \geq 0$ and a word $w \in \{A, B\}^n$ called the *turn order*, where A stands for Alice and B for Bob. The players construct a word $v \in \{0,1\}^n$ so that, for each $i = 0, 1, \ldots, n-1$ in this order, the player specified by w_i chooses the symbol v_i. If $v \in L$, then Alice wins the game, and otherwise Bob wins. The existence of a winning strategy for Alice depends on both the target set and the turn order. We fix the target set L and define its *winning set* $W(L)$ as the set of those words over $\{A, B\}$ that result in Alice having a winning strategy.

Winning sets were defined under this name in [9] in the context of symbolic dynamics, but they have been studied before that under the name of *order-shattering sets* in [1,4]. The winning set has several interesting properties: it is downward closed in the index-wise partial order induced by $A < B$ (as changing B to A always makes the game easier for Alice) and it preserves the number of words of each length. This latter property was used in [8] to study the growth rates of substitutive subshifts.

If the language L is regular, then so is $W(L)$, as it can be recognized by an alternating finite automaton (AFA) [9], which only recognizes regular languages [3]. Thus we can view W as an operation on the class of binary regular

---

I. Törmä—Author supported by Academy of Finland grant 295095.

G. Jiráskova and G. Pighizzini (Eds.): DCFS 2020, LNCS 12442, pp. 130–141, 2020.
https://doi.org/10.1007/978-3-030-62536-8_11

languages, and in this article we study its state complexity in the general case and in several subclasses. In our construction the AFA has the same state set as the original DFA, so our setting resembles parity games, where two players construct a path in a finite automaton [10]. The main difference is that in a parity game, the player who chooses the next move is the owner of the current state, whereas here it is determined by the turn order word.

In the general case, the size of the minimal DFA for $W(L)$ can be doubly exponential in that of L. We derive a lower, but still superexponential, upper bound for bounded regular languages (languages that satisfy $L \subseteq w_1^* w_2^* \cdots w_k^*$ for some words w_i). We also study certain bounded permutation invariant languages, where membership is defined only by the number of occurrences of each symbol. In particular, we explicitly determine the winning sets of the languages $L_k = (0^*1)^k 0^*$ of words with exactly k occurrences of 1.

In this article we only consider the binary alphabet, but we note that the definition of the winning set can be extended to languages $L \subseteq \Sigma^*$ over an arbitrary finite alphabet Σ in a way that preserves the properties of downward closedness and $|L| = |W(L)|$. The turn order word is replaced by a word $w \in \{1, \ldots, |\Sigma|\}^*$. On turn i, Alice chooses a subset of size w_i of Σ, and Bob chooses the letter v_i from this set.

2 Definitions

We present the standard definitions and notations used in this article. For a set Σ, we denote by Σ^* the set of finite words over it, and the length of a word $w \in \Sigma^n$ is $|w| = n$. The notation $|w|_a$ means the number of occurrences of symbol $a \in \Sigma$ in w. The empty word is denoted by λ. For a language $L \subseteq \Sigma^*$ and $w \in \Sigma^*$, denote $w^{-1} L = \{v \in \Sigma^* \mid wv \in L\}$. We say L is *(word-)bounded* if $L \subseteq w_1^* \cdots w_k^*$ for some words $w_1, \ldots, w_k \in \Sigma^*$. Bounded languages have been studied from the state complexity point of view in [5].

A finite state automaton is a tuple $\mathcal{A} = (Q, \Sigma, q_0, \delta, F)$ where Q is a finite state set, Σ a finite alphabet, $q_0 \in Q$ the initial state, δ is the transition function and $F \subseteq Q$ is the set of final states. The language accepted from state $q \in Q$ is denoted $\mathcal{L}_q(\mathcal{A}) \subseteq \Sigma^*$, and the language of $\mathcal{A}$ is $\mathcal{L}(\mathcal{A}) = \mathcal{L}_{q_0}(\mathcal{A})$. The type of δ and the definition of $\mathcal{L}(\mathcal{A})$ depend on which kind of automaton $\mathcal{A}$ is.

- If $\mathcal{A}$ is a deterministic finite automaton, or DFA, then $\delta : Q \times \Sigma \to Q$ gives the next state from the current state and an input symbol. We extend it to $Q \times \Sigma^*$ by $\delta(q, \lambda) = q$ and $\delta(q, sw) = \delta(\delta(q, s), w)$ for $q \in Q$, $s \in \Sigma$ and $w \in \Sigma^*$. The language is defined by $\mathcal{L}_q(\mathcal{A}) = \{w \in \Sigma^* \mid \delta(q, w) \in F\}$.
- If $\mathcal{A}$ is a nondeterministic finite automaton, or NFA, then $\delta : Q \times \Sigma \to 2^Q$ gives the set of possible next states. We extend it to $Q \times \Sigma^*$ by $\delta(q, \lambda) = \{q\}$ and $\delta(q, sw) = \bigcup_{p \in \delta(q,s)} \delta(p, w)$ for $q \in Q$, $s \in \Sigma$ and $w \in \Sigma^*$. The language is defined by $\mathcal{L}_q(\mathcal{A}) = \{w \in \Sigma^* \mid \delta(q, w) \cap F \neq \emptyset\}$.
- If $\mathcal{A}$ is an alternating finite automaton, or AFA, then $\delta : Q \times \Sigma \to 2^{2^Q}$. We extend δ to $Q \times \Sigma^*$ by $\delta(q, \lambda) = \{S \subseteq Q \mid q \in S\}$ and $\delta(q, sw) = \{S \subseteq$

$Q \mid \{p \in Q \mid S \in \delta(q,w)\} \in \delta(q,s)\}$ for $q \in Q$, $s \in \Sigma$ and $w \in \Sigma^*$. The language is defined by $\mathcal{L}_q(\mathcal{A}) = \{w \in \Sigma^* \mid F \in \delta(q,w)\}$.

All three types of finite automata recognize exactly the regular languages. An AFA can be converted into an equivalent NFA, and an NFA into a DFA, by the standard subset constructions. A standard reference for DFAs and NFAs is [6].

Two states $p, q \in Q$ of $\mathcal{A}$ are equivalent, denoted $p \sim q$, if $\mathcal{L}_p(\mathcal{A}) = \mathcal{L}_q(\mathcal{A})$. Every regular language $L \subseteq \Sigma^*$ is accepted by a unique DFA with the minimal number of states, which are all nonequivalent, and every other DFA that accepts L has an equivalent pair of states. Two words $v, w \in \Sigma^*$ are congruent by L, denoted $v \equiv_L w$, if for all $u_1, u_2 \in \Sigma^*$ we have $u_1 v u_2 \in L$ iff $u_1 w u_2 \in L$. They are right-equivalent, denoted $v \sim_L w$, if for all $u \in \Sigma^*$ we have $vu \in L$ iff $wu \in L$. The set of equivalence classes $\Sigma^*/\equiv_L$ is the syntactic monoid of L, and if L is regular, then it is finite. In that case the equivalence classes of $\sim_L$ can be taken as the states of the minimal DFA of L.

Let $\mathcal{P} : 2^{\Sigma^*} \to 2^{\Sigma^*}$ be a (possibly partially defined) operation on languages. The (regular) state complexity of $\mathcal{P}$ is $f : \mathbb{N} \to \mathbb{N}$, where $f(n)$ is the maximal number of states in a minimal automaton of $\mathcal{P}(\mathcal{L}(\mathcal{A}))$ for an n-state DFA $\mathcal{A}$.

We say that a function $f : \mathbb{N} \to \mathbb{R}$ grows doubly exponentially if there exist $a, b, c, d > 1$ with $a^{b^n} \leq f(n) \leq c^{d^n}$ for large enough n, and superexponentially if for all $a > 1$, $f(n) > a^n$ holds for large enough n.

3   Winning Sets

In this section we define winning sets of binary languages, present the construction of the winning set of a regular language, and prove some general lemmas. We defined the winning set informally at the beginning of Sect. 1. Now we give a more formal definition which does not explicitly mention games.

Definition 1 (Winning Set). Let $n \in \mathbb{N}$ and $T \subseteq \{0,1\}^n$ be arbitrary. The winning set of T, denoted $W(T) \subseteq \{A,B\}^n$, is defined inductively as follows. If $n = 0$, then T is either the empty set or $\{\lambda\}$, and $W(T) = T$. If $n \geq 1$, then $W(T) = \{Aw \mid w \in W(0^{-1}T) \cup W(1^{-1}T)\} \cup \{Bw \mid w \in W(0^{-1}T) \cap W(1^{-1}T)\}$. For a language $L \subseteq \{0,1\}^*$, we define $W(L) = \bigcup_{n \in \mathbb{N}} W(L \cap \{0,1\}^n)$.

For Alice to win on a turn order of the form Aw, she has to choose either 0 or 1 as the first letter v_0 of the constructed word v, and then follow a winning strategy on the target set $v_0^{-1}T$ and turn order w. On a word Bw, Alice must have a winning strategy on $v_0^{-1}T$ and w no matter how Bob chooses v_0.

A language L over a linearly ordered alphabet Σ is downward closed if $v \in L$, $w \in \Sigma^{|v|}$ and $w_i \leq v_i$ for each $i = 0, \ldots, |v| - 1$ always implies $w \in L$.

Proposition 1 (Propositions 3.8 and 5.4 in [9]). The winning set $W(L)$ of any $L \subseteq \{0,1\}^*$ is downward closed (with the ordering $A < B$) and satisfies $|W(L) \cap \{A,B\}^n| = |L \cap \{0,1\}^n|$ for all n. If L is regular, then so is $W(L)$.

From a DFA $\mathcal{A}$, we can easily construct an alternating automaton for $W(\mathcal{A})$.

Definition 2 (Winning Set Automaton). *Let* $\mathcal{A} = (Q, \{0,1\}, q_0, \delta, F)$ *be a binary DFA. Define a "canonical" AFA for* $W(\mathcal{L}(\mathcal{A}))$ *as* $(Q, \{A, B\}, q_0, \delta', F)$ *where* $\delta'(q, A) = \{S \subset Q \mid \delta(q, 0) \in S \text{ or } \delta(q, 1) \in S\}$ *and* $\delta'(q, B) = \{S \subset Q \mid \delta(q, 0) \in S \text{ and } \delta(q, 1) \in S\}$. *This AFA clearly recognizes* $W(\mathcal{L}(\mathcal{A}))$. *We transform it into the equivalent NFA* $(2^Q, \{A, B\}, \{q_0\}, \delta'', 2^F)$, *where*

$$\delta''(S, A) = \{\{\delta(q, f(q)) \mid q \in S\} \mid f : S \to \{0,1\}\}$$
$$\delta''(S, B) = \{\{\delta(q, b) \mid q \in S, b \in \{0,1\}\}\}.$$

We usually work on the determinization of this NFA, which we denote by $W(\mathcal{A}) = (2^{2^Q}, \{A, B\}, \{\{q_0\}\}, \delta_W, F_W)$. *Here* $F_W = \{\mathsf{G} \in 2^{2^Q} \mid \exists S \in \mathsf{G} : S \subseteq F\}$ *and* $\delta_W(\mathsf{G}, c) = \bigcup_{S \in \mathsf{G}} \delta''(S, c)$ *for* $\mathsf{G} \subset 2^Q$ *and* $c \in \{A, B\}$.

Intuitively, as Alice and Bob construct a word, they also play a game on the states of $\mathcal{A}$ by choosing transitions. A state G of $W(\mathcal{A})$ is called a *game state*, and it represents a situation where Alice can force the game to be in one of the sets $S \in \mathsf{G}$, and Bob can choose the actual state $q \in S$. From the definition of the AFA it follows that exchanging the labels 0 and 1 on the two outgoing transitions of any one state of $\mathcal{A}$ does not affect δ'. In other words, the winning set of a DFA's language is independent of the labels of its transitions.

For example, take $L = 0^*1(0^*10^*1)0^*$, the language of words with an odd number of 1-symbols. Its winning set is $W(L) = (A + B)^*A$, as the last player has full control of the parity of occurrences of 1s. Fig. 1 shows the minimal DFA for L and the NFA derived from it that recognizes $W(L)$. One can check that the language recognized by this NFA is indeed $(A + B)^*A$. Note how reading A lets each state of a set evolve independently by 0 or 1, while B makes both choices for all states simultaneously and results in one large set.

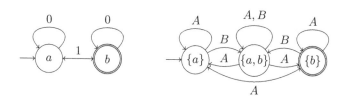

Fig. 1. A DFA for $L = 0^*1(0^*10^*1)0^*$, and the derived NFA for $W(L)$.

The following properties follow easily from the definition of $W(\mathcal{A})$.

Lemma 1. *Let $\mathcal{A}$ be a binary DFA, $W(\mathcal{A})$ the winning set DFA from Definition 2, and δ_W the iterated transition function for $W(\mathcal{A})$. Let G and H be game states of $W(\mathcal{A})$, $R, S, T, V \subseteq 2^Q$ sets of states, and w a word over $\{A, B\}$.*

(a) Sets in game states evolve independently: $\delta_W(\mathsf{G} \cup \mathsf{H}, w) = \delta_W(\mathsf{G}, w) \cup \delta_W(\mathsf{H}, w)$.

(b) *States in sets evolve almost independently: If $S, R \subseteq Q$ are disjoint, then*
$$\delta_W(\{S \cup R\}, w) = \{T \cup V \mid T \in \delta_W(\{S\}, w), V \in \delta_W(\{R\}, w)\}.$$

(c) *Supersets can be removed from game states (since δ_W is monotone in its first argument by (a) and (b)): If $S, R \in G$ and $S \subsetneq R$, then $G \sim G \setminus \{R\}$.*

(d) *Sets containing nonaccepting sink states can be removed from game states: If $S \in G$ and some $q \in S$ has no path to a final state, then $G \sim G \setminus \{S\}$.*

(e) *Accepting sink states can be removed from sets: If $S \in G$ and there is a sink state $q \in S \cap F$, then $G \sim (G \setminus \{S\}) \cup \{S \setminus \{q\}\}$.*

The next lemma helps prove equivalences of game states and words. The first part follows from monotonicity of δ_W, the second from Lemma 1(a).

Lemma 2. *Recall the assumptions of Lemma 1.*

(a) *Suppose that for each $S \in G$ there is $R \in H$ with $R \subseteq S$, and reciprocally. Then $G \sim H$.*

(b) *Let $v, w \in \{A, B\}^*$. If for all $q \in Q$, the game states $\delta_W(\{\{q\}\}, v)$ and $\delta_W(\{\{q\}\}, w)$ are either both accepting or both rejecting, then $v \equiv_{W(\mathcal{L}(A))} w$.*

Recall the *Dedekind numbers* $D(n)$, which count the number of antichains of subsets of $\{1, \ldots, n\}$ with respect to set inclusion. Their growth is doubly exponential: $a^{a^n} < D(n) < b^{b^n}$ holds for large enough n if $a < 2 < b$. This follows from $\binom{n}{\lceil n/2 \rceil} \leq \log_2 D(n) \leq (1 + O(\log n/n))\binom{n}{\lceil n/2 \rceil}$ [7] and the well known asymptotic formula $\binom{n}{\lceil n/2 \rceil} = \Theta(2^n/\sqrt{n})$.

Proposition 2. *Let A an n-state DFA. The number of states in the minimal DFA for $W(\mathcal{L}(A))$ is at most the Dedekind number $D(n)$.*

Proof. Every game state is equivalent to an antichain by Lemma 1(c), so the number of nonequivalent game states is at most $D(n)$.   □

We have computed the exact state complexity of the winning set operation for DFAs with at most 5 states; the 6-state case is no longer feasible with our program and computational resources. The sequence begins with $1, 4, 16, 62, 517$.

4   Doubly Exponential Lower Bound

In this section we construct a family of automata for which the number of states in the minimal winning set automaton is doubly exponential. The idea is to reach any desired antichain of subsets of a special subset of states, and then to make sure these game states are nonequivalent. To do this we split the automaton into several components. First we present a "subset factory gadget" that allows to reach any set of the form $\{S\}$ where S is a subset of a specific length-n path in the automaton. This gadget will be used several times to accumulate subsets in the game state. Then we present a "testing gadget" that lets us distinguish between game states by whether they contain a (subset of a) given set or not.

Recall that the transition labels of a binary DFA are irrelevant to the winning set of its language. In this section we define automata by describing their graphs, and a node with two outgoing transitions can have them arbitrary labeled by 0 and 1. Incoming and outgoing transitions in the figures indicate how the gadgets connect to the rest of the automaton.

Lemma 3 (Subset factory gadget). *Let* $\mathrm{GenSubset}_n$ *be the graph in Fig. 2. For* $i \in \{1,\dots,n\}$, *denote* $o_i = e_{2n+i-1}$ *(the* n *rightmost states labeled by* e*). For* $S \subseteq \{1,\dots,n\}$, *let* w_S^{gen} *be the concatenation* $w_1 w_2 \dots w_n$ *where* $w_i = BA$ *if* $i \in S$, *and* $w_i = AB$ *if* $i \notin S$. *Then* $\delta_W(\{\{b_1\}\}, w_S^{\mathrm{gen}})) \sim \{\{o_i \mid i \in S\}\}$ *for each binary DFA that contains* $\mathrm{GenSubset}_n$ *as a subgraph.*

The idea is that at step i, reading B adds c_i to each subset of the game state, and then reading A avoids the sink s_i. On the other hand reading A creates two versions of each subset of the game state, one that continues on the upper row, and one that falls into the sink s_i when B is read, and can then be ignored.

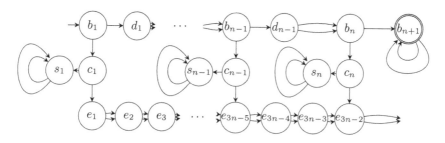

Fig. 2. $\mathrm{GenSubset}_n$, the subset factory gadget.

Lemma 4 (Game state factory gadget). *Let* $\mathrm{GenState}_n$ *be the graph in Fig. 3 and* $\mathcal{A}$ *any DFA over* $\{0,1\}$ *that contains it. For all* $G = \{S_1,\dots,S_\ell\}$ *where each* $S_i \subseteq \{r_1,\dots,r_n\}$, *let* $w_G^{\mathrm{gen}} \in \{A,B\}^{\ell(3n+1)}$ *be the concatenation of* $A w_{S_i}^{\mathrm{gen}} A^n$ *for* $i \in \{0,\dots,\ell\}$. *Then* $\delta_W(\{\{a_1\}\}, w_G^{\mathrm{gen}}) \sim G \cup \{\{a_1\}\} \cup G'$ *for some game state* G' *that does not contain a subset of the states of* $\mathrm{GenState}_n$.

The idea is to successively add new sets S_i to the game state, while previously made subsets will wait by rotating in the r-cycle. A singleton set rotates in the a-cycle so that reading A from the state a_1 creates a new singleton set in the subset factory gadget. The word $w_{S_i}^{\mathrm{gen}}$ transforms it into a set of the correct form, and then reading A^n both moves this new subset to the r-cycle with the previously created sets and rotates the singleton set back to a_i.

Lemma 5 (Testing gadget). *Let* $\mathrm{Testing}_n$ *be the graph in Fig. 4.*

(a) For $P \subseteq \{1,\dots,n\}$, *define* $w_P^{\mathrm{test}} \in \{A,B\}^n$ *by* $w_P^{\mathrm{test}}[i] = A$ *iff* $n-i+1 \in P$. *Then for each* $I \subseteq \{1,\dots,n\}$, *the game state* $\delta_W(\{\{q_i \mid i \in I\}\}, w_P^{\mathrm{test}})$ *is accepting iff* $I \subseteq P$.

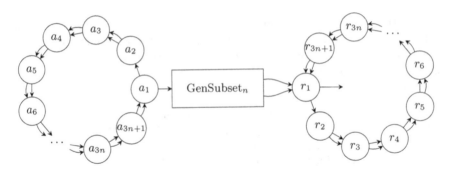

Fig. 3. GenState$_n$, the game state factory gadget.

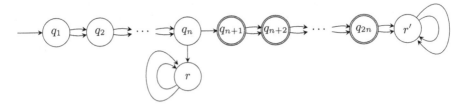

Fig. 4. Testing$_n$, the testing gadget.

(b) Let V be the set of nodes of the graph Testing$_n$. Then for all $\mathsf{G} \in 2^{2^V}$ and $w \in \{A, B\}^{\geq 2n}$, the game state $\delta_W(\mathsf{G}, w)$ is not accepting.

The idea is that reading A or B moves the game state toward r', except when the set contains the state q_n and B is read, causing it to fall into the sink r.

Theorem 1. For each $n > 0$ there exists a DFA $\mathcal{A}_n$ over $\{0, 1\}$ with $15n + 3$ states such that the minimal DFA for $W(\mathcal{L}(\mathcal{A}_n))$ has a least $D(n)$ states.

Together with Proposition 2, this implies that the state complexity of W restricted to regular languages grows doubly exponentially.

Proof (sketch). Let $\mathcal{A}_n$ be the DFA obtained by combining Testing$_n$ with the outgoing arrow of GenState$_n$ and assigning a_1 as the initial state. For an antichain G on the powerset of $\{r_1, \ldots, r_n\}$, let $X_\mathsf{G} = \delta_W(\{\{a_1\}\}, w_\mathsf{G}^{\text{gen}})$. Lemma 4 gives $X_\mathsf{G} \sim \{\{a_1\}\} \cup \mathsf{G} \cup \mathsf{G}'$ where each set in G' contains a state of Testing$_n$.

We show that distinct antichains G result in nonequivalent states. Let $P \subseteq \{1, \ldots, n\}$ and consider $X_\mathsf{G}' = \delta_W(X_\mathsf{G}, AB^{2n}A^{2n+1}w_P^{\text{test}})$. We claim that X_G' is accepting iff some element of G is a subset of $\{r_i \mid i \in P\}$. By Lemma 1(a) we may analyze the components of X_G separately.

- We have $\delta_W(\{\{a_1\}\}, A) = \{\{a_2\}, \{b_1\}\}$. The part $\{b_1\}$ is destroyed by the sink state s_1 when we read Bs, and the part $\{a_2\}$ rotates in the a-cycle without encountering accepting states.

- Each set of G' contains a state of Testing_n, which will reach one of the nonaccepting sinks r or r'.
- The game state $\delta_W(G, AB^{2n}A^{2n+1})$ consists of the sets $\{q_i \mid r_i \in S\}$ for $S \in G$, as well as sets that contain at least one element of $\{r_2, \ldots, r_{n+1}\}$. The latter will rotate in the r-cycle. By Lemma 5, the former sets produce an accepting game state in X'_G iff some $S \in G$ is a subset of $\{r_i \mid i \in P\}$.

We have found $D(n)$ nonequivalent states in $W(\mathcal{A})$. $\square$

5   Case of the Bounded Regular Languages

In this section we prove an upper bound on the complexity of the winning set of a bounded regular language. Our motivation comes from the fact that bounded regular languages correspond to so-called *zero entropy sofic shifts* in symbolic dynamics, which are defined by the number of words of given length that occur in them, and the fact that the winning set operation preserves this number. Our proof technique is based on tracing the evolution of individual states of a DFA $\mathcal{A}$ in the winning set automaton $W(\mathcal{A})$ when reading several A-symbols in a row.

Definition 3 (Histories of Game States). *Let $\mathcal{A} = (Q, \{0,1\}, q_0, \delta, F)$ be a DFA. Let $G \in 2^{2^Q}$ be a game state of $W(\mathcal{A})$, and for each $i \geq 0$, let $G_i \sim \delta_W(G, A^i)$ be the game state with all supersets removed as per Lemma 1(c). A history function for G is a function h that associates to each $i > 0$ and each set $S \in G_i$ a parent set $h(i, S) \in G_{i-1}$, and to each state $q \in S$ a set of parent states $h(i, S, q) \subseteq h(i, S)$ such that*

- *$\{q\} \in \delta_W(\{h(i, S, q)\}, A)$ for all $q \in S$, and*
- *$h(i, S)$ is the disjoint union of $h(i, S, q)$ for $q \in S$.*

Note that this implies $S \in \delta_W(\{h(i, S)\}, A)$ for each i.
   The history of a set $S \in G_i$ from i under h is the sequence $S_0, S_1, \ldots, S_i = S$ with $S_{j-1} = h(j, S_j)$ for all $0 < j \leq i$. A history of a state $q \in S$ in S under h is a sequence $q_0, \ldots, q_i = q$ with $q_{j-1} \in h(j, S_j, q_j)$ for all $0 < j \leq i$.

Every game state has at least one history function: each $S \in G_i$ has at least one set $R \in G_{i-1}$ with $S \in \delta_W(\{R\}, A)$, so we can choose $R = h(i, S)$, and similarly for the $h(i, S, q)$. It can have several different history functions, and each of them defines a history for each set S. A state of S can have several histories under a single history function.
   For the rest of this section, we fix an n-state DFA $\mathcal{A} = (Q, \{0,1\}, q_0, \delta, F)$ that recognizes a bounded binary language and has disjoint cycles. Let the lengths of the cycles be $k_1, \ldots, k_p$, and let ℓ be the number of states not part of any cycle.
   We define a preorder $\leq$ on the state set Q by reachability: $p \leq q$ holds if and only if there is a path from p to q in $\mathcal{A}$. For two history functions h, h' of a game state G, we write $h \leq h'$ if for each $i > 0$, each $S \in G_i$ and each $q \in S$, there exists a function $f : h(i, S, q) \rightarrow h'(i, S, q)$ with $p \leq f(p)$ for all $p \in h(i, S, q)$. This defines a preorder on the set of history functions of G. We write $h < h'$ if

$h \leq h'$ and $h' \not\leq h$. A history function h is *minimal* if there exists no history function h' with $h' < h$. Intuitively, a minimal history function is one where the histories of states stay in the early cycles of $\mathcal{A}$ as long as possible. Since the choices of $h(i, S)$ and $h(i, S, q)$ can be made independently, minimal history functions always exist.

Lemma 6. *Let* $\mathsf{G} \in 2^{2^Q}$ *be any game state of* $W(\mathcal{A})$. *Then there exist* $k \leq \mathrm{lcm}(k_1, \ldots, k_p) + 2n + \max_{x \neq y} \mathrm{lcm}(k_x, k_y)$ *and* $m \leq \mathrm{lcm}(k_1, \ldots, k_p)$ *such that* $\delta_W(\mathsf{G}, A^k) \sim \delta_W(\mathsf{G}, A^{k+m})$.

The idea of the proof is that under a minimal history function, no state $q \in S \in \mathsf{G}$ can spend too long in a cycle it did not start in: the maximal number of steps is comparable to the lcm of the lengths of successive cycles.

Theorem 2. *Let* $\mathcal{A}$ *be an* n-*state binary DFA whose language is bounded. Then there is a partition* $\ell + k_1 + \cdots + k_p = n$ *such that the minimal DFA for* $W(\mathcal{L}(\mathcal{A}))$ *has at most* $\sum_{m=0}^{\ell+p+1}(p \cdot \max_{x \neq y} \mathrm{lcm}(k_x, k_y) + 2\ell + 2\mathrm{lcm}(k_1, \ldots, k_p))^m$ *states.*

Proof. Denote the minimal DFA for $W(\mathcal{L}(\mathcal{A}))$ by $\mathcal{B}$. We may assume that $\mathcal{A}$ is minimal, and then it has disjoint cycles, as otherwise the number of length-n words in $\mathcal{L}(\mathcal{A})$ would grow exponentially while in a bounded language this growth is at most polynomial. Let $k_1, \ldots, k_p$ be the lengths of the cycles and ℓ the number of remaining states, and denote $P = p \cdot \max_{x \neq y} \mathrm{lcm}(k_x, k_y) + 2\ell + 2\mathrm{lcm}(k_1, \ldots, k_p)$. Then any $w \in \mathcal{L}(W(\mathcal{A}))$ has $|w|_B \leq \ell + p$, as otherwise Bob can win by choosing to leave a cycle whenever possible.

Consider a word $w = A^{t_0}BA^{t_1}B \cdots BA^{t_m}$ with $0 \leq m \leq \ell + p$. If $t_i \geq P$ for some i, then Lemma 6 implies $\delta_W(\mathsf{G}, A^{t_i}) \sim \delta_W(\mathsf{G}, A^t)$ for the game state $\mathsf{G} = \delta_W(\{\{q_0\}\}, A^{t_0}B \cdots A^{t_{i-1}}B)$ and some $t < t_i$. Thus the number of distinct states of $\mathcal{B}$ reachable by such words is at most P^{m+1}. The claim follows.   □

The upper bound we obtain (the maximum of the expression taken over all partitions of n) is at least n^n. We do not know whether the actual complexity is superexponential for bounded languages. If we combine the gadgets $\mathrm{GenSubset}_n$ and $\mathrm{Testing}_n$, the resulting DFA recognizes a language whose winning set requires at least 2^n states, so for finite (and thus bounded) regular languages the state complexity of the winning set is at least exponential.

6   Chain-Like Automata

In this section we investigate a family of binary automata consisting of a chain of states with a self-loop on each state. More formally, define a 1-*bounded chain DFA* as $\mathcal{A} = (Q, \{0, 1\}, q_0, \delta, F)$ where $Q = \{0, 1, \ldots, n-1\}$, $q_0 = 0$, $\delta(i, 0) = i$ and $\delta(i, 1) = i + 1$ for all $i \in Q$ except $\delta(n-1, 1) = n-1$, and $n - 1 \notin F$. See Fig. 5 for an example. It is easy to see that these automata recognize exactly the regular languages L such that $w \in L$ depends only on $|w|_1$, and $|w|_1$ is also bounded. Of course, the labels of the transitions have no effect on the winning set $W(\mathcal{L}(\mathcal{A}))$ so the results of this section apply to every DFA with the structure of a 1-bounded chain DFA.

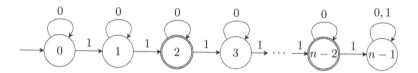

Fig. 5. A 1-bounded chain DFA. Any states except $n-1$ can be final.

Lemma 7. *Let $\mathcal{A}$ be an n-state 1-bounded chain DFA. Let $\equiv$ stand for $\equiv_{W(\mathcal{L}(\mathcal{A}))}$.*

(a) For every state $q \in Q$ and every $S \in \delta_W(\{\{q\}\}, AB)$, there exists $R \in \delta_W(\{\{q\}\}, BA)$ with $R \subseteq S$.
(b) For all $k \in \mathbb{N}$, $B^k A^k B^{k+1} \equiv B^{k+1} A^k B^k$.
(c) For all $k \in \mathbb{N}$, $A^{k+1} B^k A^k \equiv A^k B^k A^{k+1}$.
(d) $A^{n-1} \equiv A^n$ and $B^{n-1} \equiv B^n$.

The intuition for (a) is that the turn order BA is better for Alice than AB, since she can undo any damage Bob just caused. The other items are proved by concretely analyzing the evolution of game states, which A intuitively "moves around with precise control" and B "thickens". Lemma 2 simplifies the analysis.

Theorem 3. *Let $\mathcal{A}$ be a 1-bounded chain DFA with n states. The number of states in the minimal DFA of $W(\mathcal{L}(\mathcal{A}))$ is $O(n^{1/5} e^{4\pi \sqrt{\frac{n}{3}}})$.*

Proof. Since $\mathcal{A}$ does not accept any word with n or more 1-symbols, $W(\mathcal{L}(\mathcal{A}))$ contains no word with n or more B-symbols. Lemma 7(b) and (c) allow us to rewrite every word of $W(\mathcal{L}(\mathcal{A}))$ in the form $A^{n_1} B^{n_2} A^{n_3} B^{n_4} \cdots A^{n_{2r-1}} B^{n_{2r}}$ where the sequence $n_1, \ldots, n_{2r}$ is first nondecreasing and then noninncreasing, and $n_2 + n_4 + \cdots + n_{2r} < n$. With Lemma 7(d) we can also guarantee $n_1, n_3, \ldots, n_{2r-1} < n$, so that $\sum_i n_i < 4n$. In [2], Auluck showed that the number $Q(m)$ of partitions $m = n_1 + \ldots n_r$ of an integer m that are first nondecreasing and then noninncreasing is $\Theta(m^{-4/5} e^{2\pi \sqrt{m/3}})$. Of course, $v \equiv w$ implies $v \sim w$. Thus the number of non-right-equivalent words for $W(\mathcal{L}(\mathcal{A}))$, and the number of states in its minimal DFA, is at most $1 + \sum_{m=0}^{4n-1} Q(m) = O(n^{1/5} e^{4\pi \sqrt{\frac{n}{3}}})$. $\square$

7   Case Study: Exact Number of 1-Symbols

In the previous section we bounded the complexity of the winning set of certain bounded permutation invariant languages. Here we study a particular case, the language of words with exactly n ones, or $L = (0^*1)^n 0^*$. We not only compute the number of states in the minimal automaton (which is cubic in n), but also describe the winning set. Throughout the section $\mathcal{A}$ is the minimal automaton for L, described in Fig. 6. For $S \subseteq Q$, we denote $\overline{S} = \{\min(S), \min(S) + 1, \ldots, \max(S)\}$, and for any game state G of $W(\mathcal{A})$, denote $\overline{\mathsf{G}} = \{\overline{S} \mid S \in \mathsf{G}\}$.

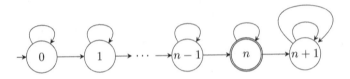

Fig. 6. The minimal DFA for $L = (0^*1)^n 0^*$.

Lemma 8. *Each game state* G *of* $W(\mathcal{A})$ *is equivalent to* $\overline{\mathsf{G}}$.

The idea is that the left and right ends of sets in G evolve independently of their other elements, and their positions determine whether G is final.

Lemma 9. *Let T be the set of integer triples (i, ℓ, N) with $0 \le i \le n$, $1 \le \ell \le n - i + 1$ and $1 \le N \le n - i - \ell + 2$. For $(i, \ell, N) \in T$, let*

$$\mathsf{G}(i, \ell, N) := \{\{i, \ldots, i+\ell-1\}, \{i+1, \ldots, i+\ell\}, \ldots, \{i+N-1, \ldots, i+\ell+N-2\}\}.$$

(a) Each reachable game state of $W(\mathcal{A})$ is equivalent to some $\mathsf{G}(i, \ell, N)$ for $(i, \ell, N) \in T$, or to $\emptyset$.
(b) The game states $\mathsf{G}(i, \ell, N)$ for $(i, \ell, N) \in T$ are nonequivalent.
(c) Every $\mathsf{G}(i, \ell, N)$ for $(i, \ell, N) \in T$ is equivalent to some reachable game state.

The game state $\mathsf{G}(i, \ell, N)$ is an interval of intervals, where i is the leftmost position of the first interval, ℓ is their common length, and N is their number. The first item is proved by induction, and the others by exhibiting a word over $\{A, B\}$ that produces or separates given game states. Then the minimal DFA for $W(L)$ has $|T| + 1$ states, and counting them yields the following.

Proposition 3. *The minimal DFA for $W(L)$ has $\frac{n^3}{6} + n^2 + \frac{11n}{6} + 2$ states.*

Proposition 4. $W(L)$ *is exactly the set of words $w \in \{A, B\}^*$ such that $|w|_A \ge n$, $|w|_B \le n$, and every suffix v of w satisfies $|v|_A \ge |v|_B$.*

Proof (sketch). Every $w \in W(L)$ satisfies $|w|_A \ge n$ since Bob can play only 0s, and $|w|_B \le 1$ since he can play only 1s. Only game states of the form $\mathsf{G}(i, 1, N)$ can be accepting. Since reading A decreases the parameter ℓ by one, and B increases ℓ by one, words of $W(L)$ must have after each B an associated A somewhere in the word. This is equivalent to the suffix condition. Conversely, on words of the given form Alice can win by associating to each $w_i = B$ some $w_j = A$ that occurs after it, choosing $v_j \ne v_i$ for the constructed word $v \in \{0, 1\}^*$, and choosing the remaining symbols so that $|v|_1 = n$. □

8   A Context-Free Language

In this section we prove that the winning set operator does not in general preserve context-free languages by studying the winning set of the Dyck language $D \subseteq \{0, 1\}^*$ of balanced parentheses. In our formalism, 0 stands for an opening parenthesis and 1 for a closing parenthesis.

Proposition 5. *The winning set of the Dyck language is not context-free.*

Proof (sketch). Take $L = W(D) \cap (AA)^*(BB)^*(AA)^*$, which is context-free if $W(D)$ is. We claim that $L = \{A^{2i}B^{2j}A^{2k} \mid i \geq j, k \geq 2j\}$. First, if Bob closes $2j$ parentheses, Alice must open at least $2j$ parentheses beforehand, so $i \geq j$ is necessary. If Bob opens $2j$ parentheses instead, when Alice plays a second time, she has to close $4j$ parentheses, hence $k \geq 2j$. Thus the right hand side contains L. Conversely, Alice can win on $A^{2i}B^{2j}A^{2k}$ by leaving exactly $2j$ parentheses open before Bob's turns and then closing all open parentheses, so L contains the right hand side. It's a standard exercise to prove that L is not context-free. $\square$

References

1. Anstee, R., Rónyai, L., Sali, A.: Shattering News. Graph. Comb. **18**(1), 59–73 (2002). https://doi.org/10.1007/s003730200003
2. Auluck, F.: On some new types of partitions associated with generalized Ferrers graphs. In: Mathematical Proceedings of the Cambridge Philosophical Society, vol. 47, pp. 679–686. Cambridge University Press (1951). https://doi.org/10.1017/S0305004100027134
3. Chandra, A.K., Kozen, D.C., Stockmeyer, L.J.: Alternation. J. ACM **28**(1), 114–133 (1981). https://doi.org/10.1145/322234.322243
4. Friedl, K., Rónyai, L.: Order shattering and Wilson's theorem. Discrete Math. **270**(1), 127–136 (2003). https://doi.org/10.1016/S0012-365X(02)00869-5
5. Herrmann, Andrea., Kutrib, Martin., Malcher, Andreas, Wendlandt, Matthias: Descriptional complexity of bounded regular languages. In: Câmpeanu, Cezar, Manea, Florin, Shallit, Jeffrey (eds.) DCFS 2016. LNCS, vol. 9777, pp. 138–152. Springer, Cham (2016). https://doi.org/10.1007/978-3-319-41114-9_11
6. Hopcroft, J.E., Motwani, R., Ullman, J.D.: Introduction to Automata Theory, Languages, and Computation, 3rd edn. Addison-Wesley Longman Publishing Co., Inc, USA (2006)
7. Kleitman, D., Markowsky, G.: On Dedekind's problem: the number of isotone Boolean functions. II. Trans. Am. Math. Soc. **213**, 373–390 (1975). https://doi.org/10.2307/1998052
8. Peltomäki, J., Salo, V.: On winning shifts of marked uniform substitutions. RAIRO-Theor. Inform. Appl. **53**(1–2), 51–66 (2019). https://doi.org/10.1051/ita/2018007
9. Salo, V., Törmä, I.: Playing with subshifts. Fundamenta Informaticae **132**(1), 131–152 (2014). https://doi.org/10.3233/FI-2014-1037
10. Zielonka, W.: Infinite games on finitely coloured graphs with applications to automata on infinite trees. Theor. Comput. Sci. **200**(1), 135–183 (1998). https://doi.org/10.1016/S0304-3975(98)00009-7

State Complexity of GF(2)-inverse and GF(2)-star on Binary Languages

Alexander Okhotin[1] and Elizaveta Sazhneva[1,2]([✉])

[1] Department of Mathematics and Computer Science, St. Petersburg State University, 7/9 Universitetskaya Nab., Saint Petersburg 199034, Russia
alexander.okhotin@spbu.ru, sazhneva.eliza@yandex.ru
[2] Department of Mechanics and Mathematics, Moscow State University, Moscow 119991, Russia

Abstract. The GF(2)-inverse operation on formal languages is known to have state complexity $2^n + 1$ for alphabets with at least three symbols, and $2^{n-1} + 1$ for a one-symbol alphabet. In this paper, it is shown that, for a two-symbol alphabet, its state complexity is exactly $\frac{3}{4}2^n + 3$. For a more general operation of GF(2)-star, its state complexity for a binary alphabet remains $2^n + 1$.

1 Introduction

GF(2)-operations on formal languages were recently defined by Bakinova et al. [1]. These operations are variants of the classical concatenation and Kleene star, in which the disjunction in the definition is replaced with exclusive OR. Consider that the classical concatenation of languages K and L is the set of all such strings w, that there exists *at least one* partition $w = uv$ with $u \in K$ and $v \in L$, which is a disjunction of $|w| + 1$ conjunctions. Replacing this disjunction with exclusive OR leads to the following new operation called *GF(2)-concatenation*.

$$K \odot L = \{ w \mid \# \text{ of partitions } w = uv, \text{ with } u \in K \text{ and } v \in L, \text{ is odd} \}$$

Similarly, the Kleene star L^* is defined as the set of all strings, for which there is *at least one* partition into a concatenation of substrings from L; a similar modification leads to another new operation, the *GF(2)-star*.

$$L^{\circledast} = \{ w \mid \# \text{ of partitions } w = u_1 \ldots u_k,$$
$$\text{with } k \geqslant 0 \text{ and } u_1, \ldots, u_k \in L \setminus \{\varepsilon\}, \text{ is odd} \}$$

Formal languages form a *ring*, with GF(2)-concatenation as multiplication and symmetric difference as addition [1]. Furthermore, every language L containing the empty string has an *inverse* with respect to GF(2)-concatenation: a language

Supported by Russian Science Foundation, project 18-11-00100.

Table 1. State complexity of GF(2)-concatenation, GF(2)-inverse and GF(2)-star for alphabets of different size.

	$|\Sigma| = 1$	$|\Sigma| = 2$	$|\Sigma| \geqslant 3$
GF(2)-concatenation ($\odot$)	$2mn$ [13,14]	$m2^n$ [1]	$m2^n$ [1]
GF(2)-inverse ($^{-1}$)	$2^{n-1} + 1$ [13,14]	?	$2^n + 1$ [1]
GF(2)-star ($\circledast$)	2^n [14]	?	$2^n + 1$ [1]

L^{-1} satisfying $L \odot L^{-1} = L^{-1} \odot L = \{\varepsilon\}$. The GF(2)-inverse L^{-1} actually equals $L^{\circledast}$. In view of their pleasant algebraic properties, these new operations might lead to interesting results in the future; a few results on formal grammars with GF(2)-operations have recently been obtained [10,11].

Classical and GF(2)-operations on languages are different in requiring "at least one partition" vs. "an odd number of partitions". These two conditions become equivalent if there can be at most one partition; the resulting *unambiguous concatenation* and *unambiguous star* are often studied in formal language theory. In particular, their state complexity is known [3,8].

Since all GF(2)-operations are known to preserve regularity [1], their state complexity also deserves investigation. The following results are known. For an m-state DFA and an n-state DFA, their GF(2)-concatenation is representable by a DFA with $m2^n$ states, and this number of states is known to be necessary, with witness languages defined over a two-symbol alphabet [1]. GF(2)-star and GF(2)-inverse of an n-state DFA can be represented with $2^n + 1$ states, and this upper bound is known to be tight for a three-symbol alphabet.

In the unary case, GF(2)-concatenation is representable with $2mn$ states, which is tight for infinitely many values of m and n. Unary GF(2)-inverse takes $2^{n-1} + 1$ states in the worst case, whereas unary GF(2)-star has state compexity 2^n. The state complexity of GF(2)-operations for alphabets of different size is compared in Table 1.

These results leave open the state complexity of GF(2)-inverse and GF(2)-star in the case of a two-symbol alphabet. Investigating this remaining case and determining whether the state complexity for binary alphabet is the same as for ternary is a typical research task in the area of state complexity: the earliest state complexity results [2,12,15] later had the size of the alphabet refined [6,7]. So far, for GF(2)-inverse, the bounds differ by a factor of two: the lower bound is $2^{n-1} + 1$ and the upper bound is $2^n + 1$; for GF(2)-star, the gap is minimal, with the state complexity contained between 2^n and $2^n + 1$. Both problems are settled in this paper.

In the case of GF(2)-inverse over a binary alphabet, the exact state complexity turns out to be $\frac{3}{4}2^n + 3$. The upper bound is established in Sect. 3 by analyzing the set of reachable states: it is proved that, using only two symbols, around one quarter of all states always remain unreachable. In Sect. 4, a matching lower bound of $\frac{3}{4}2^n + 3$ states is obtained: the argument expands on the analysis of primitive polynomials over GF(2) used in the proof for the unary case [13,14], with $2^{n-2} + 2$ extra states reached using the second symbol.

For the GF(2)-star over a binary alphabet, a new lower bound of $2^n + 1$ states is established in Sect. 5, thus improving the size of the alphabet in the earlier result [1].

2   GF(2)-star and GF(2)-inverse

This paper is concerned with one operation, the GF(2)-star, as well as with its special case, the GF(2)-inverse.

Definition 1. *For every language L, its GF(2)-star, denoted by $L^\circledast$, is the set of all strings w that have an odd number of representations of the form $w = w_1 w_2 \ldots w_k$, with $k \geqslant 0$ and $w_1, \ldots, w_k \in L \setminus \{\varepsilon\}$.*

For every language $L \subseteq \Sigma^*$ with $\varepsilon \in L$, the GF(2)-star $L^\circledast$ is the GF(2)-inverse L^{-1} [1, Thm. 2], that is, $L^{-1} \odot L = L \odot L^{-1} = \{\varepsilon\}$. Languages not containing the empty string do not have inverses.

If a language is recognized by an n-state DFA, then one can construct a DFA with $2^n + 1$ states recognizing its GF(2)-star. Since a few details of this construction shall be used in this paper, its summary is given below.

Theorem A (Bakinova et al. [1]). *For every n-state DFA $\mathcal{A} = (\Sigma, Q, q_0, \delta, F)$, the language $L(\mathcal{A})^\circledast$ is recognized by a DFA with the set of states $2^Q \cup \{q_0'\}$.*

Proof (Sketch of a proof.). The new automaton $\mathcal{B} = (\Sigma, 2^Q \cup \{q_0'\}, q_0', \delta', F')$ is defined as follows. Its states are all subsets of Q and an extra initial state q_0'. Its transition function is $\delta' \colon (2^Q \cup \{q_0'\}) \times \Sigma \to 2^Q \cup \{q_0'\}$. The transition in the state q_0' by each symbol $a \in \Sigma$ produces a singleton state corresponding to a single computation of $\mathcal{A}$.

$$\delta'(q_0', a) = \{\delta(q_0, a)\}$$

In a state $S \subseteq Q$, upon reading the next symbol $a \in \Sigma$, the automaton knows the set S' of states that occur in an odd number of computations.

$$S' = \{\, q \mid \text{the number of states } p \in S \text{ with } \delta(p, a) = q \text{ is odd} \,\}$$

Furthermore, a new simulated computation is started if the number of accepting states at the previous step was odd. The transition of $\mathcal{B}$ is thus defined as follows.

$$\delta'(S, a) = \begin{cases} S', & \text{if } |S \cap F| \text{ is even} \\ S' \triangle \{\delta(q_0, a)\}, & \text{if } |S \cap F| \text{ is odd} \end{cases}$$

The set of accepting states is $F' = \{\, S \mid |S \cap F| \text{ is odd} \,\} \cup \{q_0'\}$.

3 Upper Bound for the GF(2)-inverse

The starting point for the new upper bound on the state complexity of GF(2)-inverse for a two-symbol alphabet is the following observation. It turns out that, in the automaton constructed in Theorem A, the transition from a subset does not depend on whether the state 0 is in this subset.

Lemma 1. *Let $\mathcal{A} = (\Sigma, Q, 0, \delta, F)$ be an n-state DFA with $0 \in F$. Let $\mathcal{B} = (\Sigma, 2^Q \cup \{q_0'\}, q_0', \delta', F')$ be the DFA that recognizes the GF(2)-inverse of $L(\mathcal{A})$, constructed as in Theorem A. Then, $\delta'(S, a) = \delta'(S \cup \{0\}, a)$ for all $S \subseteq Q \setminus \{0\}$ and $a \in \Sigma$.*

The upper bound argument is based on the notion of an enterable state. Let $\mathcal{A} = (\Sigma, Q, q_0, \delta, F)$ be a DFA. A state $q \in Q$ is said to be *enterable*, if $q = \delta(p, a)$ for some $p \in Q$ and $a \in \Sigma$.

Lemma 2. *Let $\mathcal{A} = (\{a\}, Q, 0, \delta, F)$ be an n-state DFA with $0 \in F$. Let $\mathcal{B} = (\{a\}, 2^Q \cup \{q_0'\}, q_0', \delta', F')$ be the DFA recognizing the GF(2)-inverse of $L(\mathcal{A})$, defined as in Theorem A. Then, the DFA $\mathcal{B}$ has at most $2^{n-1} + 1$ enterable states.*

Consider a DFA for the GF(2)-inverse of a language over a two-symbol alphabet. An upper bound on the number of reachable states is obtained by analyzing the states enterable by the first and by the second symbol.

Theorem 1. *Let $\mathcal{A} = (\{a, b\}, Q, 0, \delta, F)$ be an n-state DFA with $0 \in F$. Then, the DFA for the GF(2)-inverse $L(\mathcal{A})^{-1}$, as defined in Theorem A, has at most $\frac{3}{4}2^n + 2$ enterable states, and accordingly at most $\frac{3}{4}2^n + 3$ reachable states.*

Depending on the form of $\mathcal{A}$, the proof is handled separately in the following three cases.

I. The only accepting state is 0.
II. There are accepting states besides 0, and there exists a state not enterable by some symbol.
III. There are accepting states besides 0, and each state is enterable by both symbols.

In the first case, the DFA $\mathcal{B}$ is proved to have at most $n + 2$ reachable states. Proofs of the remaining two cases rely on the following technical statement.

Lemma 3. *Let $\mathcal{A} = (\{a\}, Q, 0, \delta, F)$ be a DFA with n states, in which $0 \in F$ and $|F| \geqslant 2$. Let all states of $\mathcal{A}$ be enterable. Let $\mathcal{B} = (\{a\}, 2^Q \cup \{q_0'\}, q_0', \delta', F')$ be the DFA recognizing the GF(2)-inverse of $L(\mathcal{A})$, defined as in Theorem A. Then, for every state $q \in Q$, the automaton $\mathcal{B}$ has at most $2^{n-2} + 1$ enterable subset-states containing the state q.*

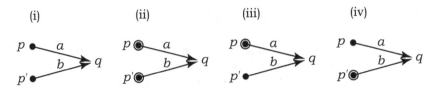

Fig. 1. Four cases of states enterable by a and by b from states with different acceptance status.

Case II in the proof of Theorem 1 is established by a direct application of this lemma. Indeed, if a state q is not enterable by b in $\mathcal{A}$, then, in $\mathcal{B}$, all 2^{n-1} subsets containing q are not enterable by b, and, according to Lemma 3, at most $2^{n-2} + 1$ of them are enterable by a. Then, a quarter of states are not enterable by either symbol.

It remains to prove the theorem in the case when every state in $\mathcal{A}$ is enterable both by a and by b, and 0 is not the only accepting state. Let $r_a = \delta(0, a)$ and $r_b = \delta(0, b)$.

All states in $\mathcal{A}$ are enterable by a, and hence, for every state $q \in Q$, there exists a unique state $p \in Q$ with $\delta(p, a) = q$. Similarly, there is a unique state $p' \in Q$ with $\delta(p', b) = q$. Depending on whether each of these states p and p' is accepting or rejecting, the set of states of $\mathcal{A}$ is split into the following five classes, as illustrated in Fig. 1.

$$Q_i = \{q \mid \exists p, p' \in Q \setminus F : \delta(p, a) = \delta(p', b) = q\},$$
$$Q_{ii} = \{q \mid \exists p, p' \in F \setminus \{0\} : \delta(p, a) = \delta(p', b) = q\},$$
$$Q_{iii} = \{q \mid \exists p \in F \setminus \{0\}, p' \in Q \setminus F : \delta(p, a) = \delta(p', b) = q\},$$
$$Q_{iv} = \{q \mid \exists p \in Q \setminus F, p' \in F \setminus \{0\} : \delta(p, a) = \delta(p', b) = q\},$$
$$Q_v = \{r_a, r_b\}.$$

Proof (Proof of Theorem 1, case III). Assume that, in $\mathcal{A}$, there are accepting states besides 0, and each state is enterable by both symbols.

The argument is based on a proof that the automaton $\mathcal{B}$ has at least 2^{n-2} subset-states enterable both by a and by b at once. This shall easily imply an upper bound on the number of states enterable by at least one symbol. Indeed, by Lemma 2, the image of the transition function by each symbol contains at most $2^{n-1} + 1$ subsets. Since 2^{n-2} subsets are enterable by both symbols, the overall number of enterable states is at most $(2^{n-1} + 1) \cdot 2 - 2^{n-2} = \frac{3}{4}2^n + 2$.

It remains to prove the existence of 2^{n-2} subsets enterable both by a and by b. The proof is split into five cases depending on the structure of the automaton $\mathcal{A}$.

Case 0. $r_a = r_b = r$.

Then it is claimed that for every subset-state $T \subseteq Q \setminus \{r\}$ the following subsets are enterable both by a and by b, and their total number is at least 2^{n-2}.

a. T, if $|T \cap (Q_{ii} \cup Q_{iii})| \equiv |T \cap (Q_{ii} \cup Q_{iv})| \equiv 0 \pmod 2$;

b. $T \cup \{r\}$, if $|T \cap (Q_{ii} \cup Q_{iii})| \equiv |T \cap (Q_{ii} \cup Q_{iv})| \equiv 1 \pmod 2$.

For every T, let $S = \{ s \mid \delta(s, a) \in T \}$ and $S' = \{ s \mid \delta(s, b) \in T \}$, be the sets of pre-images of the states in T by the symbols a and b.

– In the case (a), the condition implies that both subsets S and S' are rejecting. Then a transition by a from the subset S does not create extra states and leads to the subset T.

$$\delta'(S, a) = \{ \delta(s, a) \mid s \in S \} = T$$

A transition from S' by b similarly leads to T.

$$\delta'(S', b) = \{ \delta(s, b) \mid s \in S' \} = T$$

– In the case (b), it follows from the condition that both subsets S and S' turn out to be accepting. Then, both the transition from S by a, as well as the transition from S' by b create an extra state r and lead to the same subset.

$$\delta'(S, a) = \{ \delta(s, a) \mid s \in S \} \cup \{r\} = T \cup \{r\}$$
$$\delta'(S', b) = \{ \delta(s, b) \mid s \in S' \} \cup \{r\} = T \cup \{r\}$$

It is left to prove that at least 2^{n-2} subsets can be accessed in this way.

If $Q_{iii} \neq \varnothing$, then there exists a state $\hat{q} \in Q_{iii}$. The claim is applicable to 2^{n-1} subsets $T \subseteq Q \setminus \{r\}$, and for every pair of subsets T and $T \triangle \{\hat{q}\}$, one of them satisfies the condition (a–b). This provides 2^{n-2} desired subsets. The proof in the case $Q_{iv} \neq \varnothing$ is symmetric.

Finally, if $Q_{iii} = Q_{iv} = \varnothing$, then every T satisfies the condition (a–b), and 2^{n-1} subsets of the desired form shall be reached. This completes the proof of Case 0.

Now let $r_a \neq r_b$. Denote by s_a the state, from which there is a transition by a to r_b. The state with a transition by b to r_a is denoted by s_b. Depending on whether s_a is accepting or not, and whether s_b is accepting or not, there are four cases to consider. Each of them is handled by an argument generally similar to the one for Case 0; these proofs are omitted due to space constraints.

Overall, it has been shown that there are at least $\frac{3}{4}2^n + 2$ enterable subsets in the automaton $\mathcal{B}$, and each of them is potentially reachable from q_0'. The initial state q_0' is the only state that is reachable but not enterable, whence the upper bound $\frac{3}{4}2^n + 3$ on the number of reachable subsets. $\square$

4   Lower Bound for the GF(2)-inverse

The upper bound on the state complexity of the GF(2)-inverse over a binary alphabet established in Theorem 1 is $\frac{3}{4}2^n + 3$, and the aim of this section is to obtain a matching lower bound.

The proof elaborates on the method used to establish the state complexity of this operation in the unary case. It was shown that, for every $n \geqslant 2$, there exists a unary language $L \subseteq a^*$, with $\varepsilon \in L$, which is recognized by an n-state cyclic DFA, whereas the minimal DFA recognizing its GF(2)-inverse L^{-1} has $2^{n-1} + 1$ states [13].

Automata with this property are constructed on the basis of *primitive polynomials over GF(2)*, that is, polynomials $f(x) = a_{n-1}x^{n-1} + \ldots + a_1x + a_0$ of degree $n - 1$ over GF(2), with $a_0, \ldots, a_{n-1} \in \{0, 1\}$ and $a_{n-1} = 1$, such that the sequence $\{x^i \bmod f(x)\}_{i \geqslant 0}$ contains all $2^{n-1} - 1$ non-zero polynomials. For each $n \geqslant 2$, primitive polynomials are known to exist, and all of them have $a_0 = 1$ [9].

Next, for every primitive polynomial $f(x)$ of degree $n - 1$, one can construct the corresponding *cyclic DFA* $\mathcal{A}_f = (\{a\}, Q, 0, \delta, F)$, with $Q = \{0, \ldots, n - 1\}$, $\delta(i, a) = i + 1 \bmod n$ for all i, and $F = \{n - 1 - i \mid a_i = 1\}$. Then, the automaton for the GF(2)-inverse of $L(\mathcal{A}_f)$, constructed by Theorem A, is in a certain correspondence with the sequence $\{x^i \bmod f(x)\}$, and has exactly $2^{n-1} + 1$ reachable and pairwise incomparable states.

In this paper, this proof method needs to be refined by ensuring a small detail: there is such an automaton $L(\mathcal{A}_f)$ as described above, with the additional condition that it accepts a one-symbol string a. In order to obtain such an automaton from a primitive polynomial $f(x)$ by the above correspondence, this polynomial should have a coefficient $a_{n-2} = 1$. As proved by Davenport [4] and Han [5], for every n there is a primitive polynomial $f(x) = a_{n-1}x^{n-1} + \ldots + a_1x + a_0$ of degree $n - 1$ over GF(2), with $a_{n-2} = 1$, $a_{n-1} = 1$ and $a_0 = 1$. This is enough to construct the desired automaton.

An example of an automaton corresponding to such a polynomial is given below.

Example 1. Consider the primitive polynomial $f(x) = x^4 + x^3 + 1$. The cyclic automaton $\mathcal{A}_f$ corresponding to $f(x)$ is defined as $\mathcal{A}_f = (\{a\}, Q, 0, \delta, F)$, with $Q = \{0, 1, 2, 3, 4\}$, $\delta(i, a) = i + 1 \bmod 5$ and $F = \{0, 1, 4\}$.

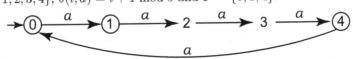

The DFA for its inverse, constructed as in Theorem A, is shown in Fig. 2. The automaton has 17 reachable states. Its cycle consists of 15 states, and 8 of them are accepting. Further 16 states are unreachable.

Lemma 4 ([13, **Lemmata 12, 13, 16**]). *Let $f(x) = a_{n-1}x^{n-1} + \ldots + a_1x + a_0$ be a primitive polynomial over GF(2), with $a_{n-1} = a_0 = 1$. Let $\mathcal{A}_f = (\{a\}, Q, 0, \delta, F)$, with $Q = \{0, \ldots, n-1\}$, $\delta(i, a) = i+1 \bmod n$ and $F = \{n-1-i \mid 0 \leqslant i \leqslant n - 1, a_i = 1\}$ be a cyclic automaton correponding to this polynomial. Let $\mathcal{B}_f$ be the automaton for $L(\mathcal{A}_f)^{-1}$ constructed as in Theorem A. Then this automaton is comprised of a tail of length 2 and a cycle of length $2^{n-1} - 1$, and all its states are pairwise distinguishable.*

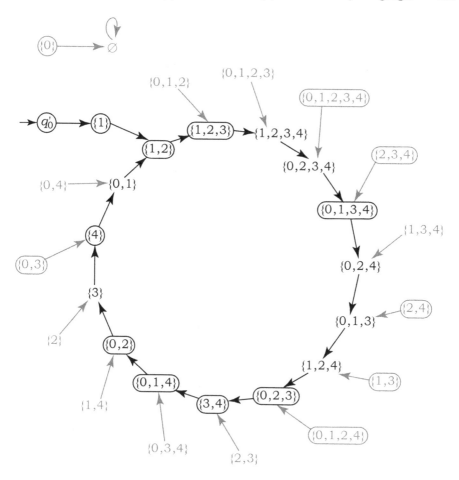

Fig. 2. DFA for the GF(2)-inverse of the language in Example 1.

In this paper, the number of accepting states in the cycle in $\mathcal{B}_f$ becomes essential. For each i, with $0 \leqslant i \leqslant 2^{n-1}$, let $\alpha_i = 1$ if $a^i \in L(\mathcal{B}_f)$, and $\alpha_i = 0$ otherwise. Then, the binary sequence $\alpha_2, \alpha_3, \ldots, \alpha_{2^{n}-1}$ represents the acceptance status of the states in the cycle of $\mathcal{B}_f$. The number of accepting states in this sequence is calculated as follows.

Lemma 5. *Let* $f(x) = a_{n-1}x^{n-1} + \ldots + a_1 x + a_0$ *be a primitive polynomial over* $GF(2)$*, with* $a_{n-1} = a_0 = 1$*, let* $\mathcal{A}_f$ *and* $\mathcal{B}_f$ *be as in Lemma 4. Then, the binary sequence* $\{\alpha_i\}_{i=2}^{2^{n}-1}$ *defined above contains exactly* $2^{n-2} - 1$ *zeroes and* 2^{n-2} *ones.*

Proof. The sequence $\alpha_2, \ldots, \alpha_{2^{n}-1}$ is naturally regarded as a cyclic sequence. Then, it is known to contain all binary substrings of length $n - 1$, except for 0^{n-1} [13, Lemmata 12, 14].

Consider a partition of these binary substrings into pairs: the string 1^{n-1} is left without a pair, and each substring of the form $0, x_2, \ldots, x_{n-1}$ corresponds

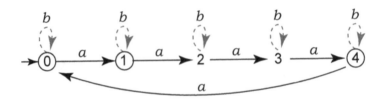

Fig. 3. A 5-state DFA in Example 2.

to the negated substring $1, \neg x_2, \ldots, \neg x_{n-1}$. In each of these 2^{n-2} pairs, there is substring beginning with 1 and a substring beginning with 0. Furthermore, the substring 1^{n-1} begins with an extra 1. Overall, the number of accepting states in the cycle is greater by 1 than the number of rejecting states.   □

Example 2. The automaton in Example 1 is expanded by adding transitions by another symbol b: for each state $q \in Q$, let $\delta(q, b) = q$. The resulting automaton in given in Figure 3.

The automaton for the GF(2)-inverse of this language, constructed according to Theorem A, is presented in Figure 4. It has 27 reachable subsets, and none of these states could be merged.

This example matches the upper bound $\frac{3}{4}2^n + 3$ obtained in Theorem 1, for $n = 5$. It turns out that matching witness languages to this upper bound can be obtained for all values of n.

Theorem 2. *For every $n \geqslant 2$, there exists a language L over an alphabet $\Sigma = \{a, b\}$, with $\varepsilon \in L$, recognized by n-state DFA, for which the minimal DFA recognizing its GF(2)-inverse L^{-1} has $\frac{3}{4}2^n + 3$ states.*

Proof. The witness language is given by an n-state DFA $\mathcal{A} = (\Sigma, Q, 0, \delta, F)$ with the set of states $Q = \{0, \ldots, n-1\}$, where 0 is the initial state.

Let $f(x) = a_{n-1}x^{n-1} + \ldots + a_1 x + a_0$ be a primitive polynomial, with $a_{n-1} = 1$ and $a_0 = 1$, which further satisfies $a_{n-2} = 1$. Then the set of accepting states is defined as $F = \{n - 1 - i \mid a_i = 1\}$.

The transitions in each state $i \in Q$ are defined as follows.

$$\delta(i, a) = i + 1 \pmod{n}$$
$$\delta(i, b) = i$$

Let $\mathcal{B} = (\{a, b\}, 2^Q \cup \{q_0'\}, q_0', \delta', F')$ be the DFA defined in Theorem A, which recognizes the GF(2)-inverse of $L(\mathcal{A})$.

If only transitions by a are considered, the automaton $\mathcal{B}$ degrades to the unary DFA described in Lemma 4, which consists of a tail of length 2 and a cycle of length 2^{n-1}. Let $C = \{\delta'(q_0', a^i) \mid i \geqslant 2\}$ be the states in this cycle.

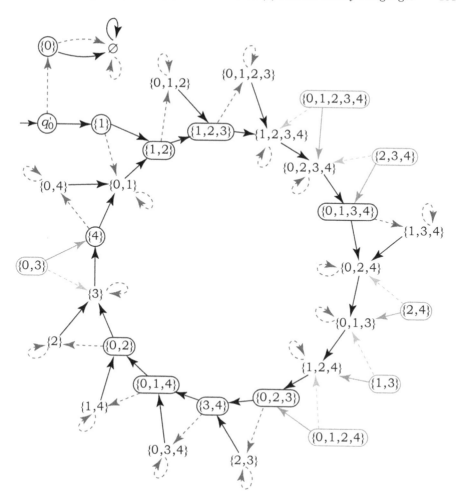

Fig. 4. DFA for the GF(2)-inverse of the language in Example 2.

By Lemma 5, the set C contains 2^{n-2} accepting states of $\mathcal{B}$. For each of them—that is, for each subset $T \in C \cap F'$—a transition by b simply toggles the membership of the state 0.

$$\delta'(T, b) = \bigcup_{t \in T} \{\delta(t, b)\} \triangle \{0\} = T \triangle \{0\}$$

By Lemma 1, transitions by a from the subsets T and $T \triangle \{0\}$ led to the same subset, which belongs to the cycle C by definition. Since only one pre-image of the subset could be in the cycle, it follows that all subsets $T \triangle \{0\}$, with $T \in C \cap F'$, do not belong to the cycle.

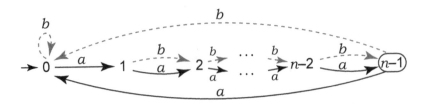

Fig. 5. Witness DFA for the GF(2)-star used in Theorem 3.

Thus, using transitions by the symbol b from accepting subsets in C, as many as 2^{n-2} subsets not in C have been reached. The resulting set of subsets is denoted by $C' = \{ T\triangle\{0\} \mid T \in C \text{ and } T \in F' \}$.

This is the essential point of the proof. The rest of the proof confirms that none of these subsets are reachable by a, two more subsets, $\varnothing$ and $\{0\}$, are reachable by b but not by a, and finally, that all the states in $\mathcal{B}$ are pairwise distinguishable, in the sense that for every pair of states there is a string accepted from one of them but not from the other. The proofs of these details are omitted due to space constraints.

This completes the proof of the state complexity of GF(2)-inverse over a binary alphabet: it is $\frac{3}{4}2^n + 3$, cf. $2^{n-1} + 1$ in the unary case and $2^n + 1$ in the ternary case.

In the case of the GF(2)-star, the result is more expected: the state complexity in the binary case turns out to be the same as for larger alphabets.

5   Lower Bound for the GF(2)-star

Theorem 3. *For every $n \geqslant 3$, there exists a language L over an alphabet $\Sigma = \{a, b\}$, with $\varepsilon \notin L$, which is recognized by a DFA with n states, whereas every DFA recognizing its GF(2)-star $L^{\circledast}$ must have at least $2^n + 1$ states.*

Proof. The witness language is given by an n-state DFA $\mathcal{A} = (\Sigma, Q, 0, \delta, F)$ with the set of states $Q = \{0, \ldots, n-1\}$, where 0 is the initial state, and the only accepting state is $n-1$. The transitions in each state $i \in Q$ are defined as follows.

$$\delta(i, a) = i+1 \pmod{n}$$

$$\delta(i, b) = \begin{cases} 0, & \text{if } i = 0 \\ i+1 \pmod{n}, & \text{if } 1 \leqslant i \leqslant n-1 \end{cases}$$

This DFA is illustrated in Fig. 5.

Let $\mathcal{B} = (\Sigma, 2^Q \cup \{q_0'\}, q_0', \delta', F')$ be the DFA constructed for $\mathcal{A}$ by Theorem A. It is claimed that every subset $S \subseteq Q$ is reachable from the initial state q_0' by some string, and that for every two states of $\mathcal{B}$, there exists a string that is accepted from one of them and not from the other. This shall confirm that every DFA recognizing the same language must have at least $2^n + 1$ states. The details of the proof are omitted due to space constraints.

6   Conclusion

The state complexity of GF(2)-concatenation, GF(2)-inverse and GF(2)-star has now been determined precisely for every alphabet size. The suggested topics for future research include estimating the state complexity of these operations for NFA and 2DFA, and perhaps investigating other possible GF(2)-based operations and their state complexity.

References

1. Bakinova, E., Basharin, A., Batmanov, I., Lyubort, K., Okhotin, A., Sazhneva, E.: Formal languages over GF(2). In: Klein, S.T., Martín-Vide, C., Shapira, D. (eds.) LATA 2018. LNCS, vol. 10792, pp. 68–79. Springer, Cham (2018). https://doi.org/10.1007/978-3-319-77313-1_5
2. Birget, J.-C.: Partial orders on words, minimal elements of regular languages and state complexity. Theor. Comput. Sci. **119**, 267–291 (1993). https://doi.org/10.1016/0304-3975(93)90160-U
3. Daley, M., Domaratzki, M., Salomaa, K.: Orthogonal concatenation: Language equations and state complexity. J. Univ. Comput. Sci. **16**(5), 653–675 (2010). https://doi.org/10.3217/jucs-016-05-0653
4. Davenport, H.: Bases for finite fields. J. London Math. Soc. **s1–43**(1), 21–39 (1968)
5. Han, W.-B.: The coefficients of primitive polynomials over finite fields. Math. Comput. **65**(213), 331–340 (1996). http://www.jstor.org/stable/2153850
6. Jirásková, G.: State complexity of some operations on binary regular languages. Theor. Comput. Sci. **330**, 287–298 (2005). https://doi.org/10.1016/j.tcs.2004.04.011
7. Jirásková, G., Okhotin, A.: State complexity of cyclic shift. RAIRO Informatique Théorique et Appl. **42**(2), 335–360 (2008). https://doi.org/10.1051/ita:2007038
8. Jirásková, G., Okhotin, A.: State complexity of unambiguous operations on deterministic finite automata. Theor. Comput. Sci. **798**, 52–64 (2019). https://doi.org/10.1016/j.tcs.2019.04.008
9. Lidl, R., Niederreiter, H.: Introduction to Finite Fields and their Applications. Cambridge University Press, Cambridge (1994). https://doi.org/10.1017/CBO9781139172769
10. Makarov, V.: Bounded languages described by GF(2)-grammars. CoRR abs/1912.13401 https://arxiv.org/abs/1912.13401 (2019)
11. Makarov, V., Okhotin, A.: On the expressive power of GF(2)-grammars. In: Catania, B., Královič, R., Nawrocki, J., Pighizzini, G. (eds.) SOFSEM 2019. LNCS, vol. 11376, pp. 310–323. Springer, Cham (2019). https://doi.org/10.1007/978-3-030-10801-4_25
12. Maslov, A.N.: Estimates of the number of states of finite automata. Sov. Math. Dokl. **11**, 1373–1375 (1970)
13. Okhotin, Alexander, Sazhneva, Elizaveta: State complexity of GF(2)-concatenation and GF(2)-inverse on unary languages. In: Hospodár, Michal, Jirásková, Galina, Konstantinidis, Stavros (eds.) DCFS 2019. LNCS, vol. 11612, pp. 248–259. Springer, Cham (2019). https://doi.org/10.1007/978-3-030-23247-4_19

14. Okhotin, A., Sazhneva, E.: State complexity of GF(2)-operations on unary languages, submitted
15. Yu, S., Zhuang, Q., Salomaa, K.: The state complexity of some basic operations on regular languages. Theor. Comput. Sci. **125**, 315–328 (1994). https://doi.org/10.1016/0304-3975(92)00011-F

Complexity of Two-Dimensional Rank-Reducing Grammars

Daniel Průša[✉]

Faculty of Electrical Engineering, Czech Technical University, Karlovo nám. 13,
12135 Prague 2, Czech Republic
daniel.prusa@fel.cvut.cz

Abstract. We study properties of a two-dimensional grammar introduced recently for use in document analysis and recognition. The grammar is obtained from the two-dimensional context-free grammar by restricting the form of productions. Variants (ranks) of the grammar with regard to productions complexity are defined. It is suggested that the lowest-rank variant can be considered as a natural generalization of the regular matrix grammar, which in addition has good properties with respect to the membership and emptiness problems. However, it is also showed that the higher-rank variants do not loosen complexity of the context-free grammar too much. There is a conditional lower bound preventing to propose a linear-time parsing algorithm. Moreover, the grammar is able to simulate the 2-counter Minsky machine, which results in non-recursive trade-offs and undecidability of the emptiness problem.

Keywords: Picture language · Two-dimensional context-free grammar · Regular matrix grammar · Parsing complexity · Decidability · Descriptional complexity

1 Introduction

The two-dimensional (2D) context-free grammar, also known as Kolam grammar, was proposed by Siromoney et al. in 1972 [18] and later independently by other authors [9,17]. It is a natural generalization of the context-free grammar in the Chomsky normal form. It uses productions of the forms $N \to A$, $N \to A\,B$, $N \to {A \atop B}$ to generate 2D arrays of symbols (so called pictures) by concatenating subpictures produced by A and B.

The grammar proved to be useful in the field of document analysis and recognition if it is relaxed to generate planar layouts of printed or handwritten characters [1,8,14]. The parsing algorithms used by the related recognition systems are generalizations of the CYK [20] or Earley [3] algorithm. Although the systems can apply certain types of document domain-related constraints to speed up the parsing, they still inherit the worst case time complexity from the 2D

The author was supported by the Czech Science Foundation grant no. 19-21198S.

G. Jirásková and G. Pighizzini (Eds.): DCFS 2020, LNCS 12442, pp. 155–166, 2020.
https://doi.org/10.1007/978-3-030-62536-8_13

context-free grammar by Siromoney. As it was shown in [2,17], the generalized CYK algorithm works in $\mathcal{O}(m^2n^2(m+n))$ time for pictures of size $m \times n$.

A subclass of the grammar, called a 2D rank-reducing grammar, was proposed in an attempt to suppress the parsing complexity [13]. The grammar introduces nonterminal ranks and allows only those productions $N \to AB$, $N \to \frac{A}{B}$ where the rank of B does not exceed the rank of N and the rank of A is strictly less than the rank of B. It was showed in [13] that such a restricted grammar is powerful enough to describe logical layouts of documents. A simple text document and a fragment of a rank-reducing grammar expressing the document structure is given in Fig. 1. A top-down parsing algorithm for the grammar, which uses regular expressions to find feasible splits, was proposed and empirically evaluated [13].

<table>
<tr><td>

Little Math Test

1. What is the GCD of 18 and 24 ?
a) 4   b) 6   c) 8

2. What is x when $2x + 4 = 3x - 3$?
a) 5   b) 6   c) 7

(a)
</td><td>

Document $\to$ Title / Tasks
Tasks $\to$ Task / Tasks
Tasks $\to$ Task
Task $\to$ Question / Answers
Answers $\to$ Answer | Answers
Answers $\to$ Answer

(b)
</td></tr>
</table>

Fig. 1. (a) A document sample. (b) A subset of productions defining the document logical layout ('/' and '|' represent vertical and horizontal concatenation, respectively).

If there are no productions of the form $N \to \frac{A}{B}$, the rank-reducing grammar generates just regular languages. It can thus be seen as a candidate for a 2D generalization of the regular grammar. It is definitely more practical than the regular matrix grammar [18] or other proposals of 2D regular-like grammars (see, e.g., [4]), since their abilities to model documents are limited.

In this paper we slightly revise the rank-reducing grammar definition (Sect. 3), show a conditional lower bound on the parsing complexity (Sect. 4) and prove pumping lemmas that imply (un)decidability of the emptiness problem, an infinite hierarchy of generated languages with respect to the maximum rank and non-recursive trade-offs among the corresponding grammar classes (Sect. 5).

2   Preliminaries

$\mathbb{N} = \{0, 1, 2, \ldots\}$ is the set of natural numbers, $\mathbb{N}^+ = \mathbb{N} \setminus \{0\}$.

We use the common notation and terms on *pictures* and *picture languages* (see, e.g., [5]). If Σ is a finite alphabet, then $\Sigma^{*,*}$ denotes the set of all pictures over Σ, that is, if $P \in \Sigma^{*,*}$, then P is a matrix of symbols from Σ. If P has m rows and n columns, we say it is of size $m \times n$, and we write $P \in \Sigma^{m,n}$. We also write $a^{m,n}$ to denote the picture over $\{a\}$ of size $m \times n$. The symbol in the i-th row and j-th column of P is referred by $P(i,j)$. The *empty picture* of size 0×0

is denoted by Λ. Moreover, $\Sigma^{+,+} = \Sigma^{*,*} \setminus \{\Lambda\}$ is the set of non-empty pictures. Each $a \in \Sigma$ is also treated as the picture $a^{1,1}$.

For integers $1 \le i \le k \le m$, $1 \le j \le \ell \le n$, and a picture $P \in \Sigma^{m,n}$, we use $P(i, j : k, \ell)$ to denote the non-empty *subpicture* of P of size $(k-i+1) \times (\ell - j + 1)$ whose top-left and bottom-right corners are in P at coordinates (i, j) and (k, ℓ), respectively. Moreover, we say that a picture P' is a *submatrix* of P if P' can be obtained from P by deleting a collection of its rows and columns. Namely, $\left(\begin{smallmatrix} a & b \\ c & d \end{smallmatrix}\right)$ is a submatrix of P if there are integers i, j, k, ℓ such that $P(i, j) = a$, $P(i, \ell) = b$, $P(k, j) = c$ and $P(k, \ell) = d$.

Two partial binary operations are introduced to concatenate pictures. Let P be a picture of size $k \times \ell$ such that p_{ij} is the symbol in the i-th row and j-th column. Similarly, let Q be a picture of size $m \times n$ with symbols q_{ij}. The *column concatenation* $P \oplus Q$ is defined if $k = m$, and the *row concatenation* $P \ominus Q$ is defined if $\ell = n$. The products are given by the following schemes:

$$P \oplus Q = \begin{pmatrix} p_{11} & \cdots & p_{1\ell} & q_{11} & \cdots & q_{1n} \\ \vdots & \ddots & \vdots & \vdots & \ddots & \vdots \\ p_{k1} & \cdots & p_{k\ell} & q_{m1} & \cdots & q_{mn} \end{pmatrix}, \quad P \ominus Q = \begin{pmatrix} p_{11} & \cdots & p_{1\ell} \\ \vdots & \ddots & \vdots \\ p_{k1} & \cdots & p_{k\ell} \\ q_{11} & \cdots & q_{1n} \\ \vdots & \ddots & \vdots \\ q_{m1} & \cdots & q_{mn} \end{pmatrix}.$$

Beside that, both operations are always defined when at least one of the operands is Λ. In this case, Λ is the neutral element, so $\Lambda \ominus P = P \ominus \Lambda = \Lambda \oplus P = P \oplus \Lambda = P$ for any picture P.

Definition 1. *A two-dimensional context-free grammar (2CFG) is a tuple* $\mathcal{G} = (V_N, V_T, \mathcal{P}, S)$, *where* V_N *is a set of nonterminals,* V_T *is a set of terminals,* $S \in V_N$ *is the initial nonterminal and* $\mathcal{P}$ *is a set of productions in one of the following forms:*

(1a) $N \to A$,   (1b) $S \to \Lambda$,   (1c) $N \to AB$,   (1d) $N \to \dfrac{A}{B}$

where $N \in V_N$ *and* $A, B \in V_T \cup V_N$.

We say that a production of type (1c) is *horizontal* as it generates a horizontal line composed of A and B. Analogously, a production of type (1d) is *vertical*.

Definition 2. *Let* $\mathcal{G} = (V_N, V_T, \mathcal{P}, S)$ *be a 2CFG. The set of pictures generated by* $\mathcal{G}$ *from any* $N \in V_N$, *denoted* $L(\mathcal{G}, N)$, *is the smallest set fulfilling:*

a) *If* $N \to A$ *is in* $\mathcal{P}$, *and* $P = A \in V_T$ *or* $P \in L(\mathcal{G}, A)$, *then* $P \in L(\mathcal{G}, N)$,
b) *if* $S \to \Lambda$ *is in* $\mathcal{P}$, *then* $\Lambda \in L(\mathcal{G}, S)$,
c) *if* $N \to AB$ *is in* $\mathcal{P}$, $P_1 = A \in V_T$ *or* $P_1 \in L(\mathcal{G}, A)$, $P_2 = B \in V_T$ *or* $P_2 \in L(\mathcal{G}, B)$, *and* $P = P_1 \oplus P_2$, *then* $P \in L(\mathcal{G}, N)$, *and*
d) *if* $N \to \dfrac{A}{B}$ *is in* $\mathcal{P}$, $P_1 = A \in V_T$ *or* $P_1 \in L(\mathcal{G}, A)$, $P_2 = B \in V_T$ *or* $P_2 \in L(\mathcal{G}, B)$, *and* $P = P_1 \ominus P_2$, *then* $P \in L(\mathcal{G}, N)$.

The picture language generated by $\mathcal{G}$ is defined as $L(\mathcal{G}) = L(\mathcal{G}, S)$.

Remark 1. To simply proofs in the next sections, we will assume without loss of generality that whenever a grammar contains the production of type (1b), then the initial nonterminal does not appear at the right-hand side of any production.

3   Two-Dimensional Rank-Reducing Grammar

We introduce a 2D rank-reducing grammar as a 2CFG $\mathcal{G} = (V_N, V_T, \mathcal{P}, S)$ equipped with a *ranking relation* $\preccurlyeq$, which is a linear order on $V_N \cup V_T$ fulfilling for all $A, B \in V_N \cup V_T$ that $(A \preccurlyeq B) \vee (B \preccurlyeq A)$ whereas it may be true that $(A \preccurlyeq B) \wedge (B \preccurlyeq A)$. For every $a, b \in V_T$ and $N \in V_N$, it is also required that $a \preccurlyeq b$ and $\neg(N \preccurlyeq a)$. It means that $\preccurlyeq$ induces a partition of $V_N \cup V_T$ into sets $R_0 = V_T, R_1, \ldots, R_n$ where, for all $0 \le i \le n$ and $\{A, A'\} \subseteq R_i$, it holds that $(A \preccurlyeq A') \wedge (A' \preccurlyeq A)$, and, for all $0 \le i < j \le n$, $A \in R_i$, $B \in R_j$, it holds that $(A \preccurlyeq B) \wedge \neg(B \preccurlyeq A)$. Based on the partition, we define *rank* of $A \in R_i$ to be i (we write $\mathrm{rank}(A) = i$). For $i = 1, \ldots, n$, we also write $V_N(i) = R_i$.

Definition 3. *A two-dimensional rank-reducing grammar of rank k (2RRG(k)) is a tuple $\mathcal{G} = (V_N, V_T, \mathcal{P}, S, \preccurlyeq)$ where $(V_N, V_T, \mathcal{P}, S)$ is a 2CFG, $\preccurlyeq$ is a ranking relation, $k = \mathrm{rank}(S) = \max_{N \in V_N} \mathrm{rank}(N)$, each $N \to B \in \mathcal{P} \setminus \{S \to \Lambda\}$ satisfies $\mathrm{rank}(B) \le \mathrm{rank}(N)$, and each $N \to AB$ and $N \to \begin{smallmatrix} A \\ B \end{smallmatrix}$ in $\mathcal{P}$ satisfies $\mathrm{rank}(A) < \mathrm{rank}(B) = \mathrm{rank}(N)$.*

If $\mathcal{G}$ is a 2RRG(1), then the horizontal and vertical productions are of the form $N \to a\,B$ and $N \to \begin{smallmatrix} a \\ B \end{smallmatrix}$, respectively, where a is a terminal. This means that $L(\mathcal{G})$ contains only one-row and one-column pictures generated by regular grammars.

2RRG(2) generalizes the regular matrix grammar, which uses horizontal regular productions to generate a string of nonterminals from an initial meta-nonterminal, and vertical regular productions to generate columns of the same height to replace the nonterminals – see Fig. 2(a). Compared to that, a 2RRG(2) generates a picture by repeatedly appending one-row and one-column subpictures. Each generated picture is thus a concatenation of subpictures, where each subpicture is generated from a nonterminal of rank 1. Moreover, these nonterminals can be visualized as a connected chain – see Fig. 2(b).

The next proposition proves that the 2D rank-reducing grammar can rather be viewed as a generalization of the regular than context-free grammar.

Theorem 1. *Let $\mathcal{G}$ be a 2RRG(k) ($k \ge 1$) with n nonterminals that does not contain vertical productions. There is a regular grammar with at most n^k nonterminals equivalent to $\mathcal{G}$.*

Proof. Let $\mathcal{G} = (V_N, V_T, \mathcal{P}, S, \preccurlyeq)$ be a 2RRG(k) without any vertical production. We first show how to construct a 2RRG($k-1$) $\mathcal{G}' = (V'_N, V_T, \mathcal{P}', S, \preccurlyeq')$ such that $L(\mathcal{G}) = L(\mathcal{G}')$ and $|V'_N| = |V_N| + |V_N(k)| \cdot |V_N(k-1)|$.

Denote $\mathcal{P}_1 = \{N \to A\,M \mid N, M \in V_N(k) \wedge A \in V_N(k-1)\}$. Since $\mathcal{P}_1$ consists exactly of those productions that prevent nonterminals in $V_N(k) \cup V_N(k-1)$ to be

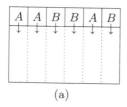
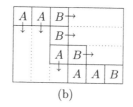

(a)   (b)

Fig. 2. A picture generated by (a) a regular grammar, (b) a 2RRG(2). Symbols A and B are nonterminals (of rank 1 in case (b)). The arrows represent expansions of nonterminals to one-column and one-row pictures (if there is no arrow, then the nonterminal is replaced by a terminal).

of the same rank, our idea is to introduce new nonterminals of the form (A, M) to represent the sentential form AM generated by a production $N \to A\,M \in \mathcal{P}_1$. Hence, for all $i = 1, \ldots, k-2$, we define $V'_N(i) = V_N(i)$, and $V'_N(k-1) = V_N(k-1) \cup V_N(k) \cup (V_N(k-1) \times V_N(k))$. Moreover, we define $\mathcal{P}' = (\mathcal{P} \setminus \mathcal{P}_1) \cup \mathcal{P}'_2$ where $\mathcal{P}'_2$ is the minimum set of productions that fulfill the following rules:

- If $N \to A\,M \in \mathcal{P}_1$, then $N \to (A, M) \in \mathcal{P}'_2$,
- if $A \in V_N(k-1)$, $M \in V_N(k)$, $A \to C\,B \in \mathcal{P}$, then $(A, M) \to C\,(B, M) \in \mathcal{P}'_2$,
- if $\{A, B\} \subseteq V_N(k-1)$, $M \in V_N(k)$, $A \to B \in \mathcal{P}$, then $(A, M) \to (B, M) \in \mathcal{P}'_2$,
- if $A \in V_N(k-1)$, $B \notin V_N(k-1)$, $M \in V_N(k)$ and $A \to B \in \mathcal{P}$, then $(A, M) \to B\,M \in \mathcal{P}'_2$.

For each $N \to A\,M \in \mathcal{P}_1$, the productions of $\mathcal{P}'_2$ ensure that $A \stackrel{*}{\Rightarrow}_\mathcal{G} B_1 \ldots B_s$ if and only if $(A, M) \stackrel{*}{\Rightarrow}_{\mathcal{G}'} B_1 \ldots B_s M$ for B_i's in $V_N \cup V_T$ of rank lower than $k-1$. Hence, it holds that $L(\mathcal{G}) = L(\mathcal{G}')$.

The procedure can be repeated to get grammars $\mathcal{G}_k, \ldots, \mathcal{G}_1$ where $\mathcal{G}_k$ is the given 2RRG(k) $\mathcal{G}$ and, for $i = 1, \ldots, k-1$, $\mathcal{G}_i$ is the 2RRG(i) obtained from $\mathcal{G}_{i+1}$.

It remains to show that $\mathcal{G}_1$ has at most $|V_N|^k$ nonterminals. For $i = 1, \ldots, k$, let $n_i = |V_N(i)|$ and let σ_i denote the number of nonterminals of rank i in $\mathcal{G}_i$. We can observe that $\sigma_k = n_k$ and $\sigma_i = n_i + \sigma_{i+1} + n_i \cdot \sigma_{i+1}$ for $i = 1, \ldots, k-1$.

We prove $\sigma_i \leq (n_i + \ldots + n_k)^{k-i+1}$ by induction on i. The inequality trivially holds for σ_k. If $i < k$, we use the induction hypotheses and derive

$$\sigma_i = \sigma_{i+1}\,(1 + n_i) + n_i \leq (n_{i+1} + \ldots + n_k)^{k-i}\,(1 + n_i) + n_i$$
$$\leq (n_i + \ldots + n_k)^{k-i}\,(n_i + \ldots + n_k) = (n_i + \ldots + n_k)^{k-i+1},$$

which implies that $\sigma_1 \leq \left(\sum_{i=1}^{k} n_i\right)^k = |V_N|^k$. $\square$

4   Parsing Complexity

We will show that the membership problem for 2RRG(3) is not easier than the Triangle Finding problem which aims to decide whether a given undirected graph with n vertices contains a triangle (3-clique). This problem can be solved by Boolean matrix multiplication in time $\mathcal{O}(n^{\omega})$ [6], where $\omega < 2.373$ denotes the matrix multiplication exponent [19]. However, it is currently unknown whether Triangle Finding can be solved in time $\mathcal{O}(n^2)$. Note that conditional lower bounds based on Triangle Finding are known for several problems [7, 11].

Let L_{TF} be a picture language over $\Sigma = \{0, 1, 2\}$ such that $P \in \Sigma^{*,*}$ is in L_{TF} if and only if $\left(\begin{smallmatrix} 1 & 2 \\ 1 & 1 \end{smallmatrix}\right)$ is a submatrix of P.

Lemma 1. *Triangle Finding in an undirected graph with n vertices reduces in $\mathcal{O}(n^2)$ time to the membership problem for L_{TF}.*

Proof. According to [10], a graph $G = (\{v_1, \ldots, v_n\}, E)$ has a triangle if and only if $\left(\begin{smallmatrix} 1 & 2 \\ 1 & 1 \end{smallmatrix}\right)$ is a submatrix of the n by n matrix M_G satisfying $M_G(i, i) = 2$ for all $i = 1, \ldots, n$, $M_G(i, j) = 1$ whenever $\{v_i, v_j\} \in E$ and $i < j$, and $M_G(i, j) = 0$ in all the other cases. Hence, G contains a triangle iff $M_G \in L_{\mathrm{TF}}$. $\quad\square$

Lemma 2. *There is a 2RRG(3) grammar $\mathcal{G}$ such that $L(\mathcal{G}) = L_{TF}$.*

Proof. Let $\mathcal{G} = (V_N, \Sigma, \mathcal{P}, S, \preccurlyeq)$ be a 2RRG(3) where $V_N(3) = \{S, T, F\}$, $V_N(2) = \{U, U_1, U_2\}$, $V_N(1) = \{A_r, A_c, R_1, R_1', R_2, R_2'\}$, $\Sigma = \{0, 1, 2\}$ and $\mathcal{P}$ is the set of productions (we use the $N \to A \mid B$ notation to represent $N \to A$ and $N \to B$)

$$S \to \begin{matrix} A_r \\ S \end{matrix} \mid A_c\, S \mid T, \quad T \to U\, F \mid U, \quad U \to \begin{matrix} R_1 \\ U_1 \end{matrix}, \quad F \to U_2, \quad U_2 \to \begin{matrix} A_r \\ U_2 \end{matrix} \mid A_r,$$

$$U_1 \to \begin{matrix} A_r \\ U_1 \end{matrix} \mid \begin{matrix} R_2 \\ U_2 \end{matrix} \mid R_2, \quad A_r \to a\, A_r \mid a \quad (\forall a \in \Sigma), \quad A_c \to \begin{matrix} a \\ A_c \end{matrix} \mid a \quad (\forall a \in \Sigma),$$

$$R_1 \to 1\, R_1', \quad R_2 \to 1\, R_2', \quad R_1' \to a\, R_1' \mid 2 \quad \text{and} \quad R_2' \to a\, R_2' \mid 1 \quad (\forall a \in \Sigma).$$

It holds that $L(\mathcal{G}, F) = L(\mathcal{G}, U_2) = \Sigma^{+,+}$. Moreover, $L(\mathcal{G}, U)$ consists of pictures containing the submatrix $\left(\begin{smallmatrix} 1 & 2 \\ 1 & 1 \end{smallmatrix}\right)$ aligned with both top corners, $L(\mathcal{G}, T)$ consists of pictures containing $\left(\begin{smallmatrix} 1 & 2 \\ 1 & 1 \end{smallmatrix}\right)$ aligned with the top-left corner and $L(\mathcal{G}, S)$ consists of pictures containing $\left(\begin{smallmatrix} 1 & 2 \\ 1 & 1 \end{smallmatrix}\right)$ positioned arbitrarily. $\quad\square$

Corollary 1. *There is no algorithm deciding the membership problem for 2RRG(3) in $\mathcal{O}(mn)$ time for $m \times n$ pictures unless Triangle Finding can be decided in $\mathcal{O}(n^2)$ time for graphs with n vertices.*

Theorem 2. *Let $\mathcal{G}$ be a 2RRG(2). There is an algorithm deciding the membership problem for $\mathcal{G}$ in $\mathcal{O}(mn)$ time for pictures of size $m \times n$.*

Proof. Let $\mathcal{G} = (V_N, V_T, \mathcal{P}, S, \preccurlyeq)$ be a 2RRG(2). Let P be a nonempty picture over V_T of size $m \times n$. To decide if $P \in L(\mathcal{G})$, construct three m by n matrices: M_R and M_C whose entries are subsets of $V_N(1)$, and M whose entries are subsets of $V_N(2)$. Entries are defined as follows. For all feasible (i, j), it holds that $N \in M_R(i, j)$ if and only if $P(i, j : i, n) \in L(\mathcal{G}, N)$. Analogously, $N \in M_C(i, j)$ if and only if $P(i, j : m, j) \in L(\mathcal{G}, N)$. Finally, $N \in M(i, j)$ if and only if $P(i, j : m, n) \in L(\mathcal{G}, N)$. Notice that $P \in L(\mathcal{G}) \Leftrightarrow S \in M(1, 1)$.

Entries of M_R and M_C can be computed in $\mathcal{O}(mn)$ time. It suffices to construct finite automata accepting the mirror image of $L(\mathcal{G}, A)$ where $A \in V_N(1)$

and apply the automata over rows and columns of P. Entries of M are computed using dynamic programming. First we compute $M(m, j)$ and $M(i, n)$ for $j = 1, \ldots, n$ and $i = 1, \ldots, m$, which is similar to the computation of M_R and M_C. The other entries are computed row by row. For (i, j) where $i < m$ and $j < n$, we decide whether $N \in M(i, j)$ based on productions of the forms $N \to A$, $N \to AB$, $N \to {}^A_B$ and the previously computed entries. For example, if $N \to AB \in \mathcal{P}$, $A \in M_C(i, j)$ and $B \in M(i + 1, j)$, then N belongs to $M(i, j)$. Each entry is computed in a constant time, hence the time complexity is $\mathcal{O}(mn)$.

$\square$

L_{TF} is a candidate for showing that 2RRG(3) is more powerful than 2RRG(2). The next lemma confirms that this is indeed true.

Lemma 3. L_{TF} *is not generated by any* 2RRG(2).

Proof. By contradiction. Let $\mathcal{G} = (V_N, \{0, 1, 2\}, \mathcal{P}, S, \preceq)$ be a 2RRG(2) such that $L(\mathcal{G}) = L_{TF}$. Let $n = 4 \cdot |V_N| + 1$. For $i = 1, \ldots, n - 1$, $k = 1, \ldots, n - i$, define a picture $P_{i,k}$ over $\{0, 1, 2\}$ of size $n \times n$ as follows: $P_{i,k}(i, i) = P_{i,k}(i + k, i) = P_{i,k}(i + k, i + k) = 1$, $P_{i,k}(i, i + k) = 2$, and the other entries of $P_{i,k}$ equal 0. The definition ensures that $P_{i,k} \in L_{TF}$. There are $\frac{n}{2}(n - 1)$ pictures $P_{i,k}$ in total.

Consider $P_{i,k}$ written as a concatenation of one-row and one-column subpictures as depicted in Fig. 2(b). Let $R_{i,k}$ be the one-row or one-column subpicture containing the cell (i, i) of $P_{i,k}$. Without loss of generality, there is an $A \in V_N(1)$ and a set S containing at least $\frac{n(n-1)}{4 \cdot |V_N|}$ pictures $P_{i,k}$ for which $R_{i,k}$ is a one-row picture in $L(\mathcal{G}, A)$. The lengths of $R_{i,k}$'s are in $[2, n]$. Since $n = 4 \cdot |V_N| + 1$, the pigeonhole principle implies that we can find two different pictures P_{i_1,k_1}, P_{i_2,k_2} in S such that $|R_{i_1,k_1}| = |R_{i_2,k_2}|$. Observe that the definition of $P_{i,k}$ ensures that $R_{i_1,k_1} \neq R_{i_2,k_2}$. If R_{i_1,k_1} in P_{i_1,k_1} is replaced by R_{i_2,k_2}, we obtain a picture that is also generated by $\mathcal{G}$, but this picture is not in L_{TF}, which is a desired contradiction.

$\square$

5 Decidability and Descriptional Complexity

In this section we present pumping lemmas for 1) "large" pictures generated by a unary 2RRG(2), and 2) sufficiently "wide" pictures generated by a unary 2RRG(k), $k \geq 3$. The lemmas imply results on decidability and grammar trade-offs.

Lemma 4. *Let L be a unary regular language over $\{a\}$ accepted by an n-state deterministic finite automaton $\mathcal{A}$. Then, $L = L_{fin} \cup \bigcup_{i=1}^{k} L_i$ where $k \leq n$, L_{fin} is a finite set containing only words of length up to n, and there are integers $0 \leq d, c_1, \ldots, c_k \leq n$ such that $L_i = \{a^{c_i + d \cdot j} \mid j \in \mathbb{N}\}$ for all $i = 1, \ldots, k$.*

Proof. The proof can be easily done by analyzing the underlying directed graph of $\mathcal{A}$ formed of states and transitions.

$\square$

Lemma 5. *Let $\mathcal{G} = (V_N, \{a\}, \mathcal{P}, S, \preceq)$ be a 2RRG(2). If $L(\mathcal{G})$ contains a picture $a^{m,n}$ such that $\max\{m, n\} \geq 2|V_N|^2 \cdot 8^{|V_N|^2}$, then there are integers c, d such that $0 \leq c < m$, $0 \leq d < n$, $c + d \geq 1$ and $a^{m-c+c \cdot i, n-d+d \cdot i} \in L(\mathcal{G})$ for all $i \in \mathbb{N}$.*

Proof. Let $P = a^{m,n} \in L(\mathcal{G})$ where $\max\{m,n\} \geq 2|V_N|^2 \cdot 8^{|V_N|^2}$. For each $A \in V_N$, let $L_R(\mathcal{G}, A)$ and $L_C(\mathcal{G}, A)$ denote the subset of all one-row and one-column pictures in $L(\mathcal{G}, A)$, respectively.

For each $A \in V_N(1)$, there is a regular grammar with $|V_N(1)| < |V_N|$ nonterminals generating $L_C(A, \mathcal{G})$, hence, there is a deterministic finite automaton with at most $2^{|V_N|}$ states accepting $L_C(A, \mathcal{G})$. By Lemma 4, there is an integer $1 \leq d_A \leq 2^{|V_N|}$ and a finite set of integers $\mathcal{I}_A$ such that any one-column picture $a^{k,1}$ of height $k > 2^{|V_N|}$ is in $L_C(A, \mathcal{G})$ if and only if $(k \bmod d_A) \in \mathcal{I}_A$. Let $\mathcal{D}_C = \{d_A \mid A \in V_N(1)\}$. Let $\mathcal{D}_R$ be analogously defined for the case when languages $L_R(A, \mathcal{G})$ are considered instead of languages $L_C(A, \mathcal{G})$.

Case I: $\min\{m,n\} > |V_N| \cdot 4^{|V_N|^2} + 2^{|V_N|}$. For $P_1 = a^{m_1,n_1}$, $P_2 = a^{m_2,n_2}$ and a nonterminal $N \in V_N$, let us write $P_1 \approx_N P_2$ if and only if $P_1, P_2 \in L(\mathcal{G}, N)$, $m_1, m_2, n_1, n_2 > 2^{|V_N|}$, $m_1 \equiv m_2 \pmod{d}$ for all $d \in \mathcal{D}_C$ and $n_1 \equiv n_2 \pmod{d}$ for all $d \in \mathcal{D}_R$. Observe the following fact. If $P_1 \approx_N P_2$ and $M \to AN \in \mathcal{P}$ can be used to produce $P_1' = a^{m_1,n_1+1} \in L(\mathcal{G}, M)$ from P_1, then it can also be used to produce $P_2' = a^{m_2,n_2+1} \in L(\mathcal{G}, M)$ from P_2, and it further holds that $P_1' \approx_M P_2'$. A completely analogous observation can be made for productions $M \to \genfrac{}{}{0pt}{}{A}{N}$. In addition, it is also evident that every production $M \to N$ yields $P_1 \approx_M P_2$.

In accordance to the scheme depicted in Fig. 2(b), there is a sequence of pictures $P_1, \ldots, P_s$ and nonterminals $N_1, \ldots, N_s$ from $V_N(2)$ such that $s \geq \min\{m,n\} - 2|V_N|$, $P = P_1$, $N_1 = S$, $P_i = a^{m_i,n_i} \in L(\mathcal{G}, N_i)$, $\min\{m_i, n_i\} > 2^{|V_N|}$, and P_i is generated by concatenating a column or row picture and P_{i+1}.

Since $s > |V_N| \cdot 4^{|V_N|^2} \geq |V_N| \cdot (2^{|V_N|})^{|\mathcal{D}_C|} \cdot (2^{|V_N|})^{|\mathcal{D}_R|}$, there are two distinct indexes k and ℓ such that $k < \ell$, $N_k = N_\ell = N \in V_N(2)$ and $P_k \approx_N P_\ell$. This means that 1) we can apply a sequence of productions $\mathcal{S}$, which produce $P = a^{m,n}$ from $P_k = a^{m_k,n_k}$, to produce $a^{m-(m_k-m_\ell),n-(n_k-n_\ell)} \in L(\mathcal{G})$ from $P_\ell = a^{m_\ell,n_\ell} \in L(\mathcal{G}, N)$, and 2) we can i times apply a sequence of productions that produce P_k from P_ℓ to produce $P_i' = a^{m_k+i\cdot(m_k-m_\ell),n_k+i\cdot(n_k-n_\ell)} \in L(\mathcal{G}, N)$ from P_k and then the sequence $\mathcal{S}$ to produce $a^{m+i\cdot(m_k-m_\ell),n+i\cdot(n_k-n_\ell)} \in L(\mathcal{G})$ from P_i'.

Case II: $\min\{m,n\} \leq |V_N| \cdot 4^{|V_N|^2} + 2^{|V_N|}$. Without loss of generality, let $n \geq 2|V_N|^2 \cdot 8^{|V_N|^2}$. We adjust the equivalence $\approx_N$ to the new setting: For $P_1 = a^{m_1,n_1}$, $P_2 = a^{m_2,n_2}$ and $N \in V_N$, we write $P_1 \approx_N' P_2$ if and only if $P_1, P_2 \in L(\mathcal{G}, N)$, $n_1, n_2 > 2^{|V_N|}$, $m_1 = m_2$ and $n_1 \equiv n_2 \pmod{d}$ for all $d \in \mathcal{D}_R$.

There is a sequence of pictures $P_1, \ldots, P_s$ and nonterminals $N_1, \ldots, N_s$ from $V_N(2) \cup V_N(1)$ such that $s \geq n - 2|V_N|$, $P = P_1$, $N_1 = S$, $P_i = a^{m_i,n_i} \in L(\mathcal{G}, N_i)$, $n_i > 2^{|V_N|}$ and P_i is produced from P_{i+1} by appending a column or row to P_{i+1}. Moreover, if P_i is a one-row picture, then $P_i = a \oplus P_{i+1}$. Since

$$s \geq n - 2|V_N| = 2|V_N|^2 \cdot 8^{|V_N|^2} - 2|V_N| \geq |V_N|^2 \cdot 8^{|V_N|^2} + |V_N| \cdot 2^{|V_N|^2} \cdot 2^{|V_N|}$$

$$= |V_N| \cdot 2^{|V_N|^2} \cdot \left(|V_N| \cdot 4^{|V_N|^2} + 2^{|V_N|}\right) > |V_N| \cdot m \cdot \left(2^{|V_N|}\right)^{|\mathcal{D}_R|},$$

there are two indexes k and ℓ such that $k < \ell$, $N_k = N_\ell = N \in V_N(1) \bigcup V_N(2)$ and $P_k \approx_N' P_\ell$, hence we can draw the same conclusion as in Case I. $\square$

Lemma 6. *Let* $\mathcal{G} = (V_N, \{a\}, \mathcal{P}, S, \preccurlyeq)$ *be a* 2RRG(k) *where* $k \geq 1$. *For every nonterminal* $N \in V_N$ *and picture* $a^{m,n} \in L(\mathcal{G}, N)$ *it holds that if* $n > |V_N|^k \cdot m^{k-1}$, *then* $a^{m,n+i\cdot n!} \in L(\mathcal{G}, N)$ *for all* $i \in \mathbb{N}$.

Proof. We will prove the lemma by induction on the grammar rank k and the number of picture rows m. Without loss of generality, we assume that $\mathcal{P}$ does not contain productions $N \to M$ such that $\mathrm{rank}(N) = \mathrm{rank}(M)$.

Base Case I: $m = 1$ and $k \geq 1$. If $P = a^{1,n} \in L(\mathcal{G}, N)$ where $n > |V_N|^k$, then P is a string generated by $\mathcal{G}$ from N without using vertical productions. By Theorem 1, there is a regular grammar $\mathcal{G}' = (V_N', \{a\}, \mathcal{P}', N)$ such that $|V_N'| \leq |V_N|^k$ and $P \in L(\mathcal{G}') \subseteq L(\mathcal{G}, N)$. The standard pumping lemma applied to $\mathcal{G}'$ yields that $a^{1,n+i\cdot p} \in L(\mathcal{G}')$ for a suitable $p \leq n$ and all $i \in \mathbb{N}$, hence $a^{1,n+i\cdot n!} \in L(\mathcal{G}, N)$ for all $i \in \mathbb{N}$.

Base Case II: $k = 1$ and $m \geq 1$. Since $\mathcal{G}$ is of rank 1, it generates only one-row and one-column pictures. If $P = a^{m,n} \in L(\mathcal{G}, N)$ where $n > |V_N| \geq 1$, then P is a one-row picture, hence Base case II is included in Base case I.

Induction Step: Let $k > 1$ and $m > 1$. Moreover, let $n > |V_N|^k \cdot m^{k-1}$. We will inspect how $P = a^{m,n} \in L(\mathcal{G}, N)$ is generated by $\mathcal{G}$ from N.

Let $\{N_i \to A_i N_{i+1}\}_{i=1}^{s}$ be a maximum length sequence of productions from $\mathcal{P}$ satisfying $N_1 = N$ and there are pictures $P_1, \ldots, P_{s+1}$ such that $P_i \in L(\mathcal{G}, A_i)$ if $i \in \{1, \ldots, s\}$, $P_{s+1} \in L(\mathcal{G}, N_{s+1})$ and $P = P_1 \oplus \ldots \oplus P_s \oplus P_{s+1}$. We examine three cases.

(1) If there is $i \in \{1, \ldots, s\}$ such that $P_i = a^{m,n'}$ and $n' > |V_N|^{k-1} \cdot m^{k-2}$, then the induction hypotheses applies to P_i.

(2) If $s > |V_N|$, then $N \overset{*}{\Rightarrow}_{\mathcal{G}} A_1 \ldots A_s N_{s+1}$ implies that

$$N \overset{*}{\Rightarrow}_{\mathcal{G}} A_1 \ldots A_{k-1} \left(A_k \ldots A_\ell\right)^i A_{\ell+1} \ldots A_s N_{s+1}$$

for some $1 \leq k \leq \ell \leq s$, hence $a^{m,n+p\cdot i} \in L(\mathcal{G})$ for all $i \in \mathbb{N}$ and p equal to the number of columns of $P_k \oplus \cdots \oplus P_\ell$ where it holds that p divides $n!$.

(3) Since $\{N_i \to A_i N_{i+1}\}_{i=1}^{s}$ is a maximum length sequence, $\mathcal{P}$ contains a production $N_{s+1} \to \begin{smallmatrix} B \\ N_{s+2} \end{smallmatrix}$ and there are pictures Q_1, Q_2 such that $Q_1 \in L(\mathcal{G}, B)$, $Q_2 \in L(\mathcal{G}, N_{s+2})$ and $P_{s+1} = Q_1 \ominus Q_2$. If P_{s+1} has more than $|V_N|^k \cdot (m-1)^{k-1}$ columns, then the induction hypotheses applies to Q_1 as well as to Q_2.

All three cases (1), (2) and (3) yield that $a^{n,n+i\cdot n!} \in L(\mathcal{G}, N)$ for all $i \in \mathbb{N}$. At the same time, one of these cases must occur. If none of them occurs, it holds

$$n \leq |V_N| \cdot |V_N|^{k-1} \cdot m^{k-2} + |V_N|^k \cdot (m-1)^{k-1} \leq |V_N|^k \cdot m^{k-1},$$

which contradicts the assumption on n. $\square$

For each $k \geq 1$, it is possible to propose a 2RRG(k+1) $\mathcal{G}_k$ which shows that the picture width assumption in Lemma 6 is asymptotically optimal.

Lemma 7. *For every* $k \in \mathbb{N}^+$, *there is a* 2RRG(k+1) *grammar* $\mathcal{G}_k$ *such that* $L(\mathcal{G}_k) = \{a^{i,i^k} \mid i \in \mathbb{N}^+\}$.

Proof. Let us denote $L_k = \{a^{i,i^k} \mid i \in \mathbb{N}^+\}$. Define $\mathcal{G}_1 = (V_\mathrm{N}^1, \{a\}, \mathcal{P}_1, S_1, \preccurlyeq_1)$ where $V_\mathrm{N}^1(2) = \{S_1, T_1\}$, $V_\mathrm{N}^1(1) = \{R, C\}$ and $\mathcal{P}_1$ consists of productions

$$S_1 \to \frac{R}{T_1} \,\Big|\, a\,, \qquad T_1 \to C\,S_1\,, \qquad R \to a\,R \,|\, a\,, \qquad C \to \frac{a}{C} \,\Big|\, a\,.$$

It is easy to check that $L(\mathcal{G}_1)$ consists of all nonempty square pictures.

To generate a $P \in L_2$, the equality $(n+1)^2 = 1 + 2n + n^2$ suggests to write

$$a^{n+1,(n+1)^2} = a^{1,n+1} \ominus \left(a^{n,1} \oplus a^{n,n} \oplus a^{n,n} \oplus a^{n,n^2} \right).$$

It leads to a 2RRG(3) $\mathcal{G}_2 = (V_\mathrm{N}^1 \cup V_\mathrm{N}^2, \{a\}, \mathcal{P}_1 \cup \mathcal{P}_2, S_2, \preccurlyeq_2)$ where $V_\mathrm{N}^2(3) = \{S_2, T_2, U_2, V_2\}$, $V_\mathrm{N}^2(2) = V_\mathrm{N}^1(2)$, $V_\mathrm{N}^2(1) = V_\mathrm{N}^1(1)$ and $\mathcal{P}_2$ consists of productions

$$S_2 \to \frac{R}{T_2} \,\Big|\, a\,, \qquad T_2 \to C\,U_2\,, \qquad U_2 \to S_1\,V_2\,, \qquad V_2 \to S_1\,S_2\,.$$

The above approach generalizes to any $k \geq 3$. Utilizing the binomial expansion formula, the picture from L_k of size $(n+1) \times (n+1)^k$ can be expressed as

$$a^{n+1,(n+1)^k} = a^{1,n+1} \ominus \left(a^{n,1} \oplus P_2 \oplus \cdots \oplus P_{2^k} \right)$$

where $P_{2^k} = a^{n,n^k} \in L_k$ and all pictures $P_2, \ldots, P_{2^k-1}$ are in $L_1 \cup \ldots \cup L_{k-1}$. Hence, a 2RRG($k+1$) generating L_k can be constructed. □

Theorem 3. *For each $k \geq 1$, the picture languages generated by 2RRG(k) form a proper subset of the picture languages generated by 2RRG($k+1$).*

Proof. By Lemma 7, $L_k = \{a^{i,i^k} \mid i \in \mathbb{N}^+\}$ is generated by a 2RRG($k+1$). Assume that $\mathcal{G}_k = (V_\mathrm{N}, \{a\}, \mathcal{P}, S, \preccurlyeq)$ is a 2RRG(k) and $L(\mathcal{G}_k) = L_k$. Let $m = |V_\mathrm{N}|^k + 1$ and $n = m^k$. Since $a^{m,n} \in L_k$ and $n = m^k > |V_\mathrm{N}|^k \cdot m^{k-1}$, Lemma 6 implies that $a^{m,n+n!} \in L_k$, which is a contradiction. □

It was proved in [15, Theorem 1] that 2CFG is powerful enough to simulate the 2-counter Minsky machine. The proof can be easily adapted to 2RRG(3).

Theorem 4. *For every deterministic n-state 2-counter Minsky machine $\mathcal{M}$, there is a 2RRG(3) $\mathcal{G}$ with $\mathcal{O}(n)$ nonterminals fulfilling: If $\mathcal{M}$ halts in time t when launched with initially zeroed counters, then $L(\mathcal{G}) = \{a^{\ell,\ell}\}$ for some $\ell \geq t$; if $\mathcal{M}$ does not halt, then $L(\mathcal{G}) = \emptyset$.*

Theorem 5. *The emptiness problem is decidable for 2RRG(2) and undecidable for 2RRG(k) if $k \geq 3$.*

Proof. By Theorem 4, the halting problem reduces to the emptiness for 2RRG(3).

Let $\mathcal{G} = (V_\mathrm{N}, V_\mathrm{T}, \mathcal{P}, S, \preccurlyeq)$ be a 2RRG(2) and $\pi : V_\mathrm{T} \to \{a\}$ be a projection. Deciding whether $L(\mathcal{G}) = \emptyset$ is equivalent to deciding whether $\pi(L(\mathcal{G})) = \emptyset$. The family of picture languages generated by 2RRG(2) is apparently closed under projection, hence, without loss of generality we can assume that $V_\mathrm{T} = \{a\}$.

By Lemma 5, $L(\mathcal{G}) \neq \emptyset$ iff there is $a^{m,n} \in L(\mathcal{G})$ with $\max\{m,n\} < 2|V_\mathrm{N}|^2 8^{|V_\mathrm{N}|^2}$, it thus suffices to check membership to $L(\mathcal{G})$ for finitely many pictures. □

The next theorem characterizes descriptional complexity of $2\mathsf{RRG}(k)$. Size of a grammar is measured as the number of its nonterminals. In the proof we work with the non-recursive *busy beaver function* $\mathrm{bb} : \mathbb{N} \to \mathbb{N}$ [16].

Theorem 6. *The trade-off between* $2\mathsf{RRG}(k+1)$ *and* $2\mathsf{RRG}(k)$ *is non-recursive for every* $k \geq 2$.

Proof. Let $\{\mathcal{M}_j\}_{j=1}^{\infty}$ be a sequence of deterministic 2-counter Minsky machines where each $\mathcal{M}_j$ is equivalent to a j-th busy beaver Turing machine. By Theorem 4, for each $\mathcal{M}_j$, there is a $2\mathsf{RRG}(3)$ $\mathcal{G}_j^1$ with $\mathcal{O}(j)$ nonterminals generating $\{a^{\ell,\ell}\}$ where $\ell \geq \mathrm{bb}(j)$.

Case I: $k \geq 3$. By Lemma 7, there is a $2\mathsf{RRG}(k+1)$ grammar $\mathcal{G}_j^2$ generating the picture language $\{a^{i,i^k} \mid i \in \mathbb{N}^+\}$. Assume that $\mathcal{G}_j^1$ and $\mathcal{G}_j^2$ do not share any nonterminal. Let S_j^1 and S_j^2 be the initial nonterminal of $\mathcal{G}_j^1$ and $\mathcal{G}_j^2$, respectively. Define a $2\mathsf{RRG}(k+1)$ $\mathcal{G}_j$ which inherits all nonterminals and productions in $\mathcal{G}_j^1$ and $\mathcal{G}_j^2$, preservers the rank of all nonterminals, and introduces a new initial nonterminal S_j of rank $k+1$ and an extra production $S_j \to S_j^1 \, S_j^2$. It holds that $L(\mathcal{G}_j) = \{a^{\ell_1,\ell_2}\}$ where $\ell_1 \geq \mathrm{bb}(j)$ and $\ell_2 = \ell_1 + \ell_1^k > \ell_1^k$.

Since $L(\mathcal{G}_j)$ is finite, there is a $2\mathsf{RRG}(k)$ $\mathcal{G}_j^3$ such that $L(\mathcal{G}_j^3) = L(\mathcal{G}_j)$. Let n_j be the number of nonterminals in $\mathcal{G}_j^3$. It must fulfill $\ell_2 \leq (n_j)^k \ell_1^{k-1}$, otherwise Lemma 6 applies and contradicts that $|L(\mathcal{G}_j^3)| = 1$. Hence, $(n_j)^k \geq \ell_2/\ell_1^{k-1} \geq \mathrm{bb}(j)$, which implies that $\{n_j\}_{j=1}^{\infty}$ grows faster than any recursive function.

Case II: $k = 2$. For each $j \in \mathbb{N}^+$, it suffices to consider a $2\mathsf{RRG}(2)$ $\mathcal{G}_j$ which generates $L(\mathcal{G}_j^1) = \{a^{\ell,\ell}\}$ with $\ell \geq \mathrm{bb}(j)$. Lemma 5 enforces $\ell < 2 \cdot (n_j)^2 \cdot 8^{(n_j)^2}$, hence $\{n_j\}_{j=1}^{\infty}$ grows again faster than any recursive function. □

6 Conclusion

We studied theoretical properties of the two-dimensional rank-reducing grammar. We showed that the variant of rank 2 generalizes the principle of the regular matrix grammar and still has quite good properties. However, from a practical point of view, it is not powerful enough since the grammars used in [13] to describe the structure of common documents are of rank at least 5.

We demonstrated that the grammar properties greatly change when going from rank 2 to rank 3. As in the case of 2CFG, the grammar of rank 3 is able to encode computations of the 2-counter Minsky machine. The subsequently induced non-recursive trade-offs are then in a line with the results in [12].

There are some interesting topics that remained untouched by this paper, like closure properties, or parsing algorithms for the grammar of rank 3 and 4. These topics may therefore be the subject of future research.

References

1. Álvaro, F., Cruz, F., Sánchez, J.A., Ramos Terrades, O., Benedí, J.M.: Structure detection and segmentation of documents using 2D stochastic context-free grammars. Neurocomputing **150**(PA), 147–154 (2015)

2. Crespi Reghizzi, S., Pradella, M.: A CKY parser for picture grammars. Inf. Process. Lett. **105**(6), 213–217 (2008)
3. Earley, J.: An efficient context-free parsing algorithm. Commun. ACM **13**(2), 94–102 (1970)
4. Fernau, H., Paramasivan, M., Schmid, M.L., Thomas, D.G.: Simple picture processing based on finite automata and regular grammars. J. Comput. Syst. Sci. **95**, 232–258 (2018)
5. Giammarresi, D., Restivo, A.: Two-dimensional languages. In: Rozenberg, G., Salomaa, A. (eds.) Handbook of Formal Languages, vol. 3, pp. 215–267. Springer, New York (1997). https://doi.org/10.1007/978-3-642-59126-6_4
6. Itai, A., Rodeh, M.: Finding a minimum circuit in a graph. In: Proceedings of the 9th Annual ACM Symposium on Theory of Computing (STOC 1977), STOC 1977, pp. 1–10. ACM, New York (1977)
7. Lee, L.: Fast context-free grammar parsing requires fast Boolean matrix multiplication. J. ACM **49**(1), 1–15 (2002)
8. Lemaitre, A., Mouchère, H., Camillerapp, J., Coüasnon, B.: Interest of syntactic knowledge for on-line flowchart recognition. In: 9th IAPR International Workshop on Graphics Recognition, 2011, GREC 2011, pp. 85–88 (2011)
9. Matz, O.: Regular expressions and context-free grammars for picture languages. In: Reischuk, R., Morvan, M. (eds.) STACS 1997. LNCS, vol. 1200, pp. 283–294. Springer, Heidelberg (1997). https://doi.org/10.1007/BFb0023466
10. Mráz, F., Průša, D., Wehar, M.: Two-dimensional pattern matching against basic picture languages. In: Hospodár, M., Jirásková, G. (eds.) CIAA 2019. LNCS, vol. 11601, pp. 209–221. Springer, Cham (2019). https://doi.org/10.1007/978-3-030-23679-3_17
11. de Oliveira Oliveira, M., Wehar, M.: Intersection non-emptiness and hardness within polynomial time. In: Hoshi, M., Seki, S. (eds.) DLT 2018. LNCS, vol. 11088, pp. 282–290. Springer, Cham (2018). https://doi.org/10.1007/978-3-319-98654-8_23
12. Průša, D.: Non-recursive trade-offs between two-dimensional automata and grammars. Theor. Comput. Sci. **610**, 121–132 (2016)
13. Průša, D., Fujiyoshi, A.: Rank-reducing two-dimensional grammars for document layout analysis. In: 14th IAPR International Conference on Document Analysis and Recognition (ICDAR 2017), vol. 01, pp. 1120–1125 (2017)
14. Průša, D., Hlaváč, V.: Mathematical formulae recognition using 2D grammars. In: 9th International Conference on Document Analysis and Recognition (ICDAR 2007), pp. 849–853. IEEE Computer Society (2007)
15. Průša, D., Reinhardt, K.: Undecidability of the emptiness problem for context-free picture languages. Theor. Comput. Sci. **679**, 118–125 (2017)
16. Radó, T.: On non-computable functions. Bell Syst. Tech. J. **41**(3), 877–884 (1962)
17. Schlesinger, M.I., Hlaváč, V.: Ten Lectures on Statistical and Structural Pattern Recognition (Computational Imaging and Vision), 1st edn. Springer, Dordrecht (2012)
18. Siromoney, G., Siromoney, R., Krithivasan, K.: Abstract families of matrices and picture languages. Comput. Graph. Image Process. **1**(3), 284–307 (1972)
19. Williams, V.V.: Multiplying matrices faster than Coppersmith-Winograd. In: 44th Annual ACM Symposium on Theory of Computing (STOC 2012), pp. 887–898. ACM, New York (2012)
20. Younger, D.: Recognition of context-free languages in time n^3. Inf. Control **10**, 189–208 (1967)

Palindromic Length of Words with Many Periodic Palindromes

Josef Rukavicka[✉]

Department of Mathematics, Faculty of Nuclear Sciences and Physical Engineering,
Czech Technical University in Prague, Prague, Czech Republic
josef.rukavicka@seznam.cz

Abstract. The palindromic length $\mathrm{PL}(v)$ of a finite word v is the minimal number of palindromes whose concatenation is equal to v. In 2013, Frid, Puzynina, and Zamboni conjectured that: If w is an infinite word and k is an integer such that $\mathrm{PL}(u) \leq k$ for every factor u of w then w is ultimately periodic.

Suppose that w is an infinite word and k is an integer such $\mathrm{PL}(u) \leq k$ for every factor u of w. Let $\Omega(w, k)$ be the set of all factors u of w that have more than $\sqrt[k]{k^{-1}|u|}$ palindromic prefixes. We show that $\Omega(w, k)$ is an infinite set and we show that for each positive integer j there are palindromes a, b and a word $u \in \Omega(w, k)$ such that $(ab)^j$ is a factor of u and b is nonempty. Note that $(ab)^j$ is a periodic word and $(ab)^i a$ is a palindrome for each $i \leq j$. These results justify the following question: What is the palindromic length of a concatenation of a suffix of b and a periodic word $(ab)^j$ with "many" periodic palindromes?

It is known that if u, v are nonempty words then $|\mathrm{PL}(uv) - \mathrm{PL}(u)| \leq \mathrm{PL}(v)$. The main result of our article shows that if a, b are palindromes, b is nonempty, u is a nonempty suffix of b, $|ab|$ is the minimal period of aba, and j is a positive integer with $j \geq 3\mathrm{PL}(u)$ then $\mathrm{PL}(u(ab)^j) - \mathrm{PL}(u) \geq 0$.

1 Introduction

In 2013, Frid, Puzynina, and Zamboni introduced a *palindromic length* of a finite word [6]. Recall that the word $u = x_1 x_2 \ldots x_n$ of length n is called a *palindrome* if $x_1 x_2 \ldots x_n = x_n \ldots x_2 x_1$, where x_i are letters and $i \in \{1, 2, \ldots, n\}$. The palindromic length $\mathrm{PL}(u)$ of the word u is defined as the minimal number k such that $u = u_1 u_2 \ldots u_k$ and u_j are palindromes, where $j \in \{1, 2, \ldots, k\}$; note that the palindromes u_j are not necessarily distinct. Let ϵ denote the empty word. We define that $\mathrm{PL}(\epsilon) = 0$.

In general, the factorization of a finite word into the minimal number of palindromes is not unique; for example $\mathrm{PL}(011001) = 3$ and the word 011001 can be factorized in two ways: $011001 = (0110)(0)(1) = (0)(1)(1001)$.

The authors of [6] conjectured that:

Conjecture 1. If w is an infinite word and P is an integer such that $\mathrm{PL}(u) \leq P$ for every factor u of w then w is ultimately periodic.

© Springer Nature Switzerland AG 2020
G. Jiráisková and G. Pighizzini (Eds.): DCFS 2020, LNCS 12442, pp. 167–179, 2020.
https://doi.org/10.1007/978-3-030-62536-8_14

So far, Conjecture 1 remains open. We call an infinite word that satisfies the condition from Conjecture 1 a word with a *bounded palindromic length*. Note that there are infinite periodic words that do not have a bounded palindromic length; for example $(012)^\infty$. Hence the converse of Conjecture 1 does not hold.

In [6] the conjecture was proved for infinite words that are k-power free for some positive integer k. It follows that if w is an infinite word with a bounded palindromic length, then for each positive integer j there is a nonempty factor r such that r^j is a factor of w.

In [11], another variation of Conjecture 1 was considered:

Conjecture 2. Every aperiodic (not ultimately periodic) infinite word has prefixes of arbitrarily high palindromic length.

In [11], the author proved that Conjecture 1 and Conjecture 2 are equivalent. More precisely, it was proved that if every prefix of an infinite word w is a concatenation of at most n palindromes then every factor of w is a concatenation of at most $2n$ palindromes. It follows that Conjecture 2 remains also open.

In [7] Conjecture 1 and Conjecture 2 have been proved for all Sturmian words. The properties of the palindromic length of Sturmian words have been investigated also in [2]. In [1], the authors study the palindromic length of factors of fixed points of primitive morphisms. In [8], the lower bounds for the palindromic length of prefixes of infinite words can be found.

In [4], a left and right greedy palindromic length have been introduced as a variant to the palindromic length. It is shown that if the left (or right) greedy palindromic lengths of prefixes of an infinite word w is bounded, then w is ultimately periodic.

In addition, algorithms for computing the palindromic length were researched [3,5,10]. In [10], the authors present a linear time online algorithm for computing the palindromic length.

In the current paper we investigate infinite words with a bounded palindromic length. Let k be a positive integer, let w be an infinite word such that $k \geq \mathrm{PL}(t)$ for every factor t of w, and let $\Omega(w, k)$ be the set of all factors u of w that have more than $\sqrt[k]{k^{-1}|u|}$ palindromic prefixes. We show that $\Omega(w, k)$ is an infinite set and we show that for each positive integer j there are palindromes a, b and a word $u \in \Omega(w, k)$ such that $(ab)^j$ is a factor of u and b is nonempty. Note that $(ab)^j$ is a periodic word and $(ab)^i a$ is a palindrome for each $i \leq j$. In this sense we can consider that w has infinitely many periodic palindromes with an arbitrarily high exponent j.

The existence of infinitely many periodic palindromes in w is not surprising. It can be deduced also from the result in [6], which says, as mentioned above, that if w is an infinite word with a bounded palindromic length, then for each positive integer j there is a nonempty factor r such that r^j is a factor of w.

These results justify the following question: What is the palindromic length of a concatenation of a suffix of b and a periodic word $(ab)^j$ with "many" periodic palindromes?

It is known that if u, v are nonempty words then $|\mathrm{PL}(uv) - \mathrm{PL}(u)| \leq \mathrm{PL}(v)$ [11]. Less formally said, it means that by concatenating a word v to a word u the change of the palindromic length is at most equal to the palindromic length of v. The main result of our article shows that if a, b are palindromes, b is nonempty, u is a nonempty suffix of b, $|ab|$ is the minimal period of aba, and j is a positive integer with $j \geq 3\mathrm{PL}(u)$ then $\mathrm{PL}(u(ab)^j) - \mathrm{PL}(u) \geq 0$.

The results of our article should shed some light on infinite words for which Conjecture 1 and Conjecture 2 remain open. For the moment, for given factor u, we identified factors v such that $\mathrm{PL}(uv) - \mathrm{PL}(v) \geq 0$. The idea for the future development of this result is, for given $k \in \mathbb{N}$, to identify factors u, v such that $\mathrm{PL}(u) = k$ and $\mathrm{PL}(uv) - \mathrm{PL}(u) > 0$. The existence of such factors would, in consequence, allow us to prove the Conjecture 1 and Conjecture 2.

2 Preliminaries

Let $\mathbb{N}$ denote the set of all positive integers, let $\mathbb{N}_0 = \mathbb{N} \cup \{0\}$ denote the set of all nonnegative integers, let $\mathbb{R}$ denote the set of all real numbers, and let $\mathbb{R}^+$ denote the set of all positive real numbers.

Let A denote a finite alphabet with $|A| \geq 2$ letters. Let A^+ denote the set of all finite nonempty words over the alphabet A and let $A^* = A^+ \cup \{\epsilon\}$; recall that ϵ denotes the empty word. Let $A^{\mathbb{N}}$ denote the set of all right infinite words.

Let $n \in \mathbb{N}$ and let $w = w_1 w_2 \ldots w_n \in A^*$ (or $w = w_1 w_2 \cdots \in A^{\mathbb{N}}$), where $w_i \in A$ and $i \in \{1, 2, \ldots, n\}$ (or $i \in \{1, 2, \ldots\}$). We denote by $w[i, j] = w_i w_{i+1} \ldots w_j$ the factor of w starting at position $i \in \mathbb{N}$ and ending at position $j \in \mathbb{N}$, where $i, j \in \mathbb{N}$ and $i \leq j \leq n$

We call the word $v \in A^*$ a *factor* of the word $w \in A^* \cup A^{\mathbb{N}}$ if there are words $a \in A^*$ and $b \in A^* \cup A^{\mathbb{N}}$ such that $w = avb$. Given a word $w \in A^* \cup A^{\mathbb{N}}$, we denote by $\mathrm{Fac}(w)$ the set of all factors of w. It follows that $\epsilon \in \mathrm{Fac}(w)$ and if $w \in A^*$ then also $w \in \mathrm{Fac}(w)$.

We call the word $v \in A^*$ a *prefix* of the word $w \in A^* \cup A^{\mathbb{N}}$ if there is $t \in A^* \cup A^{\mathbb{N}}$ such that $w = vt$. Given a word $w \in A^* \cup A^{\mathbb{N}}$, we denote by $\mathrm{Prf}(w)$ the set of all prefixes of w. It follows that $\epsilon \in \mathrm{Prf}(w)$ and if $w \in A^*$ then also $w \in \mathrm{Prf}(w)$.

We call the word $v \in A^*$ a *suffix* of the word $w \in A^*$ if there is $t \in A^*$ such that $w = tv$. Given a word $w \in A^*$, we denote by $\mathrm{Suf}(w)$ the set of all suffixes of w. It follows that $\epsilon, w \in \mathrm{Suf}(w)$.

Let $w = w_1 w_2 \ldots w_n \in A^+$, where $w_i \in A$ and $i \in \{1, 2, \ldots, n\}$. Let w^R denote the *reversal* of the word $w \in A^+$; it means $w^R = w_n w_{n-1} \ldots w_2 w_1$. In addition we define that the reversal of the empty word is the empty word; formally $\epsilon^R = \epsilon$.

Realize that $w \in A^*$ is a *palindrome* if and only if $w^R = w$. Let $\mathrm{Pal} \subset A^*$ denote the set of all palindromes over the alphabet A. We define that $\epsilon \in \mathrm{Pal}$. Let $\mathrm{Pal}^+ = \mathrm{Pal} \setminus \{\epsilon\}$ be the set of all nonempty palindromes.

Given $w \in A^* \cup A^{\mathbb{N}}$, let $\mathrm{PalPrf}(w) = \mathrm{Pal} \cap \mathrm{Prf}(w)$ be the set of all palindromic prefixes of w.

Given $w \in A^+$, let $\mathrm{MPF}(w)$ denote the set of all k-tuples of palindromes whose concatenation is equal to w and $k = \mathrm{PL}(w)$; formally

$$\mathrm{MPF}(w) = \{(t_1, t_2, \ldots, t_k) \mid k = \mathrm{PL}(w) \text{ and } t_1 t_2 \ldots t_k = w \text{ and } \\ t_1, t_2, \ldots, t_k \in \mathrm{Pal}^+\}.$$

We call a k-tuple $(t_1, t_2, \ldots, t_k) \in \mathrm{MPF}(w)$ a *minimal palindromic factorization* of w.

Let $\mathbb{Q}$ denote the set of all rational numbers. We say that the word $w \in A^+$ is a *periodic* word, if there are $\alpha \in \mathbb{Q}$, $r \in \mathrm{Prf}(w)\backslash\{\epsilon\}$, and $\bar{r} \in \mathrm{Prf}(r)\backslash\{r\}$ such that $\alpha > 1$, $w = rr \ldots r\bar{r}$, and $\frac{|w|}{|r|} = \alpha$; note that $\bar{r}$ is uniquely determined by r. We write $w = r^\alpha$ and the period of w is equal to $|r|$. For example $12341 = (1234)^{\frac{5}{4}}$ and $12341234123 = (1234)^{\frac{11}{4}}$.

Given $w \in A^+$, let

$$\mathrm{Period}(w) = \{(r, \alpha) \mid r^\alpha = w \text{ and } r \in \mathrm{Prf}(w) \setminus \{\epsilon\} \text{ and } \alpha \in \mathbb{Q} \text{ and } \alpha > 1\}.$$

The set $\mathrm{Period}(w)$ contains all couples (r, α) such that $r^\alpha = w$. Let

$$\mathrm{MinPer}(w) = \min\{|r| \mid (r, \alpha) \in \mathrm{Period}(w)\} \in \mathbb{N}.$$

The positive integer $\mathrm{MinPer}(w)$ is the *minimal period* of the word w. The word $w \in A^+$ has a period $\delta \in \mathbb{Q}$ if there is a couple $(r, \alpha) \in \mathrm{Period}(w)$ such that $|r| = \delta$.

We will deal a lot with periodic palindromes. The two following known lemmas will be useful for us.

Lemma 1 *(see [9, Lemma 1]). Suppose p is a period of a nonempty palindrome w; then there are palindromes a and b such that $|ab| = p$, $b \neq \epsilon$, and $w = (ab)^* a$.*

Lemma 2 *(see [9, Lemma 2]). Suppose w is a palindrome and u is its proper suffix-palindrome or prefix-palindrome; then the number $|w| - |u|$ is a period of w.*

3   Periodic Palindromic Factors

We start the section with a definition of a set of real non-decreasing functions that diverge as n tends towards the infinity.

Let Λ denote the set of all functions ϕ such that

- $\phi(n) : \mathbb{N} \to \mathbb{R}$,
- $\phi(n) \leq \phi(n+1)$, and
- $\lim_{n \to \infty} \phi(n) = \infty$.

Let $k \in \mathbb{N}$, let $\tau(n, k) = \sqrt[k]{k^{-1}n} \in \Lambda$, let $w \in A^{\mathbb{N}}$, and let

$$\Omega(w, k) = \{t \in \mathrm{Fac}(w) \mid |\mathrm{PalPrf}(t)| \geq \tau(|t|, k)\}.$$

The definition says that the set $\Omega(w, k)$ contains a factor t of w if the number of palindromic prefixes of t is larger than or equal to $\tau(|t|, k) = \sqrt[k]{k-1|t|}$.

The next proposition asserts that if w is an infinite word with a bounded palindromic length, then the set of factors that have more than $\tau(n, k)$ palindromic prefixes is infinite, where n is the length of the factor in question and $k \geq \mathrm{PL}(t)$ for each factor t of w.

Proposition 1. *If $w \in A^{\mathbb{N}}$, $k \in \mathbb{N}$ and $k \geq \max\{\mathrm{PL}(t) \mid t \in \mathrm{Fac}(w)\}$ then $|\Omega(w, k)| = \infty$.*

Proof. Suppose that $|\Omega(w, k)| < \infty$ and let

$$K = \max\{|\mathrm{PalPrf}(t)| \mid t \in \Omega(w, k)\}.$$

Less formally said, the value K is the maximal value from the set of numbers of palindromic prefixes of factors t of w that have more than $\tau(|t|, k)$ palindromic prefixes. Clearly $K < \infty$, because of the assumption $|\Omega(w, k)| < \infty$.

Let $p \in \mathrm{Prf}(w)$ be the shortest prefix of w such that $\tau(|p|, k) > K$. Since $\lim_{n \to \infty} \tau(n, k) = \infty$, it is clear that such prefix p exists.

To get a contradiction suppose that $|\mathrm{PalPrf}(t)| \geq \tau(|p|, k)$ for some $t \in \mathrm{Fac}(p)$. Since $\tau(|t|, k) \leq \tau(|p|, k)$ and thus $|\mathrm{PalPrf}(t)| \geq \tau(|t|, k)$, it follows that $t \in \Omega(w, k)$ and consequently $|\mathrm{PalPrf}(t)| \leq K$. It is a contradiction, because $K < \tau(|p|, k)$. Hence we have that

$$|\mathrm{PalPrf}(t)| < \tau(|p|, k) \text{ for each } t \in \mathrm{Fac}(p). \tag{1}$$

Let $n, j \in \mathbb{N}$ and let

$$\Theta(n, j) = \{(v_1, v_2, \ldots, v_j) \mid v_i \in \mathrm{Pal}^+ \text{ and } i \in \{1, 2, \ldots, j\} \text{ and}$$
$$|v_1 v_2 \ldots v_j| \leq n \text{ and } v_1 v_2 \ldots v_j \in \mathrm{Prf}(w)\}.$$

The set $\Theta(n, j)$ contains j-tuples of nonempty palindromes whose concatenation is of length smaller than or equal to n and also the concatenation is a prefix of w.

Thus from (1) we get that

$$|\Theta(|p|, j)| < (\tau(|p|, k))^j. \tag{2}$$

The Eq. (2) follows from the fact that each factor of p has at most $\tau(|p|, k)$ palindromic prefixes. In consequence there are at most $(\tau(|p|, k))^j$ of j-tuples of palindromes.

Let $\bar{\Theta}(|p|, j) = \bigcup_{j>0}^{k} \Theta(|p|, j)$. Since $\tau(n, k) \leq \tau(n + 1, k)$ we have from (2) that

$$|\bar{\Theta}(|p|, k)| \leq k|\Theta(|p|, k)| < k(\tau(|p|, k))^k \leq k\left(\sqrt[k]{k-1|p|}\right)^k = |p|. \tag{3}$$

The inequality (3) says that the number of prefixes of p having the form $v_1 v_2 \ldots v_j$, where $j \leq k$ and $v_i \in \mathrm{Pal}^+$ is smaller than the length of p. But p has $|p|$ nonempty prefixes. It is a contradiction. Since $\bigcup_{r \in \mathrm{Prf}(p)} \mathrm{MPF}(r) \subseteq \bar{\Theta}(|p|, k)$ we conclude that $\Omega(w, k)$ is an infinite set.

Remark 1. In the proof of Proposition 1, we used the idea that the number of prefixes of a word of length n that are a concatenation of at most k palindromes is smaller than n. This idea was used also in Theorem 1 in [6].

We show that if Σ is an infinite set of words r such that the number of nonempty palindromic prefixes of r grows more than $\ln |r|$ as $|r|$ tends towards infinity then for each positive integer j there are palindromes a, b and a word $t \in \Sigma$ such that $(ab)^j$ is a prefix of t and b is nonempty. Realize that $(ab)^j a$ is a palindrome for each $j \in \mathbb{N}_0$. This means that Σ contains infinitely many words that have a periodic palindromic prefix of arbitrarily high exponent j.

Proposition 2. *If $\Sigma \subseteq A^*$, $|\Sigma| = \infty$, $\phi(n) \in \Lambda$, $\lim_{n \to \infty} (\phi(n) - \ln n) = \infty$, and $|\mathrm{PalPrf}(t) \setminus \{\epsilon\}| \geq \phi(|t|)$ for each $t \in \Sigma$ then for each $j \in \mathbb{N}$ there are palindromes $a \in \mathrm{Pal}$, $b \in \mathrm{Pal}^+$ and a word $t \in \Sigma$ such that $(ab)^j \in \mathrm{Prf}(t)$.*

Proof. Given $t \in \Sigma$, let $\mu(t, i)$ be the lengths of all palindromic prefixes of t such that $\mu(t, 1) = 1$ (a letter is a palindrome) and $\mu(t, i) < \mu(t, i + 1)$, where $i \in \{1, 2, \ldots, h_t\}$. For example if $t = 0100010111$, then $\mu(t, 1) = |0| = 1$, $\mu(t, 2) = |010| = 3$, $\mu(t, 3) = |0100010| = 7$. Let $h_t = |\mathrm{PalPrf}(t) \setminus \{\epsilon\}|$; the integer h_t is the number of nonempty palindromic prefixes of t. Let $i \in \{1, 2, \ldots, h_t - 1\}$. It is clear that

$$\mu(t, i + 1) = \mu(t, i) \frac{\mu(t, i + 1)}{\mu(t, i)}. \tag{4}$$

From (4) we have that

$$\frac{\mu(t, h_t)}{\mu(t, h_t - 1)} \frac{\mu(t, h_t - 1)}{\mu(t, h_t - 2)} \frac{\mu(t, h_t - 2)}{\mu(t, h_t - 3)} \cdots \frac{\mu(t, 2)}{\mu(t, 1)} = \mu(t, h_t) \leq |t|. \tag{5}$$

Suppose that there is $\alpha \in \mathbb{R}$ such that $\alpha > 1$ and for each $t \in \Sigma$ and for each $i \in \{1, 2, \ldots, h_t - 1\}$ we have that $\frac{\mu(t, i+1)}{\mu(t, i)} \geq \alpha$. It follows from (5) that

$$\alpha^{h_t - 1} \leq h_t \leq |t|. \tag{6}$$

Let $c = \frac{1}{\ln \alpha} \in \mathbb{R}^+$. Then $|t| = \alpha^{c \ln |t|}$. Since $h_t \geq \phi(|t|)$ we get that

$$\frac{\alpha^{h_t - 1}}{|t|} \geq \frac{\alpha^{\phi(|t|) - 1}}{|t|} = \frac{\alpha^{\phi(|t|) - 1}}{\alpha^{c \ln |t|}} = \alpha^{\phi(|t|) - 1 - c \ln |t|}. \tag{7}$$

Because $\lim_{n \to \infty} (\phi(n) - \ln n) = \infty$ the Eq. (7) implies that there is n_0 such that for each $t \in \Sigma$ with $|t| > n_0$ we have that

$$\frac{\alpha^{h_t - 1}}{|t|} \geq \alpha^{\phi(|t|) - 1 - c \ln |t|} > 1. \tag{8}$$

From (6) and (8) we have that $\alpha^{h_t - 1} \leq |t|$ and $\frac{\alpha^{h_t - 1}}{|t|} > 1$, which is a contradiction. We conclude there is no such α. In consequence, for each $\beta \in \mathbb{R}^+$ with $\beta > 1$ there is $t \in \Sigma$ and $i \in \{1, 2, \ldots, h_t - 1\}$ such that $\frac{\mu(t, i+1)}{\mu(t, i)} \leq \beta$.

Let $j \in \mathbb{N}$, let

$$\gamma \le \frac{1}{j} + 1 \in \mathbb{R}^+, \tag{9}$$

let $t \in \Sigma$, and $i \in \{1, 2, \ldots, h_t\}$ be such that $\frac{\mu(t,i+1)}{\mu(t,i)} \le \gamma$. Let $\delta = \frac{\mu(t,i+1)}{\mu(t,i)} \le \gamma$. Let $u, v \in \mathrm{Prf}(t)$ be such that $|u| = \mu(t,i)$ and $|v| = \mu(t, i+1)$. Then v is a periodic palindrome with a period $|v| - |u| = \mu(t, i+1) - \mu(t, i) = \mu(t, i)\delta - \mu(t, i) = \mu(t, i)(\delta - 1)$; see Lemma 2. Lemma 1 implies that there are $a \in \mathrm{Pal}$ and $b \in \mathrm{Pal}^+$ such that $(ab)^k a = v$ for some $k \in \mathbb{N}$. From Lemma 1 we have also that $|ab|$ is the period of v. Thus

$$|ab| = \mu(t, i)(\delta - 1) \le \mu(t, i)(\gamma - 1). \tag{10}$$

From (9) and (10) it follows that

$$|ab| \le \mu(t, i)(\gamma - 1) \le \mu(t, i)\frac{1}{j}. \tag{11}$$

Note that $v = (ab)^k a$ and $u \in \mathrm{Prf}((ab)^k)$. Since $\mu(t, i) = |u|$ we get that $\frac{\mu(t,i)}{|ab|} \le k$. From (11) we have that

$$j \le \frac{\mu(t, i)}{|ab|} \le k.$$

Thus for arbitrary $j \in \mathbb{N}$ we found t, a, b, k such that $(ab)^k \in \mathrm{Prf}(t)$ and $j \le k$. The proposition follows.

A corollary of Proposition 1 and Proposition 2 says that if w is an infinite word with a bounded palindromic length then for each positive integer j there are palindromes a, b such that $(ab)^j$ is a factor of w and ab is a nonempty word.

Corollary 1. *If $w \in A^{\mathbb{N}}$, $k \in \mathbb{N}$, and $k \ge \max\{\mathrm{PL}(t) \mid t \in \mathrm{Fac}(w)\}$ then for each $j \in \mathbb{N}$ there are $a \in \mathrm{Pal}$ and $b \in \mathrm{Pal}^+$ such that $(ab)^j \in \mathrm{Fac}(w)$.*

Proof. Just take $\Sigma = \Omega(w, k)$. Obviously $\lim_{n \to \infty} (\tau(n, k) - \ln n) = \infty$. Then Proposition 2 implies the corollary.

4 Palindromic Length of Concatenation

In this section we present some known results about the palindromic length of concatenation of two words.

The first lemma shows the very basic property of the palindromic length that the palindromic length of concatenation of two words x and y is smaller than or equal to the sum of palindromic length of x and y. We omit the proof.

Lemma 3. *If $x, y \in A^*$ then $\mathrm{PL}(xy) \le \mathrm{PL}(x) + \mathrm{PL}(y)$.*

An another basic property says that if $(t_1, t_2, \ldots, t_k) \in \mathrm{MPF}(w)$ is a minimal palindromic factorization of the word w then the palindromic length of the factor $t_i t_{i+1} \ldots t_j$ is equal to $j - i + 1$ for each $i, j \in \{1, 2, \ldots, k\}$ and $i \leq j$. We omit the proof.

Lemma 4. *If $w \in \mathrm{A}^+$, $k = \mathrm{PL}(w)$, and $(t_1, t_2, \ldots, t_k) \in \mathrm{MPF}(w)$ then for each $i, j \in \{1, 2, \ldots, k\}$ with $i \leq j$ we have that $\mathrm{PL}(t_i t_{i+1} \ldots t_j) = j - i + 1$.*

The following result has been proved in [11]. It says that if x, y are words then the palindromic length of y is the maximal absolute difference of palindromic lengths of x and xy; i.e. $|\mathrm{PL}(x) - \mathrm{PL}(xy)| \leq \mathrm{PL}(y)$.

Lemma 5 *(see [11, Lemma 6]).* *If $x, y \in \mathrm{A}^*$ then*

- $\mathrm{PL}(y) \leq \mathrm{PL}(x) + \mathrm{PL}(xy)$ *and*
- $\mathrm{PL}(x) \leq \mathrm{PL}(y) + \mathrm{PL}(xy)$.

We have two following immediate corollaries of Lemma 5.

Corollary 2. *If $x, y \in \mathrm{A}^*$ and $y \in \mathrm{Pal}$ then $|\mathrm{PL}(xy) - \mathrm{PL}(x)| \leq 1$.*

Proof. It is enough to consider y in Lemma 5 to be a palindrome. Thus we have $\mathrm{PL}(y) = 1$ if $y \neq \epsilon$ or $\mathrm{PL}(y) = 0$ if $y = \epsilon$. The corollary follows.

Corollary 3. *If $x, y \in \mathrm{A}^*$ and $xy \in \mathrm{Pal}$ then $|\mathrm{PL}(x) - \mathrm{PL}(y)| \leq 1$.*

Proof. If $x = y^R$ then $\mathrm{PL}(x) - \mathrm{PL}(y) = 0$, because clearly $\mathrm{PL}(y) = \mathrm{PL}(y^R)$. Suppose that $x \neq y^R$. It follows that $|x| \neq |y|$, since $xy \in \mathrm{Pal}$. Without loss of generality suppose that $|x| > |y|$. Let $\bar{x}$ be such that $x = y^R \bar{x}$. Then $xy = y^R \bar{x} y$. Thus $\bar{x} \in \mathrm{Pal}^+$. Corollary 2 implies that $|\mathrm{PL}(y^R \bar{x}) - \mathrm{PL}(y)| \leq 1$. The corollary follows.

5   Concatenation of Periodic Palindromes

To simplify the notation of the next two lemmas and the theorem we define an auxiliary set Δ. Let Δ be the set of all 4-tuples (u, d, v, n) such that

- $d \in \mathrm{Pal}^+$,
- $v \in \mathrm{Pal}$,
- $u \in \mathrm{Suf}(d) \setminus \{\epsilon\}$,
- $n \in \mathbb{N}$,
- $|dv| = \mathrm{MinPer}(dvd)$, and
- $n \geq 3\mathrm{PL}(u)$.

Remark 2. The set Δ contains all 4-tuples (u, v, d, n) such that d is a nonempty palindrome, v is a palindrome (possibly empty), u is a nonempty suffix of d, $|dv|$ is the minimal period of the word dvd, and n is a positive integer such that $n \geq 3\mathrm{PL}(u)$. It follows that $n \geq 3$, since u is nonempty and thus $\mathrm{PL}(u) \geq 1$.

Lemma 6. *If $(u, v, d, n) \in \Delta$, $r \in \mathrm{Fac}(u(vd)^n)$, and $|r| \geq 3|vd|$ then $dvd \in \mathrm{Fac}(r)$.*

Proof. Let $\bar{w} = u(vd)^n$, let $p \in \mathrm{Prf}(r)$ be such that $|p| = 3|vd|$, and let $\bar{i}, \bar{j} \in \{1, 2, \ldots, |\bar{w}|\}$ be such that $p = \bar{w}[\bar{i}, \bar{j}]$. Let $\bar{u} \in \mathrm{Prf}(d)$ be such that $d = \bar{u}u$. Note that $|uv\bar{u}| = |vd|$ and thus $(uv\bar{u}, \beta) \in \mathrm{Period}(\bar{w})$, where $\beta = \frac{|\bar{w}|}{|uv\bar{u}|} > 1$.

Let $k \in \mathbb{N}_0$ and $w \in \mathrm{Suf}(\bar{w})$ be such that $\bar{w} = (uv\bar{u})^k w$, $\bar{i} > |(uv\bar{u})^k|$, and $\bar{i} \leq |(uv\bar{u})^{k+1}|$. Obviously such k and w exist. Let $i = \bar{i} - k|uv\bar{u}|$ and $j = \bar{j} - k|uv\bar{u}|$. It is easy to see that $p = w[i, j]$.

We distinguish:

- If $i \in \{1, 2, \ldots, |u|\}$ then $p = tvdvd v \bar{t}$ for some $t \in \mathrm{Suf}(u)$ and for $\bar{t}$ such that $d = \bar{t}t$.
- If $i \in \{|u| + 1, |u| + 2, \ldots, |uv|\}$ then $p = tdvdvd \bar{t}$ for some $t \in \mathrm{Suf}(v)$ and for $\bar{t}$ such that $v = \bar{t}t$.
- If $i \in \{|uv| + 1, |uv| + 2, \ldots, |uv| + |\bar{u}|\}$ then $p = tvdvd v\bar{t}$ for some $t \in \mathrm{Suf}(d)$ and for $\bar{t}$ such that $d = \bar{t}t$.

In all three cases one can see that $dvd \in \mathrm{Fac}(p)$. It is easy to see that if $dvd \in \mathrm{Fac}(p)$ then $dvd \in \mathrm{Fac}(r)$ for each $r \in \mathrm{Fac}(w)$ with $p \in \mathrm{Prf}(r)$. The lemma follows.

Remark 3. Note in the previous proof that with the condition $|r| \geq |(vd)^2|$ it would be possible that $dvd \notin \mathrm{Fac}(p)$. In the cases 1 and 3 we would have $p = tvdv\bar{t}$. That is why the condition $|r| \geq |(vd)^3|$ is necessary. For this reason in the definition of Δ we state that $n \geq 3\mathrm{PL}(u)$.

The next lemma shows that if $(u, v, d, n) \in \Delta$, k is the palindromic length of u, and $(t_1, t_2, \ldots, t_k) \in \mathrm{MPF}(u(vd)^n)$ is a minimal palindromic factorization of $u(vd)^n$ then there is $j \in \{1, 2, \ldots, k\}$ such that t_j is a palindrome having the factor dvd in the "center" of t_j; formally $t_j = pd(vd)^\gamma p^R$ for some positive integer γ and for some proper suffix p of dv.

Lemma 7. *If $(u, v, d, n) \in \Delta$, $w = u(vd)^n$, $k = \mathrm{PL}(w)$, and $(t_1, t_2, \ldots, t_k) \in \mathrm{MPF}(w)$ then there are $j \in \{1, 2 \ldots, k\}$, $p \in \mathrm{Suf}(dv) \setminus \{dv\}$, and $\gamma \in \mathbb{N}$ such that $t_j = pd(vd)^\gamma p^R$.*

Proof. Suppose that $|t_i| < 3|vd|$ for each $i \in \{1, 2, \ldots, k\}$. It follows that

$$|t_1 t_2 \ldots t_k| < 3k|vd|.$$

Since $u(vd)^n = t_1 t_2 \ldots t_k$ and $n \geq 3k \geq 3$ it is a contradiction. It follows that there is j such that $|t_j| \geq |(vd)^3|$. Lemma 6 asserts that $dvd \in \mathrm{Fac}(t_j)$. Then clearly there are $\gamma \in \mathbb{N}$ and $p_1, p_2 \in A^*$ such that $p_1 \in \mathrm{Suf}(dv) \setminus \{dv\}$, $p_2 \in \mathrm{Prf}(vd) \setminus \{vd\}$, and $t_j = p_1 d(vd)^\gamma p_2$.

To get a contradiction suppose that $p_1 \neq p_2^R$. Without loss of generality suppose that $|p_1| > |p_2|$. It follows that $p_2 \in \mathrm{Prf}(p_1^R)$. Obviously $p_1 d(vd)^\gamma p_1^R \in$

Pal. Thus we have two palindromes $p_1 d(vd)^\gamma p_1^R$ and $p_1 d(vd)^\gamma p_2$. Lemma 2 implies that $p_1 d(vd)^\gamma p_1^R$ is periodic with a period

$$\delta = |p_1 d(vd)^\gamma p_1^R| - |p_1 d(vd)^\gamma p_2| = |p_1| - |p_2|.$$

Clearly $\delta < |dv|$. This is a contradiction to the condition $|dv| = \mathrm{MinPer}(dvd)$, see Definition of Δ. We conclude that $p_1 = p_2^R$. The lemma follows.

We step to the main theorem of the article.

Theorem 1. *If $(u, v, d, n) \in \Delta$, $m = \mathrm{PL}(u)$, and $w = u(vd)^n$ then $\mathrm{PL}(w) \geq m$.*

Proof. Let $(t_1, t_2, \ldots, t_k) \in \mathrm{MPF}(w)$. Lemma 7 asserts that there are $\gamma \in \mathbb{N}$, $j \in \{1, 2, \ldots, k\}$, and $p \in \mathrm{Suf}(dv) \setminus \{dv\}$ such that $t_j = pd(vd)^\gamma p^R$.
Let $a \in \mathrm{Prf}(w)$ and $b \in \mathrm{Suf}(w)$ be such that $w = at_j b$. Realize that $a = t_1 t_2 \ldots t_{j-1}$ and $b = t_{j+1} t_{j+2} \ldots t_k$. Note that a or b can be the empty word; then $j = 1$ or $j = k$ respectively. Lemma 4 implies that

$$\mathrm{PL}(w) = \mathrm{PL}(t_1 t_2 \ldots t_{j-1}) + \mathrm{PL}(t_j) + \mathrm{PL}(t_{j+1} t_{j+2} \ldots t_k) = \mathrm{PL}(a) + \mathrm{PL}(t_j) + \mathrm{PL}(b). \tag{12}$$

We distinguish three distinct cases.

1. $u \notin \mathrm{Prf}(a)$: This case is depicted in Table 1. Let $u_2 \in \mathrm{Suf}(u)$ be such that $u = au_2$. Let $\bar{p} \in \mathrm{Suf}(d)$ be such that $\bar{p}u_2 = d$. It follows that $u_2^R \bar{p}^R = d$ and $p^R \bar{p}^R = vd$.
Then we have that $u_2^R b = u_2^R \bar{p}^R (vd)^\beta = d(vd)^\beta \in \mathrm{Pal}^+$ for some $\beta \in \mathbb{N}_0$. Hence $\mathrm{PL}(u_2^R \bar{p}^R (vd)^\beta) = 1$. In consequence $\mathrm{PL}(u_2) \geq \mathrm{PL}(b) - 1$ and

$$\mathrm{PL}(b) \geq \mathrm{PL}(u_2) - 1, \tag{13}$$

since $\mathrm{PL}(u_2^R) = \mathrm{PL}(u_2)$ and $u_2^R b \in \mathrm{Pal}^+$; see Corollary 3. Lemma 3 implies that

$$\mathrm{PL}(a) + \mathrm{PL}(u_2) \geq \mathrm{PL}(u). \tag{14}$$

From (12), (13), and (14) we have that

$$\mathrm{PL}(w) = \mathrm{PL}(a) + \mathrm{PL}(t_j) + \mathrm{PL}(b) \geq \mathrm{PL}(a) + 1 + \mathrm{PL}(u_2) - 1 \geq \mathrm{PL}(u).$$

Table 1. Case 1: The structure of the word w with $u \notin \mathrm{Prf}(a)$.

a	t_j			b	$\cdot$
a	p	$d(vd)^\gamma$	p^R	$\bar{p}^R$	$(vd)^\beta$
a	u_2	v	$d(vd)^\gamma$	v	u_2^R	$\bar{p}^R$	$(vd)^\beta$
u		$(vd)^{\gamma+1}$		v	d	$(vd)^\beta$

2. $u \in \mathrm{Prf}(a)$ and $p \in \mathrm{Suf}(v)$: This case is depicted in Table 2. Let $\bar{p} \in \mathrm{Prf}(v)$ be such that $\bar{p}p = v$. Note that if $p = v$ then $\bar{p} = \epsilon$, and if $p = \epsilon$ then $\bar{p} = v$. It is easy to verify that $b = \bar{p}^R d(vd)^\beta$ for some $\beta \in \mathbb{N}_0$ and $a = u(vd)^\alpha \bar{p}$ for some $\alpha \in \mathbb{N}_0$.

Let $\bar{a}$ be such that $a = u\bar{a}$. We have that $\bar{a} = (vd)^\alpha \bar{p}$ and $b = \bar{p}^R d(vd)^\beta$. It follows that either $\bar{a} = b^R d(vd)^\delta$ or $b = \bar{a}^R d(vd)^\delta$ for some $\delta \in \mathbb{N}_0$. Since $d(vd)^\delta \in \mathrm{Pal}$, Corollary 2 implies that

$$|\mathrm{PL}(\bar{a}) - \mathrm{PL}(b)| \leq 1. \tag{15}$$

It follows from Lemma 5 that

$$\mathrm{PL}(a) + \mathrm{PL}(\bar{a}) \geq \mathrm{PL}(u). \tag{16}$$

From (12), (15), and (16) we have that

$$\mathrm{PL}(w) = \mathrm{PL}(a) + \mathrm{PL}(t_j) + \mathrm{PL}(b) \geq \mathrm{PL}(a) + 1 + \mathrm{PL}(\bar{a}) - 1 \geq \mathrm{PL}(u).$$

Table 2. Case 2: The structure of the word w with $u \in \mathrm{Prf}(a)$ and $p \in \mathrm{Suf}(v)$.

a			t_j			b	
u	$(vd)^\alpha$	$\bar{p}$	p	$d(vd)^\gamma$	p^R	$\bar{p}^R$	$d(vd)^\beta$
	$\bar{a}$				v		

3. $u \in \mathrm{Prf}(a)$ and $p \notin \mathrm{Suf}(v)$: This case is depicted in Table 3. Since $p \in \mathrm{Suf}(vd) \setminus \{vd\}$ and $p \notin \mathrm{Suf}(v)$ it follows that $p \in \mathrm{Suf}(dv) \setminus (\mathrm{Suf}(v) \cup \{dv\})$.

Table 3. Case 3: The structure of the word w with $u \in \mathrm{Prf}(a)$ and $p \notin \mathrm{Suf}(v)$.

a			t_j			b	
u	$v(dv)^\alpha$	$\bar{p}$	p	$d(vd)^\gamma$	p^R	$\bar{p}^R$	$(vd)^\beta$
	$\bar{a}$				vd		

Let $\bar{p} \in \mathrm{Prf}(d)$ be such that $\bar{p}p = dv$ and consequently $p^R \bar{p}^R = vd$. Then $a = u(vd)^\alpha \bar{p}$ for some $\alpha \in \mathbb{N}_0$ and $b = \bar{p}(vd)^\beta$ for some $\beta \in \mathbb{N}_0$.

Let $\bar{a}$ be such that $a = u\bar{a}$. We have that $\bar{a} = v(dv)^\alpha \bar{p}$. It follows that either $\bar{a} = b^R(vd)^\delta v$ or $b = \bar{a}^R(vd)^\delta v$ for some $\delta \in \mathbb{N}_0$.

The rest of the proof of Case 3 is analogue to Case 2: Since $v(dv)^\delta \in \mathrm{Pal}$, Corollary 2 implies that

$$|\mathrm{PL}(\bar{a}) - \mathrm{PL}(b)| \leq 1. \tag{17}$$

It follows from Lemma 5 that

$$\mathrm{PL}(a) + \mathrm{PL}(\bar{a}) \geq \mathrm{PL}(u). \tag{18}$$

From (12), (17), and (18) we have that

$$\mathrm{PL}(w) = \mathrm{PL}(a) + \mathrm{PL}(t_j) + \mathrm{PL}(b) \geq \mathrm{PL}(a) + 1 + \mathrm{PL}(\bar{a}) - 1 \geq \mathrm{PL}(u).$$

We proved for each case that $\mathrm{PL}(w) \geq \mathrm{PL}(u)$. Since obviously for each u and each p one of the three cases applies, this completes the proof.

Acknowledgments. This work was supported by the Grant Agency of the Czech Technical University in Prague, grant No. SGS20/183/OHK4/3T/14.

References

1. Ambrož, P., Kadlec, O., Masáková, Z., Pelantová, E.: Palindromic length of words and morphisms in class P. Theor. Comput. Sci. **780**, 74–83 (2019). https://doi.org/10.1016/j.tcs.2019.02.024
2. Ambrož, P., Pelantová, E.: On palindromic length of Sturmian sequences. In: Hofman, P., Skrzypczak, M. (eds.) Developments in Language Theory, pp. 244–250. Springer International Publishing, Cham (2019). https://doi.org/10.1007/978-3-030-24886-4_18
3. Borozdin, K., Kosolobov, D., Rubinchik, M., Shur, A.M.: Palindromic length in linear time. In: Kärkkäinen, J., Radoszewski, J., Rytter, W. (eds.) 28th Annual Symposium on Combinatorial Pattern Matching (CPM 2017). Leibniz International Proceedings in Informatics (LIPIcs), vol. 78, pp. 23:1–23:12. Schloss Dagstuhl-Leibniz-Zentrum fuer Informatik, Dagstuhl, Germany (2017). https://doi.org/10.4230/LIPIcs.CPM.2017.23
4. Bucci, M., Richomme, G.: Greedy palindromic lengths. Int. J. Found. Comput. Sci. **29**(03), 331–356 (2018). https://doi.org/10.1142/S0129054118500077
5. Fici, G., Gagie, T., Kräkkäinen, J., Kempa, D.: A subquadratic algorithm for minimum palindromic factorization. J. Discrete Algorithms **28**, 41–48 (2014). https://doi.org/10.1016/j.jda.2014.08.001. stringMasters 2012 & 2013 Special Issue (Volume 1)
6. Frid, A., Puzynina, S., Zamboni, L.: On palindromic factorization of words. Adv. Appl. Math. **50**(5), 737–748 (2013). https://doi.org/10.1016/j.aam.2013.01.002
7. Frid, A.E.: Sturmian numeration systems and decompositions to palindromes. Eur. J. Comb. **71**, 202–212 (2018). https://doi.org/10.1016/j.ejc.2018.04.003
8. Frid, A.E.: First lower bounds for palindromic length. In: Hofman, P., Skrzypczak, M. (eds.) Developments in Language Theory, pp. 234–243. Springer International Publishing, Cham (2019). https://doi.org/10.1007/978-3-030-24886-4_17
9. Kosolobov, D., Rubinchik, M., Shur, A.M.: Pal^k is linear recognizable online. In: Italiano, G.F., Margaria-Steffen, T., Pokorný, J., Quisquater, J.J., Wattenhofer, R. (eds.) SOFSEM 2015: Theory and Practice of Computer Science, pp. 289–301. Springer, Berlin Heidelberg, Berlin, Heidelberg (2015). https://doi.org/10.1007/978-3-662-46078-8_24

10. Rubinchik, M., Shur, A.M.: EERTREE: an efficient data structure for processing palindromes in strings. In: Lipták, Z., Smyth, W.F. (eds.) IWOCA 2015. LNCS, vol. 9538, pp. 321–333. Springer, Cham (2016). https://doi.org/10.1007/978-3-319-29516-9_27

11. Saarela, A.: Palindromic length in free monoids and free groups. In: Brlek, S., Dolce, F., Reutenauer, C., Vandomme, É. (eds.) WORDS 2017. LNCS, vol. 10432, pp. 203–213. Springer, Cham (2017). https://doi.org/10.1007/978-3-319-66396-8_19

Operational Complexity of Straight Line Programs for Regular Languages

Hannes Seiwert[✉][iD]

Institute of Computer Science, Goethe University Frankfurt, Frankfurt, Germany
seiwert@em.uni-frankfurt.de

Abstract. A *straight line program (SLP)* is a circuit with letters as inputs and gates performing one of the operations union, concatenation, or star; its size is the number of its nodes. Every SLP describes a regular language in a natural manner. We study the complexity of language operations on SLPs and show that the complexity is exponential for intersection and shuffle, and double exponential for complementation. These results carry over to constant height pushdown automata and non-self-embedding grammars, since these models and SLPs are polynomially equivalent. We also examine *extended* SLPs that may perform additional operations and show that the cost of simulating an extended SLP with shuffle or intersection by a conventional SLP is double exponential.

Keywords: Regular language · Straight line program · Lower bound · Operational complexity · Shuffle · Constant height pushdown automaton

1 Introduction

There are many ways to describe a regular language, e.g. various kinds of automata, regular expressions, or grammars. Recently, the model of *straight line programs (SLPs)* was investigated by Geffert et al. [8]. An SLP is a circuit whose input nodes hold a letter $a \in \Sigma$, the empty word ε or the empty language $\emptyset$, and whose gates perform one of the operations union $(+)$, concatenation $(\cdot)$ or star $(*)$. Thus, an SLP is nothing else than a regular expression (RE) with its syntax tree replaced by a directed acyclic graph. The possibility to use a node several times allows exponential savings in size. For example, the language $L = \{a^n\}$ can be described by an SLP of size $O(\log n)$ (via iterated squaring), while every RE requires length $\Omega(n)$. SLPs are tightly related to automata and grammars, namely, they are polynomially equivalent to constant height pushdown automata (h-PDAs) [8] and to non-self-embedding context-free grammars [14].

Given a language operation and a descriptional model, a classical question is, by how much can the size increase when applying this operation. For example, there are languages L_1, L_2 with REs of length n, but their intersection $L_1 \cap L_2$ requires REs of length $2^{\Omega(n)}$ [10,11]; hence the complexity of intersection for REs is exponential. A lot of research was done in this area, including operational

G. Jirásková and G. Pighizzini (Eds.): DCFS 2020, LNCS 12442, pp. 180–192, 2020.
https://doi.org/10.1007/978-3-030-62536-8_15

complexity for finite automata (see [7] for a survey), REs [10–13] and h-PDAs [1,2,4]. Also, the descriptional complexity of *extended* REs that may perform additional operations was studied. For example, the cost of simulating a RE with intersection or shuffle by a conventional RE is double exponential [9,13].

In this paper, we study the complexity of operations on SLPs (thereby also continuing the study of operations for h-PDAs by Bednárová et al. [1,2,4]) and show that it is exponential for intersection and shuffle, and double exponential for complementation. The results for intersection and complementation already follow from the corresponding results for h-PDAs [1,4], however, we present alternative proofs that are considerably simpler. Secondly, we investigate *extended* *SLPs* in analogy to extended REs and show the same double exponential simulation costs for SLPs with intersection or shuffle. All results are achieved on *finite* languages over constant size alphabets.

2   Preliminaries

Throughout let $\mathbb{N} = \{0, 1, 2, \dots\}$ be the set of all nonnegative integers and $[n] = \{1, 2, \dots, n\}$. We assume the reader to be familiar with basics of formal languages. For a word w its *length* $|w|$ is the number of its letters. *Regular expressions* (*REs*, or just *expressions*) over an alphabet Σ are defined as follows: The empty word ε, the empty language $\emptyset$ and all letters $a \in \Sigma$ are expressions. If R and R' are expressions, then so are $(R+R')$, $(R \cdot R')$ and R^*. Every expression R *describes* a regular language $L(R)$ defined as

$$L(\varepsilon) = \{\varepsilon\}, \ L(\emptyset) = \emptyset, \ L(a) = \{a\},$$
$$L(R + R') = L(R) \cup L(R'), \ L(R \cdot R') = L(R) \cdot L(R'), \ L(R^*) = (L(R))^*. \tag{1}$$

The *length* of an expression is the number of nodes in its syntax tree. With a slight abuse of notation we identify expressions with their described languages, e.g. $(a+b)$ stands for the language $\{a, b\}$. The *shuffle* operation $\sqcup\!\sqcup$ (also called *interleaving*) is defined as follows: For two words v, w, their shuffle $v \sqcup\!\sqcup w$ is the set of all words $v_1 w_1 v_2 w_2 \cdots v_k w_k$ where $k \in \mathbb{N}$, $v_i, w_i \in \Sigma^*$ for all i, $v_1 v_2 \cdots v_k = v$ and $w_1 w_2 \cdots w_k = w$. The shuffle of two languages is $L_1 \sqcup\!\sqcup L_2 = \bigcup_{v \in L_1, w \in L_2} v \sqcup\!\sqcup w$. Since shuffle is associative, we write $\sqcup\!\sqcup_{i=1}^n L_i$ for $L_1 \sqcup\!\sqcup \cdots \sqcup\!\sqcup L_n$. The *reversal* w^R of a word $w = w_1 \cdots w_n$ is $w^R = w_n \cdots w_1$.

Straight Line Programs for Regular Languages. There are several equivalent ways to define straight line programs, we here choose *circuits*. A *straight line program (SLP) for a regular language* [8] is a directed acyclic graph (DAG) with one sink; parallel edges are allowed. Each in-degree-zero node holds either a letter $a \in \Sigma$, the empty word ε or the empty language $\emptyset$. Every other node, a *gate*, either has in-degree two and performs one of the operations union $(+)$ or concatenation $(\cdot)$ or has in-degree one and performs the star operation $(^*)$. An SLP whose underlying graph is a tree is just a regular expression.

Every node u *describes* a regular language $L(u)$ defined analogously to Eq. (1). The language $L(S)$ *described by an SLP* S is the language described by its sink. The *size* of S is the number of its nodes and its *depth* is the length of a longest path. For a regular language L let $\mathsf{slp}(L)$ be the size of a smallest SLP describing L.

An equivalent definition, explaining the name "straight line program", is the following: An SLP S consists of *variables* $V_1, \ldots, V_k$ and *instructions* of the form $V_i = R_i$ where R_i is a RE over the alphabet $\Sigma \cup \{\varepsilon, \emptyset\} \cup \{V_j : j < i\}$.[1] Every variable V_i describes a language $L(V_i) := L(R_i)$, and S describes the language $L(S) := L(V_k)$; its size is the sum of lengths of all expressions R_i. We will use the two definitions interchangeably. For further reading we refer to [8].

Example 1. Let $\Sigma = \{a_1, \ldots, a_k\}$ be an alphabet, n be a power of two and $I = \{1, 2, 4, \ldots, n/2\}$. Then the languages Σ^i for $i \in I$ and Σ^{n-1} can simultaneously be described the variables S_i and S_{n-1} of the following SLP of size $O(k + \log n)$:

$$S_1 = a_1 + \cdots + a_k, \quad S_{2i} = S_i S_i \ \forall i \in I, \quad S_{n-1} = S_1 S_2 S_4 \cdots S_{n/2} \qquad (2)$$

Analogously, the languages $\Sigma^{\leq n}$ or $\Sigma^{\geq n}$ can be described if we replace each letter a by $(a + \varepsilon)$ or aa^*. We will use these SLPs later implicitly in our proofs.

Example 2. The *palindrome language* $L_n^{\mathrm{pal}} := \{ww^{\mathrm{R}} : w \in \Sigma^n\}$ over an alphabet $\Sigma = \{a_1, \ldots, a_k\}$ can be described by the following program P_n of size $O(kn)$:

$$P_0 = \varepsilon, \qquad P_i = a_1 P_{i-1} a_1 + \cdots + a_k P_{i-1} a_k \ \forall i \in [n] \qquad (3)$$

A similar (but not identical) model is that of non-self-embedding grammars. A context-free grammar is *non-self-embedding (NSE)* if there is no derivation $A \Rightarrow^* \alpha A \beta$ (a "cycle") with both α and β being non-empty [5]. Any SLP can be transformed into an NSE grammar, and vice versa, with only polynomially increasing size [14] – just simulate cycles by star operations, and vice versa.

A language L is *homogeneous* if all its words have same length, and its *degree* $\deg L$ is the length of its words. An SLP is *homogeneous* if every of its nodes g describes a homogeneous language $L(g)$; the *degree* of such a node is $\deg g = \deg L(g)$. We assume w.l.o.g. that an SLP for a homogeneous language is homogeneous, and that an SLP for a finite language contains no star operation. So, for finite languages, NSE grammars and SLPs are *identical* models, since there are neither stars nor cycles.

Constant Height Pushdown Automata. We assume the reader to be familiar with nondeterministic finite automata (NFAs) and pushdown automata (PDAs). For a regular language L denote by $\mathsf{nsc}(L)$ the minimal number of states of an NFA that accepts L. Following [8], a *constant height pushdown automaton (h-PDA)* $A = (Q, \Sigma, \Gamma, \delta, q_0, F, h)$ of *height* h is a PDA whose pushdown store never contains more than h symbols; a *deterministic h-PDA (h-DPDA)* is defined in the natural way. For a comparison between h-PDAs and h-DPDAs see [3]. The connection between automata and SLPs is given by the two facts below.

---

[1] For convenience and in contrast to [8], we allow arbitrary regular expressions (possibly with many operations) on the RHS of instructions instead of just single operations.

Fact 1 (Geffert et al. [8, Thm. 1]).

(a) *Every NFA with n states can be simulated by an SLP of size $O(n^3)$.*
(b) *Every h-PDA $A = (Q, \Sigma, \Gamma, \delta, q_0, F, h)$ can be simulated by an SLP of size $O(h|Q|^4|\Gamma| + |Q|^2|\Sigma|)$.*

Fact 2 (Geffert et al. [8, Thm. 2]). *Every SLP of size n can be simulated by an*

(a) *NFA with $O(2^n)$ states,*
(b) *h-PDA with $O(n)$ states, height $h \leq n$ and pushdown alphabet size $|\Gamma| \leq n$.*

3   Lower Bound Techniques

In this section we prepare our lower bound methods. For SLPs describing *finite* languages – hence, not containing any gates performing star operations – we can use methods from circuit complexity. The following lemma is due to Hrubeš, Wigderson and Yehudayoff [15]. Originally, they stated it for non-commutative arithmetic polynomials, here we reformulate it in terms of languages. Filmus [6] used a similar method to obtain lower bounds for context-free grammars.

Definition 1 (Rectangle). Let X be a homogeneous language and Y a set of pairs of words $(y, \tilde{y})$ such that all words $y\tilde{y}$ have same length. We call the language $\{yx\tilde{y} : x \in X, (y, \tilde{y}) \in Y\}$ a *semi-rectangle* and denote it by $X \otimes Y$. If all words y have same length d and all words $\tilde{y}$ have same length $\tilde{d}$, then $X \otimes Y$ is a *rectangle*. A rectangle is *balanced* if $n/3 \leq \deg X \leq 2n/3$ holds for $n := d + \tilde{d} + \deg X$.

In other words, a rectangle is just a cyclic permuted *concatenation* $X \cdot Y$ of two homogeneous languages X and Y, and is balanced if the degrees of both parts X, Y differ at most by a factor of 2.

To get some intuition, consider an SLP for a homogeneous language L. If we delete one incoming edge of all union gates, we obtain a tree that consists solely of concatenation gates and describes a single word $w \in L$. Every tree has a node v_x whose subtree contains about half of its leaves. This gives us a "balanced" decomposition $w = yx\tilde{y}$ of w, where x is the word described by the node v_x. If we repeat this for all words in L and collect all the decompositions, we obtain a set of balanced rectangles such that every word in L lies in at least one of them.

Lemma 2 ([15, Prop. 3.2]). *Let $n \geq 2$ and $L \subseteq \Sigma^n$ be a homogeneous language. Then L is a union of $s \leq n \cdot \mathsf{slp}(L)$ balanced rectangles $X_1 \otimes Y_1, \ldots, X_s \otimes Y_s$.*

Proof. Let S be a homogeneous SLP for L, let $g_1, \ldots, g_t$ be all nodes g_i in S with $n/3 \leq \deg g_i < 2n/3$ and let $X_i := L(g_i)$ be their described languages.

Claim 1. *For every node f in S with $\deg f \geq n/3$, its described language $L(f)$ is a union of semi-rectangles $L(f) = \bigcup_{i=1}^{t} X_i \otimes Y_i(f)$ for some sets $Y_1(f), \ldots, Y_t(f)$.*

Proof of Claim 1. Proceed by induction on the depth. If $\deg f < 2n/3$, then $f = g_i$ for an $i \in [t]$ and we set $Y_i(f) = \{(\varepsilon, \varepsilon)\}$ and $Y_j(f) = \emptyset$ for all $j \in [t]\setminus\{i\}$. Otherwise, $\deg f \geq 2n/3$ holds. If $f = h_1 + h_2$ is a union gate, then $\deg f = \deg h_1 = \deg h_2$. By induction there are sets $Y_i(h_j)$ for $i \in [t], j \in \{1,2\}$ such that $L(h_j) = \bigcup_{i=1}^t X_i \otimes Y_i(h_j)$ is a union of semi-rectangles. Then let $Y_i(f) := Y_i(h_1) \cup Y_i(h_2)$ for all $i \in [t]$. If $f = h_1 \cdot h_2$ is a concatenation gate, then $\deg f = \deg h_1 + \deg h_2$. Since $\deg f \geq 2n/3$, we have $\deg h_1 \geq n/3$ or $\deg h_2 \geq n/3$. Assume $\deg h_1 \geq n/3$, the other case is analogous. By induction, there are sets $Y_i(h_1)$ for $i \in [t]$ such that $L(h_1) = \bigcup_{i=1}^t X_i \otimes Y_i(h_1)$ is a union of semi-rectangles. Then let $Y_i(f) := \{(y, \tilde{y}w) : (y, \tilde{y}) \in Y_i(h_1), w \in L(h_2)\}$ for all $i \in [t]$. $\qquad\square$Claim 1

Applying Claim 1 to the sink z of S yields a union of semi-rectangles $L(z) = \bigcup_{i=1}^t X_i \otimes Y_i(z)$. For every $i \in [t]$ and $d \in \{0, \ldots, n - \deg X_i\}$ define $Y_i^{(d)} := \{(y, \tilde{y}) \in Y_i(z) : |y| = d\}$. Then every set $X_i \otimes Y_i^{(d)}$ is a balanced rectangle and we obtain $L = L(z) = \bigcup_{i=1}^t \bigcup_{d=0}^{n - \deg X_i} X_i \otimes Y_i^{(d)}$. $\qquad\square$

To show a lower bound on $\mathsf{slp}(L)$ for a homogeneous language L, it suffices to upper bound the number of words in every balanced rectangle $X \otimes Y \subseteq L$.

Theorem 3 (Rectangle bound). *Let $L \subseteq \Sigma^n$ be a homogeneous language. If $|X \otimes Y| \leq h$ holds for every balanced rectangle $X \otimes Y \subseteq L$, then $\mathsf{slp}(L) \geq |L|/nh$.*

Proof. Let S be an SLP of size s for L and assume $|X \otimes Y| \leq h$ for all balanced rectangles $X \otimes Y \subseteq L$. By Lemma 2, L is a union of at most sn such rectangles. At least $sn \geq |L|/h$ such rectangles are necessary to describe all words in L. $\quad\square$

We will deal with languages that give restrictions of the form: For some indices i, j and all words $w = w_1 \cdots w_n \in L$, the letters w_i and w_j must coincide. This motivates the following notion. For a homogeneous language $L \subseteq \Sigma^n$ we call a (maximal) set $M \subseteq [n]$ a *mirror set of L* if $w_i = w_j$ holds for every word $w \in L$ and all $i, j \in M$. For example, the *copy language* $L_n^{\mathrm{copy}} := \{ww : w \in \Sigma^n\}$ has the mirror sets $M_i = \{i, n+i\}$ for all $i \in [n]$ and the palindrome language $L_n^{\mathrm{pal}} = \{ww^{\mathrm{R}} : w \in \Sigma^n\}$ has the mirror sets $M_i = \{i, 2n+1-i\}$ for all $i \in [n]$.

We will use mirror sets to upper bound the cardinality of balanced rectangles. Roughly speaking, if a mirror set contains positions of *both* parts X and Y of a rectangle, then the corresponding letters are identical in every word $x \in X$ and pair $(y, \tilde{y}) \in Y$. Formally, given a homogeneous language $L \subseteq \Sigma^n$ and a rectangle $X \otimes Y \subseteq L$ with $|y| = d$ and $|\tilde{y}| = \tilde{d}$ for all $(y, \tilde{y}) \in Y$, we say that Y *covers* the positions $1, \ldots, d, n-\tilde{d}+1, \ldots, n$, and X *covers* the positions $d+1, \ldots, d+\deg X$. That is, for any word $y x \tilde{y} \in X \otimes Y$, the positions of the letters belonging to x are covered by X and the positions of the letters belonging to $y\tilde{y}$ are covered by Y. A mirror set M is *separated* (w.r.t. $X \otimes Y$), if there are $i, j \in M$ such that i is covered by X and j is *not* covered by X (and, hence, is covered by Y).

Lemma 4. *Let L be a homogeneous language, $X \otimes Y \subseteq L$ a rectangle and M a separated mirror set of L. Then $w_j = w'_j$ holds for all words $w, w' \in X \otimes Y$ and all $j \in M$.*

We call the letters w_j with $j \in M$ *fixed* and call $\{w_j : j \in M\}$ a *group* of letters.

Proof. Let M be a separated mirror set of L such that X covers $k \in M$ and Y covers $\ell \in M$. Assume to the contrary that there are words $w, w' \in X \otimes Y$ with $w_j \neq w'_j$ for a $j \in M$. The rectangle $X \otimes Y$ gives unique decompositions of w and w': There are words $x, x' \in X$ and pairs $(y, \tilde{y}), (y', \tilde{y}') \in Y$ such that $w = yx\tilde{y}$ and $w' = y'x'\tilde{y}'$. So, also the word $u := y'x\tilde{y}'$ lies in $X \otimes Y$. Since X covers k, the letter u_k belongs to x, implying $u_k = w_k$, and since Y covers ℓ, the letter u_ℓ belongs to $y'\tilde{y}'$, implying $u_\ell = w'_\ell$. Since j, k, ℓ are in the same mirror set M, we have $w_k = w_j$ and $w'_\ell = w'_j$. Thus, $u_k = w_k = w_j \neq w'_j = w'_\ell = u_\ell$. But since $k, \ell \in M$ and $u \in X \otimes Y \subseteq L$, we must have $u_k = u_\ell$, a contradiction.   □

We demonstrate how to apply Theorem 3 and Lemma 4 on the copy language. In fact, all lower bounds in this paper are based on this language or variations of it.

Corollary 5 (Copy language). *Let Σ be a non-unary alphabet. Then the copy language $L_n^{\text{copy}} = \{ww : w \in \Sigma^n\}$ requires SLPs of size $\text{slp}(L_n^{\text{copy}}) \geq |\Sigma|^{\Omega(n)}$.*

Proof. Let $X \otimes Y \subseteq L_n^{\text{copy}}$ be a balanced rectangle with $2n/3 \leq \deg X \leq 4n/3$. Our goal is to upper bound the number of words in $X \otimes Y$. The language L_n^{copy} has the mirror sets $M_i = \{i, n+i\}$ for all $i \in [n]$. We claim that at least $2n/3$ mirror sets are separated. Distinguish two cases.

Case 1: If $\deg X \leq n$, then X covers at most one position of every mirror set. Hence, all mirror sets that contain a position covered by X are separated, and since $\deg X \geq 2n/3$, there are at least $2n/3$ such positions.

Case 2: If $\deg X \geq n$, then X covers at least one position of every mirror set. Hence, all mirror sets that contain a position *not* covered by X are separated, and since $\deg X \leq 4n/3$, there are at least $2n - 4n/3 = 2n/3$ such positions.

So, from Lemma 4 follows that at least $2n/3$ groups of letters are fixed in every word in $X \otimes Y$, and therefore $|X \otimes Y| \leq |\Sigma|^{n-2n/3} = |\Sigma|^{n/3}$. Hence, by Theorem 3 we have $\text{slp}(L_n^{\text{copy}}) \geq |\Sigma|^n / (2n|\Sigma|^{n/3}) \geq |\Sigma|^{\Omega(n)}$.   □

The class of context-free languages is closed under intersection with regular languages. So, a standard trick for showing that a language L is *not* context-free is to pick a *regular* language L' and show that $L \cap L'$ is not context-free, intending that $L \cap L'$ is easier to analyze. Similarly, for a regular language L, we can obtain a lower bound on $\text{slp}(L)$ from the intersection $L \cap L'$ for an "easy" language L'.

Lemma 6. *Let L and L' be regular languages. Then L requires SLPs of size at least $\text{slp}(L) \geq \Omega\left(\sqrt[6]{\text{slp}(L \cap L')/\text{nsc}(L')}\right)$.*

In particular, if $\text{slp}(L \cap L') \geq 2^{\Omega(n)}$ and $\text{nsc}(L') = 2^{o(n)}$, then $\text{slp}(L) \geq 2^{\Omega(n)}$ follows.

Proof. Let S be an SLP for L of size n and N be an NFA for L' with m states. By Fact 2(b), S can be simulated by an h-PDA A with $O(n)$ states, height $h \leq n$ and pushdown alphabet of size $|\Gamma| \leq n$. By [4, Thm. 3.1], the intersection $L \cap L'$

can be accepted by an h-PDA A' with at most nm states and same pushdown alphabet and height as A. Finally, by Fact 1(b) the h-PDA A' can be simulated by an SLP of size $O((nm)^4 \cdot n^2) \leq O((nm)^6)$. Thus, $\mathsf{slp}(L \cap L') \leq O((nm)^6)$, and rearranging yields $\mathsf{slp}(L) = n \geq \Omega(\sqrt[6]{\mathsf{slp}(L \cap L')/m})$. □

4   SLP-Complexity of Operations

We now examine the complexity of operations on SLPs, i.e. by how much the size can increase when applying an operation. Bednárová et al. showed that the complexity of intersection for h-PDAs is exponential [4, Thm. 3.4]. Their result already carries over to SLPs, however, we here give a simpler proof without taking a "detour" over h-PDAs.

Theorem 7 (Intersection, [4]). *There are finite languages L_1 and L_2 such that $\mathsf{slp}(L_1), \mathsf{slp}(L_2) \leq O(n)$ but $\mathsf{slp}(L_1 \cap L_2) \geq 2^{\Omega(n)}$.*

Proof. Let $\Sigma = \{a, b\}$. We use the witness languages $L_1 = \{ww^{\mathsf{R}}w' : w, w' \in \Sigma^n\}$ and $L_2 = \{w'w^{\mathsf{R}}w : w, w' \in \Sigma^n\}$. Since $L_1 = L_n^{\mathrm{pal}} \cdot \Sigma^n$ and $L_2 = \Sigma^n \cdot L_n^{\mathrm{pal}}$, both languages can be described by SLPs of size $O(n)$ (see Example 2).

The intersection of the above languages is $L := L_1 \cap L_2 = \{ww^{\mathsf{R}}w : w \in \Sigma^n\}$. In order to apply Theorem 3 to L, take a balanced rectangle $X \otimes Y \subseteq L$ satisfying $n \leq \deg X \leq 2n$. The language L has the mirror sets $M_i = \{i, 2n+1-i, 2n+i\}$ for all $i \in [n]$. Since $\deg X \leq 2n$, for every $i \in [n]$ not both i and $2n+i$ can be covered by X. Since $\deg X \geq n$, at least $n/2$ sets M_i contain a position covered by X. Thus, all these mirror sets are separated. By Lemma 4 all $n/2$ corresponding groups of letters are fixed in every word in $X \otimes Y$. Therefore $|X \otimes Y| \leq 2^{n-n/2} = 2^{n/2}$, and Theorem 3 yields $\mathsf{slp}(L) \geq 2^n/(3n2^{n/2}) = 2^{\Omega(n)}$. □

Next, we turn to the shuffle operation which was not studied for h-PDAs yet.

Theorem 8 (Shuffle). *There are finite languages L_1 and L_2 such that $\mathsf{slp}(L_1), \mathsf{slp}(L_2) \leq O(n)$ but $\mathsf{slp}(L_1 \sqcup \!\!\! \sqcup L_2) \geq 2^{\Omega(n)}$.*

Proof. Let $\Sigma_1 = \{0, 1\}$ and $\Sigma_2 = \{a, b\}$ be two disjoint alphabets. We use the witness languages $L_1 = \{uu^{\mathsf{R}} : u \in \Sigma_1^n\}$ and $L_2 = \{vv^{\mathsf{R}} : v \in \Sigma_2^n\}$. Their shuffle is the language $L := L_1 \sqcup \!\!\! \sqcup L_2 = \{uu^{\mathsf{R}} \sqcup \!\!\! \sqcup vv^{\mathsf{R}} : u \in \Sigma_1^n, v \in \Sigma_2^n\}$. As shown in Example 2, L_1 and L_2 can be described by programs of size $O(n)$.

To prove the lower bound on $\mathsf{slp}(L)$, consider the sublanguage $L' := L \cap \Sigma_1^n \Sigma_2^n \Sigma_1^n \Sigma_2^n = \{uvu^{\mathsf{R}}v^{\mathsf{R}} : u \in \Sigma_1^n, v \in \Sigma_2^n\}$. Clearly $\mathsf{nsc}(\Sigma_1^n \Sigma_2^n \Sigma_1^n \Sigma_2^n) \leq O(n)$, so by Lemma 6 it suffices to prove an exponential lower bound on $\mathsf{slp}(L')$. We apply Theorem 3 to L'. Let $X \otimes Y \subseteq L'$ be a balanced rectangle satisfying $4n/3 \leq \deg X \leq 8n/3$. The language L' has the mirror sets $M_i = \{i, 3n+1-i\}$ and $M_{n+i} = \{n+i, 4n+1-i\}$ for all $i \in [n]$. We claim that at least $n/3$ mirror sets of L' are separated. Split the range $[4n]$ into four quarters $Q_1, \ldots, Q_4$ defined as $Q_j = \{(j-1)n+1, \ldots, jn\}$. So, for every mirror set M either $M \subseteq Q_1 \cup Q_3$ or $M \subseteq Q_2 \cup Q_4$ holds. Distinguish two cases.

Case 1: Assume that X covers *no* position in Q_1. Then, since $\deg X \geq 4n/3$, the first or the last $n/3$ positions in Q_3 must be covered by X. Thus, the corresponding mirror sets of these $n/3$ positions are separated.

Case 2: Assume that X covers *at least one* position in Q_1. Then, since $\deg X \geq 4n/3$, the first $n/3$ positions in Q_2 must be covered by X. Since $\deg X \leq 8n/3$, the last $n/3$ positions in Q_4 *cannot* be covered by X. Thus, the corresponding mirror sets $M_{n+1}, \ldots, M_{n+n/3}$ are separated.

By Lemma 4, at least $n/3$ groups of letters are fixed in every word in $X \otimes Y$. So, $|X \otimes Y| \leq 2^{2n-n/3} =: h$ and Theorem 3 yields $\mathsf{slp}(L') \geq 2^{2n}/4nh = 2^{\Omega(n)}$. $\square$

The exponential blow-up for shuffle in Theorem 8 can be shown also for deterministic h-PDAs by the same witness languages, we leave the proof to the reader. Thus, the following corollary answers questions from Bednárová et al. asking for the complexity of other language operations for h-PDAs [4] resp. h-DPDAs [2].

Corollary 9. *There are finite languages L_1, L_2 that can be accepted by h-DPDAs of size $O(n)$, but any h-PDA accepting $L_1 \sqcup\!\sqcup L_2$ has size $2^{\Omega(n)}$.*

The complexity of complementation also was studied for h-PDAs [1,4], Bednárová and Geffert [1] showed that it is double exponential. Again, this result implies double exponential complexity also for SLPs. Nevertheless, we give a simpler, direct proof, and in particular with a *cofinite* witness language.

Theorem 10 (Complementation, [1]). *There are cofinite languages L such that $\mathsf{slp}(L) \leq O(n)$ but $\mathsf{slp}(\Sigma^* \setminus L) \geq 2^{\Omega(2^n)}$.*

Proof. Let $\Sigma = \{a, b\}$, let $n \in \mathbb{N}$ and $k = 2^n$. By Corollary 5 the copy language $L_k^{\mathrm{copy}} = \{ww : w \in \Sigma^k\}$ requires SLPs of size $2^{\Omega(k)} = 2^{\Omega(2^n)}$. Now we give an SLP of size $O(n)$ for its complement $L := \Sigma^* \setminus L_k^{\mathrm{copy}} = \{ww' : w, w' \in \Sigma^k, w \neq w'\} \cup \{w \in \Sigma^* : |w| \neq 2k\}$. The latter part of L is trivial (see Example 1). To describe the first part we simulate a binary search for a position on which the words w and w' differ. Define variables S_i describing the languages $L_i := \{ub v \bar{b} u' : b \neq \bar{b} \in \Sigma, v \in \Sigma^{k-1}, uu' \in \Sigma^{i-1}\}$ recursively by

$$S_1 = a\Sigma^{k-1}b + b\Sigma^{k-1}a,$$
$$S_{2i} = S_i \Sigma^i + \Sigma^i S_i \quad \forall i \in \{1, 2, 4, \ldots, k/2\}. \tag{4}$$

The variable S_{2i} correctly describes L_{2i} since the first term $S_i \Sigma^i$ describes all words with $|u'| \geq i$ and the second term $\Sigma^i S_i$ describes all words with $|u| \geq i$.

So, S_k describes the language $L_k = \{ww' : w, w' \in \Sigma^k, w \neq w'\}$ with $O(\log k)$ variables and a constant number of operations per variable. Additional size $O(\log k)$ is sufficient for all Σ^i- and Σ^{k-1}-terms (see Example 1). Finally the program $S := S_k + \Sigma^{<2k} + \Sigma^{>2k}$ of size $O(\log k) = O(n)$ describes L. $\square$

Matching upper bounds for intersection and complementation, showing that Theorems 7 and 10 are tight, were given by Bednárová et al. [4]. For shuffle a similar construction as given in [4, Thm. 3.1] for intersection is possible, this shows that Theorem 8 is tight. Since the proof is straightforward, we omit it.

Proposition 11. *Let L_1, L_2 be languages with $\mathsf{slp}(L_1) \leq n$ and $\mathsf{slp}(L_2) \leq m$. Then their shuffle can be described by an SLP of size $\mathsf{slp}(L_1 \sqcup\!\sqcup L_2) \leq 2^{O(m + \log n)}$.*

5   Complexity of Extended SLPs

We now investigate SLPs that may perform additional operations. For a set $\mathcal{O} \subseteq \{\cap, \sqcup\!\sqcup\}$ of operations, an *extended regular expression* $\mathrm{RE}[\mathcal{O}]$ (resp. an *extended straight line program* $\mathrm{SLP}[\mathcal{O}]$) is an expression (resp. SLP) that may additionally perform operations from $\mathcal{O}$. Any extended RE or SLP describes a regular language in the obvious way, i.e. $L(R \circ R) = L(R) \circ L(R)$ for $\circ \in \{\cap, \sqcup\!\sqcup\}$. For a regular language L, denote by $\mathsf{slp}[\mathcal{O}](L)$ the size of a smallest $\mathrm{SLP}[\mathcal{O}]$ describing L. We do *not* consider complementation here, since already the blow-up for REs with complementation is *non-elementary* [16], i.e. larger than any function $\exp(\exp(\ldots \exp(n)\ldots))$.

Theorem 12 (SLPs with intersection). *There are finite languages L such that $\mathsf{slp}[\cap](L) \leq O(n)$ but $\mathsf{slp}(L) \geq 2^{\Omega(2^n)}$.*

Proof. Let $\Sigma = \{a, b\}$, let $n \in \mathbb{N}$ and $k = 2^n$. We use again the witness language $L := L_k^{\mathrm{copy}} = \{ww : w \in \Sigma^k\}$. In Corollary 5 we showed a lower bound $\mathsf{slp}(L) \geq 2^{\Omega(k)} = 2^{\Omega(2^n)}$. Now we design an $\mathrm{SLP}[\cap]$ of size $O(\log k) = O(n)$ for L. Define variables S_i for the languages $L_i := \{wuw : w \in \Sigma^i, u \in \Sigma^{k-i}\}$ recursively by[2]

$$\begin{aligned}
S_1 &= a\Sigma^{k-1}a + b\Sigma^{k-1}b, \\
S_{2i} &= (S_i\Sigma^i) \cap (\Sigma^i S_i) \quad \forall i \in \{1, 2, 4, \ldots, k/2\}.
\end{aligned} \qquad (5)$$

The variable S_{2i} describes L_{2i}, since for every word $w = w_1 \cdots w_{k+2i} \in L(S_{2i})$ the first term $(S_i \Sigma^i)$ ensures that the first i letters $w_1 \cdots w_i$ coincide with their counterparts $w_{k+1} \cdots w_{k+i}$, and the second term $(\Sigma^i S_i)$ ensures that the last i letters $w_{k+i+1} \cdots w_{k+2i}$ coincide with their counterparts $w_{i+1} \cdots w_{2i}$.

So, the program S_k describes the language $L_k = L_k^{\mathrm{copy}}$ with $O(\log k)$ variables and a constant number of operations per variable. Additional size $O(\log k)$ is sufficient to compute all Σ^i- and Σ^{k-1}-terms (see Example 1). $\square$

Theorem 13 (SLPs with shuffle). *There are finite languages L such that $\mathsf{slp}[\sqcup\!\sqcup](L) \leq O(n)$ but $\mathsf{slp}(L) \geq 2^{\Omega(2^n)}$.*

The idea is to generalize the proof of Theorem 8 using a shuffle of $m = 2^n$ distinguishable instances of $L_i^{\mathrm{pal}} = \{ww^{\mathrm{R}} : w \in \Sigma^i\}$ (it turns out that already $i = 1$ suffices) and then focus on words of the form $w_1 w_2 \cdots w_m w_1^{\mathrm{R}} w_2^{\mathrm{R}} \cdots w_m^{\mathrm{R}}$. However, we cannot use distinct alphabets for all instances, because already the size needed to describe every letter once would be too large. Instead, we use binary numbers to identify start and end of each instance and mark its middle by the symbol $.

---

[2] Note the duality to the program given in Eq. 4 for the language $\Sigma^{2k} \backslash L_k^{\mathrm{copy}}$.

Proof. Let $\Sigma = \{0, 1, a, b, \$\}$, let $n \in \mathbb{N}$ and $m = 2^n$. For k being a power of two and a number $j \in [k]$, denote by $\langle j \rangle_k$ the word in $\{0, 1\}^{\log_2 k}$ that corresponds to the binary representation of $j-1$ and let $\langle j \rangle_k^{\mathsf{R}}$ be its reversal. For example, $\langle 1 \rangle_k = 0^{\log_2 k}$, $\langle k \rangle_k = 1^{\log_2 k}$ and $\langle 1 \rangle_1 = \varepsilon$. Define variables S_k for the languages $L_k := \bigsqcup_{j=1}^{k} \left(\langle j \rangle_k (a\$a + b\$b) \langle j \rangle_k^{\mathsf{R}} \right)$ recursively by

$$S_1 = a\$a + b\$b,$$
$$S_{2k} = (0^k S_k 0^k) \sqcup (1^k S_k 1^k) \quad \forall k \in \{1, 2, 4, \ldots, m/2\}. \tag{6}$$

For brevity let $c\$c := a\$a + b\$b$. Since $\sigma^k(\bigsqcup_{i=1}^{k} T_i)\sigma^k = \bigsqcup_{i=1}^{k}(\sigma T_i \sigma)$ holds for any languages T_i and letter σ, the variable S_{2k} correctly describes L_{2k}:

$$(0^k L_k 0^k) \sqcup (1^k L_k 1^k) = \left(0^k \bigsqcup_{j=1}^{k} (\langle j \rangle_k c\$c \langle j \rangle_k^{\mathsf{R}}) 0^k \right) \sqcup \left(1^k \bigsqcup_{j=1}^{k} (\langle j \rangle_k c\$c \langle j \rangle_k^{\mathsf{R}}) 1^k \right)$$

$$= \bigsqcup_{j=1}^{k} \left((\underbrace{0\langle j \rangle_k}_{\langle j \rangle_{2k}} c\$c \underbrace{\langle j \rangle_k^{\mathsf{R}} 0}_{\langle j \rangle_{2k}^{\mathsf{R}}}) \sqcup (\underbrace{1\langle j \rangle_k}_{\langle 2^k+j \rangle_{2k}} c\$c \underbrace{\langle j \rangle_k^{\mathsf{R}} 1}_{\langle 2^k+j \rangle_{2k}^{\mathsf{R}}}) \right) = \bigsqcup_{j=1}^{2k} (\langle j \rangle_{2k} c\$c \langle j \rangle_{2k}^{\mathsf{R}}) = L_{2k}.$$

So, the program S_m describes the language $L := L_m$, this will be our witness language. The program has $O(\log m)$ variables and uses a constant number of operations for each. Additionally, size $O(\log m)$ is sufficient for all 0^k- and 1^k-terms (see Example 1). Hence, in total size $O(\log m) = O(n)$ suffices.

We now show the lower bound on $\mathsf{slp}(L)$. Let $\langle j \rangle := \langle j \rangle_m$. In order to apply Lemma 6, take the language $H := \langle 1 \rangle (a+b) \cdots \langle m \rangle (a+b) \$^m (a+b) \langle 1 \rangle^{\mathsf{R}} \cdots (a+b) \langle m \rangle^{\mathsf{R}}$.

Claim 2. $L \cap H = L' := \{\langle 1 \rangle c_1 \cdots \langle m \rangle c_m \$^m c_1 \langle 1 \rangle^{\mathsf{R}} \cdots c_m \langle m \rangle^{\mathsf{R}} : c \in \{a, b\}^m\}.$

Proof of Claim 2. The direction $L' \subseteq L \cap H$ is trivial. We show the other direction $L \cap H \subseteq L'$. Let w be an arbitrary word in $L \cap H$. Since $w \in L$, there are letters $c_1, \ldots, c_m \in \{a, b\}$ such that $w \in \bigsqcup_{i=1}^{m}(u_i \$ v_i)$ for $u_i := \langle i \rangle c_i$ and $v_i := c_i \langle i \rangle^{\mathsf{R}}$. Since $w \in H$, it must be of the form $w = \langle 1 \rangle c_{j_1} \cdots \langle m \rangle c_{j_m} \$^m c_{j'_1} \langle 1 \rangle^{\mathsf{R}} \cdots c_{j'_m} \langle m \rangle^{\mathsf{R}}$ where $j_1, \ldots, j_m$ and $j'_1, \ldots, j'_m$ are permutations of $[m]$.

We claim that $w = u_1 \cdots u_m \$^m v_1 \cdots v_m$ must hold, i.e. $j_i = j'_i = i$ for all $i \in [m]$. The block $\$^m$ in the middle of w ensures that the left part of w is a shuffle of the u_i's and the right part is a shuffle of the v_i's. We show inductively for $i = 0, \ldots, m$ that $u_1 \cdots u_i$ is a prefix of w. By an analogous argument follows that $v_1 \cdots v_m$ is a suffix of w.

For $i = 0$ there is nothing to prove. Assume that the claim holds for $i-1 < m$, thus, $u_1 \cdots u_{i-1} \langle i \rangle c_{j_i}$ is a prefix of w. Since $u_{j_i} = \langle j_i \rangle c_{j_i}$, the word $\langle j_i \rangle$ must stand somewhere before c_{j_i}, potentially "shuffled". But since all letters in front of $\langle i \rangle$ by induction belong to the words $u_1, \ldots, u_{i-1}$, the word $\langle j_i \rangle$ can only stand (as continuous factor) *right before* c_{j_i}, implying $\langle j_i \rangle = \langle i \rangle$; hence, $c_{j_i} = c_i$ must hold. Thus, $j_i = i$ and $\langle i \rangle c_{j_i} = u_i$, as desired.

Finally, from $w = u_1 \cdots u_m \$^m v_1 \cdots v_m$ follows $w \in L'$. $\square_{\text{Claim 2}}$

Clearly, H can be described by an expression of length $O(m \log m)$, and thus, also by an NFA of size $\mathsf{nsc}(H) \leq O(m \log m)$. Hence, in order to show $\mathsf{slp}(L) \geq 2^{\Omega(m)}$, by Lemma 6 together with Claim 2 it suffices to show $\mathsf{slp}(L') \geq 2^{\Omega(m)}$.

Let L'' be the language that results from L' by deleting all letters 0, 1 and \$. Then, $L'' = \{cc : c \in \{a,b\}^m\}$ is the copy language L_m^{copy} over the alphabet $\{a,b\}$. Clearly $\mathsf{slp}(L') \geq \mathsf{slp}(L'')$ holds, since any SLP for L' can be transformed into an SLP for L'' by just deleting all occurrences of 0, 1 and \$ without increasing size. In Corollary 5 we showed $\mathsf{slp}(L'') \geq 2^{\Omega(m)}$ which completes the proof. $\square$

We now show how to simulate extended SLPs by extended REs and by conventional SLPs, thereby proving the tightness of Theorems 12 and 13. The simulation is an easy adaption of results from Gelade [9] and Geffert et al. [8].

Proposition 14. *Every $SLP[\cap, \sqcup]$ of size n can be simulated by an $RE[\cap, \sqcup]$ of length $2^{O(n)}$ or by an SLP of size $2^{2^{O(n)}}$.*

Proof. Take an $SLP[\cap, \sqcup]$ S of size n and depth $d \leq n$. Since every gate has fan-in at most 2, we can simulate S by a $RE[\cap, \sqcup]$ R of length $r = 2^{O(d)} \leq 2^{O(n)}$ by expanding its underlying DAG as tree, analogously to [8, Prop. 2]. According to [9, Prop. 4], R can be simulated by an NFA of size $2^{O(r)} \leq 2^{2^{O(n)}}$. Translating this NFA into an SLP increases size at most polynomially according to Fact 1(a). $\square$

Table 1. Complexity of conversions for non-unary, constant size alphabets.

Conversion	Upper bound	Lower bound
$SLP \cap SLP \to SLP$	$2^{O(n)}$ [4, Thm. 3.1]	$2^{\Omega(n)}$ [4, Thm. 3.4], [**Thm. 7**]
$SLP \sqcup SLP \to SLP$	$2^{O(n)}$ [**Prop. 11**]	$2^{\Omega(n)}$ [**Thm. 8**]
$\Sigma^* \backslash SLP \to SLP$	$2^{2^{O(n)}}$ [4, Thm. 4.2]	$2^{2^{\Omega(n)}}$ [1, Thm. 3.5], [**Thm. 10**]
$h\text{-DPDA} \sqcup h\text{-DPDA} \to h\text{-PDA}$		$2^{\Omega(n)}$ [**Cor. 9**]
$\left.\begin{array}{l} SLP[\cap], SLP[\sqcup], \\ SLP[\cap, \sqcup] \end{array}\right\} \to SLP$	$2^{2^{O(n)}}$ [**Prop. 14**]	$2^{2^{\Omega(n)}}$ [**Thm. 12, Thm. 13**]

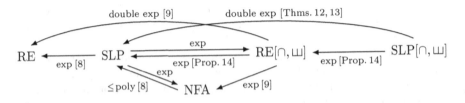

Fig. 1. Simulation costs between (extended) REs, (extended) SLPs and NFAs. The edges from SLP to NFA and $RE[\cap, \sqcup]$ trivially follow from the language $L = \{a^n\}$.

6   Conclusion

We determined the complexity of the shuffle operation for SLPs as well as for (deterministic) h-PDAs, thereby answering questions from [2,4]. For the complexities of intersection and complementation we gave alternative proofs. The lower bound method based on non-commutative circuit complexity (see Sect. 3) might be of independent interest, not only for SLPs but also for h-PDAs or NSE grammars. We also determined the complexity of extended SLPs with shuffle or intersection. The results are summarized in Table 1 and the hierarchy between conventional and extended REs and SLPs is depicted in Fig. 1.

All shown blow-ups are in analogy with closure properties of context-free languages (this class is *not* closed under ∩, ⧢ or complementation; cf. [2]) and with REs (exactly the same blow-ups occur here [9–11,13]). However, let us emphasize that the lower bounds here were obtained already on *finite* languages (*cofinite* for complementation). This stands in contrast to these analogies:

- The class of context-free languages (trivially) *is* closed under ∩ and ⧢ of finite and complement of cofinite languages.
- The blow-up of REs is at most $n^{O(\log n)}$ for ∩ and ⧢ on finite and $2^{O(n^2)}$ for complement on cofinite languages and the simulation cost of RE[∩, ⧢]s for finite languages is at most $2^{O(n^2)}$.

The latter claim can be seen by considering the standard conversion chain "REs → NFAs → product NFA/powerset DFA → RE". For finite languages, the cost of the last step is only $n^{\Theta(\log n)}$ (while $2^{\Theta(n)}$ for infinite ones). Surprisingly, for SLPs there is no such difference between finite and infinite languages.

Acknowledgments. We thank the referees for their helpful comments.

References

1. Bednárová, Z., Geffert, V.: Two double-exponential gaps for automata with a limited pushdown. Inf. Comput. **253**, 381–398 (2017). https://doi.org/10.1016/j.ic.2016.06.005
2. Bednárová, Z., Geffert, V., Mereghetti, C., Palano, B.: The size-cost of boolean operations on constant height deterministic pushdown automata. Theor. Comput. Sci. **449**, 23–36 (2012). https://doi.org/10.1016/j.tcs.2012.05.009
3. Bednárová, Z., Geffert, V., Mereghetti, C., Palano, B.: Removing nondeterminism in constant height pushdown automata. Inf. Comput. **237**, 257–267 (2014). https://doi.org/10.1016/j.ic.2014.03.002
4. Bednárová, Z., Geffert, V., Mereghetti, C., Palano, B.: Boolean language operations on nondeterministic automata with a pushdown of constant height. J. Comput. Syst. Sci. **90**, 99–114 (2017). https://doi.org/10.1016/j.jcss.2017.06.007
5. Chomsky, N.: On certain formal properties of grammars. Inf. Control. **2**(2), 137–167 (1959). https://doi.org/10.1016/S0019-9958(59)90362-6
6. Filmus, Y.: Lower bounds for context-free grammars. Inf. Process. Lett. **111**(18), 895–898 (2011). https://doi.org/10.1016/j.ipl.2011.06.006

7. Gao, Y., Moreira, N., Reis, R., Yu, S.: A survey on operational state complexity. J. Autom. Lang. Comb. **21**(4), 251–310 (2016). https://doi.org/10.25596/jalc-2016-251

8. Geffert, V., Mereghetti, C., Palano, B.: More concise representation of regular languages by automata and regular expressions. Inf. Comput. **208**(4), 385–394 (2010). https://doi.org/10.1016/j.ic.2010.01.002

9. Gelade, W.: Succinctness of regular expressions with interleaving, intersection and counting. Theor. Comput. Sci. **411**(31), 2987–2998 (2010). https://doi.org/10.1016/j.tcs.2010.04.036

10. Gelade, W., Neven, F.: Succinctness of the complement and intersection of regular expressions. ACM Trans. Comput. Logic (TOCL) **13**(1), 4 (2012). https://doi.org/10.1145/2071368.2071372

11. Gruber, H., Holzer, M.: Finite automata, digraph connectivity, and regular expression size. In: ICALP, pp. 39–50 (2008). https://doi.org/10.1007/978-3-540-70583-3_4

12. Gruber, H., Holzer, M.: Language operations with regular expressions of polynomial size. Theor. Comput. Sci. **410**(35), 3281–3289 (2009). https://doi.org/10.1016/j.tcs.2009.04.009

13. Gruber, H., Holzer, M.: Tight bounds on the descriptional complexity of regular expressions. In: Developments in Language Theory, pp. 276–287. Springer, Heidelberg (2009). https://doi.org/10.1007/978-3-642-02737-6_22

14. Guillon, B., Pighizzini, G., Prigioniero, L.: Non-self-embedding grammars, constant-height pushdown automata, and limited automata. In: CIAA, pp. 186–197 (2018). https://doi.org/10.1007/978-3-319-94812-6_16

15. Hrubes, P., Wigderson, A., Yehudayoff, A.: Non-commutative circuits and the sum-of-squares problem. In: STOC, pp. 667–676 (2010). https://doi.org/10.1145/1806689.1806781

16. Stockmeyer, L.J., Meyer, A.R.: Word problems requiring exponential time: preliminary report. In: STOC, pp. 1–9 (1973). https://doi.org/10.1145/800125.804029

Classifying ω-Regular Aperiodic k-Partitions

Victor Selivanov[✉]

A.P. Ershov Institute of Informatics Systems and Saint Petersburg State University,
St. Petersburg, Russia
vseliv@iis.nsk.su

Abstract. We develop a theory of ω-regular aperiodic k-partitions (for arbitrary $k \geq 2$) that extends existing results for the ω-regular k-partitions and for the fine hierarchy of regular aperiodic ω-languages (which coincide with 2-partitions). In particular, we characterize the structure of Wadge degrees of ω-regular aperiodic k-partitions, prove the decidability of many related problems, and discuss their complexity.

Keywords: Aperiodic k-partition · Acceptor · Transducer · Iterated labeled tree · Fine hierarchy · Reducibility

1 Introduction

In [20] K. Wagner discovered a topological classification of regular ω-languages which is in a sense the finest possible. In [12] the Wagner hierarchy was related to the Wadge hierarchy [19] and to the author's fine hierarchy (see also [1, 2, 4] for an alternative approach). Later some results from [12, 20] were extended to languages recognized by more complicated computing devices (see e.g. [3, 5, 13]) for which some important properties of the Wagner hierarchy (e.g., the decidability of levels) usually fail. It is also natural to investigate variants of the Wagner hierarchy for popular subclasses of regular languages the most important of which is certainly the class of regular aperiodic ω-languages (for brevity, just aperiodic sets). In [15] a complete analogue of the Wagner hierarchy for aperiodic sets was developed which has its own flavour.

In this paper we extend the latter theory from the aperiodic sets to the aperiodic k-partitions $A : X^\omega \to k$ of the set X^ω of ω-words over a finite alphabet X, i.e. k-tuples $(A_0, \ldots, A_{k-1})$ of pairwise disjoint aperiodic sets satisfying $A_0 \cup \cdots \cup A_{k-1} = X^\omega$ (the ω-languages are in a bijective correspondence with the 2-partitions of X^ω). Motivations for this generalization come from the fact that similar objects are noticeable in descriptive set theory, computability theory and complexity theory (see e.g. the introduction to [10] for useful examples of similar objects).

Supported by the Russian Science Foundation, project 18-11-00100.

G. Jiráskova and G. Pighizzini (Eds.): DCFS 2020, LNCS 12442, pp. 193–205, 2020.
https://doi.org/10.1007/978-3-030-62536-8_16

A similar theory for regular k-partitions was roughly sketched in [16] which required to develop a machinery of iterated labeled trees and of the fine hierarchy (FH) of k-partitions (systematized in [17]) which turned out crucial for the corresponding extension of Wadge theory to k-partitions in [18] and, as a concluding step, to the of Borel Q-partitions, for arbitrary better quasiorder Q [8]. This machinery is recalled and systematized in Sect. 2. In Sect. 3 we use the notions and results from [15–18] to further develop the fruitful interaction between descriptive set theory and automata theory.

This yields principal facts about aperiodic k-partition, and simplifies rather technical results in [16] (in fact, the current work subsumes the results in [16] which are obtained by changing "aperiodic" to "regular"). We characterize the degree structures of aperiodic k-partitions under natural reducibilities and hierarchies, and establish several facts on the computability and complexity of the corresponding decision problems which are new even for the case of sets.

2   Preliminaries

In this section we recall (with some modification and adaptation) notation, notions and facts used in subsequent sections. We use standard set-theoretic notation. For sets A and S, $P(S)$ is the class of subsets of S and S^A is the class of all functions from A to S. For a class $\mathcal{C} \subseteq P(S)$, $\check{\mathcal{C}}$ is the dual class $\{S \setminus C \mid C \in \mathcal{C}\}$, and $BC(\mathcal{C})$ is the Boolean closure of $\mathcal{C}$. We assume familiarity with notions from first-order logic, including the notions of structure and quotient-structure.

2.1   Aperiodic Acceptors and k-partitions

Fix a finite alphabet X containing more than one symbol (for simplicity we may assume that $X = m = \{x \mid x < m\}$ for a natural number $m > 1$, so $0, 1 \in X$). Note that usually we work with the fixed alphabet X but sometimes we are forced to consider several alphabets simultaneously. The "fixed-alphabet mode" is the default one.

Let X^*, X^+, and X^ω denote resp. the sets of all words, all nonempty words, and all ω-words over X. Let ε be the empty word and $X^{\leq\omega} = X^* \cup X^\omega$. We use standard notation concerning words and ω-words. For $w \in X^*$ and $\xi \in X^{\leq\omega}$, $w \sqsubseteq \xi$ means that w is a substring of ξ, $w \cdot \xi = w\xi$ denote the concatenation, $l = |w|$ is the length of $w = w(0) \cdots w(l-1)$. For $w \in X^*, W \subseteq X^*$ and $A \subseteq X^{\leq\omega}$, let $w \cdot A = \{w\xi : \xi \in A\}$ and $W \cdot A = \{w\xi : w \in W, \xi \in A\}$. For $k, l < \omega$ and $\xi \in X^{\leq\omega}$, let $\xi[k, l) = \xi(k) \cdots \xi(l-1)$ and $\xi \restriction k = \xi[0, k)$.

By an *automaton* (over X) we mean a triple $\mathcal{M} = (Q, f, in)$ consisting of a finite non-empty set Q of states, a transition function $f : Q \times X \to Q$ and an initial state $in \in Q$. The function f is extended to the function $f : Q \times X^* \to Q$ by induction $f(q, \varepsilon) = q$ and $f(q, u \cdot x) = f(f(q, u), x)$, where $u \in X^*$ and $x \in X$. Similarly, we may define the function $f : Q \times X^\omega \to Q^\omega$ by $f(q, \xi)(n) = f(q, \xi \restriction n)$. Associate with any automaton $\mathcal{M}$ the set of *cycles*

$C_{\mathcal{M}} = \{f_{\mathcal{M}}(\xi) \mid \xi \in X^\omega\}$ where $f_{\mathcal{M}}(\xi)$ is the set of states which occur infinitely often in the sequence $f(in, \xi) \in Q^\omega$. A *Muller acceptor* is a pair $(\mathcal{M}, \mathcal{F})$ where $\mathcal{M}$ is an automaton and $\mathcal{F} \subseteq C_{\mathcal{M}}$; it recognizes the set $L(\mathcal{M}, \mathcal{F}) = \{\xi \in X^\omega \mid f_{\mathcal{M}}(\xi) \in \mathcal{F}\}$. The Muller acceptors recognize exactly the *regular ω-languages*.

An automaton $\mathcal{M} = (Q, X, f)$ is *aperiodic* if for all $q \in Q$, $u \in X^+$ and $n > 0$ the equality $f(q, u^n) = q$ implies $f(q, u) = q$. This is equivalent to saying that for all $q \in Q$ and $u \in X^+$ there is $m < \omega$ with $f(q, u^{m+1}) = f(q, u^m)$. An acceptor is aperiodic if so is the corresponding automaton. A language $A \subseteq X^*$ ($A \subseteq X^\omega$) is *aperiodic* if it is recognized by an aperiodic (Muller) acceptor. Aperiodic sets are precisely those which satisfy a fixed first-order sentence (see e.g. [11] for details). We denote by $\mathcal{A}$ and $\mathcal{A}_k$ the classes of aperiodic ω-languages and aperiodic k-partitions of X^ω resp.; note that $\mathcal{A} = \mathcal{A}_2$. We need a characterisation of the aperiodic k-partitions similar to Proposition 1 of [14]. An *aperiodic k-acceptor* is a pair $(\mathcal{M}, c)$ where $\mathcal{M}$ is an aperiodic automaton and $c : C_{\mathcal{M}} \to k$ is a k-partition of $C_{\mathcal{M}}$. It recognizes the aperiodic k-partition $L(\mathcal{M}, c) = c \circ f_{\mathcal{M}}$ where $f_{\mathcal{M}} : X^\omega \to C_{\mathcal{M}}$ is defined above.

Proposition 1. *A k-partition $A : X^\omega \to k$ is aperiodic iff it is recognized by an aperiodic k-acceptor.*

Proof. We consider only the non-trivial direction. Let A be an aperiodic k-partition and $k > 2$ (for $k = 2$ the assertion is obvious). Then A_l is aperiodic for every $l < k$, hence $A_l = L(\mathcal{M}_l, \mathcal{F}_l)$ for some aperiodic acceptors $(\mathcal{M}_l, \mathcal{F}_l)$. Let $\mathcal{M} = (Q, f, in)$ where $Q = Q_0 \times \cdots \times Q_{k-2}$, $f((q_0, \ldots, q_{k-2}), x) = (f_0(q_0, x), \ldots, f_{k-2}(q_{k-2}, x))$ and $in = (in_0, \ldots, in_{k-2})$. By Proposition 4 in [15], $\mathcal{M}$ is aperiodic. We have $pr_l(f_{\mathcal{M}}(\xi)) = f_{\mathcal{M}_l}(\xi)$ for all $l < k - 1$ and $\xi \in X^\omega$, where $pr_l : Q \to Q_l$ is the projection to the l-th coordinate. Since A_l are pairwise disjoint, so are also $pr_l^{-1}(\mathcal{F}_l)$. Let $c : C_{\mathcal{M}} \to k$ be the unique partition of $C_{\mathcal{M}}$ satisfying $c^{-1}(l) = pr_l^{-1}(\mathcal{F}_l)$ for all $l < k - 1$. Then $(\mathcal{M}, c)$ recognizes A. $\qquad\square$

2.2 Aperiodic Transducers and Games

The set X^ω carries the *Cantor topology* with the open sets $W \cdot X^\omega$, where $W \subseteq X^*$. The *Borel sets* in X^ω are obtained by closing the class of open sets by the operations of complement and countable unions. Let $\mathbf{\Sigma}_n^0, \mathbf{\Pi}_n^0, \mathbf{\Delta}_n^0$ denote the levels of the Borel hierarchy in X^ω [7], then $\mathcal{A} \subset BC(\mathbf{\Sigma}_2^0) \subset \mathbf{\Delta}_3^0$.

The continuous functions on X^ω are also called here, following [20], *continious asynchronous functions*, or CA-functions. A *continuous synchronous function*, or just CS-function, is a function $f : X^\omega \to X^\omega$ satisfying $f(\xi)(n) = \phi(\xi \restriction_{(n+1)})$ for some $\phi : X^* \to X$; in descriptive set theory such functions are known as Lipschitz functions. Clearly, every CS-function is a CA-function. Both classes of functions are closed under composition.

A *synchronous transducer* (over X, Y) is a tuple $\mathcal{T} = (Q, X, Y, f, g, in)$, also written as $\mathcal{T} = (\mathcal{M}, Y, g, in)$, consisting of an automaton $\mathcal{M}$ as above, an initial state in and an output function $g : Q \times X \to Y$. The output function is extended to the function $g : Q \times X^* \to Y^*$ defined by induction $g(q, \varepsilon) = \varepsilon$ and $g(q, u \cdot x) = g(q, u) \cdot g(f(q, u), x)$, and to the function $g : Q \times X^\omega \to Y^\omega$ defined by

$$g(q, \xi) = g(q, \xi(0)) \cdot g(f(q, \xi(0)), \xi(1)) \cdot g(f(q, \xi[0, 2)), \xi(2)) \cdots . \qquad (1)$$

In other notation, $g(q, \xi) = \lim_n g(q, \xi \restriction_n)$. The transducer $\mathcal{T}$ *computes* the function $g_{\mathcal{T}} : X^\omega \to Y^\omega$ defined by $g_{\mathcal{T}}(\xi) = g(in, \xi)$.

Asynchronous transducers are defined in the same way, only now the output function g maps $Q \times X$ into Y^*. As a result, the value $g(q, \xi)$ defined as in (1) is now in $Y^{\leq \omega}$, and $g_{\mathcal{T}} : X^\omega \to Y^{\leq \omega}$. Functions computed by synchronous (resp. asynchronous) transducers are called *DS-functions* (resp. *DA-functions*). Both classes of functions are closed under composition [20]. A transducer $\mathcal{T} = (\mathcal{M}, Y, g, in)$ is *aperiodic* if $\mathcal{M}$ is aperiodic. Functions computed by aperiodic synchronous (resp. asynchronous) transducers are called *AS-functions* (resp. *AA-functions*). By Proposition 10 in [15], both classes of functions are closed under composition. Obviously, every *AS*-function (resp. *AA*-function) is a *DS*-function (resp. *DA*-function), and every *DS*-function (resp. *DA*-function) is a *CS*-function (resp. *CA*-function).

We associate with any $A \subseteq (X \times Y)^\omega$ the *Gale-Stewart game* $G(A)$ played by two players 0 and 1 as follows. Player 0 chooses a letter $x_0 \in X$, then player 1 chooses a letter $y_0 \in Y$, then 0 chooses $x_1 \in X$, then 1 chooses $y_1 \in Y$ and so on. Each player knows all the previous moves. After ω moves, player 0 (resp. player 1) has constructed a word $\xi = x_0 x_1 \cdots \in X^\omega$ (resp. $\eta = y_0 y_1 \cdots \in Y^\omega$). Player 1 wins if $\xi \times \eta = (x_0, y_0)(x_1, y_1) \cdots \in A$, otherwise player 0 wins.

A *strategy for player* 1 (player 0) in the game $G(A)$ is a function $h : X^+ \to Y$ (respectively, $h : Y^* \to X$) that prompts the player 1's move (respectively, the player 0's move) for any finite string of the opponent's previous moves. The strategies for player 1 (for 0) are in a bijective correspondence with the *CS*-functions $h : X^\omega \to Y^\omega$ (respectively, with the delayed *CS*-functions $h : Y^\omega \to X^\omega$) [15]; we identify strategies with the corresponding *CS*-functions.

A strategy h for player 1 (player 0) in the game $G(A)$ is *winning* if the player always wins following the strategy, i.e. if $\xi \times h(\xi) \in A$ for all $\xi \in X^\omega$ (resp. $h(\eta) \times \eta \in \overline{A}$ for all $\eta \in Y^\omega$). For any aperiodic set $A \subseteq (X \times Y)^\omega$, one of the players has a winning strategy in $G(A)$, the winner is computable and has an *AS*-winning strategy which is also computed effectively (Theorem 1 in [15]). Below we refer to this result as the *aperiodic determinacy theorem*.

2.3   Semilattices and Labeled Posets

We assume the reader to be familiar with the standard terminology and notation related to parially ordered sets (posets) and preorders; we often apply the terminology about posets to preorders meaning the corresponding quotient-poset. Recall that a *semilattice* is a structure $(S; \sqcup)$ with binary operation $\sqcup$ such that $(x \sqcup y) \sqcup z = x \sqcup (y \sqcup z)$, $x \sqcup y = y \sqcup x$ and $x \sqcup x = x$, for all $x, y, z \in S$. By $\leq$ we denote the induced partial order on S: $x \leq y$ iff $x \sqcup y = y$. The operation $\sqcup$ can be recovered from $\leq$ since $x \sqcup y$ is the supremum of x, y w.r.t. $\leq$. The semilattice is *distributive* if $x \leq y \sqcup z$ implies that $x = y' \sqcup z'$ for some $y' \leq y$ and $z' \leq z$. All semilattices considered in this paper are distributive (sometimes after adjoining a new smallest element).

Element x of the semilattice S is *join-reducible* if it is non-zero and can be represented as the supremum of some elements strictly below x. Element x is *join-irreducible* if it is not σ-join-reducible. If S is distributive then x is join-irreducible iff $x \leq y \sqcup z$ implies that $x \leq y$ or $x \leq z$. By a *decomposition* of x we mean a representation $x = x_0 \sqcup \cdots \sqcup x_n$ where the components x_i are join-irreducible and pairwise incomparable. Such a decomposition is *canonical* if it is unique up to a permutation of the components.

We associate with any preorder Q the preorder $(Q^*; \leq^*)$ where Q^* is the set of non-empty finite subsets of Q and $S \leq^* R$ iff $\forall s \in S \exists r \in R(s \leq r)$. Let $Q^{\sqcup}$ be the quotient-poset of $(Q^*; \leq^*)$ and $\sqcup$ be the operation on S induced by the operation of union on Q^*. Then $Q^{\sqcup}$ is a semilattice the join-irreducible elements of which coincide with the elements induced by the singleton sets in Q^*. The semilattice $Q^{\sqcup}_{\perp}$ with the adjoint new bottom element (corresponding to the empty subset of Q) is distributive. Any element of $Q^{\sqcup}$ has a canonical decomposition. We will use the following easy fact: Let $f : Q \to I(S)$ be a monotone function from a poset Q to the set of join-irreducible elements of a semilattice S. Then there is a unique semilattice homomorphism $f^{\sqcup} : Q^{\sqcup} \to S$ extending f. If f is an embedding and S is distributive then $f^{\sqcup}$ is an embedding.

Let $(P; \leq)$ be a finite poset; if $\leq$ is clear from the context, we simplify the notation of the poset to P. Any subset of P may be considered as a poset with the induced partial ordering. The *rank of a finite poset P* is the cardinality of a longest chain in P. By a *forest* we mean a finite poset in which every upper cone $\uparrow x$ is a chain. A *tree* is a forest having the largest element (called the *root* of the tree).

Let $(Q; \leq)$ be a preorder. A *Q-poset* is a triple $(P, \leq, c)$ consisting of a finite nonempty poset $(P; \leq)$, $P \subseteq \omega$, and a labeling $c : P \to Q$. A *morphism* $f : (P, \leq, c) \to (P', \leq', c')$ between Q-posets is a monotone function $f : (P; \leq) \to (P'; \leq')$ satisfying $\forall x \in P(c(x) \leq c'(f(x)))$. The *h-preorder* $\leq_h$ on $\mathcal{P}_Q$ is defined as follows: $P \leq_h P'$, if there is a morphism $f : P \to P'$. Let $\mathcal{P}_Q$, $\mathcal{F}_Q$, and $\mathcal{T}_Q$ denote the sets of all finite Q-posets, Q-forests, and Q-trees, respectively. For the particular case $Q = \bar{k} = \{0, \cdots, k-1\}$ of antichain with k elements we denote the corresponding preorders by $\mathcal{P}_k$, $\mathcal{F}_k$, and $\mathcal{T}_k$. For any $q \in Q$ let $s(q) \in \mathcal{T}_Q$ be the singleton tree labeled by q; then $q \leq r$ iff $s(q) \leq_h s(r)$. Identifying q with $s(q)$, we may think that Q is a substructure of $\mathcal{T}_Q$.

The structure $(\mathcal{F}_Q; \leq_h, \sqcup)$ is a semilattice equivalent to $(\mathcal{T}^{\sqcup}_Q; \leq_h, \sqcup)$ above. The supremum operation is given by the disjoint union $F \sqcup G$ of Q-forests F, G, the join-irreducible elements are precisely the elements h-equivalent to trees. In this paper, the iterations $Q \mapsto \mathcal{T}_{\mathcal{T}_Q}$, $Q \mapsto \mathcal{F}_{\mathcal{T}_Q}$, and $Q \mapsto \mathcal{P}_{\mathcal{P}_Q}$ of these constructions are relevant. Using the identification $q = s(q)$, we may think that $\mathcal{T}_Q$ is a substructure of $\mathcal{T}_{\mathcal{T}_Q}$. Define the binary operation $\cdot$ on $\mathcal{F}_{\mathcal{T}_Q}$ as follows: $F \cdot G$ is obtained by adjoining a copy of G below any leaf of F. One easily checks that this operation is associative (i.e. $(F \cdot G) \cdot H \equiv_h F \cdot (G \cdot H)$) but not commutative

(this was the reason for changing the notation + for this operation in [16] to ·).
For $F \in \mathcal{F}_Q$, let $r(F) = \bigsqcup\{c(x) \mid x \in F\}$; then $r : \mathcal{F}_Q \to Q^{\sqcup}$ is a semilattice
homomorphism such that $q = r(s(q))$ for every $q \in Q$.

By Proposition 8.7(2) of [17], for any finite Q-poset $(P, \leq, c)$ there exist a
finite Q-forest $F = F(P)$ of the same rank as P (obtained by a top-down
unfolding of P) and a morphism f from F onto P which is a bijection between
the maximal elements of F, P, and for any non-minimal element $x \in F$, f is a
bijection between the predecessors of x in F and the predecessors of $f(x)$ in P.
Moreover, F is a largest element in $(\{G \in \mathcal{F}_Q \mid G \leq_h P\}; \leq_h)$. This extends to
the iterated version (Proposition 8.7(1) in [17]): for any $(P, \leq, c) \in \mathcal{P}_{\mathcal{P}_Q}$ there is
an $\leq_h$-largest element $(F(P) \leq, d) \in \mathcal{F}_{\mathcal{F}_Q}$ below P: it suffices to set $d = F \circ c \circ f$.
If $c(p)$ has a largest element for every $p \in P$ then $(F(P) \leq, d) \in \mathcal{F}_{T_Q}$.

A *finite Q-labeled 2-preorder* is a tuple $(S; \leq_0, \leq_1, c)$ where S is a finite
nonempty set, $c : S \to k$, and $\leq_0, \leq_1$ are preorders on S such that $x \leq_1 y$ implies
$x \equiv_0 y$. A *morphism of k-labeled 2-preorders* S, S_1 is a function $g : S \to S_1$ that
respects the preorders and satisfies $\forall x \in S(c(x) \leq c_1(g(x)))$. By Proposition 8.8
in [17], the category of finite Q-labeled 2-preorders is equivalent to the category
$\mathcal{P}_{\mathcal{P}_Q}$. The Q-poset corresponding to $(S; \leq_0, \leq_1, c)$ is $(P; \leq, d)$ where $(P : \leq)$ is
the quotient-poset of $(S; \leq_0)$ and $d([x]_0) = ([x]_0; \leq_1, c)$ for $x \in S$.

Recall that a *well quasiorder* (wqo) is a preorder that has neither infinite
descending chains nor infinite antichains A famous Kruskal's theorem implies
that if Q is a wqo then $(\mathcal{F}_Q; \leq_h)$ and $(\mathcal{T}_Q; \leq_h)$ are wqo's; it is not hard to see
that $(\mathcal{P}_Q; \leq_h)$ is, in general, not a wqo. Note that the iterated preorders $\mathcal{T}_{T_Q}$
and $\mathcal{F}_{T_Q}$ are wqo's whenever Q is a wqo.

3   Classifying Aperiodic k-partitions

In this section we briefly describe the main results of this work and discuss
remaining open questions.

3.1   Reducibilities and Operations on k-partitions

Let $\mathcal{F}$ be a set of unary functions on X^ω which is closed under composition
and contains the identity function. For $A, B \in k^{X^\omega}$, A is said to be $\mathcal{F}$-*reducible*
to B (in symbols $A \leq_{\mathcal{F}} B$), if $A = B \circ f$ for some $f \in \mathcal{F}$. The relation $\leq_{\mathcal{F}}$
is a preorder on X^ω, the induced equivalence relation is denoted by $\equiv_{\mathcal{F}}$; the
$\equiv_{\mathcal{F}}$-equivalence classes are called $\mathcal{F}$-*degrees*. For $\mathcal{C} \subseteq k^{X^\omega}$, a k-partition C is
$\mathcal{F}$-*complete in* $\mathcal{C}$ if $C \in \mathcal{C}$ and any $A \in \mathcal{C}$ is $\mathcal{F}$-reducible to C.

For the functions in Subsect. 2.2, we obtain reducibilities $\leq_{CA}, \leq_{CS}, \leq_{DA}$
, $\leq_{DS}, \leq_{AA}, \leq_{AS}$. By Σ_2^0-function we mean a unary function f on X^ω such that
$f^{-1}(A) \in \Sigma_2^0$ for every $A \in \Sigma_2^0$; we denote the corresponding reducibility by
$\leq_2$. Clearly, $\leq_{AS} \subseteq \leq_{CS} \subseteq \leq_{CA} \subseteq \leq_2$ and $\leq_{AA} \subseteq \leq_{CA}$. From the results in [15] it
follows that $\mathcal{A}_k$ is closed downwards under $\leq_{AA}, \leq_{AS}$ but not under $\leq_{CS}$.

We define the binary operation $A \oplus B$ on k^{X^ω} by: $(A \oplus B)(0\xi) = A(\xi)$ and
$(A \oplus B)(i\xi) = B(\xi)$ for all $0 < i < m$ and $\xi \in X^\omega$ (recall that $X = m$).

Then $(k^{X^\omega}; \leq_{CA}, \oplus)$ is a semilattice which becomes distributive after adjoining a new smallest element; the same holds for $\leq_{CS}, \leq_2$. Since $\mathcal{A}_k$ is closed under $\oplus$, $(\mathcal{A}_k; \leq_{AA}, \oplus)$ and $(\mathcal{A}_k; \leq_{AS}, \oplus)$ have the same property. Similar facts hold for the other reducibilities. We abbreviate $I(\mathcal{A}_k; \leq_{AA}, \oplus)$ to I_{AA}, and similarly for the other reducibilities.

We are ready to formulate our first main result which will follow from Facts 1 — 6 in this and the next subsection.

Theorem 1. *1. The relations $\leq_{CA}$ and $\leq_{AA}$ coincide on $\mathcal{A}_k$, and we have $(\mathcal{A}_k; \leq_{AA}, \oplus) \simeq (\mathcal{F}_{\mathcal{T}_k}; \leq_h, \sqcup)$.*
2. The relations $\leq_{CA}, \leq_{AA}, \leq_{CS}, \leq_{AS}$ coincide on $I_{CA} = I_{AA} = I_{CS} = I_{AS}$, and $(I_{AA}; \leq_{AA}) \simeq (\mathcal{T}_{\mathcal{T}_k}; \leq_h)$.
3. We have: $(\mathcal{A}_k; \leq_2, \oplus) \simeq (\mathcal{F}_k; \leq_h, \sqcup)$ and $(I_2; \leq_2) \simeq (\mathcal{T}_k; \leq_h)$.

Fact 1. For all $A, B \in \mathcal{A}_k$, $A \leq_{CS} B$ iff $A \leq_{AS} B$.

Proof. We prove the direction from left to right; the opposite direction is obvious. Let $A \leq_{CS} B$ via a CS-function $f : X^\omega \to X^\omega$. Consider the game $G(A, B)$ where players produce resp. ξ and η from X^ω as in Subsect. 2.2; let player 1 win iff $A(\xi) = B(\eta)$, i.e. $\xi \in A_i \leftrightarrow \eta \in B_i$ for every $i < k$. Then f is a winning strategy for player 1. Since all A_i, B_i are aperiodic and $\mathcal{A}$ is closed under the Boolean operations, $G(A, B)$ is aperiodic. By the aperiodic determinacy, player 1 has an AS-winning strategy g. Then $A \leq_{AS} B$ via g. □

The remaining facts are about some operations on k^{X^ω} closely related to the corresponding operations in [16,18]; modifications are designed to make the set of aperiodic k-partitions closed under these operations. First, we recall the unary operations $q_0, \ldots, q_{k-1}$ on k^{X^ω} from [16] (which extend and modify the operation $\#$ from [19]) which use a coding of alphabets to guarantee the preservation of aperiodicity. To simplify notation, we do this only for the binary alphabet $X = \{0, 1\} = 2$ (it will be clear how to modify the idea for larger alphabets). Define the function $f : 3^\omega \to 2^\omega$ by $f(x_0 x_1 \cdots) = \tilde{x}_0 \tilde{x}_1 \cdots$ where $x_0, x_1 \ldots < 3$ and $\tilde{0} = 110000, \tilde{1} = 110100, \tilde{2} = 110010$ (in the same way we may define $f : 3^* \to 2^*$). It is easy to see that f is an AA-function, its image $f(3^\omega)$ is a closed aperiodic set, and there is an AA-function $f_1 : 2^\omega \to 3^\omega$ such that $f_1 \circ f = id_{3^\omega}$. For all $i < k$ and $A \in k^{X^\omega}$, we define $q_i(A) \in k^{X^\omega}$ by

$$[q_i(A)](\xi) = \begin{cases} i, & \text{if } \xi \notin f(3^\omega) \vee \forall p \exists n \geq p(\xi[n, n+5] = \tilde{2}), \\ A(f_1(\xi)), & \text{if } \xi \in f(2^\omega), \\ A(\eta), & \text{if } \xi = f(\sigma 2\eta) \end{cases}$$

for some (unique) $\sigma \in 3^\omega$ and $\eta \in 2^\omega$.

Using the same coding of 3^ω into 2^ω, we define the binary operation $\cdot$ on k^{X^ω} (which modify the operation $+$ from [16,19]) as follows (we again consider the typical particular case $X = 2$). Define an AA-function $g : X^\omega \to X^\omega$ by $g(x_0 x_1 \cdots) = \tilde{x}_0 \tilde{2} \tilde{x}_1 \tilde{2} \cdots$ where $x_0, x_1, \ldots \in X$ (in the same way we may define $g : X^* \to X^*$). Obviously, $g(X^\omega)$ is a closed aperiodic set and there is an AA-function $g_1 : X^\omega \to X^\omega$ such that $g_1 \circ g = id_{X^\omega}$. For all k-partitions A, B of X^ω, we set

4

$$[A \cdot B](\xi) = \begin{cases} A(g_1(\xi)), & \text{if } \xi \in g(X^\omega), \\ B(\eta), & \text{if } \xi = g(u) \cdot v \cdot \eta, \end{cases}$$

where $u \in X^*, \eta \in X^\omega$, and $v \in X^+$ is the shortest word such that $g(u) \cdot v \cdot X^\omega \cap g(X^\omega) = \emptyset$. We will also use unary operations $p_i(A) \equiv_{AA} \mathbf{i} \cdot A$ where $\mathbf{i} = \lambda x.i$, $i < k$, is the constant k-partition. Equivalent operations with the names $p_0, \ldots, p_{k-1}$ were used in [16, 18].

Fact 2. The class $\mathcal{A}_k$ is closed under the introduced operations.

Proof. Let $B = q_i(A)$ and let A be aperiodic. It suffices to prove that B_j is aperiodic for any $j \in \bar{k} \setminus \{i\}$. By the definition, $\xi \in B_j$ iff $\xi \in f(3^\omega)$ and there are only finitely many n with $\xi[n, n+6) = \tilde{2}$ and either ($\xi \in f(2^\omega)$ and $f_1(\xi) \in A_j$) or $\exists n(\xi[n, n+6) = \tilde{2} \wedge \forall m > n(\xi[n, n+6) \neq \tilde{2}) \wedge \xi[n+6, \infty) \in f_1^{-1}(A_j))$. Since A_j is aperiodic, so is also B_j, by the logical characterisation of aperiodic sets.

For the operation $\cdot$, let $C = A \cdot B$ and $i < k$. Then $\xi \in C_i$ iff ($\xi \in g(X^\omega)$ and $g_1(\xi) \in A_i$) or ($\xi \notin g(X^\omega)$ and $\eta \in B_i$) where η as in the definition of C. From aperiodicity of A_i, B_i and the definition of u, v it is easy to find a first-order sentence defining C_i. Thus, C is aperiodic. □

Next we define functions μ, ν, ρ (which are variants of the corresponding functions from Sect. 6 of [18]) from labeled trees to k-partitions using the operations $p_i, q_i, \cdot$. It is technically convenient to realise finite trees as initial segments $(T; \leq)$ of $(\omega^*; \sqsubseteq)$ where ω^* is the set of finite strings of natural numbers (including the empty string ε), $\sqsubseteq$ is the substring relation, and $\leq$ is the reverse relation for $\sqsubseteq$. Then forests may be represented as $T \setminus \{\varepsilon\}$ where $T \subseteq \omega^*$ is a tree. We use some standard notation related to such "concrete" trees and forests. Clearly, any labeled tree of forest from Subsect. 2.3 is h-equivalent (even isomorphic) to such "concrete" labeled tree or forest.

Let $(T; c) \in \mathcal{T}_k$. We associate with any node $\sigma \in T$ the k-partition $\mu_T(\sigma)$ by induction on the rank $rk(\sigma)$ of σ in $(T; \sqsupseteq)$ as follows: if $rk(\sigma) = 0$, i.e. σ is a leaf of T then $\mu_T(\sigma) = \mathbf{i}$ where $i = c(\sigma)$; otherwise, $\mu_T(\sigma) = p_i(\bigoplus \{\mu_T(\sigma n) \mid n < \omega, \sigma n \in T\})$. Now we define a function $\mu : \mathcal{T}_k \to k^{X^\omega}$ by $\mu(T) = \mu_T(\varepsilon)$. We define $\nu : \mathcal{T}_k \to k^{X^\omega}$ in the same way but using q_i instead of p_i.

Now let $(T; c) \in \mathcal{T}_{\mathcal{T}_k}$. We associate with any node $\sigma \in T$ the k-partition $\rho_T(\sigma)$ by induction on the rank $rk(\sigma)$ of σ in $(T; \sqsupseteq)$ as follows: if $rk(\sigma) = 0$ then $\rho_T(\sigma) = \nu(V)$ where $V = c(\sigma) \in \mathcal{T}_k$; otherwise, $\rho_T(\sigma) = \nu(V) \cdot (\bigoplus \{\rho_T(\sigma n) \mid n < \omega, \sigma n \in T\})$. Finally, define a function $\rho : \mathcal{T}_{\mathcal{T}_k} \to k^{X^\omega}$ by $\rho(T) = \rho_T(\varepsilon)$.

Fact 3. For all $T, V \in \mathcal{T}_{\mathcal{T}_k}$ we have: $\rho(T) \in I_{CA}$, $T \leq_h V$ iff $\rho(T) \leq_{CA} \rho(V)$, and similarly for $\leq_{CS}, \leq_{AA}, \leq_{AS}$.

Proof. For $\leq_{CA}$ the assertion follows from Proposition 16 in [18]. To see this, note that the definitions of μ, ν, ρ in [18] are for k-partitions of ω^ω (ω-words over ω) rather than for X^ω. The main difference between ω^ω and X^ω is that the latter space in compact while the former is not. This difference is essential only for the countable version of $\bigoplus$; since here we deal only with finitary version of $\bigoplus$, the definitions and arguments of [18] make sense here. Another difference is that here we use some additional coding to preserve aperiodicity; this is also not essential up to $\equiv_{CA}$. For $\leq_{CS}$, the assertion follows from Proposition 6 in [18]. For $\leq_{AA}$ and $\leq_{AS}$ the assertion follows from Fact 1. $\qquad\square$

The next fact follows in the same way from Propositions 15 and 9 in [18].

Fact 4. For all $T, V \in \mathcal{T}_k$ we have: $\nu(T) \in I_2$, and $T \leq_h V$ iff $\nu(T) \leq_2 \nu(V)$. The reducibilities $\leq_{CA}, \leq_{CS}, \leq_{AA}, \leq_{AS}$ coincide with $\leq_2$ on I_2.

By the remarks in Subsect. 2.3 about semilattices, the functions μ, ν, ρ uniquely extend to labeled forests to obtain semilattice embeddings of the corresponding quotient-structures. We denote the extensions by the same letters.

Fact 5. For all $F, G \in \mathcal{F}_{T_k}$ we have: $F \leq_h G$ iff $\rho(F) \leq_{CA} \rho(G)$, and similarly for $\leq_{AA}$. For all $F, G \in \mathcal{F}_k$ we have: $F \leq_h G$ iff $\nu(F) \leq_2 \nu(G)$.

Proof. Consider e.g. $\leq_{AA}$. Let $F = \bigsqcup_i T_i$ and $G = \bigsqcup_i V_j$ be the decompositions to trees. By Fact 3, $F \leq_{AA} G$ iff $\forall i (T_i \leq_{AA} G)$ iff $\forall i \exists j (T_i \leq_{AA} V_j)$ iff $\forall i \exists j (\rho(T_i) \leq_{AA} \rho(V_j))$ iff $\forall i (\rho(T_i) \leq_{AA} \rho(G))$ iff $\rho(F) \leq_{AA} \rho(G)$. $\qquad\square$

3.2 The Fine Hierarchy of k-partitions

Here we describe the FH of aperiodic k-partitions which provides their classification in terms of set operations. We first briefly recall some relevant technical notions (slightly adapted from [17]).

A *base* in a set S is a sublattice $\mathcal{L}$ of $(P(S); \cup, \cap)$ such that $\emptyset, S \in \mathcal{L}$ and $\mathcal{L}$ has the reduction property (i.e., for any $A, B \in \mathcal{L}$ there are disjoint $A', B' \in \mathcal{L}$ such that $A' \subseteq A$, $B' \subseteq B$, and $A' \cup B' = A \cup B$). For $(T, c) \in \mathcal{T}_k$, a T-*family over* $\mathcal{L}$ is a family $\{U_\tau\}_{\tau \in T}$ of $\mathcal{L}$-sets such that $U_\varepsilon = S$, $U_\tau \supseteq U_{\tau i}$ for $\tau i \in T$, and $U_{\tau i} \cap U_{\tau j} = \emptyset$ for $\tau i, \tau j \in T$ with $i \neq j$. Any such T-family *determines* the k-partition $A : S \to \bar{k}$ by $A(x) = c(\tau)$ where τ is the unique string in T such that $x \in \tilde{U}_\tau = U_\tau \setminus \bigcup \{U_{\tau i} \mid \tau i \in T\}$. The *FH of k-partitions over* $\mathcal{L}$ is the family $\{\mathcal{L}(T)\}_{T \in \mathcal{T}_k}$ where $\mathcal{L}(T)$ is the set of k-partitions determined by T-families over $\mathcal{L}$. Examples of bases in X^ω relevant to this paper are $\Sigma_1^0, \Sigma_2^0, \mathcal{K}_0 = \mathcal{A} \cap \Sigma_1^0$, and $\mathcal{K}_1 = \mathcal{A} \cap \Sigma_2^0$ [15].

A *2-base* in a set S is a pair $\mathcal{L} = (\mathcal{L}_0, \mathcal{L}_1)$ of bases in S such that $\mathcal{L}_0 \subseteq \mathcal{L}_1 \cap \check{\mathcal{L}}_1$. For $(T, c) \in \mathcal{T}_k$, a T-*family over* $\mathcal{L}$ is a pair $(\{U_\tau\}, \{U_{\tau\sigma}\})$ where $\{U_\tau\}$ is a T-family over $\mathcal{L}_0$ and, for any $\tau \in T$, $\{U_{\tau\sigma}\}$ is a $c(\tau)$-family over the base $\{\tilde{U}_\tau \cap B \mid B \in \mathcal{L}_1\}$ in $\tilde{U}_\tau$. Any such T-family over $\mathcal{L}$ *determines* the k-partition $A : S \to \bar{k}$ by $A(x) = c_1(\sigma)$, for unique $\tau \in T$ and $\sigma \in c(\tau) = (T_1, c_1) \in \mathcal{T}_k$ such that $x \in \tilde{U}_{\tau\sigma}$. The *FH of k-partitions over* $\mathcal{L}$ is the family $\{\mathcal{L}(T)\}_{T \in \mathcal{T}_{T_k}}$ where $\mathcal{L}(T)$ is the set of k-partitions determined by T-families over $\mathcal{L}$. Examples of 2-bases in X^ω relevant to this paper are $\mathcal{S} = (\Sigma_1^0, \Sigma_2^0)$ and $\mathcal{K} = (\mathcal{K}_0, \mathcal{K}_1)$.

The next theorem relates the FHs over the mentioned bases and 2-bases to each other and to the k-partitions from the previous subsection. Items 1 and 2 follow from the results in [8,18] and extend the corresponding facts in Section III.C of [19]; together with Facts 4 and 5 they imply items 3 and 4.

Theorem 2. 1. For any $T \in \mathcal{T}_k$, the level $\Sigma_2^0(T)$ is closed downwards under $\leq_2$, and $\nu(T)$ is CS-complete in $\Sigma_2^0(T)$.

2. For any $T \in \mathcal{T}_{\mathcal{T}_k}$, the level $\mathcal{S}(T)$ is closed downwards under $\leq_{CA}$, and $\rho(T)$ is CS-complete in $\mathcal{S}(T)$.

3. For any $T \in \mathcal{T}_{\mathcal{T}_k}$, the level $\mathcal{K}(T)$ is closed downwards under $\leq_{AA}$, and $\rho(T)$ is AS-complete in $\mathcal{K}(T)$.

4. For any $T \in \mathcal{T}_{\mathcal{T}_k}$, $\mathcal{K}(T) = \mathcal{A}_k \cap \mathcal{S}(T)$.

Fact 6. For any $A \in \mathcal{A}_k$ there is $F \in \mathcal{F}_{\mathcal{T}_k}$ with $A \equiv_{AA} \rho(F)$.

Proof Sketch. Let $(\mathcal{M}, d)$ be an aperiodic k-acceptor which recognizes A. Following [20], we define the preorders $\leq_0$ and $\leq_1$ on $C_{\mathcal{M}}$ as follows: $D \leq_0 E$ iff some state in D is reachable in the graph of $\mathcal{M}$ from some state in E; $D \leq_1 E$ iff $D \subseteq E$. For any $D \in C_{\mathcal{M}}$ the $\equiv_0$-class of D contains the largest element w.r.t. $\subseteq$ (such elements are precisely the strongly connected components of the graph of $\mathcal{M}$). Then $(C_{\mathcal{M}}; \leq_0, \leq_1, d)$ is a k-labeled 2-preorder.

Let $(P_{\mathcal{M}}, c)$ be the corresponding iterated $\bar{k}$-poset (see the end of Subsection 2.3). Since any label of $P_{\mathcal{M}}$ has a largest element, the unfolding $F = F(P_{\mathcal{M}})$ is in $\mathcal{F}_{\mathcal{T}_k}$. Let $F = T_0 \sqcup \cdots \sqcup T_n$ where T_i are the trees whose roots are these largest elements (recall that the maximal elements of F are precisely those of $P_{\mathcal{M}}$). Let $C_0, \ldots, C_n$ be the strongly connected components such that their $\equiv_0$-equivalence classes are precisely the maximal elements of $P_{\mathcal{M}}$ and let f be the transition function of $\mathcal{M}$. Then for any $\xi \in X^\omega$ the set $\{f(in, \xi \restriction_j) \mid j < \omega\}$ of states visited along the run of $\mathcal{M}$ on ξ intersects C_i for precisely one $i \leq n$. Let U_i be the set of all such ξ, then $(U_0, \ldots, U_n)$ is a clopen partition of X^ω. Since any U_i is a retract of X^ω, we can think that the restriction $A|_{Y_i}$ is a k-partition of X^ω. It is not hard to show (see the proof of Theorem 3 in [16] for details) that $A|_{Y_i} \in \mathcal{K}(T_i)$, hence $A|_{Y_i} \leq_{AA} \rho(T_i)$. From the definition of $\rho(T_i)$ and the structure of T_i it is straightforward to construct an CS-reduction of $\rho(T_i)$ to $A|_{Y_i}$. By Fact 1, $\rho(T_i) \equiv_{AS} A|_{Y_i}$ for all $i \leq n$, hence $\rho(F) \equiv_{AA} A$. $\square$

It is easy to see that Theorem 1 follows from Facts 1 — 6 and the remarks in Subsection 2.3 about canonical decompositions in $\mathcal{F}_{\mathcal{T}_k}$.

3.3   Computability and Complexity Issues

There are many natural algorithmic problems related to topological properties of regular sets considered e.g. in [9,20,21]. Here we briefly discuss extensions of these problems to k-partitions, and several new algorithmic problems.

First we discuss a problem which was apparently not considered before in the literature on automata theory but is very popular in computability theory where people are interested in characterizing the complexity of presentation of natural countably infinite structures of finite signatures. Such a structure is *computably presentable* if it is isomorphic to a structure whose universe is ω and all signature functions and relations are computable. A structure is *p-presentable* if there is a surjection from a polynomial-time computable set of words over a finite alphabet onto the universe of the structure modulo which all signature functions and relations, and also the equality relation, are polynomial-time computable. We abbreviate "polynomial-time computable" to "p-computable".

In preceding subsections we (implicitly) considered natural structures like the quotient-structure $\mathbb{A}_k$ of $(\mathcal{A}_k; I_{CA}, I_2, \leq_{CA}, \leq_2, \oplus, \cdot)$ under $\equiv_{CA}$ and the quotient-structure $\mathbb{A}'_k$ of $(\mathcal{A}_k; I_2, \leq_2, \oplus, q_0, \ldots, q_{k-1})$ under $\equiv_2$. The definitions of relations and functions suggest that the presentation complexity of these structures is high but in fact the following surprising result holds.

Theorem 3. *The structures $\mathbb{A}_k$ and $\mathbb{A}'_k$ are p-presentable.*

Proof Sketch. We consider the first structure, for the second one the proof is similar. Theorem 1 suggests that we could find an isomorphic copy of $\mathbb{A}_k$ with universe $\mathcal{F}_{T_k}$. For the smaller signature $\{\leq_{CA}, \oplus\}$ the isomorphism follows from Facts 1 — 6, so it remains to describe copies of relations and functions corresponding to $I_{CA}, I_2, \leq_2, \cdot$ in $\mathcal{F}_{T_k}$. For I_{CA}, it suffices to take the relation I_h true precisely on $I(\mathcal{F}_{T_k}; \leq_h, \oplus)$. For $\cdot$, we take the operation $\cdot$ on $\mathcal{F}_{T_k}$. From associativity of this operation in both structures it is easy to check by induction on the rank that $\rho(F \cdot G) \equiv_{CA} \rho(F) \cdot \rho(G)$, for every $F, G \in \mathcal{F}_{T_k}$. For $I_2, \leq_2$, let $F \leq_{h2} G$ mean $r(F) \leq_h r(G)$ where $r : \mathcal{F}_{T_k} \to \mathcal{F}_k$ is the semilattice surjection from Subsect. 2.3, and let $I_{h2}(F)$ mean $r(F) \in I(\mathcal{F}_k; \leq_h, \sqcup)$. Theorem 3 in [10] implies that $I_{h2}(F)$ iff $I_2(\rho(F))$ and $F \leq_{h2} G$ iff $\rho(F) \leq_2 \rho(G)$.

Therefore, the quotient-structure $\mathbb{F}_{T_k}$ of $(\mathcal{F}_{T_k}; I_h, I_{h2}, \leq_h, \leq_{h2}, \sqcup, \cdot)$ under $\equiv_h$ is isomorphic to $\mathbb{A}_k$, hence it suffices to show that $\mathbb{F}_{T_k}$ is p-presentable. In the proof of Theorem 7 in [6], a coding of $\mathcal{F}_k$ by words in a p-computable set of words was defined in which the relation $\leq_h$ is p-computable. It is not hard to extend the coding and proofs in [6] to $(\mathcal{F}_{T_k}; \leq_h)$. Moreover, similar proofs show that $I_h, I_{h2}, \leq_{h2}, \sqcup, \cdot$ are also p-computable w.r.t. this coding. Thus, $\mathbb{F}_{T_k}$ is p-presentable. $\qquad\square$

The computational complexity of functions and relations about regular languages are usually studied when the languages are given by their standard "names" like automata or regular expressions. In our context it is natural to think that k-partitions are given by k-acceptors. In particular, for the relation I_2 we have to estimate the complexity of the problem: given an aperiodic k-acceptor $(\mathcal{M}; c)$, is the k-partition $L(\mathcal{M}; c)$ join-irreducible in $(\mathcal{A}_k; \leq_2, \oplus)$? For the function $\cdot$, we have to estimate the complexity of the problem: given aperiodic k-acceptors for $A, B \in \mathcal{A}_k$, find an aperiodic k-acceptor for $A \cdot B$ (up to $\equiv_{CA}$). From the results above we easily obtain the following.

Corollary 1. *All the signature functions and relations on $\mathcal{A}_k$ in Theorem 3 are computable w.r.t. the k-acceptor presentation.*

Proof. Consider e.g. the relation $\leq_{CA}$. Given acceptors $(\mathcal{M}; c)$ and $(\mathcal{M}_1; c_1)$ recognising resp. A and A_1, compute (using the algorithm in the proof of Fact 6) $F, F_1 \in \mathcal{F}_{T_k}$ such that $A \equiv_{CA} \rho(F)$ and $A_1 \equiv_{CA} \rho(F_1)$, and check $F \leq_h F_1$ using the p-presentation in the proof of Theorem 3. $\qquad\square$

The method of Corollary 1 and the computability of many other relations and functions on the wqo $\mathcal{F}_{T_k}$ imply the computability of many other topological problems about regular k-partitions. The complexity of such problems is more subtle and leads to interesting open questions. Even the p-computability of $\leq_{CA}$ for $k > 2$ is currently open because our approach needs to compute the unfolding of a $\bar{k}$-labeled 2-preorder to a forest (see the proof of Fact 6) in polynomial time which is easy for $k = 2$ but not obvious for $k > 2$. For $k = 2$ the p-computability of $\leq_{CA}$ is known from [9,21].

References

1. Carton, O., Perrin, D.: Chains and superchains for ω-rational sets, automata and semigroups. Int. J. Algebra Comput. **7**, 673–695 (1997)
2. Carton, O., Perrin, D.: The wagner hierarchy of ω-rational sets. Int. J. Algebra Comput. **9**, 673–695 (1999)
3. Duparc, J.: A hierarchy of deterministic context-free ω-languages. Theor. Comput. Sci. **290**(3), 1253–1300 (2003)
4. Duparc, J., Riss, M.: The missing link for ω-rational sets, automata, and semigroups. Int. J. Algebra Comput. **16**, 161–185 (2006)
5. Finkel, O.: Borel ranks and Wadge degrees of context-free ω-languages. Math. Struct. Comput. Sci. **16**, 813–840 (2006)
6. Hertling P., Selivanov V.L.: Complexity issues for preorders on finite labeled forests. In: Brattka, V., Diener, H., Spreen, D. (eds.) Logic, Computation, Hierarchies, pp. 165–190. Ontos Publishing, de Gruiter, Boston-Berlin (2014)
7. Kechris, A.S.: Classical Descriptive Set Theory. Springer, New York (1994). https://doi.org/10.1007/978/-1-4612-4190-4
8. Kihara, T., Montalbán, A.: On the structure of the Wadge degrees of BQO-valued Borel functions. Trans. Am. Math. Soc. **371**(11), 7885–7923 (2019)
9. Krishnan, S.C., Puri, A., Brayton, R.K.: Structural complexity of ω -automata. In: Mayr, E.W., Puech, C. (eds.) STACS 1995. LNCS, vol. 900, pp. 143–156. Springer, Heidelberg (1995). https://doi.org/10.1007/3-540-59042-0_69
10. Kihara T., Selivanov V.: Wadge-like degrees of Borel BQO-valued functions. Arxiv 1909.10835 (2019)
11. Perrin D., Pin J.-E.: Infinite Words. v. 141 of pure and applied mathematics (Elsevier, 2004)
12. Selivanov, V.L.: Fine hierarchy of regular ω-languages. Theor. Comput. Sci. **191**, 37–59 (1998)
13. Selivanov, V.L.: Wadge degrees of ω-languages of deterministic turing machines. Theor. Inf. Appl. **37**, 67–83 (2003)
14. Selivanov V.L.: Classifying omega-regular partitions. In: Preproceedings of LATA-2007, Universitat Rovira i Virgili Report Series, 35/07, pp. 529–540 (2007)
15. Selivanov, V.L.: Fine hierarchy of regular aperiodic ω-languages. Int. J. Found. Comput. Sci. **19**(3), 649–675 (2008)
16. Selivanov, V.: A fine hierarchy of ω-regualr k-partitions. In: Löwe, B., Normann, D., Soskov, I., Soskova, A. (eds.) CiE 2011. LNCS, vol. 6735, pp. 260–269. Springer, Heidelberg (2011). https://doi.org/10.1007/978-3-642-21875-0_28
17. Selivanov, V.L.: Fine hierarchies via priestley duality. Ann. Pure Appl. Logic **163**, 1075–1107 (2012)

18. Selivanov, V.L.: Extending wadge theory to k-partitions. In: Kari, J., Manea, F., Petre, I. (eds.) CiE 2017. LNCS, vol. 10307, pp. 387–399. Springer, Cham (2017). https://doi.org/10.1007/978-3-319-58741-7_36
19. Wadge W.: Reducibility and determinateness in the Baire space. PhD thesis, University of California, Berkely (1984)
20. Wagner, K.: On ω-regular sets. Inf. Control **43**, 123–177 (1979)
21. Wilke, T., Yoo, H.: Computing the Wadge degree, the Lifschitz degree, and the Rabin index of a regular language of infinite words in polynomial time. In: Mosses, P.D., Nielsen, M., Schwartzbach, M.I. (eds.) CAAP 1995. LNCS, vol. 915, pp. 288–302. Springer, Heidelberg (1995). https://doi.org/10.1007/3-540-59293-8_202

Recognition and Complexity Results for Projection Languages of Two-Dimensional Automata

Taylor J. Smith[(⊠)] and Kai Salomaa[(⊠)]

School of Computing, Queen's University, Kingston, ON K7L 2N8, Canada
{tsmith,ksalomaa}@cs.queensu.ca

Abstract. The row projection (resp., column projection) of a given two-dimensional language L is the one-dimensional language consisting of first rows (resp., first columns) of all two-dimensional words in L. The operation of row projection has previously been studied under the name "frontier language", and previous work in this area has focused primarily on one- and two-dimensional language classes.

In this paper, we study projections of languages recognized by various two-dimensional automaton classes. We show that both the row and column projections of languages recognized by (four-way) two-dimensional automata are exactly context-sensitive. We also show that the column projections of languages recognized by unary three-way two-dimensional automata can be recognized using nondeterministic logspace. Finally, we study the state complexity of projection languages for two-way two-dimensional automata, focusing on the language operations of union and diagonal concatenation.

Keywords: Language classes · Projection languages · Space complexity · Three-way automata · Two-dimensional automata · Two-way automata

1 Introduction

A two-dimensional word, also known in the literature as a picture, is a generalization of the notion of a word from a one-dimensional string to a two-dimensional array or matrix of symbols. Two-dimensional words are used as the input to two-dimensional automata, whose input heads move through the input word in a variety of ways, depending on the model.

We may define special projection operations on two-dimensional words that produce either the first row or the first column of the given word. In this way, a projection can be thought of as a conversion from a two-dimensional word to a one-dimensional word. Note that projection operations are lossy (i.e., all

Smith and Salomaa were supported by Natural Sciences and Engineering Research Council of Canada Grant OGP0147224.

G. Jirásková and G. Pighizzini (Eds.): DCFS 2020, LNCS 12442, pp. 206–218, 2020.
https://doi.org/10.1007/978-3-030-62536-8_17

but the first row/column of the two-dimensional word is lost when a projection operation is applied).

The row projection operation has been studied in the past [2,13], with a particular focus on formal language theory. (We summarize previous results in Sect. 2.1.) However, little work has yet been done on investigating projections of languages recognized by various two-dimensional automaton models.

Our results are as follows. We show that both the row and column projections of languages recognized by (four-way) two-dimensional automata are exactly context-sensitive. We also show that the column projections of languages recognized by unary three-way two-dimensional automata belong to the class NSPACE($O(\log(n))$). Finally, we study the state complexity of projection languages, focusing on the state complexity of union and diagonal concatenation for projections of languages recognized by two-way two-dimensional automata.

2   Preliminaries

A two-dimensional word is a matrix of symbols from some alphabet Σ. If a two-dimensional word w has m rows and n columns, then we say that w is of dimension $m \times n$. A two-dimensional language consists of two-dimensional words. There exist two special languages in two dimensions: $\Sigma^{m \times n}$ consists of all words of dimension $m \times n$ for some fixed $m, n \geq 1$, and Σ^{**} consists of all two-dimensional words.

The row projection (resp., column projection) of a two-dimensional language L is the one-dimensional language consisting of the first rows (resp., first columns) of all two-dimensional words in L. We formalize these notions in terms of individual two-dimensional words. In the following definition, we assume we have an $m \times n$ two-dimensional word

$$
w = \begin{bmatrix} a_{1,1} & \cdots & a_{1,n} \\ \vdots & \ddots & \vdots \\ a_{m,1} & \cdots & a_{m,n} \end{bmatrix}.
$$

Definition 1 (Row/column projection). *Given a two-dimensional word $w \in \Sigma^{m \times n}$, the row projection (resp., column projection) of w is the one-dimensional word*

$$\mathrm{pr_R}(w) = a_{1,1}a_{1,2}\cdots a_{1,n} \ (resp., \ \mathrm{pr_C}(w) = a_{1,1}a_{2,1}\cdots a_{m,1}),$$

where $a_{1,j} \in \Sigma$ for $1 \leq j \leq n$ (resp., $a_{i,1} \in \Sigma$ for $1 \leq i \leq m$).

The row/column projection of a two-dimensional language L is produced by taking the row/column projections of all words $w \in L$.

Note that one may view the column projection operation as taking the "transpose" of the first column of a two-dimensional word in order to produce a one-dimensional string. The row projection operation has been considered in previous papers, where it was called the "frontier" of a word or language [13].

When a two-dimensional word is used as the input to a two-dimensional automaton, we surround the outer border of the word with a special boundary marker #. (For example, the upper-left boundary marker is at position $(0,0)$ and the lower-right boundary marker is at position $(m+1, n+1)$ in the word.) The boundary marker prevents the input head of the automaton from leaving the input word: upon reaching the border, the input head can reverse its previous move (if possible) to reenter the word.

The formal definition of a two-dimensional automaton is as follows:

Definition 2 (Two-dimensional automaton). *A two-dimensional automaton is a tuple* $(Q, \Sigma, \delta, q_0, q_{accept})$, *where* Q *is a finite set of states,* Σ *is the input alphabet (with* $\# \notin \Sigma$ *acting as a boundary marker),* $\delta : (Q \backslash \{q_{accept}\}) \times (\Sigma \cup \{\#\}) \to Q \times \{U, D, L, R\}$ *is the partial transition function, and* $q_0, q_{accept} \in Q$ *are the initial and accepting states, respectively.*

The specific model in Definition 2 is sometimes referred to as a "four-way two-dimensional automaton". In this paper, we also consider three-way and two-way variants of two-dimensional automata. In the three-way case, the transition function is restricted to use only the directions $\{D, L, R\}$. Likewise, in the two-way case, the transition function uses only the directions $\{D, R\}$. We may optionally include a direction N, which corresponds to "no move" and does not change the recognition power of the model. We abbreviate each automaton model as 2(D/N)FA-kW(-1Σ), where D/N denotes deterministic/nondeterministic, $k \in \{2, 3, 4\}$ denotes the number of directions of input head movement, and 1Σ denotes a unary alphabet. In later sections, we will use the notation L_C to denote the set of languages recognized by some automaton model C.

2.1   Previous Work

A number of survey articles and other works have been written about both two-dimensional languages [5,14] and two-dimensional automaton models [9,15,19]. Previous work on projection operations has taken two perspectives: language-theoretic and automata-theoretic.

Language-Theoretic. One of the earliest results on two-dimensional row projection, due to Latteux and Simplot [13], showed that a one-dimensional language F is context-sensitive if and only if there exists a two-dimensional language $L \in$ REC such that $F = \text{pr}_R(L)$. The class REC denotes the class of tiling-recognizable two-dimensional languages, or languages whose words can be defined by a finite set of 2×2 tiles [4].

Anselmo et al. [2] later extended this direction of research to give equivalent characterizations for unambiguous and deterministic context-sensitive one-dimensional languages; namely, F is unambiguous (resp., deterministic) context-sensitive if and only if there exists $L \in$ UREC (resp., $L \in$ Row-UREC$_t$) such that $F = \text{pr}_R(L)$. The classes UREC and Row-UREC$_t$ are subclasses of REC, where

UREC consists of languages defined by an unambiguous tiling system [4] and Row-UREC$_t$ consists of languages that are "top-to-bottom row-unambiguous"; Anselmo et al. give a formal definition of the class Row-UREC$_t$ in an earlier paper [1].

Some classes smaller than Row-UREC$_t$ (namely, the class of deterministic recognizable languages DREC [1]) have no known characterization in terms of one-dimensional language classes.

Automata-Theoretic. A (four-way) two-dimensional automaton can recognize whether or not an input word has either an exponential or a doubly-exponential side length [11]. It is well-known that the language of unary strings of exponential length is context-sensitive but not context-free [8]. This fact implies that, if L is a language recognized by a four-way two-dimensional automaton, then both $pr_R(L)$ and $pr_C(L)$ may be non-context-free, even in the unary case.

Restricting ourselves to the three-way model, we obtain results that differ based on the projection operation under consideration. Let L be a unary language. If L is recognized by a nondeterministic three-way two-dimensional automaton, then $pr_R(L)$ is regular. On the other hand, if L is recognized by a deterministic three-way two-dimensional automaton, then $pr_C(L)$ need not be regular [20]. We can refine this result by showing that $pr_C(L)$ may be non-context-free for three-way two-dimensional automata, since the language $L_{composite}$ used in the proof of the non-regularity result is context-sensitive in both the unary and general-alphabet cases [6, 16, 17].

Finally, for the two-way model, we know that if a language L is recognized by a nondeterministic two-way two-dimensional automaton, then both $pr_R(L)$ and $pr_C(L)$ are regular [20]. This applies also to deterministic and unary two-way two-dimensional automata.

3   Recognition Power and Space Complexity

From previous work, we know that $pr_R(L)$ is context-sensitive when $L \in$ REC [13]. It is known that $L_{2DFA-4W} \subset L_{2NFA-4W} \subseteq$ REC [3, 10], so $pr_R(L)$ is also context-sensitive when $L \in L_{2DFA-4W}$. The following theorem gives the other direction of this inclusion.

Theorem 1. *Let K be a context-sensitive language. Then there exists $L \in L_{2DFA-4W}$ such that $K = pr_R(L)$.*

The proof of Theorem 1 uses the technique of recognizing computation tables of linear-bounded automata via two-dimensional automaton models. A similar technique has been used in the past, for example, to prove that the emptiness problem for the class of local picture languages is undecidable [4].

The same technique used to prove Theorem 1 also works for nondeterministic two-dimensional automata. Moreover, it is straightforward to show that $pr_C(L)$ is context-sensitive when $L \in L_{2DFA-4W}$, and so Theorem 1 can similarly be adapted to apply to column projection languages. These observations, taken together, lead to the following characterization.

Corollary 1. *Both the row and column projections of languages recognized by four-way two-dimensional automata consist exactly of the class of context-sensitive languages.*

3.1   Three-Way Two-Dimensional Automata

Recall from Sect. 2.1 that the row projection of any language accepted by a three-way two-dimensional automaton $\mathcal{A}$ is regular. Since $\mathsf{REG} \in \mathsf{DSPACE}(O(1))$ [18], we immediately get that $\mathrm{pr}_R(L(\mathcal{A})) \in \mathsf{DSPACE}(O(1))$ as well.

We further noted in the same section that the column projection of a language in $L_{\text{2NFA-3W-1}\Sigma}$ may be non-context-free, depending on the choice of language. Here, we investigate the space complexity of column projection languages for $L_{\text{2NFA-3W-1}\Sigma}$.

In what follows, we use the notation $\mathrm{rso}_i[r, s]$ to denote the subword occurrence of the ith row starting at index r and ending at index $r + s$; that is, a subword of length $s + 1$. Since we are considering unary languages, all symbols of $\mathrm{rso}_i[r, s]$ are identical and independent of the value i. Thus, by "subword occurrence", we mean the cells of the ith row at indices r through $r + s$ inclusive.

The following technical lemma states that every string w in the column projection of a language in $L_{\text{2NFA-3W-1}\Sigma}$ is a projection of a two-dimensional word z, where the number of columns of z is at most some constant multiple of the length of w. The proof, intuitively speaking, uses the fact that when we have a two-dimensional word containing a large number of columns with no downward moves, we can remove some of these columns and simulate the same computation of the three-way two-dimensional automaton.

Lemma 1. *Let $\mathcal{A}$ be a unary three-way two-dimensional automaton with k states, and consider a word $w \in \mathrm{pr}_C(L(\mathcal{A}))$. Then there exists a two-dimensional word z with $|w|$ rows and at most $(|w| + 3) \cdot (k^{2^{2k}} + 2)$ columns accepted by $\mathcal{A}$.*

Proof. Let $H = k^{2^{2k}}$. Consider a two-dimensional word $z \in L(\mathcal{A})$ of dimension $|w| \times n_1$, where

$$n_1 > (|w| + 3) \cdot (H + 2). \tag{1}$$

Let C_z be an accepting nondeterministic computation of $\mathcal{A}$ on input word z. Without loss of generality, we may assume that C_z accepts at the bottom border of z.

By the inequality in Eq. 1, the input word z must have $k^{2k} + 1$ consecutive columns such that the computation C_z does not make a downward move in any such column. Furthermore, we may assume that these consecutive columns do not include either the first H columns or the last H columns of z. That is, there exists $H \leq j \leq (n_1 - 2H)$ such that the computation C_z does not make a downward move in any of the subword occurrences

$$\mathrm{rso}_i[j, H], \quad i = \{1, \ldots, |w|\}.$$

Let Q be the set of states of $\mathcal{A}$ and define $\overline{Q} = \{\overline{q} \mid q \in Q\}$ to be a disjoint copy of states in Q. For each column $x \in \{j, j+1, \ldots, j+H\}$, define a function $f_x : Q \to 2^{Q \cup \overline{Q}}$ by setting, for all $p \in Q$,

- $q \in f_x(p)$ if, for some i, the computation C_z on the ith row in column x and state p exits the subword occurrence $\mathrm{rso}_i[j, H]$ to the left in state q; and
- $\bar{q} \in f_x(p)$ if, for some i, the computation C_z on the ith row in column x and state p exits the subword occurrence $\mathrm{rso}_i[j, H]$ to the right in state q.

Note that the computation of C_z may visit the subword occurrence multiple times. By our definition, $q \in f_x(p)$ if, at some point, C_z is in the xth column in state p and, when C_z next exits $\mathrm{rso}_i[j, H]$, it exits to the left in state q.

Note also that the accepting computation must exit each subword occurrence $\mathrm{rso}_i[j, H]$ either to the left or to the right since, by our choice of j, the computation C_z makes no downward moves in any of the columns $j, \ldots, (j + H)$.

Since the number of functions from Q to $2^{Q \cup \bar{Q}}$ is $H = k^{2^{2k}}$, there exist columns x_1 and x_2, $j \leq x_1 < x_2 \leq (j + H)$, such that $f_{x_1} = f_{x_2}$. Moreover, since the computation C_z makes no downward moves in any of the columns $j, \ldots, (j + H)$, there exists an accepting computation of $\mathcal{A}$ on the two-dimensional word z' obtained by removing the columns $x_1, \ldots, (x_2 - 1)$ from z.

The above observation relies on our earlier assumption that the designated columns $j, \ldots, (j + H)$ are at distance at least H from the left and right borders of the word. For example, consider a situation where $\bar{q} \in f_{x_2}(p)$; that is, where the computation starting in column x_2 and state p exits the subword occurrence to the right in state q. When simulating the same computation on the modified word z' starting in column x_1, the computation could, at some point, move to the left of column j. Since $j \geq H$, this guarantees that the computation would not reach the left border.

Altogether, the two-dimensional word z' has $x_2 - x_1$ fewer columns than the original word z. By repeated application of the previous argument, we see that $\mathcal{A}$ must accept a two-dimensional word of dimension $|w| \times n_2$, where $n_2 \leq H$. □

An application of Lemma 1 allows us to obtain our main space complexity result for column projections of languages recognized by unary three-way two-dimensional automata.

Theorem 2. *Let $\mathcal{A}$ be a unary three-way two-dimensional automaton. Then* $\mathrm{pr}_C(L(\mathcal{A})) \in \mathsf{NSPACE}(O(\log(n)))$.

Proof. Suppose $\mathcal{A}$ has k states. We describe the operation of a nondeterministic logspace Turing machine $\mathcal{M}$ recognizing $\mathrm{pr}_C(L(\mathcal{A}))$.

On input word w, $\mathcal{M}$ first writes to its work tape a binary representation of a nondeterministically-chosen natural number $n_1 \leq (|w| + 3) \cdot (k^{2^{2k}} + 2)$. Since k is constant, this binary representation can be written in space $O(\log(|w|))$.

The machine $\mathcal{M}$ then simulates a nondeterministic computation of $\mathcal{A}$ on a two-dimensional input word z with $|w|$ rows and n_1 columns. The input head of $\mathcal{M}$ keeps track of the current row of z, while a binary counter stored on the work tape of $\mathcal{M}$ keeps track of the current column of z. The work tape also contains the originally-guessed value n_1 so that $\mathcal{M}$ is able to determine when its simulated computation encounters the right border of the input word.

By Lemma 1, we know that if $w \in \mathrm{pr}_C(L(\mathcal{A}))$, then w must be a column projection of a two-dimensional word with at most $(|w| + 3) \cdot (k^{2^{2k}} + 2)$ columns that is accepted by $\mathcal{A}$. □

Since the language class CSL coincides with the nondeterministic space complexity class $\mathsf{NSPACE}(O(n))$ [12], one consequence of Corollary 1 is that the row and column projections of languages recognized by four-way two-dimensional automata consist exactly of languages in $\mathsf{NSPACE}(O(n))$. Theorem 2 gives a significantly improved nondeterministic space complexity upper bound for column projections of languages recognized by unary three-way two-dimensional automata.

4   State Complexity

Since projections of languages in $L_{\text{2DFA-2W}}$ and $L_{\text{2NFA-2W}}$ are known to be always regular, it is possible to consider questions of state complexity involving these projection languages.

Although they seem never to have appeared anywhere in the literature, it is straightforward to prove the following closure results for Boolean operations over two-way two-dimensional automata.

Lemma 2. *$L_{\text{2DFA-2W}}$ is not closed under union or intersection.*

Lemma 3. *$L_{\text{2NFA-2W}}$ is closed under union, but is not closed under intersection or complement.*

Moreover, the present authors previously investigated closure properties of concatenation operations over two-way two-dimensional automata [21]. In this section, therefore, we will focus on the state complexity of projections of union and concatenation operations for nondeterministic two-way two-dimensional automata.

4.1   Union of 2NFA-2W Languages

Before we proceed, we require a slight modification to the definition of a two-way two-dimensional automaton that we introduced in Sect. 2. For the remainder of this section, when we refer to a "two-way two-dimensional automaton", we use the following definition.

Definition 3 (IBR-accepting two-way two-dimensional automaton). *An IBR-accepting two-way two-dimensional automaton $\mathcal{A}$ is a tuple $(Q, \Sigma, \delta, q_0, q_{accept})$ as in Definition 2, where, when the input head reads a boundary marker #, $\mathcal{A}$ either enters q_{accept} in the next transition or the transition is undefined.*

The abbreviation "IBR-accepting" refers to the automaton "immediately-bottom-right accepting"; by this, we mean that the automaton immediately halts and accepts if, upon reading a boundary marker on the bottom or right border of the word, q_{accept} is reachable from its current state. The two-way model is the only model for which we can make this modification; neither three- nor four-way models can be made to halt immediately upon reading a boundary marker.

Remark 1. The accepting state of an IBR-accepting two-way two-dimensional automaton, q_{accept}, is a "dummy" state used only as the target of accepting transitions on the boundary marker #. Thus, by the "size" of such an automaton $\mathcal{A}$ we mean the size of the set $Q \setminus \{q_{\text{accept}}\}$. This convention ensures that an IBR-accepting two-way two-dimensional automaton recognizing single-row words has the same size as the corresponding one-dimensional automaton accepting the same string language.

The following result shows that we may convert between the usual and IBR-accepting types of two-way two-dimensional automata without incurring a penalty on the number of states.

Proposition 1 [21]. *Given a two-way two-dimensional automaton $\mathcal{A}$ with n states, there exists an equivalent IBR-accepting two-way two-dimensional automaton $\mathcal{A}'$ with n states.*

Using a construction from a previous paper investigating projections of non-deterministic two-way two-dimensional automaton languages [20], we may obtain an upper bound on the nondeterministic state complexity of projection languages for this model.

Proposition 2. *Let $\mathcal{A}$ be a nondeterministic two-way two-dimensional automaton with n states. Then both $\text{pr}_R(L(\mathcal{A}))$ and $\text{pr}_C(L(\mathcal{A}))$ are recognized by a nondeterministic one-dimensional automaton with $2n$ states.*

We can show that the following lower bound applies for the same model.

Lemma 4. *There exists a nondeterministic two-way two-dimensional automaton $\mathcal{A}$ with n states such that any nondeterministic one-dimensional automaton recognizing $\text{pr}_R(L(\mathcal{A}))$ requires at least $2n - 1$ states.*

Proof. Define $\mathcal{A}$ as follows: the alphabet is $\Sigma = \{0, 1\}$, the set of states is $Q = \{q_0, q_1, \ldots, q_{n-1}\}$ (and additionally q_{accept}), the initial state is q_0, the accepting state is q_{accept}, and the transition function δ consists of the following:

- $\delta(q_i, 0) = (q_{i+1}, R)$ for all $0 \leq i \leq n - 2$;
- $\delta(q_{n-1}, 0) = \{(q_0, R), (q_{n-1}, D)\}$; and
- $\delta(q_0, \#) = (q_{\text{accept}}, N)$.

Each rightward-moving transition counts modulo n, and the only downward-moving transition occurs in a column position congruent to $-1 \mod n$. Moreover, the downward-moving transition does not change the state (i.e., the column count is preserved). Note also that $\mathcal{A}$ makes no transitions upon reading the symbol 1; this is because, after reading $n-1$ copies of 0 and making a downward move, the first row can contain any symbols after that column position so long as the number of total columns remains a multiple of n. Combining these observations, we see that the row projection of $L(\mathcal{A})$ is

$$\mathrm{pr_R}(L(\mathcal{A})) = 0^{n-1}(0+1)((0+1)^n)^* + \epsilon.$$

To show that the nondeterministic state complexity of $\mathrm{pr_R}(L(\mathcal{A}))$ is at least $2n-1$, we use the following extended fooling set [7]:

$$S = \{(x,y) \mid xy = 0^{n-1}1^{n+1}, |y| \geq 2\}.$$

The set S contains $2n-1$ elements and, by its definition, for any pair $(x,y) \in S$, $xy = 0^{n-1}1^{n+1} \in \mathrm{pr_R}(L(\mathcal{A}))$.

Consider two distinct pairs (x,y) and (x',y'). Without loss of generality, assume x is a proper prefix of x'. If $|x'| - |x| \neq n$, then $|xy'|$ is not a multiple of n, and $xy' \notin \mathrm{pr_R}(L(\mathcal{A}))$. Otherwise, $|x'| - |x| = n$. In this case, since $|x'y'| = 2n$ and $|y'| \geq 2$, we have that $|x'| \leq 2n-2$. Thus, $|x| \leq n-2$, and so $x = 0^i$ for some $0 \leq i \leq n-2$. However, this means that $xy' \notin \mathrm{pr_R}(L(\mathcal{A}))$, because in this case y' consists only of the symbol 1.   □

Using the previous results, we can obtain a state complexity bound for the projection of the union of two languages recognized by nondeterministic two-way two-dimensional automata.

Theorem 3. *(i) If $\mathcal{A}$ and $\mathcal{B}$ are nondeterministic two-way two-dimensional automata with m and n states, respectively, then $\mathrm{pr_R}(L(\mathcal{A}) \cup L(\mathcal{B}))$ is recognized by a nondeterministic one-dimensional automaton with $2(m+n+1)$ states.*

(ii) There exist nondeterministic two-way two-dimensional automata $\mathcal{A}$ and $\mathcal{B}$ with n and m states, respectively, such that any nondeterministic one-dimensional automaton recognizing $\mathrm{pr_R}(L(\mathcal{A}) \cup L(\mathcal{B}))$ requires at least $2(m+n-1)$ states.

Since two-way two-dimensional automata operate symmetrically with respect to rows and columns, there also exist nondeterministic state complexity bounds for column projections analogous to those established in Theorem 3.

4.2   Diagonal Concatenation of 2NFA-2W Languages

Given two-dimensional words w and v of dimension $m \times n$ and $m' \times n'$ respectively, the diagonal concatenation of w and v, denoted $w \oslash v$, produces a two-dimensional language consisting of words of dimension $(m+m') \times (n+n')$ where w is in the top-left quadrant, v is in the bottom-right quadrant, and words $x \in \Sigma^{m \times n'}$ and $y \in \Sigma^{m' \times n}$ are in the top-right and bottom-left quadrants of $w \oslash v$, respectively. We assume that the symbols in x and y come from the same alphabet Σ as the symbols in w and v. The diagonal concatenation language is formed by adding to the top-right and bottom-left quadrants all possible words x and y over Σ. Note also that no boundary markers appear within a diagonal concatenation $w \oslash v$.

Nondeterministic two-way two-dimensional automata are known to be closed under diagonal concatenation over a general alphabet and, moreover, this is the only concatenation operation under which two-way two-dimensional automaton languages over general alphabets are closed [21]. Thus, the natural question arises: given a pair of nondeterministic two-way two-dimensional automata $\mathcal{A}$ and $\mathcal{B}$ recognizing languages $L(\mathcal{A})$ and $L(\mathcal{B})$, respectively, how large must such an automaton be to recognize $\text{pr}_{\text{R}}(L(\mathcal{A}) \oslash L(\mathcal{B}))$?

We begin by making an elementary observation. In one dimension, an ϵ-NFA extends an ordinary NFA by allowing ϵ-transitions; i.e., "stay-in-place" moves.

Lemma 5 (Wood [22]). *Any n-state ϵ-NFA has an equivalent n-state NFA without ϵ-transitions.*

Moreover, for a pair of nondeterministic one-dimensional automata with m' and n' states recognizing languages L_1 and L_2, respectively, a total of $m' + n'$ states are necessary and sufficient to recognize the concatenation language $L_1 \cdot L_2$ in the general alphabet case, while $m' + n' - 1$ states are necessary in the unary case [7].

Theorem 4. *(i) If $\mathcal{A}$ and $\mathcal{B}$ are nondeterministic two-way two-dimensional automata with m and n states, respectively, then $\text{pr}_{\text{R}}(L(\mathcal{A}) \oslash L(\mathcal{B}))$ is recognized by a nondeterministic one-dimensional automaton with $2m + n$ states.*

(ii) There exist nondeterministic two-way two-dimensional automata $\mathcal{A}$ and $\mathcal{B}$ with m and n states, respectively, such that any nondeterministic one-dimensional automaton recognizing $\text{pr}_{\text{R}}(L(\mathcal{A}) \oslash L(\mathcal{B}))$ requires at least $m + n - 1$ states.

Proof. We prove (i) by constructing a nondeterministic one-dimensional automaton $\mathcal{C}$ to recognize the language $\text{pr}_{\text{R}}(L(\mathcal{A}) \oslash L(\mathcal{B}))$. The following procedure allows $\mathcal{C}$ to simulate the computation of $\mathcal{A}$ and $\mathcal{B}$ on a word in the language $L(\mathcal{A}) \oslash L(\mathcal{B})$:

1. The input head of $\mathcal{C}$ begins by simulating rightward moves of the input head of $\mathcal{A}$. If the input head of $\mathcal{A}$ makes a downward move, $\mathcal{C}$ remembers that a downward move occurred and replaces it with a "stay-in-place" move.
2. At some point during its computation, $\mathcal{C}$ nondeterministically switches to simulating moves of $\mathcal{B}$. Again, the input head of $\mathcal{C}$ only simulates rightward moves, and replaces downward moves with "stay-in-place" moves.

By Lemma 5, "stay-in-place" moves can be used without affecting the number of states. However, by a construction similar to that used in Proposition 2, the requirement in Step 1 to remember whether a downward move occurred doubles the number of states needed to simulate the computation of $\mathcal{A}$. Remembering downward moves is not required when simulating the computation of $\mathcal{B}$. Furthermore, in Step 2, the input head of $\mathcal{C}$ ignores the alphabet symbols it is reading.

Since the simulation only needs to check that $\mathcal{B}$ accepts a two-dimensional word with the correct number of columns, the exact symbols being read at this stage may be ignored.

If the computation of $\mathcal{C}$ accepts, then the computation of $\mathcal{A}$ and $\mathcal{B}$ must have also accepted, and therefore $\mathcal{C}$ recognizes words in the language $\mathrm{pr}_R(L(\mathcal{A}) \oslash L(\mathcal{B}))$. Moreover, $2m + n$ states are sufficient for $\mathcal{C}$ to perform its computation in this way.

We now prove (ii). Let $\mathcal{A}'$ (respectively, $\mathcal{B}'$) be an m-state (respectively, n-state) unary nondeterministic one-dimensional automaton such that the concatenation of $L(\mathcal{A}')$ and $L(\mathcal{B}')$ requires $m + n - 1$ states [7]. The language $L(\mathcal{A}')$ can be recognized by an m-state nondeterministic two-way two-dimensional automaton $\mathcal{A}$ that recognizes words consisting of one row. Similarly, $L(\mathcal{B}')$ can be recognized by an n-state nondeterministic two-way two-dimensional automaton $\mathcal{B}$. In this case, the languages $\mathrm{pr}_R(L(\mathcal{A}) \oslash L(\mathcal{B}))$ and $L(\mathcal{A}') \cdot L(\mathcal{B}')$ are equal. It follows that $m + n - 1$ states are necessary for any nondeterministic one-dimensional automaton to recognize $\mathrm{pr}_R(L(\mathcal{A}) \oslash L(\mathcal{B}))$. □

Again, there exist nondeterministic state complexity bounds for column projections analogous to those established in Theorem 4.

5   Conclusion

In this paper, we established results linking one-dimensional language classes to two-dimensional projection languages; namely, that both the row and column projections of languages $L \in L_{\text{2DFA-4W}}$ or $L_{\text{2NFA-4W}}$ are exactly context-sensitive. This improves on the previously-known non-context-free lower bound, which remains for other two-dimensional automaton models.

We also proved space complexity results for projection languages. While both the row and column projections of languages $L \in L_{\text{2DFA-4W}}$ or $L_{\text{2NFA-4W}}$ belong to the class $\mathsf{NSPACE}(O(n))$, the column projection of languages $L \in L_{\text{2DFA-3W-1}\Sigma}$ or $L_{\text{2NFA-3W-1}\Sigma}$ belongs to the class $\mathsf{NSPACE}(O(\log(n)))$.

Finally, we investigated the state complexity of projection languages. We showed that, given a pair of nondeterministic two-way two-dimensional automata $\mathcal{A}$ and $\mathcal{B}$ with m and n states, respectively, between $2(m + n - 1)$ and $2(m + n + 1)$ states are needed to recognize $\mathrm{pr}_R(L(\mathcal{A}) \cup L(\mathcal{B}))$ and between $m + n - 1$ and $2m + n$ states are needed to recognize $\mathrm{pr}_R(L(\mathcal{A}) \oslash L(\mathcal{B}))$. These bounds apply also to the column projections of such languages.

We conclude by giving a selection of open problems arising from work done in this paper.

1. Which class of one-dimensional languages characterizes the column projection of languages in $L_{\text{2DFA-3W}}$ or $L_{\text{2NFA-3W}}$ (or their unary equivalents)?
2. Which class of one-dimensional languages characterizes either the row or column projection of languages in $L_{\text{2DFA-4W-1}\Sigma}$ or $L_{\text{2NFA-4W-1}\Sigma}$?
3. If a two-dimensional automaton $\mathcal{A}$ with n states recognizes a language L, how many states are necessary/sufficient for a one-dimensional automaton $\mathcal{A}'$ to recognize the language $\mathrm{pr}_R(L)/\mathrm{pr}_C(L)$?

Problems 1 and 2 are likely difficult; it may be more reasonable to obtain an improved upper bound on the related question of space complexity for problem 2, say $\mathsf{DSPACE}(O(n))$. Moreover, for problem 3, we can obtain a trivial lower bound of n states by constructing an n-state nondeterministic three/four-way two-dimensional automaton $\mathcal{A}$ that accepts only one-row words (i.e., words of dimension $1 \times k$, $k \geq 1$), and taking $\mathcal{A}'$ to be the minimal nondeterministic two-way one-dimensional automaton recognizing the language $\mathrm{pr}_{\mathrm{R}}(L(\mathcal{A}))$.

References

1. Anselmo, M., Giammarresi, D., Madonia, M.: Deterministic and unambiguous families within recognizable two-dimensional languages. Fund. Inform. **98**(2–3), 143–166 (2010)
2. Anselmo, M., Giammarresi, D., Madonia, M.: Classification of string languages via tiling recognizable picture languages. In: Dediu, A.-H., Inenaga, S., Martín-Vide, C. (eds.) LATA 2011. LNCS, vol. 6638, pp. 105–116. Springer, Heidelberg (2011). https://doi.org/10.1007/978-3-642-21254-3_7
3. Blum, M., Hewitt, C.: Automata on a 2-dimensional tape. In: Miller, R.E. (ed.) SWAT 1967, pp. 155–160 (1967)
4. Giammarresi, D., Restivo, A.: Recognizable picture languages. Int. J. Pattern Recogn. Artif. Intell. **6**(2–3), 241–256 (1992)
5. Giammarresi, D., Restivo, A.: Two-dimensional languages. In: Rozenberg, G., Salomaa, A. (eds.) Handbook of Formal Languages, pp. 215–267. Springer, Heidelberg (1997). https://doi.org/10.1007/978-3-642-59126-6_4
6. Hartmanis, J., Shank, H.: On the recognition of primes by automata. J. ACM **15**(3), 382–389 (1968)
7. Holzer, M., Kutrib, M.: Nondeterministic descriptional complexity of regular languages. Int. J. Found. Comput. Sci. **14**(6), 1087–1102 (2003)
8. Hopcroft, J.E., Ullman, J.D.: Introduction to Automata Theory, Languages, and Computation. Addison-Wesley, Reading (1979)
9. Inoue, K., Takanami, I.: A survey of two-dimensional automata theory. Inf. Sci. **55**(1–3), 99–121 (1991)
10. Inoue, K., Takanami, I.: A characterization of recognizable picture languages. In: Nakamura, A., Nivat, M., Saoudi, A., Wang, P.S.P., Inoue, K. (eds.) ICPIA 1992. LNCS, vol. 654, pp. 133–143. Springer, Heidelberg (1992). https://doi.org/10.1007/3-540-56346-6_35
11. Kari, J., Moore, C.: Rectangles and squares recognized by two-dimensional automata. In: Karhumäki, J., Maurer, H., Păun, G., Rozenberg, G. (eds.) Theory Is Forever. LNCS, vol. 3113, pp. 134–144. Springer, Heidelberg (2004). https://doi.org/10.1007/978-3-540-27812-2_13
12. Kuroda, S.Y.: Classes of languages and linear-bounded automata. Inf. Control **7**(2), 207–223 (1965)
13. Latteux, M., Simplot, D.: Context-sensitive string languages and recognizable picture languages. Inf. Comput. **138**(2), 160–169 (1997)
14. Morita, K.: Two-dimensional languages. In: Martín-Vide, C., Mitrana, V., Păun, G. (eds.) Formal Languages and Applications, Studies in Fuzziness and Soft Computing, vol. 148, pp. 427–437. Springer, Heidelberg (2004). https://doi.org/10.1007/978-3-540-39886-8_22

15. Rosenfeld, A.: Picture Languages: Formal Models for Picture Recognition. Computer Science and Applied Mathematics. Academic Press, New York (1979)
16. Salomaa, A.: Theory of Automata, International Series of Monographs in Pure and Applied Mathematics, vol. 100. Pergamon Press, Oxford (1969)
17. Salomaa, A.: Formal Languages. Academic Press, New York (1973)
18. Shepherdson, J.C.: The reduction of two-way automata to one-way automata. IBM J. Res. Dev. **3**(2), 198–200 (1959)
19. Smith, T.J.: Two-dimensional automata. Technical report 2019–637. Queen's University, Kingston (2019)
20. Smith, T.J., Salomaa, K.: Decision problems for restricted variants of two-dimensional automata. In: Hospodár, M., Jirásková, G. (eds.) CIAA 2019. LNCS, vol. 11601, pp. 222–234. Springer, Cham (2019). https://doi.org/10.1007/978-3-030-23679-3_18
21. Smith, T.J., Salomaa, K.: Concatenation operations and restricted variants of two-dimensional automata. arXiv:2008.11164 (2020)
22. Wood, D.: Theory of Computation. Computer Science and Technology Series. Harper & Row, New York (1987)

On the Generative Power of Quasiperiods

Ludwig Staiger[⊠]

Institut für Informatik, Martin-Luther-Universität Halle-Wittenberg,
06099 Halle (Saale), Germany
staiger@informatik.uni-halle.de

Abstract. It is shown that, for every length $l \geq 3$, a quasiperiod of the form $a^n b a^n$ (or $a^n b b a^n$ if l is even) generates the largest language Q of words having this word as quasiperiod. As a means of comparison we use the growth of the function which counts the number of words of length l in the language Q.

Moreover, we give the exact ordering of the lengths l with respect to the largest language Q generated by a quasiperiod of length l.

Keywords: Quasiperiod · Formal language · Asymptotic growth · Polynomial

1 Introduction

Informally, a word q is a quasiperiod of another word w if q is a prefix and a suffix of w and every position of w is covered by q.

In this paper we investigate the languages Q_q of words w having q as quasiperiod. We are interested in the question of which quasiperiods q generate large languages Q_q. Since different quasiperiods may have incomparable w.r.t. set inclusion languages Q_q, we compare the languages Q_q by their functions $s_q : \mathbb{N} \to \mathbb{N}$ which count the number of words of length n in Q_q. As a means of comparison we use their asymptotic growth. It turns out that the languages Q_q are essentially regular star-languages, therefore their function s_q satisfies $s_q(n) \approx \text{const.} \cdot \lambda_q^n$, where the value $\lambda_q \geq 1$ depends on the quasiperiod q.

The aim of this paper is to estimate, for every length $n \geq 3$ the words q which have the largest value λ_q. To this end we consider along with language-theoretical properties of Q_q some combinatorial properties of quasiperiods. Moreover, we need to consider a special class of integer polynomials related to quasiperiods.

The paper is organised as follows. After some preliminaries we deal with combinatorial properties of quasiperiods and the generated languages. The asymptotic growth of Q_q is the subject of Sect. 4. Then we deal with basic properties of polynomials related to quasiperiods. In these sections we mainly report results of the papers [8] and [12]. The following Sects. 6 and 7 deal with the proof of the main theorem. Here we derive also the complete ordering of the values $\lambda_n = \max\{\lambda_q : |q| = n\}$.

© Springer Nature Switzerland AG 2020
G. Jirásková and G. Pighizzini (Eds.): DCFS 2020, LNCS 12442, pp. 219–230, 2020.
https://doi.org/10.1007/978-3-030-62536-8_18

2   Notation and Preliminaries

We introduce the notation used throughout the paper. By $\mathbb{N} = \{0, 1, 2, \ldots\}$ we denote the set of natural numbers. Let X be a finite alphabet. By $a, b \in X$ we mean two different letters. X^* is the set (monoid) of words on X, including the *empty word e*.

For $w, v \in X^*$ let $w \cdot v$ be their *concatenation*. This concatenation product extends in an obvious way to subsets $W, L \subseteq X^*$. For a language W let $W^* := \bigcup_{i \in \mathbb{N}} W^i$ be the *submonoid* of X^* generated by W. The smallest subset of a language W which generates W^* is called its *star root* $\sqrt[*]{W}$ [4]. It holds

$$\sqrt[*]{W} = (W \setminus \{e\}) \setminus (W \setminus \{e\})^2 \cdot W^* .$$

Furthermore $|w|$ is the *length* of the word $w \in X^*$, and by $w \sqsubseteq v$ we denote the fact that w is a *prefix* of v.

A word $w \in X^* \setminus \{e\}$ is called *primitive* if $w = v^n$ implies $n = 1$, that is, w is not the power of a shorter word.

As usual a language $L \subseteq X^*$ is called a *code* provided $w_1 \cdots w_l = v_1 \cdots v_k$ for $w_1, \ldots, w_l, v_1, \ldots, v_k \in L$ implies $l = k$ and $w_i = v_i$. A code L is said to be a *suffix code* provided no codeword is a suffix of another codeword.

Finally, we define the language Q_q of words having $q \in X^* \setminus \{e\}$ as quasi-period.

$(0) e \in Q_q$, and
$(1) w \in Q_q$, if and only if $w \in X^* \cdot q$ and
  there is a $w' \sqsubset w, w' \in Q_q$, with $w \sqsubseteq w' \cdot q$.

3   Quasiperiodic Words

In this part we consider the finite language P_q ($\mathcal{L}(q)$ in [7]) which is tightly related to Q_q. Most of the results are contained in [7,8] and [12].

We set

$$P_q := \{v : e \sqsubset v \sqsubseteq q \sqsubset v \cdot q\} . \tag{1}$$

We have the following property.

$$Q_q \setminus \{e\} = P_q^* \cdot q \subseteq P_q^* \cap q \cdot X^* . \tag{2}$$

3.1   Combinatorial Properties of P_q

We investigate basic properties of P_q using simple facts from combinatorics on words (see [2,6,10]).

Proposition 1. $v \in P_q$ *if and only if* $|v| \leq |q|$ *and there is a prefix* $\bar{v} \sqsubset v$ *such that* $q = v^k \cdot \bar{v}$ *for* $k = \lfloor |q|/|v| \rfloor$.

Corollary 1. $v \in P_q$ *if and only if* $|v| \leq |q|$ *and there is a* $k' \in \mathbb{N}$ *such that* $q \sqsubseteq v^{k'}$.

Now set $q_0 := \min_{\sqsubseteq} P_q$. Then in view of Proposition 1 and Corollary 1 we have the following canonical representation.

$$q = q_0^k \cdot \bar{q} \text{ where } k = \lfloor |q|/|q_0| \rfloor \text{ and } \bar{q} \sqsubset q_0. \tag{3}$$

We will refer to q_0 as the *repeated prefix* and to k as the *repetition factor*. If $|q_0| > |q|/2$, that is, if $k = 1$ we will refer to q as *irreducible*.[1]

Corollary 2. *Every word $v \in \sqrt[*]{P_q}$ is primitive.*

Proof. Assume $v = v_1^l$ for some $v \in \sqrt[*]{P_q}$ and $l > 1$. Then $q \sqsubseteq v^{k'} = v_1^{l \cdot k'}$, and, according to Corollary 1 $v_1 \in P_q$ contradicting $v \in \sqrt[*]{P_q}$. ∎

Proposition 2. *Let $q \in X^*, q \neq e$, $q_0 = \min_{\sqsubseteq} P_q$, $q = q_0^k \cdot \bar{q}$ and $v \in P_q^* \backslash \{e\}$.*

1. *If $w \sqsubseteq q$ then $v \cdot w \sqsubseteq q$ or $q \sqsubseteq v \cdot w$.*
2. *If $w \cdot v \sqsubseteq q$ then $w \in \{q_0\}^*$.*
3. *If $|v| \leq |q| - |q_0|$ then $v \in \{q_0\}^*$.*

Corollary 3. *If $q \notin \{q_0\}^*$ then q_0 is not a suffix of q.*

Proof. Let $q = w \cdot q_0$. Then according to Proposition 2.2 $w \in \{q_0\}^*$. ∎

Next we derive a slight improvement of Proposition 2.3. To this end, we use the Theorem of Fine and Wilf.

Theorem 1 [5]. *Let $v, w \in X^*$. Suppose v^m and w^n, for some $m, n \in \mathbb{N}$, have a common prefix of length $|v| + |w| - \gcd(|v|, |w|)$. Then v and w are powers of a common word $u \in X^*$ of length $|u| = \gcd(|v|, |w|)$.*[2]

Proposition 3. *Let $q \in X^*, q \neq e$, $q_0 = \min_{\sqsubseteq} P_q$, $q = q_0^k \cdot \bar{q}$ and $v \in P_q$. If $|v| \leq |q| - |q_0| + \gcd(|v|, |q_0|)$ then $v \in \{q_0\}^*$.*

Proof. $q_0, v \in P_q$ imply that q is a common prefix of q_0^{k+1} and $v^{k'}$ for some $k' \in \mathbb{N}$. In view of $|v| \leq |q| - |q_0| + \gcd(|v|, |q_0|)$ Theorem 1 implies that q_0 and v are powers of a common word, that is, $v \in \{q_0\}^*$. ∎

3.2   The Reduced Quasiperiod $\hat{q}$

Next we investigate the relation between a quasiperiod $q = q_0^k \cdot \bar{q}$ where $q_0 = \min_{\sqsubseteq} P_q$ and $\bar{q} \sqsubset q_0$ and its *reduced quasiperiod* $\hat{q} := q_0 \cdot \bar{q}$. Since $q \in Q_{\hat{q}}$, we have $Q_{\hat{q}} \supseteq Q_q$.

We continue with a relation between P_q and $P_{\hat{q}}$. It is obvious that $q_0^i \in P_q$ for every $i = 1, \ldots, k$. Then Proposition 3 shows that

$$\sqrt[*]{P_q} \subseteq \{q_0\} \cup \{v' : v' \sqsubseteq q \wedge |v'| > |q| - |q_0| + \gcd(|v'|, |q_0|)\}. \tag{4}$$

---

[1] Superprimitive in the sense of [1,7] quasiperiods are irreducible but not vice versa (see [12, Section 2.3.4]).

[2] Here $\gcd(k, l)$ denotes the greatest common divisor of two numbers $k, l \in \mathbb{N}$.

Lemma 1 [12, Lemma 2.2]. *Let* $q \in X^*, q \neq e$, $q_0 = \min_{\sqsubseteq} P_q$, $q = q_0^k \cdot \bar{q}$ *and* $\hat{q} = q_0 \cdot \bar{q}$ *the reduced quasiperiod of* q. *Then*

$$P_q = \{q_0^i : i = 1, \dots, k-1\} \cup \{q_0^{k-1} \cdot v : v \in P_{\hat{q}}\}.$$

This implies

$$\sqrt[*]{P_q} \subseteq \{q_0\} \cup q_0^{k-1} \cdot (P_{\hat{q}} \setminus \{q_0\}), \text{ and} \tag{5}$$

$$P_{\hat{q}} \subseteq \{v : \hat{q}_0 \sqsubseteq v \sqsubseteq \hat{q}\} \tag{6}$$

Moreover, we have the following.

Lemma 2. *Let* $q = q_0^k \cdot \bar{q}$ *with* $k \geq 2$, $\bar{q} \sqsubset q_0$ *and* $\hat{q} = q_0 \cdot \bar{q}$.

If $\hat{q}_0 \neq q_0$ *for the repeated prefix of* $\hat{q}_0$ *then* $\bar{q} \sqsubset \hat{q}_0 \sqsubset q_0$ *and* $|\hat{q}_0| > |\bar{q}| +$ gcd$(|q_0|, |\hat{q}_0|)$. *Moreover, then there is a nonempty suffix* $v \neq e$ *of* q_0 *such that* $v \sqsubset \hat{q}_0$ *and* $v \cdot \bar{q} \sqsubset \hat{q}_0^2$.

Proof. We have $\bar{q} \sqsubseteq q_0$ and, since $q_0 \in P_{\hat{q}}$, also $\hat{q}_0 \sqsubseteq q_0$. Moreover, $\hat{q} \sqsubseteq q_0^2$ and $\hat{q} \sqsubseteq \hat{q}_0^{k'}$ for some $k' \in \mathbb{N}$. Since $q_0 \neq \hat{q}_0$ and both prefixes are primitive words, Theorem 1 shows that the common prefix $\hat{q} = q_0 \cdot \bar{q}$ has to satisfy $|\hat{q}| <$ $|q_0| + |\hat{q}_0| -$ gcd$(|q_0|, |\hat{q}_0|)$, that is, $|\hat{q}_0| > |\bar{q}| +$ gcd$(|q_0|, |\hat{q}_0|)$. The assertion $\bar{q} \sqsubset \hat{q}_0 \sqsubset q_0$ now follows from a comparison of the lengths of $\bar{q}, \hat{q}_0 \sqsubseteq q_0$.

Now, let v be the suffix of q_0 defined by $\hat{q}_0^{k'} \cdot v = q_0 \sqsubset \hat{q}_0^{k'+1}$. Then $v \sqsubset \hat{q}_0$ and $v \cdot \bar{q} \sqsubset (\hat{q}_0)^2$. ∎

4   Asymptotic Growth

In this section we use the fact that $\sqrt[*]{P_q}$ is a suffix code to estimate the exponential growth of the family $(|Q_q \cap X^n|)_{n \in \mathbb{N}}$. In view of the identity $Q_q \setminus \{e\} = P_q^* \cdot q$ we have $|Q_q \cap X^{n+|q|}| = |P_q^* \cap X^n|$. So we may use P_q^* instead of Q_q.

First we mention that $\sqrt[*]{P_q}$ is a suffix code. This generalises Proposition 7 of [7].

Proposition 4 [8,12]. $\sqrt[*]{P_q}$ *is a suffix code.*

In order to derive the announced exponential growth we refer to Corollary 4 of [11] which shows that for every regular language $L \subseteq X^*$ there are constants $c_1, c_2 > 0$ and a $\lambda \geq 1$ such that

$$c_1 \cdot \lambda^n \leq_{\text{i.o.}} |L^* \cap X^n| \leq c_2 \cdot \lambda^n. \tag{7}$$

In the remainder of this section we use, without explicit reference, known results from the theory of formal power series, in particular about generating functions of languages and codes which can be found in the literature, e.g. in [2,3] or [9].

As P_q^* is a regular language the value λ_q for $L = P_q$ in Eq. (7) is $\lambda_q =$ $\limsup_{n \to \infty} \sqrt[n]{|P_q^* \cap X^n|}$ which is the inverse of the convergence radius of the power series $\mathfrak{s}_q^*(t) := \sum_{n \in \mathbb{N}} |P_q^* \cap X^n| \cdot t^n$. The series $\mathfrak{s}_q^*$ is also known as the *structure generating function* of the language P_q^*.

Since $\sqrt[*]{P_q}$ is a code, we have $\mathfrak{s}_q^*(t) = \frac{1}{1 - \mathfrak{s}_q(t)}$ where $\mathfrak{s}_q(t) := \sum_{v \in \sqrt[*]{P_q}} t^{|v|}$ is the structure generating function of the finite language $\sqrt[*]{P_q}$. Thus λ_q^{-1} is the smallest root of $1 - \mathfrak{s}_q(t)$. Hence λ_q is the largest root of the polynomial $p_q(t) := t^{|q|} - \sum_{v \in \sqrt[*]{P_q}} t^{|q| - |v|}$.

Summarising our observations we obtain the following.

Lemma 3. *Let* $q \in X^* \backslash \{e\}$. *Then there are constants* $c_{q,1}, c_{q,2} > 0$ *such that*

$$c_{q,1} \cdot \lambda_q^n \leq_{\text{i.o.}} |P_q^* \cap X^n| \leq c_{q,2} \cdot \lambda_q^n$$

where λ_q *is the largest (positive) root of the polynomial* $p_q(t)$.

5 Polynomials

Before proceeding to the proof of our main theorem we derive some properties of polynomials of the form $p(t) = t^n - \sum_{i \in M} t^i, M \subseteq \{i : i \in \mathbb{N} \land i < n\}$. We are mainly interested in results which are useful for comparing their maximal roots.

The polynomials $p(t) \in \hat{\mathcal{P}} := \{t^n - \sum_{i \in M} t^i : \emptyset \neq M \subseteq \{0, \ldots, n-1\}\}$ have the following easily verified properties.

$$p(0) \leq 0, p(1) \leq 0, p(2) \geq 1 \text{ and } p(t) < 0 \text{ for } 0 < t < 1. \tag{8}$$

$$\text{If } \varepsilon > 0 \text{ and } p(t') \geq 0 \text{ for some } t' > 0 \text{ then } p\big((1 + \varepsilon) \cdot t'\big) > 0. \tag{9}$$

Since $p(1) \leq 0$ and $p(2) \geq 1$ for $p(t) \in \hat{\mathcal{P}}$, Eq. (9) shows that once $p(t') \geq 0$, $t' \geq 1$, the polynomial $p(t)$ has no further root in the interval (t', ∞) and $p(t) \in \hat{\mathcal{P}}$ has exactly one root in the interval $[1, 2)$. This yields the following fundamental property.

Property 1. If t_0 is the positive root of the polynomial $p(t) \in \hat{\mathcal{P}}$ in $[1, 2)$ and $1 \leq t' < 2$ then $p(t') \leq 0$ if and only if $t' \leq t_0$.

For the roots of maximal modulus we have the following theorem.

Theorem 2 (Cauchy). *Let* $p(t) = \sum_{i=0}^n a_i \cdot t^i$ *be a complex polynomial. Then every root* t' *of* $p(t)$ *satisfies* $|t'| \leq t_0$ *where* t_0 *is the maximal root of the polynomial* $|a_n| \cdot t^n - \sum_{i=0}^{n-1} |a_i| \cdot t^i$.

This implies the following property of polynomials $p(t) \in \hat{\mathcal{P}}$.

$$\text{If } p(t) = 0 \text{ then } |t| \leq t_0. \tag{10}$$

From Property 1 we derive the following criterion to compare the maximal roots of polynomials in $\hat{\mathcal{P}}$.

Criterion 1. Let $p_1(t), p_2(t) \in \hat{\mathcal{P}}$ have maximal roots t_1 and t_2, respectively. Then $p_2(t_1) > 0$ if and only if $t_1 > t_2$. In particular, $p_2(t_1) > 0$ implies $t_1 > t_2$.

We conclude this section with a bound on the maximal root of certain polynomials in $\hat{\mathcal{P}}$.

Lemma 4. Let $p(t) = t^n - \sum_{i=0}^{m} t^i, n > m \geq 1$. Then $p(t) < 0$ for $1 \leq t \leq \sqrt[2n-m]{(m+1)^2}$ and $p(t) > 0$ for $\sqrt[n-m]{m+1} \leq t$.

Proof. The assertion follows from the inequality $t^n - (m+1) \cdot t^m < p(t) < t^n - (m+1) \cdot t^{m/2}$ when $t > 1$. The first part holds for $t > 1$, and the second uses the arithmetic-geometric-means inequality $\sum_{i=0}^{m} t^i > (m+1) \cdot \sqrt[m+1]{\prod_{i=0}^{m} t^i} = (m+1) \cdot t^{m/2}$.

The following special case is needed below.

Corollary 4. If $p(t) = t^n - \sum_{i=0}^{n-3} t^i, n \geq 4$, then $p(t) < 0$ for $1 \leq t \leq \sqrt[n+3]{(n-2)^2}$.

The subsequent sections are devoted to the proof of our main theorem.

6   Irreducible Quasiperiods

We start with irreducible quasiperiods. As quasiperiods $q, |q| \leq 2$, have trivially $P_q^* = \{q\}^*$, in the subsequent sections. we confine our considerations to quasiperiods q of length $|q| \geq 3$.

6.1   Extremal Polynomials

The polynomials $p_q(t)$ of irreducible quasiperiods have non-zero coefficients only for $|q|$ and $i < \frac{|q|}{2}$. Therefore we investigate the set

$$\mathcal{P} := \left\{ t^n - \sum_{i \in M} t^i : n \geq 1 \wedge \emptyset \neq M \subseteq \{j : j \leq \frac{n-1}{2}\} \right\}.$$

Let $p_n(t) := t^n - \sum_{i=0}^{\lfloor \frac{n-1}{2} \rfloor} t^i \in \mathcal{P}$.

Property 2. Let $p(t) \in \mathcal{P}$ a polynomial of degree n. Then $p_n(t) \leq p(t)$ for $t \in [1, 2]$, and $p_n(t)$ has the largest positive root among all polynomials of degree n in $\mathcal{P}$.

Proof. This follows from $t^n - \sum_{i=0}^{\lfloor \frac{n-1}{2} \rfloor} t^i \leq p(t)$ for $p(t) \in \mathcal{P}$ when $1 < t \leq 2$ and Criterion 1.

Observe that, for $n \geq 1$,

$$p_{2n+1}(t) = t^{2n+1} - \sum_{i=0}^{n} t^i \text{ and } p_{2n+2}(t) = t^{2n+2} - \sum_{i=0}^{n} t^i.$$

Moreover, $a^n b a^n$ and $a^n w a^n, w \in \{xb, bx\}, x \in X$ are quasiperiods corresponding to the extremal polynomials $p_{2n+1}(t) \in \mathcal{P}$ and $p_{2n+2}(t) \in \mathcal{P}$, respectively.

Let $Q_{\max} := \{a^n b a^n : n \geq 1\} \cup \{a^n w a^n : w \in X \cdot b \cup b \cdot X, n \geq 1\}$.

In what follows we will always assume that the first letter of a quasiperiod q is a. Then $Q_{\max}$ is the set of quasiperiods corresponding to the extremal polynomials.

Lemma 5. $Q_{max} := \{q : q \in X^* \wedge |q| \geq 3 \wedge p_q(t) = p_{|q|}(t)\}$

Proof. If $q \in Q_{max}$ then obviously $p_q(t) = p_{|q|}(t)$. Conversely, if $p_q(t) = t^{|q|} - \sum_{v \in \sqrt[*]{P_q}} t^{|q|-|v|} = p_{|q|}(t)$ then $\sqrt[*]{P_q} = \{v : v \sqsubseteq q \wedge |v| > \frac{|q|}{2}\}$. Then, in view of $q \sqsubseteq v \cdot q$, every prefix $w \sqsubseteq q$ of length $|w| < \frac{|q|}{2}$ is also a suffix of q. This is possible only for $q \in Q_{max}$ or $q \in \{a\}^*$.

In the sequel the positive root of $p_n(t)$ is denoted by λ_n. From Criterion 1 we obtain immediately.

Criterion 2. *Let $t \geq 1$. We have $t < \lambda_n$ if and only if $p_n(t) < 0$.*

Then Property 2 implies the following.

Theorem 3. *If $q \in X^*, |q| \geq 3$, is an irreducible quasiperiod then λ_q lambda$_{|q|}$, and $\lambda_q = \lambda_{|q|}$ if and only if $q \in Q_{max}$.*

6.2 The Ordering of the Maximal Roots λ_n

Before we proceed to the case of reducible quasiperiods we determine the ordering of the maximal roots λ_n. This will not only be interesting for itself but also useful for proving $\lambda_q < \lambda_{|q|}$ when q is reducible (see Eq. (21) below).

The extremal polynomials $p_n(t)$ satisfy the following general relations.[3]

$$t \cdot p_{2n-2}(t) - 1 = p_{2n-1}(t), \tag{11}$$
$$p_{2n}(t) - t^2 \cdot p_{2n-2}(t) = t^n - t - 1, \tag{12}$$
$$t^{n-2} \cdot p_{2n+1}(t) - (t^n + 1) \cdot p_{2n-1}(t) = \sum_{i=0}^{n-3} t^i, \text{ and} \tag{13}$$
$$t^{n-2} \cdot p_{2n+3}(t) - (t^{n+1} + 1) \cdot p_{2n}(t) = -t^n + \sum_{i=0}^{n-3} t^i \tag{14}$$

Lemma 6. *The polynomials $t^3 - t - 1$ and $t^5 - t^2 - t - 1 = (t^2 + 1) \cdot (t^3 - t - 1)$ have largest positive roots $\lambda_3 = \lambda_5$ among all polynomials in $\mathcal{P}$, $\lambda_5 > \lambda_4$ and $\lambda_{2n-1} > \lambda_{2n+1} > \lambda_{2n}$ for $n \geq 3$.*

Proof. From Eq. (11) we have $p_{2n+1}(\lambda_{2n}) = -1 < 0$ and, therefore, $\lambda_{2n} < \lambda_{2n+1}$ when $n \geq 1$.

Similarly, Eq. (13) yields $p_{2n+1}(\lambda_{2n-1}) = \lambda_{2n-1}^{-(n-2)} \cdot \sum_{i=0}^{n-3} \lambda_{2n-1}^i > 0$ which implies $\lambda_{2n+1} < \lambda_{2n-1}$ for $n \geq 3$ and $\lambda_3 = \lambda_5$ when $n = 2$.

So far we have ordered the 'odd' roots: $\lambda_3 = \lambda_5 > \lambda_7 > \lambda_9 > \cdots$. Next we are going to investigate the ordering of the 'even' roots λ_{2n}, $n \geq 2$.

To this end we derive the following bounds.

Lemma 7. *1. $\sqrt[3n+1]{n^2} \leq \lambda_{2n} \leq \sqrt[n+1]{n}$ and $\sqrt[3n-1]{n^2} \leq \lambda_{2n-1} \leq \sqrt[n]{n}$ for $n \geq 2$.
2. Let $n \geq 5$. Then $\lambda_{2n} \geq \sqrt[n-1]{2}$.*

---
[3] By convention, $\sum_{i=k}^m a_i = 0$ if $k > m$.

Proof.   1. follows from Lemma 4.

2. We calculate $p_{2n}(\sqrt[n-1]{2}) = 4 \cdot \sqrt[n-1]{4} - \sum_{i=0}^{n-1} \sqrt[n-1]{2^i} \leq 4 \cdot \sqrt[4]{4} - (2 + (n - 1)) = 4 \cdot \sqrt{2} - (n+1) < 0$ if $n \geq 5$ and the assertion follows with Property 1.

Remark 1. The lower bound of Lemma 7.2 does not exceed the lower bound in Lemma 7.1. However, the latter is more convenient for the purposes of the subsequent Lemma 8.

Lemma 8. *If $n \geq 5$ then $\lambda_{2n-2} > \lambda_{2n}$ and $\lambda_{2n} > \lambda_{2n+3}$.*

Proof. If $t \geq \sqrt[n-1]{2}$ then $t^n - t - 1 \geq t - 1 > 0$. Consequently, Eq. (12) implies $p_{2n}(\lambda_{2n-2}) > 0$ whence $\lambda_{2n} < \lambda_{2n-2}$.

Equation (14), Corollary 4 and the inequality $\lambda_{2n} \leq \sqrt[n+1]{n} \leq \sqrt[n+3]{(n-2)^2}$ when $n \geq 5$ imply $\lambda_{2n} \cdot p_{2n+3}(\lambda_{2n}) = -(\lambda_{2n}^n - \sum_{i=0}^{n-3} \lambda_{2n}^i) > 0$ whence $\lambda_{2n} > \lambda_{2n+3}$ for $n \geq 5$.

Since $p_8(\sqrt[3]{2}) > 0$, the proof of Lemma 8 cannot be applied to lower values of n. Thus it remains to establish the order of the λ_i for $i \leq 13$. To this end, we consider some special identities and use Criterion 2 and Lemma 8.

$$p_{12}(t) - (t^8 + t^5 + t^4 + t^2 + t) \cdot p_4(t) = t^2 - 1 \text{ and} \tag{15}$$
$$p_{13}(t) - t \cdot (t^8 + t^5 + t^4 + t^2 + t) \cdot p_4(t) = t^3 - t - 1 = p_3(t). \tag{16}$$

Lemma 9. $\lambda_8 > \lambda_{10} > \lambda_{13} > \lambda_4 > \lambda_{12}$

Proof. Lemma 8 shows $\lambda_8 > \lambda_{10} > \lambda_{13}$. Equation (15) yields $p_{12}(\lambda_4) = \lambda_4^2 - 1 > 0$ whence $\lambda_4 > \lambda_{12}$, and Eq. (16) yields $p_{13}(\lambda_4) = p_3(\lambda_4) < 0$, that is $\lambda_{13} > \lambda_4$. This shows our assertion.

For the remaining part we consider the identities

$$t^2 \cdot p_{11}(t) - (t^5 + 1) \cdot p_8(t) = -t^4 + t + 1 = -p_4(t) \tag{17}$$
$$p_{11}(t) - (t^5 + 1) \cdot p_6(t) = t^3 \cdot p_4(t) \text{ and} \tag{18}$$
$$t \cdot p_9(t) - (t^4 + 1) \cdot p_6(t) = -t^3 + 1. \tag{19}$$

Lemma 10. $\lambda_9 > \lambda_6 > \lambda_{11} > \lambda_8$

Proof. We use Eqs. (17) to (19). Then $p_{11}(\lambda_8) = -p_4(\lambda_8) < 0$ implies $\lambda_{11} > \lambda_8$, $p_{11}(\lambda_6) = \lambda_6^3 \cdot p_4(\lambda_6) > 0$ implies $\lambda_6 > \lambda_{11}$, and, finally, $\lambda_6 \cdot p_9(\lambda_6) = -\lambda_6^3 + 1$ implies $\lambda_9 > \lambda_6$.

Now Lemmata 6, 8, 9 and 10 yield the complete ordering of the values λ_n.

Theorem 4. *Let $\lambda_n, n \geq 3$, be the maximal root of the polynomial $p_n(t)$. Then the overall ordering of the values λ_n starts with*

$$\lambda_3 = \lambda_5 > \lambda_7 > \lambda_9 > \lambda_6 > \lambda_{11} > \lambda_8 > \lambda_{10} > \lambda_{13} > \lambda_4 > \lambda_{12}$$

and continues as follows $\lambda_{2n+1} > \lambda_{2n} > \lambda_{2n+3}, n \geq 7$.

From Lemma 7.1 we obtain immediately.

Corollary 5. *Let $M \subseteq \mathbb{N}\backslash\{0,1,2\}$ be infinite. Then $\inf\{\lambda_i : i \in M\} = 1$.*

7 Reducible Quasiperiods

Reducible quasiperiods q have a repeated prefix $q_0 = \min_{\sqsubseteq} P_q$ with $|q_0| \leq |q|/2$ and a repetition factor $k \geq 2$ such that $q = q_0^k \cdot \bar{q}$ where $\bar{q} \sqsubseteq q_0$. Moreover $|\bar{q}| < |q_0| \leq |q|/2$. Observe that q_0 is primitive.

We shall consider three cases depending on the relation between the lengths $n = |q|$, $\ell = |q_0|$, the length of the suffix $|\bar{q}| < |q_0|$ and the repetition factor $k \geq 2$.

7.1 The Case $|\bar{q}| + |q_0| \leq 2$

The case $|\bar{q}| + |q_0| \leq 2$ is the simplest one. Here, in view of $\bar{q} \sqsubseteq q_0$ we have necessarily $\bar{q} = e$ and $q \in a^* \cup \{ab\}^*$, $a, b \in X, a \neq b$ and, therefore, $\lambda_q = 1$ for $q \in a^* \cup \{ab\}^*$.

The remaining cases are divided according to the additional requirement $|q| - 2|q_0| \geq 3$ and its complementary one $|q| - 2|q_0| \leq 2$.

7.2 The Case $|q| - 2|q_0| \geq 3 \wedge |\bar{q}| + |q_0| \geq 3$

Under the restricting condition $|\bar{q}| < |q_0|$ this is equivalent to the fact that $|\bar{q}| \geq 3$ or the repetition factor $k \geq 3$. Moreover, then $|q| = 7$ (where $q = (ab)^3 a$) or $|q| \geq 9$.

From Eq. (4) we have

$$\sqrt[*]{P_q} \subseteq \{q_0\} \cup \{v : v \sqsubseteq q \wedge |v| > |q| - |q_0|\} \tag{20}$$

This implies that for $|q_0| \leq |q|/2$ the polynomials $p_q(t)$ have non-zero coefficients only for $|q| = n$, $|q| - |q_0| = n - \ell$ and $i < |q_0|$, that is, are of the form $p_q(t) = t^n - t^{n-\ell} - \sum_{i \in M_q} t^i$ where $M_q \subseteq \{i : i < \ell\}$.[4] Therefore, in the sequel we consider the positive roots of polynomials in

$$\mathcal{P}_{\mathrm{red}} := \Big\{ t^n - t^{n-\ell} - \sum_{i \in M} t^i : n \geq 1 \wedge \ell \leq \frac{n}{2} \wedge M \subseteq \{i : i < \ell\} \Big\}$$

Let $p_{n,\ell}(t) := t^n - t^{n-\ell} - \sum_{i=0}^{\ell-1} t^i \in \mathcal{P}_{\mathrm{red}}$ and $\lambda_{n,\ell}$ be its maximal root. Similar to the Property 2, Criterion 2 and Theorem 3 we have the following.

Property 3. Let $n \geq 3, \ell \leq \frac{n}{2}$ and $p(t) \in \mathcal{P}_{\mathrm{red}}$. Then $p(t) \geq p_{n,\ell}(t)$ for $t \in [1, 2]$, and $p_{n,\ell}(t)$ has the largest positive root among all polynomials of degree n and parameter ℓ in $\mathcal{P}_{\mathrm{red}}$.

Lemma 11. *If $q, |q| = n$, is a quasiperiod with $|q_0| = \ell \leq n/2$ then $p_q(t) \geq p_{n,\ell}(t)$ for $t \geq 1$, in particular, $\lambda_q \leq \lambda_{n,\ell}$.*

---

[4] Eq. (4) shows that even $M_q \subseteq \{i : i < \ell - 1\}$. For the Eq. (21) below this stronger version is not needed.

We have the following relation between the polynomials $p_n(t)$ and $p_{n,\ell}(t)$.

$$p_n(t) - t^\ell \cdot p_{n-2\ell}(t) = p_{n,\ell}(t), \text{ for } n - 2\ell \geq 3 \qquad (21)$$

This yields

Corollary 6. Let $n - 2 \cdot \ell \geq 3$. If $\lambda_n < \lambda_{n-2\ell}$ then $\lambda_{n,\ell} < \lambda_n$.

Proof. If $\lambda_n < \lambda_{n-2\ell}$ then $p_{n-2\ell}(\lambda_n) < p_{n-2\ell}(\lambda_{n-2\ell}) = 0$. Thus $p_{n,\ell}(\lambda_n) = \lambda_n^\ell \cdot p_{n-2\ell}(\lambda_n) > 0$, that is, $\lambda_n > \lambda_{n,\ell}$.

Next we show the relation $\lambda_q < \lambda_{|q|}$ for all quasiperiods q having $|q_0| \leq |q|/2$ and $|q_0| + |\bar{q}| \geq 3$.

Lemma 12. Let $|q| - 2|q_0| \geq 3$ and $|q_0| + |\bar{q}| \geq 3$. Then $\lambda_q < \lambda_{|q|}$.

Proof. Above we have shown that $|q| - 2|q_0| \geq 3$ and $|q_0| + |\bar{q}| \geq 3$ imply $|q| \geq 7$ or $|q| \geq 10$ according to whether $|q|$ is odd or even.

The ordering of Theorem 4 and Corollary 6 show $\lambda_n > \lambda_{n,\ell}$ for all odd values $n \geq 7$ and for all even values $n \geq 12$.

It remains to consider the exceptional case when $|q| = 10$. Here $|q| - 2|q_0| \geq 3$ and $|q_0| + |\bar{q}| \geq 3$ imply $|q_0| = 3$. Then Eq. (4) shows $\sqrt[*]{P_q} = \{q_0, q\}$ whence $p_q(t) = t^{10} - t^7 - 1 = p_{10}(t) - t^2 \cdot p_5(t)$.

From $\lambda_5 > \lambda_{10}$ and $p_{10}(\lambda_{10}) = 0$ we have $p_q(\lambda_{10}) = -\lambda_{10}^2 \cdot p_5(\lambda_{10}) > 0$, that is, $\lambda_q < \lambda_{10}$.

Remark 2. In the exceptional case when $n = 10$ and $\ell = 3$ we have indeed $\lambda_{10,3} > \lambda_{10}$. This follows from $p_{10}(t) - p_{10,3}(t) = t^3 \cdot p_4(t)$ and $\lambda_4 < \lambda_{10}$.

This shows also that, in contrast to Property 2, not for every polynomial $p_{n,\ell}(t)$ there is a quasiperiod q such that $p_q(t) = p_{n,\ell}(t)$.

7.3   The Case $|q| - 2|q_0| \leq 2 \wedge |q_0| + |\bar{q}| \geq 3$

This amounts to $|q| = 2 \cdot |q_0| + |\bar{q}|$ where $|\bar{q}| \in \{0, 1, 2\}$.

Here we have to go into more detail and to take into consideration also the reduced quasiperiod $\hat{q} = q_0 \cdot \bar{q}$ of q and its repeated prefix $\hat{q}_0 = \min_{\sqsubseteq} P_{\hat{q}}$. Observe that both repeated prefixes $q_0, \hat{q}_0$ are primitive.

Taking into consideration the repeated prefix $\hat{q}_0$, for $q = q_0^k \cdot \bar{q}, k \geq 2$, we have from Eqs. (5) and (6)

$$p_q(t) \in \left\{ t^{|q|} - t^{|q|-|q_0|} - \sum_{i \in M} t^i : M \subseteq \{0, \ldots, |\hat{q}| - |\hat{q}_0|\} \right\}.$$

Observe that $|\hat{q}| - |\hat{q}_0| = |q_0| - (|\hat{q}_0| - |\bar{q}|) < |q_0|$.

Let $\mathcal{P}'_{red} := \left\{ t^n - t^\ell - \sum_{i \in M} t^i : n > \ell > j \wedge M \subseteq \{0, \ldots, \ell - j\} \right\}$ and $p_{n,\ell,j}(t) = t^n - t^\ell - \sum_{i=0}^{\ell-j} t^i$. Then similar to Property 3 and Lemma 11 we have

Property 4. Let $n, \ell \geq 3, \ell \leq \frac{n}{2}, \ell > j$, and $p(t) \in \mathcal{P}'_{red}$. Then $p(t) \geq p_{n,\ell,j}(t)$ for $t \in [1, 2]$, and $p_{n,\ell,j}(t)$ has the largest positive root among all polynomials of degree n and parameters ℓ and j in $\mathcal{P}'_{red}$.

Lemma 13. *If $q, |q| = n$, is a quasiperiod with $|q_0| = \ell \leq n/2$ and $|\hat{q}_0| - |\bar{q}| \geq j$ then $p_q(t) \geq p_{n,\ell,j}(t)$ for $t \geq 1$, in particular, $\lambda_q \leq \lambda_{n,\ell,j}$.*

We consider the cases $|\bar{q}| \in \{0, 1, 2\}$ separately.

The Case $q = q_0^2 \wedge |\bar{q}| = 0$. In view of Sect. 7.1 we may consider only the case when $|q_0| \geq 3$. Here we have the following relation between $p_{2\ell}(t)$ and $p_{2\ell,\ell,3}(t)$.

$$p_{2\ell}(t) - p_{2\ell,\ell,3}(t) = t^{\ell-2}(t^2 - t - 1) \tag{22}$$

Lemma 14. *If $q = q_0^2$ and $|q_0| = \ell \geq 3$ then $\lambda_q < \lambda_{|q|}$.*

Proof. First we suppose $|\hat{q}_0| \geq 3$. Then $|\hat{q}_0| - |\bar{q}| \geq 3$ and Property 4 and Lemma 13 yield $p_q(t) \geq p_{2\ell,\ell,3}(t)$ for $t \in [1, 2]$. Now Eq. (22) shows $p_q(\lambda_{2\ell}) \geq p_{2\ell,\ell,3}(\lambda_{2\ell}) = -\lambda_{2\ell}^{\ell-2}(\lambda_{2\ell}^2 - \lambda_{2\ell} - 1)$. Since $t^2 - t - 1 < 0$ and $p_q(t) \geq p_{2\ell,\ell,3}(t)$ for $1 \leq t \leq \lambda_3 = \max\{\lambda_n : n \in \mathbb{N}\}$ and $\lambda_{2\ell} < \lambda_3$, it follows $p_q(\lambda_{2\ell}) > 0$, that is $\lambda_q < \lambda_{2\ell}$.

It remains to consider $1 \leq |\hat{q}_0| \leq 2$. If $\hat{q}_0 \in a^*$ then $q_0 = a^\ell$ which is not primitive. Thus $\hat{q}_0 = ab$ and, since q_0 is primitive, $q_0 = (ab)^m a$, $m \geq 1$, and $q = q_0^2 = (ab)^m a \cdot (ab)^m a$. We obtain $\sqrt[*]{P_q} = \{(ab)^m a \cdot (ab)^i : i = 0, \ldots, m\}$ and, consequently, $p_q(t) = t^{4m+2} - \sum_{i=0}^m t^{2i+1}$. From $p_q(t) = t^{4m+2} - \sum_{i=0}^m t^{2i+1} \geq p_{4m+2}(t) - t^{2m-2}(t^3 - t^2 - 1)$ and $t^3 - t^2 - 1 < 0$ for $1 < t \leq \lambda_3$, in the same way as above, we obtain $p_q(\lambda_{4m+2}) > 0$.

The Case $q = q_0^2 \cdot \bar{q} \wedge |\bar{q}| = 1$. Here we have the following relation between $p_{2\ell+1}(t)$ and $p_{2\ell+1,\ell,2}(t)$.

$$p_{2\ell+1}(t) - p_{2\ell+1,\ell,2}(t) = t^{\ell-1}(t^2 - t - 1) \tag{23}$$

Lemma 15. *If $q = q_0^2 \cdot a, a \in X$, then $\lambda_q < \lambda_{|q|}$.*

Proof. First we suppose $|\hat{q}_0| - |\bar{q}| \geq 2$. Then $\ell = |q_0| \geq |\hat{q}_0| \geq 3$, and Property 4 and Eq. (23) yield $p_q(\lambda_{2\ell+1}) \geq p_{2\ell+1,\ell,2}(\lambda_{2\ell+1}) = p_{2\ell+1}(\lambda_{2\ell+1}) - \lambda_{2\ell+1}^{\ell-1}(\lambda_{2\ell+1}^2 - \lambda_{2\ell+1} - 1)$.

Since $t^2 - t - 1 < 0$ and $p_q(t) \geq p_{2\ell+1,\ell,2}(t)$ for $1 < t \leq \lambda_3$ and $\lambda_{2\ell+1} < \lambda_3$, it follows $p_q(\lambda_{2\ell+1}) > 0$, that is $\lambda_q < \lambda_{2\ell+1}$.

It remains to consider $|\hat{q}_0| = 2$. Then Lemma 2 implies $\hat{q}_0 = q_0$ whence $q = ababa$. Now, one easily verifies $\lambda_{ababa} < \lambda_5 = \lambda_3$

The Case $q = q_0^2 \cdot \bar{q} \wedge |\bar{q}| = 2$. Here we have the following relation between $p_{2\ell+2}(t)$ and $p_{2\ell+2,\ell,2}(t)$.

$$p_{2\ell+2}(t) - p_{2\ell+2,\ell,2}(t) = t^{\ell-1}(t^3 - t - 1) \tag{24}$$

Lemma 16. *If $q = q_0^2 \cdot \bar{q}$ with $|\bar{q}| = 2$ then $\lambda_q < \lambda_{|q|}$.*

Proof. First we suppose $|\hat{q}_0| \geq 4$. Then Property 4 and Eq. (24) yield
$p_{2\ell+2}(\lambda_{2\ell+2}) - p_q(\lambda_{2\ell+2}) \leq p_{2\ell+2}(\lambda_{2\ell+2}) - p_{2\ell+2,\ell,2}(\lambda_{2\ell+2}) = \lambda_{2\ell+2}^{\ell-1}(\lambda_{2\ell+2}^3 - \lambda_{2\ell+2} - 1)$.

Since $t^3 - t - 1 < 0$ and $p_q(t) \geq p_{2\ell+2,\ell,2}(t)$ for $1 < t \leq \max\{\lambda_{2n} : n \in \mathbb{N}\} < \lambda_3$ and $\lambda_{2\ell+2} < \lambda_3$, it follows $p_q(\lambda_{2\ell+2}) > 0$, that is, $\lambda_q < \lambda_{2\ell+2}$.

It remains to consider $|\hat{q}_0| = 3$. Again, Lemma 2 implies $\hat{q}_0 = q_0$. Then $|q_0| = 3$ and $|q| = 8$, and Eq. (4) yields $\sqrt[*]{P_q} \subseteq \{q_0, v, q\}$ where $v \sqsubset q$ and $|v| = |q| - 1 = 7$ whence $p_q(t) \geq t^8 - t^5 - t - 1 = p_8(t) - t^2 \cdot p_3(t)$ for $1 \leq t \leq \lambda_3$. This shows $p_q(\lambda_8) \geq -\lambda_8^2 \cdot p_3(\lambda_8) > 0$, that is, $\lambda_q < \lambda_8$.

Our main theorem then follows from Theorem 3 and the results of Sect. 7.

Theorem 5. *If $q \in X^*, |q| \geq 3$, is a quasiperiod then $\lambda_q \leq \lambda_{|q|}$, and $\lambda_q = \lambda_{|q|}$ if and only if $q \in Q_{max}$.*

References

1. Apostolico, A., Farach, M., Iliopoulos, C.S.: Optimal superprimitivity testing for strings. Inf. Process. Lett. **39**(1), 17–20 (1991). https://doi.org/10.1016/0020-0190(91)90056-N
2. Berstel, J., Perrin, D.: Theory of Codes. Academic Press, Orlando (1985)
3. Berstel, J., Reutenauer, C.: Rational Series and Their Languages, EATCS Monographs on Theoretical Computer Science, vol. 12. Springer, Berlin (1988)
4. Brzozowski, J.A.: Roots of star events. J. ACM **14**(3), 466–477 (1967). https://doi.org/10.1145/321406.321409
5. Fine, N.J., Wilf, H.S.: Uniqueness theorems for periodic functions. Proc. Am. Math. Soc. **16**, 109–114 (1965)
6. Lothaire, M.: Combinatorics on Words, 2nd edn. Cambridge University Press, Cambridge (1997)
7. Mouchard, L.: Normal forms of quasiperiodic strings. Theor. Comput. Sci. **249**(2), 313–324 (2000). https://doi.org/10.1016/S0304-3975(00)00065-7
8. Polley, R., Staiger, L.: The maximal subword complexity of quasiperiodic infinite words. In: McQuillan, I., Pighizzini, G. (eds.) Proceedings 12th DCFS, Electronic Proceedings in Theoretical Computer Science (EPTCS), vol. 31, pp. 169–176. Open Publishing Association (2010)
9. Salomaa, A., Soittola, M.: Automata-Theoretic Aspects of Formal Power Series. Springer, New York (1978). https://doi.org/10.1007/978-1-4612-6264-0
10. Shyr, H.J.: Free Monoids and Languages, 3rd edn. Hon Min Book Company, Taichung (2001)
11. Staiger, L.: The entropy of finite-state ω-languages. Probl. Control Inform. Theory/Problemy Upravlen. Teor. Inform. **14**(5), 383–392 (1985)
12. Staiger, L.: Quasiperiods of infinite words. In: Bellow, A., Calude, C.S., Zamfirescu, T. (eds.) Mathematics Almost Everywhere. In Memory of Solomon Marcus, pp. 17–36. World Scientific, Hackensack (2018)

Insertion-Deletion with Substitutions II

Martin Vu[1(✉)] and Henning Fernau[2(✉)] iD

[1] FB3 - Informatik, Universität Bremen, Bremen, Germany
martin.vu@uni-bremen.de
[2] Universität Trier, Fachber. 4 – Abteilung Informatikwissenschaften,
54286 Trier, Germany
fernau@uni-trier.de

Abstract. We discuss substitutions as a further type of operations, added to (in particular, one-sided) insertion-deletion systems. This way, we obtain new characterizations of classes of context-sensitive and recursively enumerable languages. Moreover, we obtain new families of languages containing all regular or contained in the context-free languages.

Keywords: Computational completeness · Context-sensitive · Insertions · Deletions · Substitutions

1 Introduction

Insertion-deletion systems, or ins-del systems for short, are well established as computational devices and as a research topic within Formal Languages throughout the past decades, starting with the works of Haussler and Kari [3,4].

However, from its very beginning, papers highlighting the potential use of such systems in modelling DNA computing also discussed the replacement of single letters (possibly within some context) by other letters, an operation called *substitution* in [2,5]. Interestingly, all theoretical studies on grammatical mechanisms involving insertions and deletions omitted including the substitution operation in their studies. We are stepping into this gap by studying ins-del systems with substitutions, or ins-del-sub systems for short. Omitted proofs are marked with a star (∗). We also refer to the master thesis [14] and the companion paper [15] for proofs and further results.

2 Basic Definitions and Observations

Definitions. We assume the reader to be familiar with the basics of formal language theory. Contrasting their traditional exposition, we are now describing *insertion-deletion-substitution* systems, or ins-del-sub systems for short, in terms of the better known category of rewriting systems. Let $u, x, y, v \in V^*$. Then, $uv \to uyv$ is called an *insertion*, $uxv \to uv$ is called a *deletion*, and $uxv \to uyv$ is called a *substitution* if $|x| = |y| = 1$. More traditionally, these types of rules are written as $(u, y, v)_{\text{ins}}$, $(u, x, v)_{\text{del}}$, or $(u, x \to y, v)$, respectively, omitting

© Springer Nature Switzerland AG 2020
G. Jirásková and G. Pighizzini (Eds.): DCFS 2020, LNCS 12442, pp. 231–243, 2020.
https://doi.org/10.1007/978-3-030-62536-8_19

the subscripts ins or del if clear from the context. Formally, we define an ins-del-sub system to be a sixtuple $ID_\varsigma = (V, T, A, I, D, S)$, where $V, T \subseteq V$ are alphabets, $A \subseteq V^*$ is a finite set of axioms, and I, D and S are finite sets of insertion, deletion and substitution rules, respectively. If $S = \emptyset$, we face an insertion-deletion system, or ins-del system for short. The system ID_ς defines the relation $\Longrightarrow \subseteq V^* \times V^*$ by $w \Longrightarrow w'$ iff $w = w_1 uxv w_2$, $w' = w_1 uyv w_2$, and $uxv \to uyv \in I \cup D \cup S$. We define the closures $\Longrightarrow^*$ and $\Longrightarrow^+$ as usual. The language generated by the ins-del-sub system ID_ς is defined as $L(ID_\varsigma) = \{w \in T^* \mid \alpha \Longrightarrow^* w, \ \alpha \in A\}$. For clarity, we write $\Longrightarrow \subseteq V^* \times V^*$ for the one-step derivation relation of an ins-del system. The *size* of ID_ς, defined by the tuple $(n, m, m'; , q, q'; r, r')$, describes its descriptional complexity, where

$$
\begin{array}{ll}
n = \max\{|y| \mid (u, y, v) \in I\}, & p = \max\{|x| \mid (u, x, v) \in D\}, \\
m = \max\{|u| \mid (u, y, v) \in I\}, & q = \max\{|u| \mid (u, x, v) \in D\}, \\
m' = \max\{|v| \mid (u, y, v) \in I\}, & q' = \max\{|v| \mid (u, x, v) \in D\}, \\
r = \max\{|u| \mid (u, x \to y, v) \in S\}, & r' = \max\{|v| \mid (u, x \to y, v) \in S\}.
\end{array}
$$

Especially, the size of an ins-del system can be described by the tuple $(n, m, m'; p, q, q')$. By $\text{INS}_n^{m,m'} \text{DEL}_p^{q,q'}$ we denote the family of all ins-del systems of size $(n, m, m'; p, q, q')$ [1,13]. Depending on the context, we also denote the family of languages characterized by ins-del systems of size $(n, m, m'; p, q, q')$ by $\text{INS}_n^{m,m'} \text{DEL}_p^{q,q'}$. We call a family $\text{INS}_n^{0,0} \text{DEL}_p^{0,0}$ a family of *context-free* ins-del systems, while we call a family $\text{INS}_n^{m,m'} \text{DEL}_p^{q,q'}$ with $(m + m' > 0 \wedge mm' = 0)$ or $(q + q' > 0 \wedge qq' = 0)$ a family of *one-sided* ins-del systems. $\text{INS}_n^{m,m'} \text{DEL}_p^{q,q'} \text{SUB}^{r,r'}$ refers to a similar convention for ins-del-sub systems.

Example 1 (An insertion-deletion system with substitution rules).

Consider the system $ID_\varsigma = (V, T, A, I, D, S)$ with $V = T = \{a, b, c, d\}$, $A = \{acd\}$, $I = \{(c, c, \lambda), (c, b, \lambda), (a, d, \lambda), (a, a, \lambda)\}$, $D = \emptyset$, $S = \{(\lambda, a \to b, \lambda)\}$. Example derivation:

$$
acd \Longrightarrow^5_{(a,a,\lambda)_{\text{ins}}} aaaaaacd \Longrightarrow^2_{(c,b,\lambda)_{\text{ins}}} aaaaaacbbd \Longrightarrow^6_{(\lambda, a \to b, \lambda)_{\text{sub}}} bbbbbbcbbd.
$$

The language generated by ID_ς is $L(ID_\varsigma) = (a|b)(a|b|d)^* c(c|b)^* d$.

Let us define the term *resolve*. Let $ID_\varsigma = (V, T, A, I, D, S)$ be an ins-del-sub system. We say that a nonterminal $X \in V \backslash T$ of ID_ς is resolved if X is either deleted or substituted. Clearly, in any terminal derivation of ID_ς, all nonterminals must be resolved at some point of the derivation. Nonterminal X may be resolved by being substituted with a nonterminal Y, which in turn must be resolved.

Results. Now, we are ready to survey old and new results in this area. Ins-del systems have been extensively studied regarding the question if they can describe all of the recursively enumerable languages. Let us summarize first computational completeness results by listing the classes of languages known to be equal to RE: $\text{INS}_1^{1,1} \text{DEL}_1^{1,1}$ [12], $\text{INS}_3^{0,0} \text{DEL}_2^{0,0}$ and $\text{INS}_2^{0,0} \text{DEL}_3^{0,0}$ [8], $\text{INS}_1^{1,1} \text{DEL}_1^{0,0}$ [10, Theorem 6.3], $\text{INS}_2^{0,0} \text{DEL}_1^{1,1}$ [6], $\text{INS}_2^{0,1} \text{DEL}_2^{0,0}$ and $\text{INS}_1^{1,2} \text{DEL}_1^{1,0}$ [9], $\text{INS}_1^{1,0} \text{DEL}_1^{1,2}$ [6].

By way of contrast, the following language families are known not to be equal to RE, the first one is even a subset of CF: $INS_2^{0,0}DEL_2^{0,0}$ [13], $INS_1^{1,1}DEL_1^{1,0}$ [9], $INS_1^{1,0}DEL_1^{1,1}$ [6], $INS_1^{1,0}DEL_2^{0,0}$ and $INS_2^{0,0}DEL_1^{1,0}$ [7].

In this paper, we put special emphasis on extending one-sided ins-del systems with substitutions, because we can conclude that $INS_1^{m,m'}DEL_1^{q,q'}SUB^{1,1} = RE$ for any $m, m', q, q' \geq 0$ from our findings on extending context-free ins-del systems with substitutions, which we collected in the *companion paper* [15]; these results are also contained in [14]. Further computationally complete classes are:

- $INS_1^{1,0}DEL_1^{1,0}SUB^{0,1}$, $INS_1^{0,1}DEL_1^{0,1}SUB^{1,0}$,
- $INS_1^{1,1}DEL_1^{1,0}SUB^{1,0}$, $INS_1^{1,1}DEL_1^{0,1}SUB^{0,1}$,
- $INS_1^{1,0}DEL_2^{0,0}SUB^{0,1}$, $INS_1^{0,1}DEL_2^{0,0}SUB^{1,0}$.

$INS_1^{0,1}DEL_1^{1,1}SUB^{0,0}$ is not computationally complete, as it cannot even describe all regular languages. Moreover, $INS_1^{1,0}DEL_0^{0,0}SUB^{0,1}$ is a proper super-class of REG and a sub-class of CS, while $INS_1^{1,0}DEL_1^{0,0}SUB^{0,0}$, which equals $INS_1^{1,0}DEL_0^{0,0}SUB^{0,0}$, is a proper sub-class of CF.

Normal Forms. As in the case of ins-del systems without substitution rules [1], we define a *normal form* for ins-del-sub systems. An ins-del-sub system

$$ID_\varsigma = (V \cup \{\$\}, T, A, I, D \cup \{(\lambda, \$, \lambda)\}, S)$$

of size $(n, m, m'; p, q, q'; r, r')$ is said to be in normal form if

- for any $(u, a, v) \in I$, it holds that $|a| = n$, $|u| = m$ and $|v| = m'$;
- for any $(u, a, v) \in D$, it holds that $|a| = p$, $|u| = q$ and $|v| = q'$;
- for any $(u, a \to b, v) \in S$, it holds that $|u| = r$ and $|v| = r'$.

Theorem 1. (*)   *For every ins-del-sub system ID_ς of size $(n, m, m'; p, q, q'; r, r')$, there is an equivalent ins-del-sub system ID'_ς of the same size in normal form.*

Further Observations. In the following, ^{R} denotes the reversal (mirror) operator.

Lemma 1. $L \in INS_n^{m,m'}DEL_p^{q,q'}SUB^{r,r'}$ *iff* $L^R \in INS_n^{m',m}DEL_p^{q',q}SUB^{r',r}$.

Lemma 2. *Let $\mathcal{L}$ be a family of languages that is closed under reversal. Then:*

1. $\mathcal{L} \subseteq INS_n^{m,m'}DEL_p^{q,q'}SUB^{r,r'}$ *iff* $\mathcal{L} \subseteq INS_n^{m',m}DEL_p^{q',q}SUB^{r',r}$.
2. $INS_n^{m,m'}DEL_p^{q,q'}SUB^{r,r'} \subseteq \mathcal{L}$ *iff* $INS_n^{m',m}DEL_p^{q',q}SUB^{r',r} \subseteq \mathcal{L}$.

Due to the definition of ins-del-sub systems, the following result is clear.

Lemma 3. $INS_n^{m,m'}DEL_p^{q,q'} \subseteq INS_n^{m,m'}DEL_p^{q,q'}SUB^{r,r'}$.

Whether this inclusion is proper is the question that will be addressed in the following sections. We will see that while in some cases an arbitrary system of size $(n, m, m'; p, q, q', r, r')$ can be simulated by a system of size $(n, m, m'; p, q, q')$, this is not the general case. Furthermore, we will see that families $INS_n^{m,m'} DEL_p^{q,q'}$, which are not computationally complete, may reach computational completeness via an extension with substitution rules. Additionally, we will see below that families of ins-del systems which are equally powerful may no longer be after being extended with the same class of substitution rules, i.e., we have $INS_{n_1}^{m_1,m_1'} DEL_{p_1}^{q_1,q_1'} = INS_{n_2}^{m_2,m_2'} DEL_{p_2}^{q_2,q_2'}$, but possibly $INS_{n_1}^{m_1,m_1'} DEL_{p_1}^{q_1,q_1'} SUB^{r,r'} \subset INS_{n_2}^{m_2,m_2'} DEL_{p_2}^{q_2,q_2'} SUB^{r,r'}$. The reverse case, i.e., not equally powerful families becoming equally powerful after being extended with substitution, might occur, as well.

As the insertion rule (u, x, v) corresponds to the monotone rewriting rule $uv \rightarrow uav$ and similarly, substitution rules are monotone, a monotone grammar can simulate derivations of an insertion-substitution system. (More technically speaking, we have to do the replacements on the level of pseudo-terminals N_a for each terminal a and also add rules $N_a \rightarrow a$, all minor details.) Hence, we can conclude:

Theorem 2. *For any integers* $m, m', n, r, r' \geq 0$, $INS_n^{m,m'} DEL_0^{0,0} SUB^{r,r'} \subseteq CS$.

3   Main Results

We will focus on non-context-free ins-del systems, which are extended with substitution rules. We will discuss the computational power of various one-sided ins-del systems extended with substitution rules. In particular, we are interested in one-sided ins-del systems which are not computationally complete and wish to answer whether extending those systems with substitution rules yields a computationally complete system. Furthermore, we wish to answer whether an extension with context-free or one-sided substitution rules is sufficient for reaching computational completeness.

Remark 1. Notice that only context-free or one-sided substitution rules are of interest here, as we have shown the equality $INS_1^{0,0} DEL_1^{0,0} SUB^{1,1} = RE$ in the companion paper [15]. Hence, $INS_1^{m,m'} DEL_1^{q,q'} SUB^{1,1} = RE$ holds for any m, m', q, q'. Additionally, we have shown that $INS_1^{0,0} DEL_0^{0,0} SUB^{1,1} = CS$ holds. Therefore, $CS = INS_1^{0,0} DEL_0^{0,0} SUB^{1,1} \subseteq INS_1^{m,m'} DEL_0^{0,0} SUB^{1,1}$ holds for any m, m'. By Theorem 2, all these classes even characterize CS.

3.1   Extension with Context-Free Substitution

In this subsection, we wish to answer the question whether, given a system ID_ς with substitution rules of size $(n, m, m'; p, q, q'; 0, 0)$ with $(m + m' > 0 \wedge mm' = 0)$ or $(q + q' > 0 \wedge qq' = 0)$, is there a system ID without substitution rules of size $(n, m, m'; p, q, q')$, such that $L(ID_\varsigma) = L(ID)$ as in the case of context-free ins-del systems extended with context-free substitution rules, as shown in the companion paper [15]. We will show that in general this is not the case, considering the language generated by the system described in Example 1.

Lemma 4. *The language $L = (a|b)(a|b|d)^*c(c|b)^*d$ cannot be generated by an ins-del system of size $(1, 1, 0; 0, 0, 0)$.*

Proof. Assume there is a system $ID = (V', T, A', I', \emptyset)$ of size $(1, 1, 0; 0, 0, 0)$ such that $L(ID) = L$. Then clearly $V' = T$, as there are no deletion rules. Furthermore, let $\gamma = \max\{|\alpha| \mid \alpha \in A'\}$. As $b^n d^n cbd \in L$, $n > \gamma$, and $L(ID) = L$, there is a derivation starting from some $\alpha \in A'$, such that $\alpha \Longrightarrow^* b^n d^n cbd$. At some point of the derivation, in order to form the substring d^n, a rule adding a letter d has to have been used, because $n > \gamma$. All possible insertion rules that could have been used are (λ, d, λ), (b, d, λ) and (d, d, λ). Analyzing the language L, we see that every word of the language includes at least one letter c which may be followed by an arbitrary number of letters c and b. However, there is only exactly one letter d appearing after the first c. Assuming that $\alpha \Longrightarrow^* b^n d^n cbd$ for some $\alpha \in A'$, either of the rules (λ, d, λ), (b, d, λ) or (d, d, λ) would allow $w \Longrightarrow^* b^n d^n cbd \Longrightarrow b^n d^n cbdd$ with $b^n d^n cbdd \notin L$, yielding a contradiction. □

Corollary 1. $INS_1^{1,0} DEL_0^{0,0} \subset INS_1^{1,0} DEL_0^{0,0} SUB^{0,0}$.

We will now show that the language generated by an ins-del-sub system ID_ς of size $(1, 1, 0; 0, 0, 0; 0, 0)$ is included in CF.

Theorem 3. *For every given ins-del-sub systems ID_ς of size $(1, 1, 0; 0, 0, 0; 0, 0)$, one can construct a context-free grammar G such that $L(ID_\varsigma) = L(G)$.*

Proof. Let ID_ς be an arbitrary ins-del-sub system of size $(1, 1, 0; 0, 0, 0; 0, 0)$ and $ID'_\varsigma = (V', T', A', I', \{(\lambda, \$, \lambda)\}, S')$ be the normal form of ID_ς. We define $G = (\{N_a \mid a \in V'\} \cup \{S\}, T, P, S)$. Without loss of generality, we assume $S \notin V'$. We define the set of context-free rules as $P = P_1 \cup P_2 \cup P_3 \cup P_4 \cup \{N_\$ \rightarrow \lambda\}$, with

$$P_1 = \{N_a \rightarrow N_a N_b \mid (a, b, \lambda) \in I'\}, \ P_2 = \{N_a \rightarrow N_b \mid (\lambda, a \rightarrow b, \lambda) \in S'\},$$
$$P_3 = \{N_a \rightarrow a \mid a \in T\}, \qquad\qquad P_4 = \{S \rightarrow N_{a_1} \dots N_{a_n} \mid a_1 \dots a_n \in A\}.$$

The basic idea is as follows. The axioms $a_1 \dots a_n \in A$ are simulated by context-free rules $S \rightarrow N_{a_1} \dots N_{a_n}$ from P_4. Every insertion rule (a, b, λ) corresponds to a context-free rule $N_a \rightarrow N_a N_b$ in P_1 and vice versa. The same correspondence exists between a substitution rule $(\lambda, a \rightarrow b, \lambda)$ and a context-free rule $N_a \rightarrow N_b$ in P_2. Furthermore, the rule $N_\$ \rightarrow \lambda$ simulates the deletion rule $(\lambda, \$, \lambda)$. Together with the rules from P_3, they terminate the derivation of G. □

Interestingly, adding context-free deletion rules does not increase the power of $INS_1^{1,0} DEL_0^{0,0} SUB^{0,0}$. Namely, deletion rules can be simulated by substitution rules, keeping in mind that the only purpose of symbols that are to be deleted is to serve as context of insertion rules. Working out this idea leads to:

Theorem 4. (*) $INS_1^{1,0} DEL_1^{0,0} SUB^{0,0} = INS_1^{1,0} DEL_0^{0,0} SUB^{0,0}$.

Let $ID = (V, T, A, I, D)$ be an ins-del system of size $(1, 1, 1; 1, 1, 1)$ in *modified normal form*, i.e., there is a single context-free deletion rule (λ, X, λ) that is only applicable to the first or last symbol of a sentential form, as discussed in [14]. Assume that all rules of ID are bijectively labelled. Define $ID_\varsigma = (V', T, A, I', D', S)$, with

$$V' = V \cup \{X_i \mid i \text{ is the label of a rule in } I \text{ or } D\},$$
$$I' = \{(u, X_i, \lambda) \mid i \text{ labels an insertion rule } (u, a, v)\} \text{ and}$$
$$D' = \{(u, X_i, \lambda) \mid i \text{ labels a deletion rule } (u, a, v) \neq (\lambda, X, \lambda)\} \cup \{(\lambda, X, \lambda)\}.$$

The set of substitution rules is defined as $S = S_1 \cup S_2$, with

$$S_1 = \{(\lambda, X_i \to a, v) \mid i \text{ labels an insertion rule } (u, a, v)\},$$
$$S_2 = \{(\lambda, a \to X_i, v) \mid i \text{ labels a deletion rule } (u, a, v) \neq (\lambda, X, \lambda)\}.$$

Construction 1: Construction of an ins-del-sub system of size $(1, 1, 0; 1, 1, 0; 0, 1)$

By way of contrast, without substitutions, we can prove by using Example 1:

Proposition 1. (∗) $INS_1^{1,0} DEL_0^{0,0} \subsetneq INS_1^{1,0} DEL_1^{0,0}$.

Due to Theorem 3, the following can be concluded:

Corollary 2. $INS_1^{1,0} DEL_0^{0,0} SUB^{0,0} = INS_1^{1,0} DEL_1^{0,0} SUB^{0,0} \subseteq CF$.

Using the regular language $(ba)^+$ (as in [1, Theorem 9.28]), we can show that the inclusion in Corollary 2 is proper.

Theorem 5. (∗) $REG \setminus INS_1^{1,0} DEL_1^{1,1} SUB^{0,0} \neq \emptyset$.

Due to Theorem 5, we reach the following conclusions.

Corollary 3. $REG \setminus INS_1^{1,0} DEL_0^{1,0} SUB^{0,0} \neq \emptyset$, $REG \setminus INS_1^{1,0} DEL_0^{0,0} SUB^{0,0} \neq \emptyset$.

Corollary 4. $INS_1^{1,0} DEL_1^{1,1} SUB^{0,0} \subset RE$.

We remark that it can be shown that analogous results hold for the respective mirror language families.

Corollary 5. *The following statements hold:*

1. $INS_1^{0,1} DEL_0^{0,0} SUB^{0,0} = INS_1^{0,1} DEL_1^{0,0} SUB^{0,0} \subset CF$.
2. $INS_1^{0,1} DEL_1^{1,1} SUB^{0,0} \subset RE$.

3.2 Extension with One-Sided Substitution

In the following paragraphs, we will show that an arbitrary ins-del system ID of size $(1, 1, 1; 1, 1, 1)$ can be simulated by an ins-del-sub system ID_ς of size $(1, 1, 0; 1, 1, 0; 0, 1)$. ID_ς is built as shown in Construction 1. Every deletion rule (u, a, v) of ID with label i corresponds (in ID_ς) to a nonterminal X_i, a substitution rule $(\lambda, a \to X_i, v) \in S_2$ and a deletion rule $(u, X_i, \lambda) \in D'$. Likewise,

Let $M = (Q, T, \delta, q_0, F)$ be a DFA accepting L. We define the ins-del-sub system of size $(1, 1, 0; 0, 0, 0; 0, 1)$ which will simulate M as $ID_\varsigma = (V, T, A, I, \emptyset, S)$, with

$$V = \{(q_i, q_j), X_{(q_i, q_j)}, (q_i, q_j)' \mid q_i, q_j \in Q, \exists t \in T : \delta(q_i, t) = q_j\} \cup \{X\},$$

$$A = \{(q_0, q_i)X \mid q_i \in Q, \exists t \in T : \delta(q_0, t) = q_i\} \cup \{w \in L \mid |w| \leq 1\},$$

$$I = \{((q_i, q_j), X_{(q_j, q_k)}, \lambda) \mid q_i, q_j, q_k \in Q, \exists t_1, t_2 \in T : \delta(q_i, t_1) = q_j, \delta(q_j, t_2) = q_k\},$$

$$S = S_1 \cup S_2 \cup S_3, \text{ where}$$

$$S_1 = \{(\lambda, X_{(q_i, q_j)} \to (q_i, q_j), X) \mid q_i, q_j \in Q, \exists t \in T : \delta(q_i, t) = q_j\},$$

$$S_2 = \{(\lambda, X \to (q_i, q_f)', \lambda) \mid q_i \in Q, q_f \in F, \exists t \in T : \delta(q_i, t) = q_f\}$$
$$\cup \{(\lambda, (q_i, q_j) \to (q_i, q_j)', (q_j, q_k)') \mid q_i, q_j, q_k \in Q\} \text{ and}$$

$$S_3 = \{(\lambda, (q_i, q_j)' \to t, \lambda) \mid q_i, q_j \in Q, t \in T, \delta(q_i, t) = q_j\}.$$

Construction 2: Simulating a DFA by a system of size $(1, 1, 0; 0, 0, 0; 0, 1)$

an insertion rule (r, s, t) of ID with label j is linked to a nonterminal X_j, an insertion rule $(r, X_j, \lambda) \in I'$ and a substitution rule $(\lambda, X_j \to s, t) \in S_1$ of ID_ς.

The basic idea of this construction is to leave checking the right context to the substitution rules, as insertion/deletion rules of size $(1, 1, 0)$ cannot perform right context checks by themselves. It is easy to see that the application of the rule $(\lambda, a \to X_i, v) \in S_2$, immediately followed by an application of the rule $(u, X_i, \lambda) \in D'$, is equivalent to the deletion rule $(u, a, v) \in D$, i.e.,

$$w_1 u a v w_2 \Longrightarrow_{(\lambda, a \to X_i, v)} w_1 u a X_i v w_2 \Longrightarrow_{(u, X_i, \lambda)_{\text{del}}} w_1 u v w_2$$

is equivalent to the application of the deletion rule $(u, a, v) \in D$. Similarly, the successive application of the rules $(r, X_j, \lambda) \in I'$ and $(\lambda, X_j \to s, t) \in S_1$ is equivalent to the insertion rule $(r, s, t) \in I$.

Theorem 6. $(*)$ *Given $ID \in INS_1^{1,1} DEL_1^{1,1}$, one can construct an ins-del-sub system $ID_\varsigma \in INS_1^{1,0} DEL_1^{1,0} SUB^{0,1}$ such that $L(ID) = L(ID_\varsigma)$.*

Note that every derivation within ID_ς can be re-ordered such that auxiliary nonterminals X_i are immediately resolved. This is essential for showing $L(ID) \supseteq L(ID_\varsigma)$. With the previous theorem, reference [12] and Lemma 2, we conclude:

Corollary 6. $RE = INS_1^{1,1} DEL_1^{1,1} = INS_1^{1,0} DEL_1^{1,0} SUB^{0,1} = INS_1^{0,1} DEL_1^{0,1} SUB^{1,0}$.

It is known that there are regular languages which ins-del systems of size $(1, 1, 0; 0, 0, 0)$ cannot generate. Consider for instance the regular language $(ba)^+$, which even systems of size $(1, 1, 0; 1, 1, 1)$ cannot generate; cf. [1]. Now, we will show that the set of all regular languages is included in $INS_1^{1,0} DEL_0^{0,0} SUB^{0,1}$. More precisely, we will show that all deterministic finite automata can be simulated by ins-del systems with substitution rules of size $(1, 1, 0; 0, 0, 0; 0, 1)$. We will build such a system as shown in Construction 2. We now describe its basic idea. Clearly $\{w \in L \mid |w| \leq 1\} \subseteq L(ID_\varsigma)$ follows from $\{w \in L \mid |w| \leq 1\} \subseteq A$. We remark that if $w \in L$ with $|w| \leq 1$ is the axiom of a derivation, then no word other than w can be derived, as no rule in I or S is applicable to the axiom.

Let $(q_0, q_{i_1})X$ with $q_{i_1} \in Q$ and $\delta(q_0, t) = q_{i_1}$ for some $t \in T$ be the axiom of a derivation. Then the idea is to generate a terminal word from a string of the form $(q_{i_0}, q_{i_1})'(q_{i_1}, q_{i_2})' \ldots (q_{i_{n-1}}, q_{i_n})'(q_{i_n}, q_{i_{n+1}})'$ such that $\delta(q_{i_m}, t_m) = q_{i_{m+1}}$ holds for every tuple $(q_{i_m}, q_{i_{m+1}})'$ for some $t_m \in T$ with $0 \leq m \leq n$, $q_0 = q_{i_0}$ and $q_{i_{n+1}} \in F$. The terminal string is generated by substituting each tuple $(q_{i_m}, q_{i_{m+1}})'$ with a letter $t_m \in T$ with the above property. A word $t_0 t_1 \ldots t_n$ obtained by such substitutions is accepted by the deterministic finite automaton M with the sequence of states that are passed while processing $t_0 t_1 \ldots t_n$ being $q_{i_0} \ldots q_{i_{n+1}}$. Details of Construction 2 are contained in [14].

Theorem 7. (∗) *For any deterministic finite automaton M, one can construct an ins-del-sub system of size $(1, 1, 0; 0, 0, 0; 0, 1)$ which generates $L(M)$.*

Proof. Consider an ins-del-sub system ID_ς of size $(1, 1, 0; 0, 0, 0; 0, 1)$ built as in Construction 2. By the above, $L(ID_\varsigma) \subseteq L(M)$ holds. We now show the converse. By construction, it is clear that $\{w \in L(M) \mid |w| \leq 1\} \subseteq L(ID_\varsigma)$ holds. Let $w \in L(M)$ with $|w| \geq 2$. Let $q_0 q_1 \ldots q_n q_f$ be the sequence of states passed by M during a run on w. Now, ID_ς can generate a string of the form

$$(q_0, q_1)'(q_1, q_2)' \ldots (q_{n-1}, q_n)'(q_n, q_f)'$$

and hence w. Therefore, $L(M) \subseteq L(ID_\varsigma)$ holds. □

Due to the theorem above, we conclude the following consequences.

Corollary 7. $INS_1^{1,0} DEL_0^{0,0} \subset INS_1^{1,0} DEL_0^{0,0} SUB^{0,1}$, $REG \subset INS_1^{1,0} DEL_0^{0,0} SUB^{0,1}$.

Proof. The first inclusion holds as it is known that the regular language $(ba)^+$ cannot be generated systems of size $(1, 1, 0; 1, 1, 1)$ [1, Theorem 9.28], while systems of size $(1, 1, 0; 0, 0, 0; 0, 1)$ can generate all regular languages.
The second inclusion follows due to the fact that even systems of size $(1, 1, 0; 0, 0, 0)$ can generate non-regular languages; see [13, Example 5.1]. □

As regular languages are closed under reversal, we conclude that, due to Lemma 2, all regular languages are included in $INS_1^{0,1} DEL_0^{0,0} SUB^{1,0}$, as well. Recall that due to Theorem 2, ins-del-sub systems without deletions always define context-sensitive languages.

While ins-del systems of size $(1, 1, 1; 1, 1, 0)$ are known to be unable to generate the language $\{a^n b^n \mid n \geq 1\}$ (see [9, Theorem 7]) and are therefore not computationally complete, we show in the following paragraphs that these systems can reach computational completeness if extended with one-sided substitution rules of the form $(a, b \to c, \lambda)$. Consider an arbitrary type-0 grammar $G = (V, T, P, S)$ in Penttonen normal form; see [11]. We show that this grammar can be simulated by an ins-del-sub system of size $(1, 1, 1; 1, 1, 0; 1, 0)$. This system is built as shown in Construction 3. The simulation of G is conducted as follows: rewriting rules of the form $AB \to AC$ and $A \to a$ with $A, B, C \in V$, $a \in T$ are simulated directly by the substitution rules $(A, B \to C, \lambda)$ and $(\lambda, A \to a, \lambda)$, respectively, while rules of the form $A \to \lambda$ are simulated by deletion rules of

Assume that all production rules in P are bijectively labelled. Let $\{\#\} \cap V = \emptyset$. We define the ins-del-sub system simulating G as $ID_{\varsigma} = (V', T, \{\#S\}, I', D', S')$, with

$$V' = V \cup T \cup \{\#\} \cup \{N_i, N_i', N_i'', N_{i,0}, N_{i,1} \mid i \text{ is the label of a rule } A \to BC\},$$

$$I' = \{(X, N_{i,0}, N_i), (N_{i,0}, N_{i,1}, N_i') \mid i \text{ labels rule } A \to BC, A \neq B, X \in V \cup \{\#\}\}$$
$$\cup \{(A, B, \lambda) \mid A \to AB \in P\},$$

$$D' = \{(X, A, \lambda) \mid A \to \lambda \in P, X \in V \cup \{\#\}\} \cup \{(\lambda, \#, \lambda)\}$$
$$\cup \{(X, N_{i_0}, \lambda) \mid i \text{ labels rule } A \to BC, X \in V \cup \{\#\}\} \text{ and}$$

$$S' = \{(A, B \to C, \lambda) \mid AB \to AC \in P\} \cup \{(\lambda, A \to a, \lambda) \mid A \to a \in P\}$$
$$\cup \{(\lambda, A \to N_i, \lambda), (N_{i,0}, N_i \to N_i', \lambda), (N_{i,1}, N_i' \to N_i'', \lambda), (N_{i,0}, N_{i,1} \to B, \lambda),$$
$$(B, N_i'' \to C, \lambda) \mid i \text{ labels rule } A \to BC\}.$$

Construction 3: Simulating a Penttonen normal form grammar $G = (V, T, P, S)$ by an ins-del-sub system of size $(1, 1, 1; 1, 1, 0; 1, 0)$.

the form (X, A, λ) with $X \in V \cup \{\#\}$. These deletion rules have this particular form instead of the form (λ, A, λ) in order to simplify subsequent proofs. In order to see that this change is insignificant, consider the following: Consider an arbitrary derivation of ID_{ς}. It is easy to see that we can assume that the deletion of the nonterminal $\#$ introduced as part of the axiom is the last action to be performed in the derivation. Additionally, we remark that no symbol can be inserted left of the nonterminal $\#$, as all insertion rules have left context. Therefore, in an arbitrary derivation of ID_{ς} any nonterminal A with $A \to \lambda \in P$ can always be deleted by the application of a rule (X, A, λ) with $X \in V \cup \{\#\}$, as A always has left context until the end of the derivation. Rule $A \to AB$ is simulated by the insertion rule (A, B, λ). Production rules of the form $A \to BC$, $A \neq B$, are simulated by the following sequence of rules. Let i be the label of $A \to BC$, $A \neq B$, then we begin with the application of the substitution rule $(\lambda, A \to N_i, \lambda)$, which in turn is followed by the application of an insertion rule $(\lambda, N_{i,0}, N_i)$, i.e.,

$$w_1 A w_2 \overset{\wedge}{\Longrightarrow} w_1 N_i w_2 \overset{\wedge}{\Longrightarrow} w_1 N_{i,0} N_i w_2.$$

The subsequent rules applied in the simulation of $A \to BC$ are:
(1) $(N_{i,0}, N_i \to N_i', \lambda)_{sub}$, (2) $(N_{i,0}, N_{i,1}, N_i')_{ins}$, (3) $(N_{i,1}, N_i' \to N_i'', \lambda)_{sub}$, (4) $(N_{i,0}, N_{i,1} \to B, \lambda)_{sub}$, (5) $(B, N_i'' \to C, \lambda)_{sub}$ and finally (6) $(\lambda, N_{i_0}, \lambda)_{del}$, i.e.,

$$w_1 N_{i,0} N_i w_2 \overset{\wedge}{\Longrightarrow} w_1 N_{i,0} N_i' w_2 \overset{\wedge}{\Longrightarrow} w_1 N_{i,0} N_{i,1} N_i' w_2 \overset{\wedge}{\Longrightarrow} w_1 N_{i,0} N_{i,1} N_i'' w_2$$
$$\overset{\wedge}{\Longrightarrow} w_1 N_{i,0} B N_i'' w_2 \overset{\wedge}{\Longrightarrow} w_1 N_{i,0} B C w_2 \overset{\wedge}{\Longrightarrow} w_1 B C w_2.$$

The basic idea is that the symbols $N_{i,0}$ and N_i (and all primed variants of N_i) delimit the insertion site. The idea of the delimiters is that the working insertion sites are separated from each other to avoid any interactions. Furthermore, the delimiters prevent any interaction between the symbols in the insertion site and all symbols outside it. (The idea behind this approach is the same as in [13, Theorem 3.5].) As mentioned before, in the course of the simulation of $A \to$

> Assuming a bijective labelling of the rules of *ID*, the ins-del-sub system which will simulate *ID* is defined as $ID_\varsigma = (V', T, A, I', D, S')$, with
>
> $$V' = V \cup \{X_i \mid i \text{ is the label of an insertion rule of } ID\}$$
> $$I' = \{(r, X_i, \lambda) \mid i \text{ is the label of an insertion rule } (r, s, t) \in I\}$$
> $$S' = \{(\lambda, X_i \to s, t) \mid i \text{ is the label of an insertion rule } (r, s, t) \in I\}.$$

Construction 4: Simulating an ins-del system $ID = (V, T, A, I, D)$ of size $(1, 1, 1; 2, 0, 0)$ in normal form by an ins-del-sub system of size $(1, 1, 0; 2, 0, 0; 0, 1)$.

BC, primed variants of N_i, that is N_i' and N_i'', will be introduced. The idea behind these symbols is that they serve as indicators that certain symbols have been introduced. For instance N_i', which is introduced by the substitution rule $(N_{i,0}, N_i \to N_i', \lambda) \in S''$, indicates that a symbol $N_{i,0}$ has been introduced to the left of N_i. Likewise N_i'', introduced by $(N_{i,1}, N_i' \to N_i'', \lambda) \in S''$, indicates the introduction of $N_{i,1}$.

It is easy to see that applying these rules in the order specified above yields a simulation of $A \to BC$. We also have to show that we can always assume this particular application order. More precisely, we can show that prematurely applying certain substitution or deletion rules results in sentential forms from which no terminal string can be derived. Due to Lemma 2, we can then state:

Theorem 8. (∗) $RE = INS_1^{1,1} DEL_1^{1,0} SUB^{1,0} = INS_1^{1,1} DEL_1^{0,1} SUB^{0,1}.$

While it is known that the family of languages generated by ins-del systems of size $(1, 1, 0; 2, 0, 0)$ is a proper subset of RE [7], we now show that extending this family of ins-del-sub systems yields computational completeness.

This claim is proved in the following paragraphs by showing that an arbitrary ins-del system of size $(1, 1, 1; 2, 0, 0)$ can be simulated by an ins-del-sub systems of size $(1, 1, 0; 2, 0, 0; 0, 1)$.

The computational completeness of $INS_1^{1,1} DEL_2^{0,0}$ has been shown in [10, Theorem 6.3]. Hence, by showing that a system of size $(1, 1, 1; 2, 0, 0)$ can be simulated by a system with substitution rules of size $(1, 1, 0; 2, 0, 0; 0, 1)$, we show that ins-del-sub systems of size $(1, 1, 0; 2, 0, 0; 0, 1)$ are computationally complete.

The basic idea of Construction 4 is the same as in Construction 1, i.e., an insertion rule (r, s, t) of *ID* is simulated by an application of an insertion rule $(r, X_i, \lambda) \in I'$ and a substitution rule $(\lambda, X_i \to s, t) \in S'$.

Let $\alpha \in A$. We prove the equality $L(ID) = L(ID_\varsigma)$ as usual by showing that for every derivation $\alpha \stackrel{\wedge}{\Longrightarrow}{}^* w \in T^*$, there is an alternative derivation from α to w in which all nonterminals $V' \backslash V$ are resolved immediately after being introduced.

Lemma 5. *Consider a derivation* $w \stackrel{\wedge}{\Longrightarrow}{}^* w' \in T^*$ *of* ID_ς *with* $w \in V^*$ *with at most* $m \in \mathbb{N}$ *insertion rules. Then there is an alternative derivation from* w *to* w' *in which nonterminals* $V' \backslash V$ *are resolved immediately after being introduced.*

Proof. We prove our claim by induction. The base case $m = 0$ is obvious. $\underline{m \to m+1}$: Consider a derivation $w \stackrel{\wedge}{\Longrightarrow}{}^* w' \in T^*$ with $w \in V^*$ where $m +$

1 insertion rules are used. Due to our construction, all inserted symbols are nonterminals in $V'\backslash V$. Clearly one of these nonterminals has to be the first to be resolved in the derivation. We denote this nonterminal by $\underline{X}_i$. Let the label i correspond to the insertion rule (r, s, t) of ID. Then $\underline{X}_i$ is introduced via an insertion rule (r, X_i, λ) and resolved via a substitution rule $(\lambda, X_i \to s, t)$. Then, the derivation $w \stackrel{\wedge}{\Longrightarrow}{}^* w' \in T^*$ is of the form

$$w \stackrel{\wedge}{\Longrightarrow}{}^* w_1 r w_2 \stackrel{\wedge}{\Longrightarrow} w_1 r \underline{X}_i w_2 \stackrel{\wedge}{\Longrightarrow}{}^* w_1' \underline{X}_i t w_2' \stackrel{\wedge}{\Longrightarrow} w_1' s t w_2' \stackrel{\wedge}{\Longrightarrow}{}^* w' \tag{1}$$

with $w_1, w_1', w_2, w_2' \in V'^*$. As the nonterminal $\underline{X}_i$ is the first symbol in $V'\backslash V$ to be resolved in the derivation, it follows that the symbol r which has been used to insert $\underline{X}_i$, as well as the symbol t which has been used to resolve $\underline{X}_i$ have been introduced as part of w. We denote this specific r and t by $\underline{r}$ and $\underline{t}$, respectively. Let $w = u_1 \underline{r} u_2 \underline{t} u_3$ with $u_1, u_2, u_3 \in V^*$. Consider the derivation

$$w = u_1 \underline{r} u_2 \underline{t} u_3 \stackrel{\wedge}{\Longrightarrow}{}^* w_1 \underline{r} w_2 \stackrel{\wedge}{\Longrightarrow} w_1 r \underline{X}_i w_2 \stackrel{\wedge}{\Longrightarrow}{}^* w_1' \underline{X}_i t w_2' \tag{2}$$

up to this point. As all rules used up to this point are either context-free deletion rules or one-sided insertion rules with only left context, it is easy to see that

$$u_1 \underline{r} \stackrel{\wedge}{\Longrightarrow}{}^* w_1 \underline{r} \stackrel{\wedge}{\Longrightarrow}{}^* w_1' \tag{3}$$

holds. Furthermore, $w_2 = w_{2,1} \underline{t} w_{2,2}$ holds as $\underline{t}$ cannot be substituted and per definition not be deleted before $\underline{t}$ has been used to resolve $\underline{X}_i$.
Additionally, $\underline{r} u_2 \underline{t} u_3 \stackrel{\wedge}{\Longrightarrow}{}^* \underline{r} w_2 = \underline{r} w_{2,1} \underline{t} w_{2,2}$ holds as only context-free deletion rules and one-sided insertion rules with left context are applied. Consequently, using the same argument as in the case of Derivation (3), we obtain

$$\underline{r} u_2 \stackrel{\wedge}{\Longrightarrow}{}^* \underline{r} w_{2,1} \text{ and } \underline{t} u_3 \stackrel{\wedge}{\Longrightarrow}{}^* \underline{t} w_{2,2} . \tag{4}$$

Due to $w_1 r \underline{X}_i w_2 = w_1 r \underline{X}_i w_{2,1} \underline{t} w_{2,2} \stackrel{\wedge}{\Longrightarrow}{}^* w_1' \underline{X}_i t w_2'$, we also conclude that $w_{2,1} \stackrel{\wedge}{\Longrightarrow}{}^* \lambda$ and $\underline{t} w_{2,2} \stackrel{\wedge}{\Longrightarrow}{}^* \underline{t} w_2'$ hold, as $\underline{X}_i$ is not used as a context in any rule. Hence, with Derivations (4) we get

$$\underline{r} u_2 \stackrel{\wedge}{\Longrightarrow}{}^* \underline{r} w_{2,1} \stackrel{\wedge}{\Longrightarrow}{}^* \underline{r} \text{ and } \underline{t} u_3 \stackrel{\wedge}{\Longrightarrow}{}^* \underline{t} w_{2,2} \stackrel{\wedge}{\Longrightarrow}{}^* \underline{t} w_2' . \tag{5}$$

We remark that we can assume that only deletion rules are used in Derivation (5). Any symbol that would be inserted in Derivation (5) is an element of $V'\backslash V$ and any symbol in $V'\backslash V$ must be substituted with a symbol in V before it can be deleted. However, up to the point specified in Derivation (2), no substitution rule is used. Consider the following derivation

$$w = u_1 \underline{r} u_2 \underline{t} u_3 \stackrel{\wedge}{\Longrightarrow}_{\text{derivation }(5)^*} u_1 \underline{r} \underline{t} u_3 \stackrel{\wedge}{\Longrightarrow} u_1 \underline{r} \underline{X}_i \underline{t} u_3 \stackrel{\wedge}{\Longrightarrow} u_1 \underline{r} s \underline{t} u_3$$
$$\stackrel{\wedge}{\Longrightarrow}_{\text{derivation }(3)^*} w_1' s \underline{t} u_3 \stackrel{\wedge}{\Longrightarrow}_{\text{derivation }(5)^*} w_1' s \underline{t} w_2' \stackrel{\wedge}{\Longrightarrow}{}^* w' \in T^*,$$

where the last part of the derivation follows due to Derivation (1). The derivation above implies $u_1 \underline{r} s \underline{t} u_3 \stackrel{\wedge}{\Longrightarrow}{}^* w' \in T^*$ and that in the derivation $u_1 \underline{r} s \underline{t} u_3 \stackrel{\wedge}{\Longrightarrow}{}^* w' \in T^*$ at most m insertion rules are used. Therefore, our claim follows with the induction hypothesis. □

With Lemma 5, we can see that the next theorem follows.

Theorem 9. $L(ID_\varsigma) = L(ID)$.

As any ins-del system of size $(1, 1, 1; 2, 0, 0)$ can be simulated by an ins-del-sub system of size $(1, 1, 0; 2, 0, 0; 0, 1)$, the following corollary holds by Lemma 2.

Corollary 8. $RE = INS_1^{1,1} DEL_2^{0,0} = INS_1^{1,0} DEL_2^{0,0} SUB^{0,1} = INS_1^{0,1} DEL_2^{0,0} SUB^{1,0}$.

4   Conclusions

We have shown that several classes of ins-del-sub systems are computationally complete. Yet, there are quite a number of classes where we do not know if they are. We rather conjecture incompleteness for $INS_1^{1,0} DEL_1^{1,0} SUB^{1,0}$ and for $INS_1^{1,0} DEL_2^{0,0} SUB^{1,0}$, because of the unidirectional flow of information; we are less sure about $INS_1^{1,0} DEL_1^{0,1} SUB^{1,0}$. We strongly conjecture that $RE = INS_1^{1,0} DEL_1^{0,0} SUB^{0,1}$.

References

1. Alhazov, A., Krassovitskiy, A., Rogozhin, Y., Verlan, S.: Small size insertion and deletion systems. In: Martin-Vide, C. (ed.) Applications of Language Methods, pp. 459–515. Imperial College Press (2010)
2. Beaver, D.: Computing with DNA. J. Comput. Biol. **2**(1), 1–7 (1995)
3. Haussler, D.: Insertion languages. Inf. Sci. **31**(1), 77–89 (1983)
4. Kari, L.: On insertions and deletions in formal languages. Ph.D. thesis, University of Turku, Finland (1991)
5. Karl, L.: DNA computing: arrival of biological mathematics. Math. Intell. **19**(2), 9–22 (1997). https://doi.org/10.1007/BF03024425
6. Krassovitskiy, A., Rogozhin, Y., Verlan, S.: Further results on insertion-deletion systems with one-sided contexts. In: Martín-Vide, C., Otto, F., Fernau, H. (eds.) LATA 2008. LNCS, vol. 5196, pp. 333–344. Springer, Heidelberg (2008). https://doi.org/10.1007/978-3-540-88282-4_31
7. Krassovitskiy, A., Rogozhin, Y., Verlan, S.: Computational power of insertion-deletion (P) systems with rules of size two. Nat. Comput. **10**, 835–852 (2011)
8. Margenstern, M., Păun, Gh., Rogozhin, Y., Verlan, S.: Context-free insertion-deletion systems. Theor. Comput. Sci. **330**(2), 339–348 (2005)
9. Matveevici, A., Rogozhin, Y., Verlan, S.: Insertion-deletion systems with one-sided contexts. In: Durand-Lose, J., Margenstern, M. (eds.) MCU 2007. LNCS, vol. 4664, pp. 205–217. Springer, Heidelberg (2007). https://doi.org/10.1007/978-3-540-74593-8_18
10. Păun, Gh., Rozenberg, G., Salomaa, A.: DNA Computing: New Computing Paradigms. Springer, Heidelberg (1998). https://doi.org/10.1007/978-3-662-03563-4
11. Penttonen, M.: One-sided and two-sided context in formal grammars. Inf. Control (now Inf. Comput.) **25**, 371–392 (1974)
12. Takahara, A., Yokomori, T.: On the computational power of insertion-deletion systems. Nat. Comput. **2**(4), 321–336 (2003)

13. Verlan, S.: Recent developments on insertion-deletion systems. Comput. Sci. J. Moldova **18**(2), 210–245 (2010)
14. Vu, M.: On insertion-deletion systems with substitution rules. Master's thesis, Informatikwissenschaften, Universität Trier, Germany (2019)
15. Vu, M., Fernau, H.: Insertion-deletion systems with substitutions I. In: Anselmo, M., Della Vedova, G., Manea, F., Pauly, A. (eds.) CiE 2020. LNCS, vol. 12098, pp. 366–378. Springer, Cham (2020). https://doi.org/10.1007/978-3-030-51466-2_33

Author Index

Printed in the United States
By Bookmasters